Black, White, and Southern

Black, White, and Southern

Race Relations and Southern Culture

1940 to the Present

DAVID R. GOLDFIELD

Louisiana State University Press
Baton Rouge and London

Designer: Albert Crochet
Typeface: Linotron Trump Mediaeval
Typesetter: The Composing Room of Michigan, Inc.

LIBRARY OF CONGRESS CATALOGING-IN-PUBLICATION DATA

Goldfield, David R., 1944–
    Black, white, and southern : race relations and southern culture,
    1940 to the present / David R. Goldfield.
        p. cm.
    Includes bibliographical references.
    ISBN 0-8071-1532-0 (cloth)
    ISBN 0-8071-1682-3 (paper)

    1. Southern States—Race relations. 2. Afro-Americans—South-
ern States—History—20th century. 3. Afro-Americans—Civil
rights—Southern States—History—20th century. I. Title.
E185.61.G584 1990
305.8'00975—dc20   89-36162
                                                         CIP

The paper in this book meets the guidelines for permanence and
durability of the Committee on Production Guidelines for Book
Longevity of the Council on Library Resources. ∞

Louisiana Paperback Edition, 1991

00 99 98 97 96 95 94 93 92 91   5 4 3 2 1

For Erik and Eleanor

We are one South, by blood and suffering, by horror and triumph.

—Maynard Jackson, mayor of Atlanta

Contents

Preface   xiii

Acknowledgments   xvii

I.   Race Relations and Southern Culture   1

II.   "A Kind of Sunlight": Depression, War, and Change, 1930–1945   25

III.   A Season of Hope, 1945–1954   45

IV.   Flight from Reality: The Rise of White Resistance, 1945–1956   63

V.   The Limits of Endurance: Buses, Books, and Balance Sheets, 1954–1960   87

VI.   The Crusade Against Segregation, 1960–1964   118

VII.   The Last Crusade: Voting Rights, 1962–1965   149

VIII.   The First Hurrah: Black Ballots   174

IX.   The Rough Side of the Mountain: The Black Economy, 1965–1976   199

X.   No Broad Highways: Class and Race in the South Since 1976   227

XI.   Mountaintops and Green Valleys: Beyond Race in the Modern South   256

Bibliographical Essay   279

Index   313

Illustrations

Map: The Civil Rights Movement in the South   *page 24*

following page 44

Black and white elementary schools
The Negro curriculum, *ca.* 1935
A Mississippi Delta sharecropper
A sharecropping family's home
Evicted sharecroppers, 1936
Black sharecroppers' shacks
Black housing in downtown Atlanta, 1938
John Hope Homes, Atlanta

following page 173

First black student in a Fort Smith elementary school, 1957
A white girl responds to integration
Turned away from church
"It's Nice to Have You in Birmingham"
Sit-in at Woolworth's lunch counter, 1961
Woolworth's response to sit-ins
Injured Freedom Rider
The children's crusade begins, 1963
Dogs and hoses
Saying grace
Rev. Martin L. King, Jr., Rev. Fred L. Shuttlesworth, and Rev. Ralph David Abernathy
The bombing of Rev. A. D. King's home, 1963
Kelly Ingram Park, Birmingham

State police clean their weapons

The bombed 16th Street Baptist Church, 1963

The damaged interior of the church

Standing in the schoolhouse door

Pickets in front of a Chattanooga swimming pool

The effort to desegregate Birmingham Public Library

following page 236

A federal registrar places a black citizen on the
   voting rolls, 1965

Waiting to register to vote at the federal courthouse,
   Birmingham

Voting in the Alabama Democratic primary, 1966

Jackson Ward makes way for the Richmond Coliseum

Douglas Wilder speaking at a banquet of Richmond's
   political leaders

Diverging societies, 1971

H. J. Russell talks with a worker at a public housing site

Tom Gilmore, sheriff, in front of his boyhood home

Richmond mayor Henry Marsh III helps host an affair

Lawrence Wade, Memphis banker and entrepreneur

Fulfilling the American Dream

Contemporary southern politics

Race and metropolitan politics, 1986

Black political power in Richmond

Preface

I had just finished giving my students a mental walking tour of Uptown (as downtown is called in this upbeat city) Charlotte some time in the 1950s. We pretended we were black. We packed a picnic lunch because no restaurants or lunch counters would serve us, and we boarded the bus and took a seat in the rear. If a department store was on our Uptown agenda, there were many items we could purchase, but few we could try on. If we were fortunate, the salesperson would serve us in turn; if not, we would wait until the white people received assistance whether they came in after us or not. The salesperson obviously had difficulty with names because she continued to call us "Auntie" or "Boy" or "Uncle," though some might venture a "Mister" or "Miss." If we had business in a public building—the county courthouse, for example—we would ride to our floor in an elevator marked *Colored*, go to the rest room with the same designation, and, if we were thirsty, drink from the separate water fountain. If we brought children with us, they could likely tell, even if they couldn't read, which facilities were "colored" and which were "white." We would hope that they would not ask any questions, at least not until we got home. We adults may have long since grown accustomed to the differences and scarcely noticed any, or we may have felt that familiar pang of humiliation or rage or frustration. As we left the courthouse, a well-dressed white man coming up the steps smiled at our young son and said, "Hey there, fellow, how ya' doin?" Charlotte was a friendly place.

The bell rang, and the students began to disperse. One student came up to me with a wry grin on her face and asked if I had put it on a little thick with that reference to separate water fountains. I assured her that such customs existed in our not-too-distant past. Her reply was, "Wow! That's weird!"

Indeed it was. And it dawned on me that it must have seemed weird to her colleagues as well. Most were not yet born when President Lyndon B. Johnson signed the Civil Rights Act into law in July, 1964. Almost all of my students, particularly those who were raised in the South, had attended integrated schools. "White" and "colored" for them were laundering instructions.

In some ways, this lack of knowing is good. White supremacy exacted a terrific toll on white and black southerners and upon the South.
It was a reality that could find no logical support in the region's
culture—its history and its religion in particular—yet past, place, and
religion had been marshaled to serve this construct. Southern writer
William Price Fox tells the story of an elderly pair of sisters in Charleston, aristocrats to the core, but of seriously reduced financial circumstances. In their younger days of better means, they had fled the city's
oven summers for Paris. Now, every summer night they steal quietly
from their shuttered home to take their constitutional on the Battery.
One night, a child recognizes them and is about to blurt out a "hello"
when her mother pulls her short and says, "No, dear, we don't speak to
them in the summertime. They're still in Paris."

Appearances are important in the South, and white southerners have
a great capacity for ignoring unpleasant things. Their capacity for ignorance has served them well, because defeat, ostracism, occupation,
poverty, and illiteracy would be more than sufficient to conquer a
lesser people. But at some point it is no longer possible to pretend; the
thing being avoided may make its presence known in a very decided
manner, or the burden of trying to square values and culture with ignorance becomes too great to bear. If the sisters invite you over for tea
one summer afternoon or if your child does finally accost them, the
fiction may be blown.

My students need no longer maintain the fiction of white supremacy. That is a strength, but ignorance of its existence can also become a
serious weakness. In the wake of racial violence on campuses across
the nation during 1987, Washington *Post* columnist Jonathan Yardley
asked, "Can it really be true that only a decade and a half after the
climax of the civil rights movement, American college students are
widely ignorant of the circumstances in which it began and the forms
it brought about?" If that is so, then, according to Yardley, it is a notion
that "is as dangerous as it is preposterous, for in essence it asserts that
history has no meaning beyond itself, that we have nothing of value
and importance to learn from it." Though some may argue that it
might be a good thing that "the young are growing up with less unpleasant racial baggage to shoulder than did their parents," the
ignorance-is-bliss school of thought has little validity. "Racial antagonism," Yardley concludes, "has not been erased from American life,
and we must always be on alert against it. If young people are to have
any hope of understanding and fulfilling their responsibilities as citi-

zens . . . they must be taught the story of [those] who sought to perpetuate discrimination and the brave ones who overcame it."

This, then, is the inspiration for this book: to recount a great moral drama that swept the South less than a generation ago; to show that what is weird to the present generation of southerners was matter-of-fact to their predecessors; to indicate that the race relations we have today—the good parts and the lingering bad—resulted from a regional trauma of immense proportions, paid for in blood and souls and minds. This is not a book on the civil rights movement, though that era, from the Montgomery bus boycott of 1955 to the voting rights marches of 1965, forms an important part of the story, of course. It is, rather, a book about redemption, a southern story that begins by defining the sin of white supremacy and how it poisoned a region and its people; it continues by relating how that sin came to be expiated, and how the sinner and the redeemer managed to be transformed without destroying their unique land, the South; and it concludes by discussing how southerners are wrestling with the legacy of redemption, groping for guideposts, hoping against backsliding, but above all, remembering. "Remembering," journalist Roy Reed stated in reference to the legacy of race relations in the South, "is not a luxury. It is an obligation."

Acknowledgments

Historians' research interests usually operate in a stream of consciousness. One topic suggests another, and that yet another, and so on. Sometimes the stream veers off into a shallow eddy from which we can hope to extricate ourselves without getting mired. On other, more fortunate occasions, the stream widens, deepens, and quickens, feeding a fertile valley of ideas, questions, interpretations, and conclusions. No historian makes this journey alone. We take along the work and ideas of students, other scholars, novelists, journalists, and the various grassroots sages we have met along the way. Southern historians have additional company. We travel with the lore and feeling of a special region.

With all this weight, it is little wonder that we need a deep channel to carry on our work. But without it, we are rudderless minds, easily disoriented. The bibliographical essay at the end of this book is a tribute to my pilots and guides. Harvard Sitkoff deserves special mention for his careful reading of the manuscript and his helpful suggestions. My students also share a hand in the book since their incredulity at what the South was like a short generation ago first prompted me to write this story. Barbara Lisenby, director of interlibrary loan at the University of North Carolina-Charlotte, was relentless in tracking down material for me. Jeff Simpson and his staff at the university's cartographic lab provided prompt and expert service. The staffs at the Library of Congress and the National Archives were helpful, as were Don Veasey of the Birmingham Public Library, Jane Smith of the Valentine Museum in Richmond, and Elaine Kirkland of the Atlanta Historical Society. A grant from the Southern Regional Education Board enabled me to travel to these sites. UNC-Charlotte generously granted me a leave of absence for a term to write this book, and Vice-Chancellor James H. Werntz, Jr., and Dean Schley Lyons have been supportive of my research and writing activities. I especially appreciate my colleagues in the history department, who have provided a stimulating and congenial atmosphere for me and my work.

This is my third book with Louisiana State University Press. As in the past, I've benefited from an array of experts who turned the publication process into a pleasurable experience. Beverly Jarrett, formerly associate director of the press, encouraged the project from the outset. Margaret Fisher Dalrymple, senior editor, not only encouraged but participated in copyediting the manuscript, as did Catherine Landry. And marketing director Cathy Silvia promises to make the book known far and wide, or at least as far as Shreveport.

Most of all, I thank my family. My parents, as well as my aunt and uncle Mary and Charles Gainor, taught me the joys of reading and writing at an early age. As a child, I recall listening intently to my parents' stories of their years in segregated Memphis. My wife, Marie-Louise, and children, Erik and Eleanor, have shown their love and particularly their patience. I dedicate this book to my children who are fortunate to be growing up in the South at this time.

Black, White, and Southern

I / Race Relations and Southern Culture

There were two races; one black and one white. They shared a common history: they had suffered together through defeat and oppression, each in its own way; they had felt the dull pain of poverty and the uprootedness of economic change; they had stumbled and fallen behind the rest of America in literacy, health, and technology. They shared the land—the land overworked by cotton or tobacco, rutted and ragged and abandoned to scrub and gullies, raw red, bleeding; and the land of running streams, of dewy mornings and indescribable fragrances, of bare feet in fresh mud, of rainbow springtimes, of white summers and gray winters. They shared a faith that God had chosen them as modern-day Hebrews to lead them to a promised land of better times, if not here and now, then assuredly in the by-and-by. Theirs was a personal relationship; they worshipped God in a familiar, conversational tone, for He was as present as the debt hanging over this year's crop. And they shared the grace of conversation, of manners and social convention, of revering the elderly and the dead most of all, of passing down family traditions orally, through word and song; the past was to be remembered, not learned.

Yet, in this region of ironies, the supreme irony was that the two races lived side by side for centuries and knew each other not at all. The sin of race pride had come between them and created an abyss so deep that few held out hope for reconciliation. The separation was an artifice, and an artifice maintained it. Through the centuries, through slavery and emancipation, an elaborate etiquette evolved to govern race relations. The etiquette of race served several functions. First, it helped to create an orderly means of discourse in a disorderly society. The South was a predominantly rural region well into the twentieth century, and its people lived in isolation, sometimes from each other, often from the outside world. They were frontiersmen long after the passing of the frontier, and the codes they lived by were private and local rather than public and national. As Chapel Hill sociologist Rupert B. Vance noted in 1932, "institutions and customs are still tinged with the shades of the forests." And these shades often revealed the darker side of regional existence, the sudden violence, as ominous as the tornadoes and rainstorms that ripped the region, and the capriciousness of justice, as fickle as the weather. Southerners, white and black, made their peace as best they could with natural and man-made uncertainties, but it was a tenuous, often heartbreaking existence that fired frustrations that turned to violence and sharp mood swings, unpredictable and hence more frightening.

To compound matters, southerners, especially whites, had adopted a siege mentality. They had been set upon, first by abolitionists, then by preachers and politicians, and eventually by an invading army. Since that time, their enemies had made periodic thrusts into the region, opening up old wounds and creating renewed turmoil. The etiquette of race evolved as a complicated set of rules and customs designed in part to "place" individuals in a racial and class hierarchy that would retain its fixity regardless of the tensions and pressures swirling in and about the South. It bound whites together, though not equally, and it relegated blacks to a permanent status of inferiority.

The Etiquette of Race

Aside from ordering an unsettled society and creating a certainty, however artificial, amidst the whimsy of man and nature, racial etiquette created a system of behavior that served to reinforce the supremacy of the white race and the inferiority of the black. In the process, the etiquette produced dire consequences for both races and for the South. The tone of speech, the gesture, what was said and not said, where and how one stood or sat became parts of the rituals of southern personal relations. It was theater. As Lillian Smith observed, "every little southern town is a fine stage-set for Southern Tradition." But it was a theater where everyone had to learn his lines and adhere to the script. An act of bad manners was not merely a regrettable faux pas, but a major social transgression that threatened order, violated expectations, called into question the rectitude of social and racial givens, and challenged integrity. The players assumed their roles carefully, especially the blacks.

The code of etiquette governed every social situation from hunting to casual meetings on the street. For blacks encountering whites, the code demanded, among other things, "sir" and "ma'am," averted eyes, preferably a smile, never imparting bad news, never discussing other whites, and always exhibiting a demeanor that would make a white comfortable in believing that this deferential mien was not only right but the way things ought to be. The white, in turn, would almost always address the black by a first name or by generic terms such as "boy," "uncle," or "aunty," regardless of age. The tone would always be condescending. And whites enforced the code on others. Swedish sociologist Gunnar Myrdal recalled visiting a small southern city during the late 1930s to seek out the principal of a black high school. Myrdal inquired after "Mr. Jim Smith" only to meet blank stares from whites. When he finally located the principal and related his story, the principal laughed and said: "You should have asked for . . . 'Jim'— sure, everybody knows me in this town."

The racial etiquette governing encounters between black and white produced a "stage Negro," and maybe the white and almost certainly the black knew it. But from this etiquette flowed an array of assumptions whites held about blacks that reinforced the inferior role of black southerners. Blacks were childlike; they were prone to steal and prone to violence; they were oversexed, stupid, lethargic, dependent on whites, and, above all, happy. And when blacks confirmed these assumptions, they were generally rewarded—with employment, a good word at the bank, food, or even money. As black author Richard Wright pointed out, "whites . . . encouraged irresponsibility; and their rewards were bestowed upon us blacks in the degree we could make them feel safe and secure." Marsh Taylor, a white landowner in Georgia during the 1930s, caught three black youngsters stealing nuts from his pecan orchard. Amused rather than outraged by their lame excuses, he gave each a nickel after a mild scolding. In a similar vein, the white grocery store owner in William Faulkner's *Intruder in the Dust* (1948) expressed his fondness for blacks, even though he knew they cheated him occasionally: "All he requires," Faulkner wrote, "is that they act like niggers." So whites came to expect, even require, less of blacks. Whites, blacks, and the South lost for the expectation.

Whites equated the black as portrayed in the staged race relations with the real black. Consequently, they fancied themselves as experts on black behavior and feeling, and they railed against outsiders who presumed to divine the minds of black southerners from afar. Racial etiquette demonstrated, among other things, that race relations were benign and harmonious. In 1948, for example, when pressure for modest racial adjustments began to build in Washington, a perplexed congressman from Mississippi, John E. Rankin, extended an invitation to his colleagues: "Go down South where I live . . . where more Negroes are employed than anywhere else in the country, where they enjoy more happiness, more peace, more prosperity, more security and protection than they ever enjoyed in all history." Northern lawmakers were incredulous, but it was likely that Rankin believed his portrayal was accurate because that was what he saw in Mississippi.

The "stage Negro" inured whites to the suffering of southern blacks. It was not that whites were cruel or unfeeling. The etiquette of race made them, as W. E. B. Du Bois put it, "discount the suffering or harm done others; . . . once it is hidden beneath a different color of skin, a different stature or a different habit of action and speech, . . . all consciousness of inflicting ill disappears." Blacks are poor and shiftless and behave in certain ways because that is the way they are, and they are happy in that way. Consider, for example, this exchange between Will Tweedy, a fourteen-year-old white boy, growing up in a small Georgia town early in this century, and his grandfather's new wife, Miss Love from Baltimore, in Olive Ann Burns's novel, *Cold Sassy Tree* (1984):

> One time I ast Queenie [the black cook] why she drinks out of a quart Mason jar instead of a glass and you know what she said? "Mr. Will dat first glassful always be's de bestis, so I makes it jes' big as I can." I laughed the way white folks do when they tell something funny a colored person said. Miss Love laughed too. Then she said, "But of course you know the real truth bout that, Will."
>
> "What do you mean?"
>
> "I mean colored cooks know white people don't want them using their dishes and things. That's why they all drink out of jars and eat out of old plates or pie pans."

Will refused to believe this, insisting that Queenie preferred pie pans because they held more than plates. Reacting as most white southerners would to any challenge to their racial perceptions, Will muttered angrily, "Miss Love couldn't understand that Queenie really just didn't care. Yankee, I thought, burning. Yankee Yankee."

By proclaiming their consummate knowledge of blacks, white southerners effectively and ironically closed off the opportunity to know and benefit from their neighbors of three centuries. Occasionally, a few whites, like Miss Love, would penetrate the charade and recognize it as such. William Alexander Percy, scion of a prominent Mississippi Delta planter family, wrote in his poignant autobiography, *Lanterns on the Levee* (1941), "It is true in the South that whites and blacks live side by side, exchange affection liberally, and believe they have an innate and miraculous understanding of one another. But the sober fact is we understand one another not at all." Another sober fact was that, despite this knowledge, Percy felt himself immobilized by the racial traditions of his region and class to end the theater.

The result of this blindness to the real Negro was to render him invisible. The black man was a collection of stereotypical characteristics confirmed by public behavior rather than a flesh-and-blood human being. As Quentin Compson, William Faulkner's tragic young protagonist in *The Sound and the Fury* (1929), put it nonchalantly, "a nigger is not a person so much as a form of behavior; a sort of obverse reflection of the white people he lives among." Ralph Ellison's prize-winning novel, *Invisible Man* (1947), offered the black perspective. He wrote of "Invisible Man": "I am invisible, simply because people refuse to see me. . . . When they approach me they only see my surroundings, themselves, or figments of their imagination—indeed, everything and anything except me."

The racial etiquette that rendered blacks invisible and whites unknowing exacted a heavy toll on both races and on the South. In a region where informal contact was a way of business and of life, where conversation and sociability softened the intruding edges of competition and anonymity, blacks and whites were cut adrift from each other's fellowship, and they and the South were the poorer for it. As Du Bois articulated it in 1903, "in a world where it means so much to take a man by the hand and sit beside him, to look frankly into his eyes and feel his heart beating with red blood; in a world where a social cigar or a cup of tea together means more than legislative halls and magazine articles and speeches,—one can imagine the consequences of the almost utter absence of such social amenities between estranged races."

The white man lost the black man as a resource. Blacks had worked whites' land for three centuries and had developed an intimate knowledge of its idiosyncrasies and of the technologies best suited to cultivate it. Whites consulted them occasionally but most often did not, and blacks rarely volunteered advice. Wisdom and knowledge were the province of one race, so ignorance covered both and the South.

The consequences were harshest on southern blacks. Etiquette required them to live and act down to white expectations. Richard Wright recalled the time that, when he was a boy, he confided to a white woman his ambition to be a writer. The woman replied angrily: "You'll never be a writer. . . . Who on earth put such ideas into your nigger head?" Somewhat later, Wright nearly received a severe beating when, working at an optical company, he asked one of the white employees to show him the trade. Racial etiquette turned the American

Dream on its head; it devalued education and ambition, and rewarded its opposite. When blacks fulfilled these low expectations, they merely reinforced white perceptions. Etiquette trapped blacks in a role that robbed them of the opportunity to attain an identity, an intellectual and social potential, and the dignity that comes with a sense of self-worth. As Wright summarized his experience, "not only had the southern whites not known me, but more important still, . . . I had not had the chance to learn who I was. The pressure of southern living kept me from being the kind of person that I might have been. I had been what my surroundings had demanded."

Black parents found it prudent to squelch their children's ambitions to accumulate knowledge or property so that whites would let them be. Mississippi civil rights activist Fannie Lou Hamer recalled that whites poisoned her father's mules to keep him from getting ahead. Ned Cobb, a black Alabama farmer, had a short career as a landowner in the 1930s. A white landlord, supported by law officers, confiscated his land and personal property on manufactured charges. Ned's brother, Peter, a victim of a cheating white merchant, concluded that hard work and financial responsibility were liabilities for Alabama blacks. As Ned explained: "He weren't goin to have anything and after that, why, nothin could hurt him."

Racial etiquette was, above all, a system of control. Whites molded blacks to suit their perceptions, and blacks had little recourse to break that mold. Willie Morris noted in his autobiographical work, *North Toward Home* (1968), that "the Negroes in the town [Yazoo City, Miss.] were there; they were ours, to do with as we wished." Blacks felt their invisibility deeply. Black writer Maya Angelou grew up in Stamps, Arkansas, in the early 1940s. She graduated from high school and looked toward her future: "It was awful to be negro and have no control over my life. . . . We should all be dead." Powerlessness generated shame, guilt, and frustration. As black author Ernest J. Gaines observed, "We had all done the same thing sometime or another; we had all seen our brother, sister, mama, daddy insulted once and didn't do a thing about it."

Black Responses to White Supremacy

Southern blacks understood that they couldn't do a thing about it, or nearly so. Whites controlled not only behavior, but employment, housing, social services, education, and the legal system. Staunch localism characterized the South before World War II, and community institutions supported and enforced white supremacy. It was not simply a matter of learning and abiding by a series of behavioral rules, for racial etiquette was never immutable over time and between places, or even at the same time and place. Whites held the power to alter the tone and form of racial etiquette, and blacks had to adjust accordingly. Gunnar Myrdal reported that "Negroes often complain about the uncertainty they experience because of the fact that the initiative in defining the personal situation always belongs to the white man. It is the white man who chooses between the alternatives as to the character of the contact to be established." Accordingly, blacks were very guarded when white strangers approached them. "The reason for this," Myrdal suggested, "is that the Negro's person and property are practically subject to the whim of any white person." Some blacks solved the dilemma by always adopting the lowest common denominator or by becoming especially adept at measuring white behavior. A few blacks never learned or refused to learn these strategies. Richard Wright was one: "The words and actions of white people were baffling signs to me . . . I had to keep remembering what others took for granted . . . I could not make subservience an automatic part of my behavior."

Wright's imperceptions were dangerous. Prudence born of fear usually inhibited retaliation or departure from behavioral norms. Stories of white brutality against blacks, often for minor transgressions, circulated through black communities. As Wright explained, "the things that influenced my conduct as a Negro did not have to happen to me directly; . . . Indeed the white brutality that I had not seen was a more effective control of my behavior than that which I knew." In 1955, Anne Moody, a black Mississippi teenager, heard news of a lynching near her Delta home. She recalled her immobilizing fear: "I didn't know what one had to do or not to do as a Negro not to be killed." So a constant tension gripped blacks in their relations with whites, an uneasiness that a wrong word or a gesture could have serious consequences.

Blacks over the centuries had devised several mechanisms to relieve the tension and assert their dignity. One method was to internalize the white image, to totally submerge identity into an extension of white imagination. In the slavery era, this was what historian Stanley Elkin called the "Sambo" personality. While there was a good deal of "puttin' on ole massa" in both eras, habits could become ingrained. "I began to marvel," Richard Wright noted, "at how smoothly the black boys acted out the roles that the white race had mapped out for them.

Most of them were not conscious of living a special separate, stunted way of life. Yet I knew that in some period of their growing up . . . there had been developed in them a delicate, sensitive controlling mechanism that shut off their minds and emotions from all that the white race had said was taboo."

Some blacks had internalized their roles so well that they chafed when fellow blacks departed from their assigned place. They were the slave drivers of the twentieth century, ensuring conformist behavior even apart from whites. When Wright published a short story in a black newspaper in Jackson, Mississippi, his friends expressed disapproval: "They looked at me with new eyes, and a distance, a suspiciousness came between us." These blacks assumed not only their own inferiority, but that of other blacks as well. A black Knoxville dentist recalled that his attempt to rally the black community to support a campaign to purchase supplies, clothing, and food for indigent black schoolchildren during the Depression elicited a lukewarm response. When the white mayor endorsed the plan, volunteers inundated the dentist. Blacks learned to take their cues from whites rather than from each other.

Another option for blacks was to release frustration and humiliation through violence. Since attacking whites was out of the question, black-on-black violence was the result. The white community tacitly acknowledged this function and treated it with diffidence. The self-hatred expressed by such violence furthered class, generational, and gender divisions in the black community. Anne Moody confessed that, growing up, she hated Negroes: "In fact, I think I had a stronger resentment toward Negroes for letting the whites kill them than toward the whites." Moody hated black men most of all. Racial etiquette bound black men to a role that negated their manhood, that questioned if not destroyed their traditional roles as protectors and breadwinners in a society where such images were important. Black novelist Alice Walker wrote of Grange Copeland's first wife, Margaret, in her novel *The Third Life of Grange Copeland* (1970): "After only two years of marriage she knew that in her plantation world the mother was second in command, the father having no command at all."

There was, of course, the option of picking up and leaving, and southern blacks exercised this choice with increasing frequency after the turn of the century. Leaving had its own satisfaction by breaking the cycle of dependency on southern whites while at the same time challenging the prevailing white belief in benign race relations. During the 1930s, years when hard times everywhere should have restricted interregional mobility, the South experienced a net loss of a half million blacks to the North—even though the network of friends and relatives already in the North had likely communicated the difficulties of Depression-era life in those locales. The North held symbolic value that transcended reality. Richard Wright, about to embark on that journey himself, explained that "the North symbolized to me all that I had not felt and seen; had no relation whatever to what actually existed. Yet, by imagining a place where everything was possible, I kept hope alive in me."

If the North was the breath of air that kept the flame of hope alive for some, the thought of revenge, however remote, prevented a total submergence into caricature for others. There were sporadic outbreaks of arson in Black Belt areas, especially during and after picking season when whites would feel the loss of a crop most severely. Direct violence was less likely because the consequences were well known, not only for the individual involved but for his or her family and friends. More common was theft, which had the double benefit of hurting the white landlord or merchant and allowing the black perpetrator to behave in what whites thought was a predictable manner—so punishment was likely to be less severe than for such "crimes" as talking back to a white or looking at a white woman. But thieving also compromised morals; it was part of a system that left the black bereft of the basic values of Western civilization. So even in acts of crime or other antiwhite violence, the black man plotted his own destruction when his unrequited desire for revenge translated into a consuming hate for the white man. As a chastened Grange Copeland advises his son at the end of Alice Walker's novel, "when they [whites] got you thinking they're to blame for everything they have you thinking they're some kind of gods! You can't do nothing wrong without them being behind it. . . . Then you begins to think up evil and begins to destroy everybody around you, and you blames it on the crackers."

These "options" were scarcely options at all. Either blacks "chose" them unconsciously or whites precipitated the choice, but even in conscious selection the option often proved defeating. It was not surprising that some blacks sought to avoid all contact with whites. This was usually more possible in urban communities where blacks lived in discrete districts than in rural areas. Segregation enhanced separateness and thus provided a cloak of protection even as it reflected an inferior status; within the bounds of segregation, blacks could be self-sufficient in a number of ways: in churches, social clubs, schools, and businesses. "In Stamps," Maya Angelou recalled, "segregation was so complete that most Black children didn't really, absolutely know what whites looked like." Journalist Patricia A. Williams remembered her segregated black Charlotte neighborhood after World War II as a place where adults "formed protective, human boundaries . . . that sheltered the children long enough for most of us to grow into ourselves before leaving our isolated little world."

In rural areas, however—and the majority of southern blacks resided in the countryside as late as the 1930s—such segregation required extraordinary measures. There, black and white mingled at country stores, gins, on the roads, and in recreational pursuits such as hunting and fishing. Even so, the Reverend Ralph David Abernathy, former head of the Southern Christian Leadership Conference (SCLC), related how he escaped from contact with whites while growing up in the Alabama Black Belt during the 1930s. His father, rather than school him in the complexities of racial etiquette—an education that required a flawless execution of lessons learned—instructed young Ralph never to talk to a white man. As Abernathy explained, "a [white] man would ask me something and I'd just shake my head, so I got the reputation of being dumb. That was my father's way of protecting me . . . I would sit in the wagon and hold the reins, but if a white man said anything to me, I'd just be dumb. So I never had any contact with white people at all. I went to a black school. I went to a black church. I was surrounded by black people."

Since the early nineteenth century, black churches were central institutions in protecting and advancing urban black communities in the South. Blacks controlled these churches, especially after the Civil War: the ministers provided leadership and succor, and the members exercised their decision-making skills. The churches often served as schools, gathering places, and social clubs, and were community focal points in the midst of the uncertainties generated by race relations and blacks' tenuous economic and political circumstances. Social clubs offered more than comradeship; they often provided funds for burial, temporary social welfare, and, occasionally, workmen's compensation. After a time, more specific black institutions evolved to take over some of these functions, such as life insurance companies, banks, and building societies. Finally, the schools, however inferior to white facilities, offered employment and later served as a training ground for black activists.

Throughout the nineteenth and early twentieth centuries, these institutions formed the bulwark of southern black protest activity. Whether the issue was black voting rights and civil rights after emancipation or challenges to Jim Crow in the early 1900s and beyond, individuals supported by a network of kin, club, and church worked diligently to expand the limited range of black rights in the South. The civil rights movement did not emerge full blown from World War II, but rather was the culmination of hundreds of local efforts across the South over the previous century. The facility with which the movement leaders would mobilize southern blacks owed to this institutional and protest experience.

Segregation had existed in the antebellum South but became more prevalent after the Civil War when, ironically, blacks and sympathetic whites promoted it as an improvement over the exclusion blacks faced from schools, theaters, parks, and public conveyances. With segregation, at least blacks could count on their own facilities. But it quickly became apparent that segregation itself was another form of exclusion—exclusion from a decent education, from public parks, from restaurants, from some theaters and from sections within other theaters, and from the clubs and churches that guided community life throughout the South. As with other elements of racial etiquette, segregation was never rigid and uniform. It was an evolving institution, an accompaniment of modernization that followed the urban and economic development of the region. Regardless of its variations, however, segregation emphasized the inferiority of black southerners.

Segregation was a world framed by "white" and "colored"—emblems meant not only to separate but to denote superior or inferior status. The expenditure in funds and effort to maintain this form of racial charade was prodigious. Separate water fountains, rest rooms, entrances, seating, eating facilities, schools, and even days to shop were among the more obvious manifestations of segregation. But signs were not the only physical reminders of separation. The unpaved streets, unpainted houses, absence of sewers, running water, and electricity, as well as the filthiness of separate accommodations provided under the rubric *colored*, spoke volumes about place in the South. These reminders spelled inferiority and humiliation on a daily basis. As black writer John Williams remarked: "Nothing is quite as humiliating, so murderously angering, as to know that because you are black you may have to walk a half mile further than whites just to urinate; that because you are black you have to receive your food through a window in the back of a restaurant or sit in a garbage-littered yard to eat."

The Beguiling Corruption of Race

Whites also paid a price for their complicity in and direction of the biracial society. As black leader Booker T. Washington noted, "the white man cannot hold the Negro in the gutter without getting in there himself." Though whites controlled the etiquette of race, they could not deviate too far from the prescribed script, especially in the rural areas of the Deep South. Ferrol Sams's autobiographical novel, *Run with the Horsemen* (1982), recalls his childhood days in rural Georgia between the two world wars. On one occasion, the main character, Porter Osborne, Jr., sees the black janitor of his high school and wonders what mischief he would cause by addressing the black man as if he were white. Young Osborne soon thinks better of his prank: "To have addressed him as 'Mister' or 'Sir' would have violated too many rural Southern taboos of that era . . . it would have been like finding a loose piece of yarn and pulling it until the entire fabric of his regional civilization lay in a tangled snarl at his feet."

The etiquette was corrupting, in part because it denied feelings of love and intimacy. Numerous white children developed close relationships with blacks, especially black women, in their earliest years, but these relationships could never be fulfilled and were stunted as white children internalized the nature of race relations. As white civil rights activist Virginia Durr recalled of her Alabama childhood, "[I was] taught little by little that it was a relationship [I] couldn't have. I was just as intimate with Sarah and Nursie and the tall yellow man as if they were members of my family. Yet I literally never knew their names."

White children learned these lessons early. Sams noted that "by the time he was four or five years old, the Southern white was . . . subliminally convinced of his superiority." Even so, there were usually occasions later in childhood when the illogic of the system would jar the senses of the indoctrinated young white. Journalist Peter Ross Range, growing up in the university town of Athens, Georgia, related that when he was ten years old he overheard a conversation between his parents and their black maid concerning which college the maid's daughter should attend. Range was surprised to hear that the prospective choices were some distance from Athens. In his naïveté he asked why the daughter would not consider the university ten blocks from his house. "A stunned silence filled the room. . . . Finally, my father spoke: 'Negroes can't go to the university,' he said quietly. 'Only white people can.' Too young to be ashamed—I hadn't created this mess—I simply felt outrage."

By the time white southerners attained adulthood, most were inured or resigned to the injustice. They came to accept the inferior, demeaning status of blacks as a natural element of the southern landscape, and they looked through or past or not at all at the contradictions of the system. The maintenance of white supremacy dominated southern institutions and thought, and whites tried to eradicate the black completely from public discourse and life. Blacks were ignored in white schools; the press shunned them, except occasionally for criminal activity; and discussions of public issues treated the black as a nonperson. The exclusion of blacks enabled whites to adhere to racial perceptions designed to justify such exclusion. As black writer James Baldwin noted, "segregation has worked brilliantly in the South. . . . It has allowed white people, with scarcely any pangs of conscience whatever, to create, in every generation, only the Negro they wished to see." This image was yet another regional fiction designed to block out unpleasantness from white southerners' lives. Indirection, circumvention, and avoidance carried the white southerner around the harsh realities of defeat, poverty, and racial and social inequality. "People," Gunnar Myrdal observed of southern whites, "become trained generally to sacrifice truth, realism, and accuracy for the sake of keeping superficial harmony in every social situation."

Even the most well-meaning, sensitive whites succumbed to the beguiling corruption of white supremacy. Anne Braden, a white southerner who carried on a sometimes lonely campaign for racial equality during the 1950s, remembered an incident from her days as a novice reporter for a Birmingham newspaper in the late 1940s. Every weekday morning, she and a friend stopped for breakfast at a downtown cafeteria. Before breakfast, she called the sheriff's office to hear if any major stories had occurred overnight. If not, she sat down and ate breakfast with her friend. On this particular morning, she returned to her table after the call and her companion asked, "Anything doing?" She replied, "No, just a colored murder." Black-on-black violence was not news to the city's white media. At the moment Braden said those words, however, a black waitress was setting down some coffee at her table, "and it suddenly dawned on me what I'd said." The waitress, of course, mindful of the behavioral code, did not register a reaction, although Braden noticed that her hand shook a bit as she placed the cups down. "I wanted to say, 'I didn't mean that. I'm not the one who says it's not news . . . .' But I didn't say anything, because as I sat there, it suddenly dawned on me that I did mean it! It was like an octopus, it was getting me too . . . you can't be neutral. You are either part of it or you are against it. And I didn't know how to be against it."

There was an additional, equally costly price whites had to pay for their adherence to white supremacy. White leaders understood that appeals to racial solidarity successfully covered severe social and economic disparities among whites. Jefferson Davis assured his constituents in 1859 that, regardless of their economic status, they were all equal because of the inferior position of blacks: "[T]he existence [of slavery] . . . raises white men to the same general level, . . . it dignifies and exalts every white man by the presence of a lower race." After the end of Reconstruction, attacks on the Democratic party encountered the obstacle of race. Politicians, unwilling to address the social and economic ills of the region, fastened on race as a strategy both to avoid those issues and to ensure their continued leadership. The prominence of race in the political arena meant that whites had disfranchised themselves. With blacks removed from political participation de jure, whites effected their own withdrawal de facto. As Baptist preacher Will Campbell observed, "it's the redneck who's been the special victim of the whole system . . . he's never really known who the enemy was . . . every time the poor white began getting together in natural alliance with the equally dispossessed black, he's been told . . . the blacks were gonna ravish his wimminfolks. . . . He's never known how he's been had."

As Campbell implied, the system also hurt white women, since the leaders argued that black males were a threat not only to the white man's status, but also to the white woman's purity. The logic elevated white women to an exaggerated chastity, persons with no sexual feelings, delicate individuals who were not supposed to do much. Such an image made the black man's yearnings more heinous, of course, but it also required white women to suppress their feelings and contradicted the hard fact that, for most, a life of leisure was impossible.

But it is incorrect to assume that political will alone held the etiquette of race in place. Whites required relatively little convincing that they needed to perpetuate the biracial society in order to preserve their status and their region. The presence of the black assured the mass of poor whites of a degree of real power, since whites, whatever their status, controlled racial etiquette and blacks were, within certain ill-defined limitations, at the mercy of their whims. The habits formed through race relations were comforting to whites; there was at least some order and stability in their lives. If they could not depend on next year's crop, or on the wife living through the winter, or on the job at the mill, they could count on "the nigger." He was always there as their creation, at least until something or someone forced the regional imagination to think otherwise.

The Culture of Bondage

And that was not likely to happen quickly, because the entire culture of the South was entwined with preserving the racial status quo. Southerners would have found their past difficult to live with on its own, but their historical distinction was perennially a subject of derision, sermonizing, or vilification, depending on the mood and purpose of outsiders. While the rest of the nation in 1930 could look back at the late nineteenth and early twentieth centuries and see a linear progression upward of their civilization and culture, southerners could not share this perception. If anything, the glory of the region resided in the distant past, in the plantation regimes of the Old South or on the battlefields of Manassas and Shiloh and Gettysburg. Though their region was changing, southerners perceived their past as immutable; they used it to explain the present and reified it to the bargain. As Gunnar Myrdal noted, "reality is actually dynamic in the South, but people's ideas about reality are usually astonishingly static. . . . History is not used, as in the North, to show how society is continuously changing, but rather, on the contrary, to justify the status quo and to emphasize society's inertia." So, just as Southern white perceptions of blacks diverged from reality, so did their interpretation of history. It was a perspective that also justified the present state of race relations and most other aspects of regional life. These historical myths not only inhibited change but denied that there was anything that required change.

The myths included foremost the Lost Cause, an impressive body of intellectual alchemy that transformed a crushing defeat into a glorious crusade accompanied by heroism and sacrifice. The outcome was at worst immaterial and at least a sign of God's favor, for "He loveth whom He chasteneth." The leaders of that conflict were not only heroes but saints—subjects of statuary, art, literature, oratory, and history lessons. If Appomattox was a crucifixion of sorts, then the Resurrection followed with the aptly named Redeemers wresting control from corrupt Yankee- and Negro-infested regimes. They not only redeemed the memory of their fallen comrades but restored the racial balance as well. And they reminded their constituents of the danger in not mastering this history lesson: as Atlanta journalist Henry Grady explained in 1889, "whites understand that the slightest division on their part will revive those desperate days [of Reconstruction]." White supremacy was itself a powerful myth: it was the historical, natural order of things and benefited the Negro race in particular, since, without the guidance of whites, the Negro would certainly fall to savagery.

Southern white children learned these lessons in school and recalled them with parents and relatives, the past becoming more romantic and less challenged by contrary opinions with each passing generation. This was a society that passed down its heritage orally. Southerners lived or visited among extended kinship groups, where at least one member could recall either directly or through a close relative the Eden of the Old South, the sacrifice and suffering of the war, and the social and racial givens that emanated from this history. Southerners worshiped their past; it became their present, and it colored their vision of the future.

The past was not only heroic; it was holy. Southerners had been a religious people long before the Civil War as the gospel of evangelical Protestantism swept through the southern frontier early in the nineteenth century and became commonplace by 1860. As the sectional conflict took on an increasingly moral tone, marked by the sundering of national evangelical sects and a proliferation of Bible-toting and -quoting politicians and intellectuals, self-righteousness permeated the thought and rhetoric of both North and South. In a verbal war for the soul, no compromise was possible—an individual or a section was a sinner or a saint, saved or damned. There was no middle ground, no moderation in such a contest.

Defeat required explanation, and the life fashioned from that catastrophe required sanction. Fashioning a historical myth was an important mechanism to deal with death and the life that followed, but such cataclysmic events required special justification beyond the collection of facts that comprise a history. The elevation of heroes to saints and of politicians to redeemers consciously invoked religious metaphors. The southern way of life was thus not only the result of a particular history; it was sanctified by the deaths of Confederate heroes. To cherish and honor their memories it was necessary to carry on a particular lifestyle, to follow and obey the Redeemers, to adhere to the etiquette of race, and to tolerate no dissent from the prevailing patterns of thought and behavior. The strain of social reform in southern evangelical thought dissolved, leaving only a pale reflection of the Social Gospel good works that characterized northern sects after the Civil War. Southerners saw no need to change a society that had already experienced redemption. Just as their history came to deny change, so did their religion, and racial etiquette became not only tradition but an element of that religion. There was irony in this, too, a wide gap between religious myth and the reality of professed evangelical principles. W. T. Couch, director of the University of North Carolina Press, expressed the contradiction in 1927:

> If Jesus Christ were to come to earth today and come into a Southern community and start preaching as we are told he did two thousand years ago, if he suggested again his teaching of the brotherhood of man, and instead of a parable were to preach against the condition that negroes cannot ride on busses in North Carolina and that they were in many things treated in a somewhat unbrotherly way, what would happen to him? . . . If he kept up his agitation the mob would rise and demand his blood. . . . Jesus Christ was a radical; his teachings, though professed, can hardly be seriously mentioned in public in the South.

The South came to prize unanimity and conformity—"social fundamentalism," as sociologist Howard W. Odum called it. Racial etiquette took on even greater importance because it represented a public display of fealty to regional myths, a public statement that the individual was safe, a good southerner, a good Christian. Southern religion was, as theologian Samuel S. Hill claimed, "an ethos without an ethic," piety without social responsibility. The result was an insular individual and an isolated society, inherently defensive, threatened by the slightest (at least to outsiders) provocation. By cutting off outside influences, southerners fell back on their own imaginations to create an ever-greater dream province, to concoct ever-more ferocious enemies, and to deny the reality of their circumstances. "The net result of this closed organization," Frank Rose, former president of the University of Alabama explained, "has been a heightened sentimentalism, a proud refusal to face the reality of poverty; a complacency with social evils as the 'givens' of God; . . . a militant reaction against self-criticism from within the South, and chauvinism against . . . 'outsiders.' In a word, the South clings to exaggerated myths of a closed and happy society."

The perception was an effective obstacle to change, "against even considering whether there was any need for change," as historian T. Harry Williams suggested. So the South sailed through defeat, Reconstruction, a prolonged agricultural depression, the industrial revolution, and a world war and remained the South.

This is not to say that all white southerners in the 1930s (or earlier) stood mute before the altar of their culture. Although World War I did not provoke any immediate alterations in southern culture, it stirred the cobwebs in the regional mind. "The South not only reentered the world with the first World War," poet Allen Tate explained, "it looked around and saw for the first time since about 1830 that the Yankees were not to blame for everything." One result was a flowering of southern literature that undertook a forbidden introspection into both the rotten condition of the contemporary South and the blasted legacy of the past. The writers—William Faulkner, Thomas Wolfe, T. S. Stribling, and Ellen Glasgow, among others—did not so much propose solutions as they offered insights. A growing number of social scientists and journalists in the 1920s and thirties began to provide empirical supports for these insights. Chapel Hill's Howard W. Odum was among the foremost of this group of critics. His monumental work, *Southern Regions of the United States* (1936), is as much a tract on the limits of southern culture as it is an economic analysis, diagnosing the region's major cultural illnesses accurately, if somewhat obtusely: "There is a like-mindedness of the region in the politics of the 'Solid South,' in the Protestant religion, in matters of racial culture and conflict, and in state and sectional patriotism, much of it tending to take the form of loyalties to the past and to outmoded patterns rather than faith in the future and confidence in achievement."

Odum, his Institute for Research in Social Science, and his able accomplice at the University of North Carolina Press, W. T. Couch, generated a prodigious body of literature probing various southern problems that was remarkable for a region that denied their existence. Odum and his colleagues held the faith that education and the dissemination of data and conclusions from the numerous articles and books would seep into the consciousness of southerners and result in a cultural revolution. The problem, they felt, was not with the South or with the white southerner, but with his confining culture. The "intrinsic truths" spoken by facts would change regional folkways and open up a closed society.

But the influence of these hearty liberals was limited as much by the fact that these men and women were also part of southern culture as by the depth and impermeability of that culture. Many of them experienced the ostracism and isolation that accompanied their outspokenness. During the mid-1920s, Odum's journal, *Social Forces*, embarked on an ambitious series of articles dealing candidly and critically with race and religion. The subsequent uproar forced Odum to measure his words more carefully, and even in *Southern Regions* he did not venture too far from the presentation of data and facts. For others, the fear of being outcast as well as the guilt of opposing beliefs learned from loved ones created great psychological pressures. Thomas Wolfe's protagonist Eugene Gant, who delighted in debunking southern myths from his voluntary exile in New York, acknowledged the irresistibility of southern culture and the dangers of opposition. Rationally, he could call the South a "barren spiritual wilderness," with its "murderous entrenchment against all new life." Yet, "so great was his fear of the legend, his fear of their antagonism, that he still pretended the most fanatic devotion to them."

Life followed fiction in the South, and the internal pressure of an omnipresent culture consumed several iconoclasts. Clarence Cason, an English professor at the University of Alabama, wrote a book, *90 Degrees in the Shade* (1935), that surveyed the South's decline since the antebellum era. Although the work decried the exploitation of textile workers and the violent excesses of poor whites, it skirted the race issue. But Cason's tone was critical, and in a society perceived as blessed, criticism was inappropriate. As the book's publication approached, Cason became increasingly anxious. He fired off a telegram to his publisher, W. T. Couch, complaining that "I have thought as much about the possible effects of the book that it will be exceedingly difficult for me to remain in Tuscaloosa after the work is published. . . . The situation appears to me to be critical indeed." Three days later, he killed himself.

Nell Battle Lewis, a columnist for the Raleigh (N.C.) *News and Observer* and daughter of a prominent family, broke numerous conventions with her hard-hitting stories on the role of women, race, lynching, and labor exploitation during the late 1920s and early 1930s. Despite her journalistic crusade, she confided, "the whole of my sentimental attachment is to the Old South order. . . . I almost feel as if I had stuck a knife in a friend." Her ambivalence precipitated a severe nervous breakdown, and when she returned to writing in 1935, it was as an arch-conservative supporter of the racial and gender status quo. Her penchant for religious mysticism and ghosts was a bizarre indication of how she had succumbed under the pressure to conform.

In order to avoid both internal and external conflicts, most Southern liberals in the 1930s acknowledged the inviolability of the racial order. When they expressed opinions on race, it was frequently as part of a larger discussion on agriculture, poverty, or health. "What confronts the Southeast today is the problem of making the best possible use of eight million blacks," Odum colleague Gerald W. Johnson admitted. "But," he continued, "this is no special problem. The same deficiencies that have wasted the energies of the white population are precisely the deficiencies that have handicapped the black. . . . From this standpoint there is no Negro problem, only a Southern problem."

Liberals prefaced discussions on race with warnings against outside interference. Odum often commented that one of the most important services of his program at Chapel Hill was to train regional leaders because change could only occur under indigenous auspices. Odum and others took the view that regional change, especially in race relations, had to occur gradually. As South Carolina journalist Ben Robertson warned, "suddenness was not the way. There was too much poverty and too much ignorance for suddenness. We would move step by step, generation by generation—from position to position."

If the South's new, young, progressive writers and academics moved with such agonizing caution, the prospect for altering the regional culture and racial etiquette in the near future looked dim. For here in the 1930s, with the New Deal swirling around them, with agriculture undergoing major changes, and with the region in the midst of a literary and intellectual flowering, timidity characterized those who perceived the region with a critical eye. Those who had never thought or who were afraid to think about bridging the gap between myth and reality remained in command. The critics, though, were performing a valuable service. Their work focused on regional culture, a culture that supported the etiquette of race, but elements of that culture, however fixed they may have appeared in the 1930s, also contained the attributes to release the South from its bondage. This would become one of the great ironies of an ironic region: the culture that enthralled would be the culture that liberated. The first step in this transformation—a change in attitude and perception—was underway in the novels and academic works of the time. As novelist and poet Robert Penn Warren observed, "if you look at a thing, the very fact of your looking changes it. . . . if you think about yourself, the very fact changes you."

The Culture of Liberation

The beginnings of analysis and introspection portended an uncovering of the positive attributes of southern culture. David Mathews, former president of the University of Alabama, noted that "all our traditions are two-sided coins . . . the very tendencies that have made Southerners reactionary could, indeed, have at times made them progressive." Southern religion sanctified and ossified southern culture, but the same evangelical Protestantism that clouded whites' image of regional ills provided vision for a growing band of progressive southerners in the 1930s. Aubrey Williams, James Dombrowski, and Will Alexander were ordained evangelical ministers who interpreted their Christian duty quite differently from their white southern brothers and sisters. In addition, the black perspective on evangelical Protestantism was less dour and placed a greater emphasis on community than did the individualistic white churches, where Jesus' crucifixion took precedence over the Resurrection. Black ministers also had greater freedom and authority than their white counterparts, which meant they could challenge and lead their congregations rather than merely reflect their will. Finally, evangelical theology that had settled into dogma could just as well inspire imagination and introspection. Anne Braden recalled that Christian doctrine as expressed by her minister in Anniston, Alabama, was her "great opening to the world," providing an alternative to the stifling localism and conformity of her town and stimulating questions that moved her to discover the buried aspects of her soul and culture.

The southerner's emphasis on the past also held positive attributes. History provides an anchor, an essential beginning point for embarking on a meaningful journey toward the future, but for a long time that anchor had been a burden immobilizing the South in its place. What was necessary was not a denial of the past, but rather an understanding of the Old South, slavery, segregation, and the Civil War. Historians had not assisted this process; instead, their works merely mimicked regional myths. But in the 1930s a young historian from Arkansas, C. Vann Woodward, began to uncover the rich tapestry of southern history that lay beneath the myth. That history revealed a common struggle of blacks and common whites, not necessarily against the omnipresent Yankee, but against grasping forces within the region. It was a history that told southerners that their differences could be their strength, their defeat could teach humility, their racial struggles could teach humanity, and their centuries of shared living would teach respect and forgiveness.

This last point was crucial, because white southerners evinced a strong sense of place along with their other cultural attachments. Their fierce localism, attachment to kin, living and dead, and their readiness to defend hearth and region reflected this connection. But blacks shared that attachment as well, even if the etiquette of race rendered whites oblivious to such feelings in blacks—a people after all with no country but the heart, who had traveled out of Africa, down the Mississippi, or to the next county often at the whim of others and rarely out of their own desires. The connection was there nevertheless. "I can deal with the South," black poet Nikki Giovanni explained, "because I love it." To northerners who find her attachment to the South difficult to understand, Alice Walker replied, "they have never lived, as I have, at the end of a long road in a house that was faced by the edge of the world on one side and nobody for miles on the other. They have never experienced the magnificent quiet of a summer day when the heat is intense and is the essence of all life."

But who should reveal this rich culture—the healing, loving force of religion, the shared understanding of history, the commonality of place? The novelists, journalists, and academics who initiated discussions in the 1920s and thirties were important catalysts, but their reach was limited. Political and economic leaders served as guardians and arbiters of the status quo, so revelation from that quarter was unlikely, and the mass of southern whites remained frozen in their culture, satisfied in their position vis-à-vis the blacks. The likelihood of outsiders—the federal government, Yankee reformers, philanthropic organizations—attaining a voice in the region was even more remote; the memories, or rather the myths, of Civil War and Reconstruction were too fresh to admit even the most benign interloper. So it would fall to southern blacks to reveal to their region the liberating qualities of its culture, thereby securing redemption for whites and humanity for themselves. South Carolina writer James McBride Dabbs projected this scenario: "A despised minority, excluded from the common life returns at last more in love than in hatred to reveal . . . not only that possibility of community that has always haunted the mind of the South, but also . . . a vision of the universal meaning of failure and defeat, revealing how men become human through the positive acceptance and affirmation of defeat. . . . For we shall understand that Southern history was God's way of leading two originally opposed people into a richer life than either could have found alone."

At the time—the 1930s—this seemed a hopeless prospect, because the racial code had locked blacks into a pattern of behavior that rendered them invisible. If they could not be seen or heard, how could they affect this revelation? But events occurring outside the South would soon provide both the context and the encouragement for southern blacks to accelerate their centuries-old challenge to the biracial society. The South had weathered national and international crises in the past, but the dimensions this time would be different—first depression, then war. A war had entombed the South, and a war would begin the process of resurrection.

The Civil Rights Movement in the South

☆ Capital

● Civil Rights Location

○ Other City

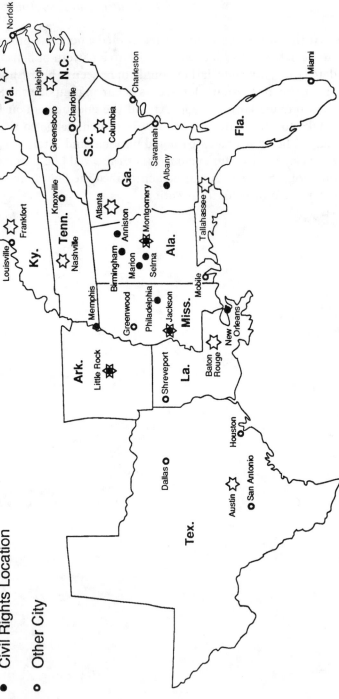

II / "A Kind of Sunlight": Depression, War, and Change, 1930–1945

"Tore Up and A-Movin'": Down and Out on the Farm

Heat shimmered from the road that bore wagons, mules, and drivers to the ungainly two-storied gin that received the cotton and devoured it. This was an autumn ritual performed by southerners, black and white, for generations. It was a ritual now performed more out of habit than with purpose, because the contraction of international markets, competition from abroad and the Southwest, the boll weevil, overproduction, ruined soils, and rising prices for fertilizer, seed, and equipment had rendered King Cotton an impotent monarch over a depleted region.

These forces were color-blind, of course. But blacks, as the poorest of the South's poor and as most likely to be sharecroppers, were least able to withstand the downward spiral of staple commodities. In good years, a sharecropper family might clear fifty to sixty dollars. More likely, they would finish the year in debt, and a series of bad years made it impossible for the family to extricate itself from financial obligation. Not surprisingly, mobility in the Cotton Belt was high. One estimate held that croppers moved once every three years. Richard Wright was nine years old before he had spent so much as one year in the same place. Blacks moved sometimes seeking better circumstances and sometimes at the whim of the landowner. Not owning land or much personal property increased the chances of a nomadic existence. "Tore up and a-movin'," lamented one North Carolina sharecropper in the early 1930s. "I wish I could have me one acre o' land dat I could call mine. I'd be willin' to eat dry bread de rest o' my life if I had a place I could settle down on and nobody could tell me I had to move no more."

But no matter how many times they moved, there was no escape from the hard times, flimsy shacks, premature death, illiteracy, and poverty that accompanied a life on the farm. As Gracie Turner, another black North Carolina sharecropper, put it in the mid-1930s: "Every year's been hard, de forty-nine years I been here. Dat's all dey is to expect—work hard and go hongry part time—long as we lives on de other man's land." This dependency and poverty merely confirmed the white man's perspective on blacks and reinforced the etiquette of race.

Worse days lay ahead for Gracie Turner and her fellow sharecroppers. The Agricultural Adjustment Act (AAA), one of the earliest New Deal measures (1933), paid farm owners to take cotton land out of production in order to drive up prices for the staple. Despite provisions protecting croppers and tenants, evictions multiplied in the Cotton Belt, and owners sometimes used their government checks to purchase tractors, further reducing the need for labor. Local officials administered the act and were unlikely to challenge influential landlords; black sharecroppers dared not register complaints, for that would violate the behavioral code and would, at the least, reduce their chances of catching on elsewhere. Between 1933 and 1940, the AAA was responsible for diminishing the number of sharecroppers in the South by one-third. Some croppers stayed on as occasional farm laborers subsisting on federal welfare and below-subsistence wages. Others pulled up and left for towns and cities where they crowded in with relatives or into boarding houses or wooden shacks in poorly drained districts, frequently without running water—urban replicas of the rural life they had left behind, except there was no land. And some journeyed to northern cities.

Those blacks who drifted into southern towns and cities (and white urban dwellers discouraged this migration) found little improvement in their situation. The employment base of southern black urbanites had been narrowing even before the Depression, with whites pushing blacks out of skilled occupations such as carpentry, masonry, and painting. Apprenticeships were drying up as well. Even in traditional "nigger work" such as barbering, waiting on tables, and hotel labor, blacks were losing ground by 1930. As the Depression deepened, so did black urban unemployment. Black historian Charles B. Rousseve described the situation in New Orleans where, historically, blacks had been engaged in a wide variety of occupations. He wrote in 1937 that "the Negro who, in antebellum days, performed all types of labor . . . found himself gradually almost eliminated from the various trades. In recent years, even from the meanest forms of servile occupations he is being excluded by his fairer-skinned fellow citizens."

As mechanization and new industries made their way into the South during the early decades of the twentieth century, blacks rarely benefited from them. In the building trades, the change from lumber to steel reduced demand for carpentry. Wheelwrights and coopers were vanishing as factory machinery overtook such work. Trucks were replacing drays—traditionally a black-dominated transport trade. Few blacks worked in the textile mills of the southern Piedmont—too many white women worked in these factories for employers to consider black male workers, and white men generally refused to work alongside blacks. The mechanization of the textile industry in the 1920s provided a further bar against black employment, since the belief was widespread that blacks were unable to master the mechanical skills necessary to operate the new machines. On the other hand, the dexterity with which blacks operated machinery in the tobacco factories of North Carolina and Virginia was usually offered as proof of their inferiority, since races of superior intellect (*i.e.,* whites) supposedly could not work as well with their hands.

Living conditions for blacks in the urban South reflected their bleak occupational prospects and were additional reminders of inferiority. In Memphis, blacks lived in neighborhoods with names such as "Slippery Log Bottoms," "Queen Bee Bottoms," and "Shinertown" that indicated their disadvantaged topographical position. Squalor confirmed racial stereotypes, and since eradicating or improving such areas would threaten that confirmation, they remained as rural vestiges in an urban milieu.

Endurance and Advance: A New Deal

But the New Deal changed some things. How much is difficult to pinpoint, because historians are still sifting through the evidence; moreover, the real change may have been more psychological than tangible, which renders an accurate assessment more difficult. In addition, the deterioration of black economic status on the farm and in the towns and cities of the South possibly made small advances seem much larger. It was not, of course, the specific purpose of New Deal programs in the South to improve the status of blacks; as elsewhere, the focus of legislation in the South was to boost the morale and employment opportunities of the middle class and enable businesses and banks to resume normal operations. In the process, the general economic recovery was expected to enhance the economic recovery of blacks, and as black status rose, white racism would diminish—or so the theory of the Roosevelt administration went.

But the New Deal operated within a federal context, and southern local and state power structures were geared toward the maintenance of white supremacy, so it was unlikely that political institutions, courts, and private agencies would apply New Deal legislation even-handedly in the region. In terms of labor policy, an early measure, the National Recovery Act (NRA), that established wage and hour guidelines probably hurt blacks more than it helped. By raising wages and shortening hours, the NRA made many menial occupations such as messengers, janitors, and elevator operators attractive to whites, who quickly displaced blacks. When the NRA increased the average wage in tobacco factories from nineteen cents to thirty-two cents an hour (subsequently raised to sixty-five cents an hour by the Fair Labor Standards Act), black employment in the industry was cut in half; white employment increased by 40 percent. Southern employers, unaccustomed to color-blind wage scales, petitioned for a racial differential, which the NRA denied, sealing the fate of black workers in many southern industries.

On the other hand, federal encouragement to labor organizations elicited a strong black response. By 1935, the United Mine Workers had recruited 23,000 black members in Alabama, though segregated from whites. And newly organized black tobacco-factory workers in Richmond held a successful strike for better wages and a forty-hour workweek. But labor unions in general were unwelcome in the South, especially outside the relatively few heavy industries, and even some of those unions, such as the Steelworkers, discriminated against black members and narrowly defined the types of jobs they could perform at the mill.

The New Deal accumulated a slightly better record for southern blacks in terms of relief, primarily due to the vigilance of Public Works Administration (PWA) chief Harold Ickes, former president of the National Association for the Advancement of Colored People (NAACP) chapter in Chicago. In addition to agricultural labor and domestic service, federal relief became the major source of black income in the South during the 1930s. Blacks also received 59 percent of federally subsidized PWA housing in the South, and PWA funds built or renovated more than eight hundred hospitals, school buildings, and libraries for southern blacks. Referring to federal relief efforts in the South, the NAACP journal, *Crisis*, declared, "Mr. Roosevelt's relief organizations . . . have made great gains for the race in areas which heretofore have set their faces steadfastly against decent relief for Negroes."

But later New Deal relief agencies, such as the Works Progress Administration (WPA), adhered more closely to regional racial customs.

In Memphis, for example, local WPA officials trained black girls in domestic service and helped them find positions earning five dollars a week. The trainees worked beneath a banner which proclaimed that "dishwashing is an ancient art but few are proficient in it." The Memphis *Press-Scimitar*, commenting on the "curriculum," boasted that the course of study "goes to make a well-rounded servant." Blacks encountered discrimination when applying for job openings in federal projects such as the Tennessee Valley Authority (TVA), and when they succeeded in landing employment, they were relegated to the most menial positions. The Authority barred them from vocational schools and from training sessions for higher-skilled jobs. In addition, there were no blacks living in the TVA model community of Norris.

Even one of the more positive accomplishments of the New Deal for blacks, the PWA housing program, had its adverse side. The government often built black housing projects in socially and physically undesirable areas. In Charleston, South Carolina, the PWA project was located on the site of the former city dump, surrounded by marshland. In Memphis and Jacksonville, a federal official noted, the housing was "virtually isolated from Negro colleges, high schools, civic and welfare organizations, churches, businesses and the better residential sections in these cities." It appears that historian Harvard Sitkoff's assessment of the New Deal's impact on the black South is generally accurate: "Black southerners endured, but did not advance in the 1930s."

But southern blacks were aware of other things apart from New Deal legislation. They heard about President Roosevelt's black cabinet; they knew that the Democratic party at its national convention in 1936 accredited black delegates for the first time in its history; and they relished stories about Eleanor Roosevelt and her defiance of southern custom, sitting in the black section of an auditorium in Birmingham, Alabama, at a Southern Conference on Human Welfare meeting in 1937. Some came into contact with whites from Washington or other parts of the country in federal employ on public works or in welfare offices who did not demand the deference of etiquette. White southerners in certain areas of the South appeared to modify the rules of racial discourse as well. Gunnar Myrdal reported that, by the late 1930s, "upper and middle class whites in the Upper South are beginning to call upper class Negroes by these titles [*Mr.*, *Mrs.*, and *Miss*]." And some newspapers had begun to capitalize the word *negro*. These were not extensive changes, to be sure, but the Depression, the sudden injection of federal money and personnel into the region, and the widespread hope generated by the jaunty president and his First Lady, were new elements in an old, tired region.

Perhaps the best indication that something different was afoot was the growing disenchantment among white southern leaders with certain aspects of the New Deal after 1936. Some of these objections were genuinely philosophical—the fear of big government usurping local prerogatives, for example, was a very sensitive issue in the South. The fact that some of the talented newcomers whom the Roosevelt administration had attracted to the nation's capital had leftist sympathies was another cause for uneasiness among southern leaders. The administration's tacit support of federal antilynching legislation and the scheme to pack the Supreme Court did not please conservative southern whites. The Memphis *Commercial-Appeal* probably spoke for many in the leadership circle when it complained in 1937 that the New Deal had succumbed to "professional agitators and adventurers" who were targeting "southern customs, southern traditions, southern institutions." By 1940, the editors noted with alarm the "pinkish rind of sociology which surrounds the core of administration policy" and the "steady and heavy pressure toward the centralization of government." While some of this criticism could be passed off as typical southern sensitivity to anything remotely threatening change, it was also an indication of a wider fear that federal intrusion portended ill for the future of the southern Eden.

An intricate web of black dependence bound southern race relations. Dissenting blacks faced loss of property, legal harassment, eviction, denial of credit at the store, and violence. Black lives and livelihood literally depended upon whites, so many blacks, especially in rural areas, ingratiated themselves with powerful whites. Ned Cobb, though proud of his independence, was savvy enough to cultivate a few well-placed whites in his community, and they returned his fealty by supporting him in disputes with other white men. As black sociologist Charles S. Johnson noted in the 1930s, "for those [blacks] still living in the country there is, it would appear, one unfailing rule of life. If they would get along with least difficulty, they should get for themselves a protecting white family." This lingering paternalism sealed black dependence. "It bound the black man to the past," C. Vann Woodward explained, "to dependence and withdrawal, to 'his place.' It avoided much competition and some overt tension, but it closed the door to independence and the future."

The New Deal held the potential for short-circuiting this dependence. When Ned Cobb looked in his mailbox for a check from the federal government to cover costs for fertilizer and seed, one strand of that web of dependence began to disintegrate. Occasionally, a Farm Security Administration agent would offer to stake a black tenant to land and supplies. The WPA opened up rare employment options for rural blacks. One white Alabama landlord complained, "Why, they [WPA] are going to take all our hands away from us and put them to work on the big road. They are going to give them two dollars a day, and it would break me to pay that much." Georgia governor Eugene Talmadge presented the hard logic to President Roosevelt: "I wouldn't plow nobody's mule for fifty cents a day when I could get $1.30 for pretending to work on the DITCH." Losing control of the black man's labor reduced the black man's dependence, which ultimately threatened the character of southern race relations.

On the Wings of War: Black Aspirations and Federal Initiatives

As the nation prepared for war, the federal presence grew and black dependence declined further. For whites, the advent of war generated renewed patriotism and an opportunity to prove their mettle on a familiar stage, but war also generated anxiety about the intrusion of the disorderly outside world into an insular community governed by a rigid set of rules. The New Deal had already brought foreboding to the surface, particularly over race relations. It was not as if white southerners could encourage and welcome change in one area of race relations without affecting other racial customs. It was all of one piece. Segregation kept the black in his appropriate place; political disfranchisement did the same; the legal system enforced that place with tortuous interpretations and applications of the law; the educational system both reinforced and justified subservience; living conditions on the farm and in towns and cities reflected black character, which, in turn, justified discrimination in these other aspects of southern life; and racial etiquette was the behavioral manifestation of institutional inferiority. For blacks it was a vicious circle, as one form of discrimination justified another which secured the first. For whites it was the natural order, and tampering with any part would doom the whole.

Southern blacks looked upon war less equivocally as they recalled that their situation had improved in the aftermath of three previous wars. The ideals of the American Revolution helped to topple slavery in many northern states, had outlawed the slave trade everywhere, and had even triggered open debate in Virginia. The Civil War brought emancipation and the promise of political and economic advancement, realized only partially and briefly during Reconstruction, and World War I encouraged massive black migration from the South to seek the first major economic opportunities opened to blacks in the urban, industrialized North. On the eve of World War II, the same rhetorical ideals that flourished during the earlier conflicts entered the public arena and, with that, black hopes as well.

The preparations for war created a stirring in the South. Defense industries offered attractive alternatives to the hardships of cultivating the land, and the prospect of fighting, even dying, for one's country touched the region's sense of romance, as did the opportunity to travel to distant lands and to be at the center of things after trolling the backwaters of American civilization for so long. Federal money— eventually twelve billion dollars—began flowing in, and blacks and whites were moving about to towns and cities and out of the region altogether.

A black sharecropper could leave his mule and plow and earn more money in one week of work in a defense plant than he ever saw at the end of a good crop year. He could enjoy the luxury of choosing a place to live, of paying other people to work for him—dry cleaners, taxi drivers, waitresses, and maintenance personnel. He could exercise choices in how and where to spend his money, assured that a drought or tumbling international markets or capricious landlords would not suddenly end his relative prosperity. Or, if he took up a gun, he could demonstrate his worthiness for first-class citizenship and visibility. And if both he and his nation were fighting to preserve democratic principles, how could his countrymen deny him his due? "Ask any Negro sharecropper or worker what his neighbor is thinking," one southern black leader noted, "and if he has sense enough to come out of the rain he will say that the white man cannot lick Hitler with his right hand and keep the Negro down with his left."

Even some southern whites recognized that the war against fascism generated too many contradictions at home to be ignored. In July, 1943, William Faulkner wrote a letter to his stepson who was serving in the armed forces. Referring to race relations, Faulkner predicted that "a change will come out of this war. If it doesn't, if the politicians and people who run this country are not forced to make good the shibboleths they glibly talk about, freedom, liberty, human rights, then you young men who have lived through it will have wasted your precious time, and those who don't live through it will have died in vain."

Black aspirations soared not only on the wings of war, but also on some more down-to-earth events. The federal government became bolder during the war years, and blacks encouraged this boldness when, through their national organizations, they pressured the Roosevelt administration for equal employment opportunities in defense industries and in the federal government. In June, 1941, an executive order established the Fair Employment Practices Committee (FEPC), designed to report and redress grievances arising from discriminatory hiring and work practices. Once the FEPC reported the violation to the appropriate government agency (the Department of Defense, for example), that agency would implement disciplinary measures. The president appointed Mark Ethridge, liberal publisher of the Louisville *Courier-Journal*, as the committee's first chairman. In addition, the United States Employment Service (USES) refused to accept ads that specified race. Partly as a result of these measures, the number of blacks in federal employ nationally tripled to 200,000 workers during the war years.

The federal government acted in other areas on behalf of blacks. In January, 1942, a mob of whites in a small southeastern Missouri town lynched Cleo Wright, a black. The Japanese, who had bombed Pearl Harbor the previous month prompting American entrance into the war, used the incident to expose the hypocrisy of the Allies' contention that they were fighting to preserve democracy and freedom. In an unprecedented move, the Justice Department, under Attorney General Francis Biddle, launched an investigation of the lynching. Though Biddle's efforts were fruitless, they signaled a policy change in Washington. Federal officials had traditionally maintained that such incidents were local matters. Since southern blacks could hardly expect local law-enforcement personnel (some of whom may have been involved in or at least knowledgeable of the attack) to undertake an inquiry, let alone to redress a denial of due process, the intervention of federal authorities established an important precedent.

The United States Supreme Court added to the growing list of black advances during the war by setting another crucial precedent. Dr. Lonnie Smith was a black Houston dentist who had unsuccessfully attempted to vote in Texas' Democratic party primary. Around the turn of the century, eight southern states, including Texas, had established the "white primary" that barred blacks from selecting Democratic candidates for the general election. Since Democrats in these states faced, at most, token opposition in the general election, the primary became the most important contest. Democratic officials contended that the party was a private organization and hence could set its own membership guidelines. The High Court, in *Smith* v. *Allwright* (1944), issued an 8-1 decision in favor of Smith, rejecting the state's argument and contending that, to the contrary, political parties were agents of the state and could not therefore discriminate in their membership. Primaries were not private races, but public elections open to every eligible voter. Southern blacks, most of whom had been effectively disfranchised since early in the century, could now look forward to regaining their political voice.

The impact of these encouraging federal decisions, however, was more apparent than real. They scarcely budged regional racial traditions and, in fact, generated strong resistance from whites whose sense of history told them to expect the worst. The FEPC, which had promised to eliminate job discrimination, accomplished much less than that. Southern white leaders greeted the committee with derision—"dat cummittee fer de pertecshun of Rastus and Sambo"—and indignation. Mississippi congressman John E. Rankin feared that the FEPC was the opening wedge for a "communistic dictatorship," while L. Mendel Rivers, a South Carolina congressman, predicted racial "bloodshed" if the committee pursued its objectives. The committee stirred up the usual sexual fantasies that accompanied any civil rights proposal. Mississippi senator Theodore G. Bilbo lectured that "every Negro in America who is behind movements of this kind . . . dream[s] of social equality and intermarriage between whites and blacks."

As with New Deal legislation, the implementation of federal policies during the war usually necessitated the cooperation and participation of local officials. FEPC procedures required blacks to file the initial complaint—a stipulation fraught with considerable economic, if not personal, danger in many areas of the South. Also, Mark Ethridge moved cautiously, fearful of white reaction in his native region. He strongly opposed antidiscriminatory legislation and counted on voluntarism among white southerners.

By 1942, it was apparent that discrimination was rife in federal agencies and defense plants throughout the South. Ella Dotson, for example, a black southerner, wrote to the president in October, 1942, that the USES office in Memphis refused her application for work in a local defense plant: "They could give me white lady day work in their homes . . . which they have always gave me . . . but that is not defense work to help my country. . . . Please sir if it is in your power, write these people." The experience of Doris Jones was equally frustrating:

she had worked in Washington as a clerk-typist and had scored a 95.52 (out of a possible 100) on her federal civil-service exam. When she returned home to New Orleans, no federal agency would hire her.

Southern racial customs compromised efficiency in the war effort. The Southern Welding Institute in Memphis, for example, trained and qualified 180 blacks by 1943 in the trade of arc welding. None of these graduates was able to secure a welding position at the numerous defense installations in the South, though plants and shipyards elsewhere quickly hired those who were willing to relocate out of the region. At the Charleston, South Carolina, Navy Yard, black employees in the powerhouse trained whites to serve as engineers in the engine room. Despite the superior experience of these black teachers, they did not advance to engineer positions. The mechanics union, for one thing, prohibited black membership.

Federal officials were aware of the persistent discrimination in the South. Those stationed in southern communities, however, felt constrained by indigenous customs: hiring black women for defense work meant upsetting the local source for domestic labor; forcing contractors to hire skilled blacks risked violence, because white workers frequently stated their aversion to working alongside blacks; and many shipyards had negotiated closed-shop agreements with labor unions that required union membership to work in the yard.

FEPC was not a complete failure; for an underfunded and undersupported agency, it accomplished modest gains. The committee occasionally held hearings in southern communities to determine the extent of discrimination, and it succeeded in removing some of the more blatant abuses, especially in job advertising. Also, the committee effected compromises at some shipyards and defense plants by acquiescing in segregated work arrangements if the facility hired blacks.

But the case of the Alabama Dry Dock and Shipbuilding Company (ADDSCO) in Mobile illustrated the tenuous nature of such compromises. Mobile's population had doubled to 200,000 inhabitants between the outbreak of war and 1943. Severe housing shortages and the breakdown of urban services generated chaos. Blacks comprised 30 percent of the city's population, and since they could not find skilled work in the shipyard, their idleness contributed to a pyramiding of the population. The FEPC sought modest relief by convincing ADDSCO to upgrade twelve blacks to welders from the seven thousand blacks who occupied menial positions at the yard (out of a total employment base of 30,000). ADDSCO officials placed these blacks on the night

shift. White workers, surprised by the sudden presence of black welders, attacked them, and a riot erupted that injured fifty blacks. Federal
troops eventually quelled the disturbance. The FEPC and ADDSCO
quickly modified the experiment by segregating the black welders and
all of the unskilled black laborers as well.

The conflict of black aspirations and white resistance to altering the
color line produced a volatile atmosphere at defense installations and
military bases. In June, 1943, a race riot occurred at the Pennsylvania
Shipyards in Beaumont, Texas, as a rumor spread that a black worker
had raped the wife of a white employee. In six hours of rioting that
spread to the city and destroyed parts of Beaumont's black section, two
blacks and one white died and nearly four hundred were injured. The
rumor, incidentally, proved to be false.

Racial violence flared at military bases in Georgia, Mississippi,
Texas, and Louisiana. In many of these incidents, blacks retaliated
against marauding whites. More than 80 percent of the nation's blacks
in military service trained at southern bases, and those from other
parts of the country were unaccustomed to the racial mores of the
South. The vision (and reality) of blacks training on an equal basis with
whites, toting guns, and receiving an education in combat tactics,
explosives, and ammunition aroused white animosities and fears both
on and especially off base. At Camp Van Dorn in Mississippi, black
soldiers broke into a stockade and took up arms against local authorities after the sheriff shot a black enlisted man attempting to avoid
arrest. In a more obvious reversal of roles, blacks at Camp Stewart,
Georgia, heard rumors that white soldiers had raped a black woman. In
retaliation, some blacks seized submachine guns, killed a military
policeman, and wounded four others.

Southern Whites and the Inner War

For many southern whites, there was a direct connection between the
FEPC and the growing aggressiveness of blacks. They believed that
Washington was operating from ignorance and arrogance. White
southerners, after all, were living with a large, dependent black population, and they believed they were more knowledgeable and even more
compassionate on the subject of race relations than outsiders. If problems existed with these relations, the feeling went, only those competent to understand the complexities of race should deal with them. The
widespread resentment against the FEPC, then, hardly stemmed from
its effectiveness but from its symbolic import as another intrusion into

the etiquette of race, upsetting established patterns of relations and perceptions. Other meddling would inevitably follow. Whites took alarm at the real and potential dangers of outside intervention; blacks took hope. And white southerners would now be confronted by challenges from both within and outside the South.

In the insular South, rumors fed upon themselves until they attained the shape of reality. There were warnings that blacks planned to "take over" white women once white men went off to war, that blacks were arming themselves with ice picks, and that black women were forming "Eleanor Clubs" (named after the First Lady) whose slogan was "put a white woman in every kitchen by 1943." Rumors of a rise in black insolence confirmed these and other rumors. Some whites believed that direct action was necessary before these attitudes infected the entire black population. Lynchings increased, and segregation in some areas became more rigid. Alabama judge Horace C. Wilkinson suggested that "there is a need of a League to Maintain White Supremacy. . . . The time to act is now. An organization should be formed so strong, so powerful, and so efficient, that this menace to our national security and our local way of life will rapidly disappear."

Some whites petitioned Washington not to train black soldiers in the South; others suggested not drafting them into the armed forces at all. In targeting some of their appeals to the federal government, white southerners—already uneasy with the Roosevelt administration's liberal drift and the growing power of the multiethnic urban North within the Democratic party—were tacitly acknowledging that they were not in total control of their race relations. One Alabama leader warned the president that unless the administration left white supremacy undisturbed, "we are going to face a crisis in the South . . . [and] witness the annihilation of the Democratic Party in this section." In 1944, Memphis political boss Edward H. Crump confided to Tennessee senator Kenneth McKellar that his constituents were chafing under administration overtures to blacks and that "the Negro question is looming big in this part of the country—in fact, all over the South." Some southern politicians were so concerned about the drift of policy and party that they considered the unspeakable—the Republican party. As one southern legislator admitted to a reporter from *Fortune* magazine in 1943, "if the Republican party would come out on the issue of white supremacy, it would sweep the South."

The decision in the white primary case exercised white southerners, particularly since Roosevelt appointees now occupied a majority of positions on the Supreme Court. In fact, the lone dissenter in the case was the only justice appointed by a previous administration. Regional leaders perceived the Court's action as part of a broader strategy "to ram social equality down the throats of the white people of the South." Even such staunch New Dealers as Florida senator Claude Pepper vowed after *Smith* v. *Allwright* that "the South will allow nothing to impair white supremacy." South Carolina governor Olin D. Johnston called a special session of the legislature to consider the case. Accompanied by rebel yells, the lawmakers sought to evade, if not nullify, the Court's ruling by repealing all laws regulating primaries, thus removing the state's legal connection to the system. Though an appeals court disallowed this attempt, the legislation demonstrated the concern of leaders for the integrity of their whites-only political system.

That system, which worked on the twin principles of black disfranchisement and low white participation, was threatened by the white primary decision and increased agitation in the Congress and the administration against the poll tax. The Black Belt districts of the Deep South and the rural areas of other southern states dominated state politics. These sparsely settled regions, often with majority black populations, were traditional strongholds of an agricultural-mercantile clique that manipulated state constitutions and legislative procedures to secure and maintain power. The political machine controlled by Senator Harry F. Byrd in Virginia, the Barnwell Ring in South Carolina, and the Black Belt oligarchies in Georgia, Alabama, and Mississippi typified the regional disdain for democracy and service. As journalist Charles McDowell described these regimes in the mid-1940s, "there was an assumption that the poll tax was right. There was an assumption that a country school with four teachers teaching sixty kids apiece was just fine. There was an assumption that the state owed the citizens very little in the way of service."

The combination of poll taxes, literacy tests, complicated registration procedures, and handpicked candidates reduced the numbers of whites and blacks casting ballots. In 1940, only 26 percent of the adult population voted in the South, compared with 53 percent in the North. Though roughly 80,000 blacks voted in the general election in the South, almost none cast ballots in the crucial primaries. Even if they had been eligible to vote in primary elections, their choices would have been limited, since only thirty-six of the seventy-eight Democratic primaries across the region in 1940 were contested. And even when voters could exercise a choice, they often did so in full view and knowledge of the local leadership, since the secret, printed uniform ballot—the Australian ballot—was not common in many parts of the South, especially in rural areas.

The attempt of Virginia Durr to register and vote in Virginia, where she resided during the early 1940s, demonstrated how the political system worked to limit voter participation. The procedure involved going to the registrar, paying the poll tax, and presenting the receipt upon voting, but it turned out to be considerably more complicated than it sounded. The registrar worked at home far out in the rural reaches of the county. He did not have a telephone, so Durr had to take a chance on finding him in. She drove to his house, and the woman who answered the door said the registrar was not there and she did not know when he would return. Durr waited until nightfall and left. She returned another day and repeated the scenario. Finally, on the third try, the registrar was at home. He would be delighted to register Durr, but first he had to locate the poll book. His wife eventually found it in an old trunk in the attic. Durr asked the registrar for a pen to sign her name in the book. Again he launched a search, this time for a writing implement, and, again, his wife saved the situation by finding a rusty pen. Unfortunately, there was no ink in the house. Durr, determined and undaunted, fixed her own ink from a mixture of mercurochrome from the medicine cabinet and soot from the fireplace. She produced a pale red-blue mixture that sufficed. Durr signed the book and received her receipt to show that she had registered.

Durr next went to the Fairfax County Courthouse to pay her poll tax. Nine states in the country (all in the South, including Virginia) required a poll tax, a modest annual sum of $1.50 on the average. But it was an amount that cash-poor rural southerners, black and white, found difficult to raise, and falling behind one year meant an additional assessment the following year, and so on. It was common for candidates to pay the poll tax for poor whites in exchange for votes, especially in rural portions of the Deep South and in the mountain areas of the region. The tax served the dual function of further restricting black suffrage and enabling political leaders to manipulate the white vote.

The clerk at the Fairfax County Courthouse assessed Durr $4.50 for two years' back poll tax. Durr paid it, and on election day she went to her polling place to cast her ballot. But her name was not in the poll book. Indignant, she presented her registration and poll tax receipts. The clerk informed her that she had forgotten to pay the interest on the poll tax in arrears and thus had not been entered in the book. Durr went back to the courthouse, paid the twenty-seven cents in interest, finally got her name inscribed in the poll book, and voted.

It was easy to understand why southern leaders were anxious over *Smith* v. *Allwright* and the growing sentiment in Congress against the poll tax. Both events threatened the exclusivity of southern politics. Durr recalled an incident involving Mississippi senator James O. Eastland that revealed the fear generated by these threats. She escorted a group of white churchwomen from the Women's Society for Christian Service into the senator's office one day during the war. The women were lobbying for an end to the poll tax, and Eastland, as head of the Senate Judiciary Committee, was a logical target. The meeting began pleasantly until the women broached the subject of the poll tax. As Durr remembered, Eastland "jumped up. His face turned red. . . . And he screamed out, 'I know what you women want—black men laying on you!'"

The oft-proclaimed southern white solidarity on race was as artificial a creation as the racial etiquette it supported, and it required constant reinforcement. The events of the 1930s and during the early years of the war, both in Washington and among an increasingly vocal group of southern liberals, black and white, indicated yet again that white supremacy and black subservience were ideals that did not enjoy unanimous subscription, despite claims to the contrary. The virulence of southern reaction stemmed not so much from the FEPC (whose impact was marginal at best) or the white primary decision (southern states could manage ingenious circumventions) or the attack on the poll tax (there were numerous other weapons southern leaders had at their disposal to limit the franchise) or the increasing boldness of blacks and white liberals (neither of whom could command broad support from either race) as from what the combination of these events might accomplish in generating more serious assaults on regional racial traditions. And these traditions were fragile because, regardless of the region's perception of history, they were ever-changing.

Race relations were never stationary or monolithic in the South. They varied within and between states. In the Black Belt, where blacks usually outnumbered whites, controls were likely to be tighter than in the predominantly white Piedmont or in cities such as Charlotte, Richmond, or Dallas. Whites of high social status often prided themselves on their civility and courtesy toward black neighbors, while other whites took pleasure in harassment and persecution. Ed Pike, a sawmill operator in the Alabama piney woods, paid equal wages to his white and black operatives (who worked side-by-side). Other white employers paid blacks less (if they hired them at all) and offered lower prices for their cotton and charged more for store-bought goods. During the 1930s, interviews conducted by the Federal Writers' Project revealed several instances of rough equality between the races in social situations. Hunting and fishing, for example, had an etiquette predicated more on fairness than on racial distinctions. "[T]here existed," historian Jack Temple Kirby observed, "a bewildering variety of human relationships that almost confound attempts at generalization." The anxiety of southern white leaders reflected the variability of these relations and their vulnerability to events beyond control of the South.

The Retreat of White Liberals

The swift and seemingly disproportionate white reaction was successful in silencing white liberals in the region, who, in the short run, were more dangerous to the racial status quo than the slow-moving and still-distant federal government. As the press and political leaders mounted the barricades, white liberals retreated into a customary pessimism. Howard W. Odum averred that race relations had not been worse in the region "since the period a hundred years earlier, which led to the War between the States." James McBride Dabbs was even more disconsolate: "I do not see that we shall make any radical changes in . . . the South—in generations, perhaps in centuries."

As if to underscore that prediction, Virginius Dabney, the liberal editor of the Richmond *Times-Dispatch*, proposed in a 1943 editorial that the state abolish segregation on common carriers as an inconvenience to blacks and whites alike. Journalists from across the South condemned his modest suggestion with striking unanimity. A chastened Mark Ethridge counseled, "he [the Negro] must recognize that there is no power in the world—not even all the mechanized armies of the earth, Allied and Axis—which could now force the southern white people to the abandonment of the principle of social segregation." Even some black leaders in the South expressed fears that continued federal interest in race relations, however minimal, would generate a white backlash that would erode the modest gains of the New Deal years. C. H. Bynum, a black official with the Committee on Interracial Cooperation (CIC), a southern group begun by white liberal Will Alexander in 1919 and dedicated to improving race relations in the region, confided to Gunnar Myrdal in August, 1942, that "we [southern blacks] may suffer heartbreaking reversals in race relations when peace comes. . . . [I]mposition [from the federal government] will engender smoldering feelings which may at any hour leap into a blazing flame of madness."

The frustration felt by white liberals and some black colleagues resulted in part from the threat to the hard-won victories of the previous decade. Local chapters of the CIC, for example, had successfully lobbied for legal aid for indigent blacks, improved public services in black neighborhoods, community recreation facilities for black children, and employment of blacks in city bureaucracies. Though these advances occurred in only a few places, involving relatively small numbers of southern blacks, given the racial context of the time they were important gains. At the least, they chipped away at the grim dependence and inferiority that characterized white supremacy. But scarcely had the United States entered the war when the feeling became widespread among liberals that these gains were lost. As one lamented in a letter to Gunnar Myrdal in the summer of 1942:

> we are in the midst of a situation in the South where we seem to have been thrown back with great losses where we had expected great gain. . . . We had worked into entirely new patterns of fellowship and participation, and there were many evidences that the South was beginning to be proud of this progress. Today, as far as I know, there is practically none of this left. The South is becoming almost unanimous in a pattern of . . . white unity. The thousands of incidents and accidents in the South are being integrated into the old pattern of Southern determination against an outside aggression.

The response of white liberals may seem out of proportion to the actual circumstances in the South, but the liberals were as much prisoners of history, and of their interpretation of it, as their adversaries. They had seen and heard the demagogues, the disruptions, the violence that accompanied defenses of regional mores during periods of stress, and they appreciated their own vulnerability. This was so for even the more outspoken crusaders of previous years, such as W. T. Couch of the University of North Carolina Press. Soon after American entrance into the war, Couch contracted with black Howard University historian Rayford W. Logan to edit a symposium in which "Negroes would state what they believe and indicate what the Negro wants and what he ought to have." By the time Logan submitted the manuscript in late 1943, the racial climate in the South had deteriorated; even worse for Couch, the manuscript condemned segregation. Couch persuaded Logan to tone down his introduction and published the work, *What the Negro Wants*, in 1944 with a minimum of publicity.

The defection of white liberals was not total. Lillian Smith produced a biting exegesis on the biracial society, particularly on the difficulty of well-meaning whites to break away from regional cultural norms. The novel, *Strange Fruit* (1944), takes place in a Georgia town and concerns the love of a white man for a college-educated black woman. The woman becomes pregnant, and in a Hamlet-like sequence her lover agonizes over moral choices. Ultimately he is unable to reject his culture, which has taught him that she is "merely a nigger girl," and abandons her. The woman's brother murders him in revenge. The story underscores how the racial system infected whites as well as blacks, leaving white liberals just as culture-bound as the rest of the white South.

But the white liberal also held an inflated view of his importance to the scheme of racial progress. Part of the despairing rhetoric that projected racial progress as millennia away resulted from the belief that change could only occur from within. The liberals believed that their enlightened leadership would gradually and with sensitivity accomplish major advances in race relations, and they could point to several successes during the 1930s. But in realizing that it was prudent to withdraw under fire, they also felt that the opportunity to effect change was receding as well. Subsequent events proved these perceptions to be false. White southern liberals were not only marginal to the process of change, but in some cases actually inhibited it; and the intrusion of the outside world did not set back the cause of racial equality but, to the contrary, enhanced its chances for success.

"A Kind of Sunlight": The World Moves South

Reaction or no, a return to the status quo antebellum was unlikely. The disruptions in agriculture, the sudden presence of federal bureaucracy and funding in large doses, and the massive movement of people, black and white, from farms to cities, factories, and battlefields changed perspectives and thereby changed the South. Writer H. C. Nixon described his hometown, "Possum Trot," in north Alabama, and the impact of the war. He related that residents were "gossiping about the world and the ways of the world more than ever. They were talking about Hitler and 'them Japs,' about Russia and 'Joe,' about FDR and Churchill." They devoured the newspaper from Anniston and also sought out the Birmingham and Atlanta papers. "Workers brought in news from town and city," and letters from soldiers in far-off places "gave wider contacts." By the end of the war, Nixon concluded, "the little community has become much less isolated and much less community."

The outside world was indeed penetrating the South, and from Nixon's perspective, the prospects were exciting, and perhaps frightening. Flannery O'Connor's short story "The Displaced Person" probes the darker side of the intrusion. The story centers on Guizac, a Polish refugee. He and his family have survived a German concentration camp and emigrated to the American South, where he works as a farm laborer. The complexities of racial etiquette puzzle Guizac, and he wonders why white farmhands and the landlord tolerate malingering by black workers and their periodic theft of chickens. Through his industriousness and his management recommendations, however, the inefficient and unprofitable farm begins to prosper. The Pole's adherence to the work ethic and his desire to innovate anger his fellow workers, but his most serious transgression occurs when he offers his sixteen-year-old cousin in marriage to one of the black tenants. She is a survivor of a death camp as well, but has been detained in Poland, unable to emigrate. Marriage to an American citizen, however, would reunite her with her family in the United States. Guizac defends his proposal by explaining that, after three years in a camp, "she no care black." Before the plan proceeds, however, a runaway tractor crushes Guizac to death in full view of the landlord and many of the tenants, who fail to warn the Pole as the machine bears down on him. After his death, the farm lapses back into its familiar, unproductive routine, and eventually the owner is forced to sell at a loss and the tenants must pull up stakes and look for other work.

The Pole's intrusion into this cultural milieu eventually destroys that milieu even as its defenders succeed in destroying the Pole. The war and its consequences came to the South's isolated rural districts, and these places would never be the same again. As World War II ended, southerners, flushed with victory and imbued with the pride of a job well done and the acceptance that accompanies such effort, looked forward to the future with optimism. They were not so much prepared to accept change as they were hoping to incorporate it into their society—a process that had worked in the past. But the world, the nation, and their distinctive region had become too small to allow for a splendid isolation. As Thomas Wolfe noted, even before the war "a kind of sunlight" was beginning to penetrate the South, and the light would ultimately expose the region and lift the darkness.

Black (top) and white (bottom) elementary schools, South Boston, Virginia, *ca.* 1935.

Sewing Department.

Laundry Department.

Cooking Department.

Blacksmith Shop.

The Negro curriculum at an unidentified black school in Virginia, *ca.* 1935.

A Mississippi Delta sharecropper rests. Perthshire, Bolivar County, Mississippi, October, 1939.

A sharecropping family's home, Greensboro, Alabama, May, 1941.

Family of evicted sharecroppers, Cross County, Arkansas, January, 1936.

Black sharecroppers' shacks in Atlanta, March, 1936.

In the shadow of the state capitol, black housing in downtown Atlanta, October, 1938.

John Hope Homes, Atlanta, June, 1941, one example of how the New Deal assisted blacks in the urban South. Atlanta University is in the background.

III / A Season of Hope
1945–1954

The postwar era began with bright hope for southerners—they had proven themselves on the battlefield, tasted the rewards of prosperity, and looked forward to unprecedented employment and educational opportunities. If, amid the optimism, white southerners assumed that blacks would resume their subservient places, that was understandable. In recent memory, World War I and the prolonged economic depression had scarcely shaken the etiquette of race. Even progressive whites, such as attorney Gavin Stevens in William Faulkner's *Intruder in the Dust* (1948), figured that the black's limited aspirations would persist for the foreseeable future. Stevens attributed this perspective to the black man's inherent stoicism—"patience when he didn't have hope, the long view even when there was nothing to see at the end of it, not even just the will but the desire to endure." And he marveled at the simple comforts—"a little earth for his own sweat to fall on among his own green shoots and plants"—that reflected low black expectations.

These were comforting images for whites, progressive or otherwise, but they were mistaken. Racial etiquette had thrived on the self-reinforcing isolation of the prewar South, but it could not withstand the glare of expanded horizons and consciousness. Blacks had shared with whites similar wartime experiences—fighting, working, traveling about, and improving living standards. The placid endurance, the steely survival, the great pleasure in small things noted by Stevens would not disappear from the black character, but it was about to become part of a larger striving, a broader perspective on the possibility of improving blacks' condition.

A Political Spring

Blacks scored immediate gains in the political arena. *Smith* v. *Allwright* opened up the promise of participation in the electoral process, and they seized that opportunity. In 1940, about 2 percent of the eligible southern black population was registered to vote. By 1947, this figure had climbed to 12 percent and would increase to almost 20 percent at the end of the 1950s. Increased registration reflected less a spontaneous outpouring of political consciousness than an organized effort by Negro Voters Leagues in several southern cities. Black political organizations had existed since the Reconstruction era, but they waxed and waned depending on external political circumstances. The postwar era ushered in a renewed enthusiasm for politics, and blacks revived their organizing campaigns. In a three-week drive in 1946, the Atlanta league, for example, tripled the number of black registrants. By the early 1950s, political scientist Henry Allen Bullock noted that "practically every southern city has a Negro voter's league as a part of the institutional complex of the Negro community." The leagues served not only to encourage registration but also to lobby for black issues at city hall.

Southern urban blacks did not undertake these efforts as quixotic endeavors. The experiences of the recent past, even before the white primary decision, demonstrated that concerted effort despite limited numbers could have specific payoffs. In Greenville, South Carolina, in 1939, several hundred black voters ignored threats from the Ku Klux Klan to cast their ballots; the results were two fully equipped playgrounds. A large black turnout in Miami, also in 1939, produced improved streets and two public housing projects. Black voters in Austin, Texas, that same year saw their influence result in more public-sector jobs.

Black political power was perhaps most significant in Atlanta. The substantial black middle-class business community in that city had effected an arrangement with the white economic elite who controlled the political system to deliver votes in exchange for black appointments and improved services. William B. Hartsfield, a tinsmith's son and a local attorney, became the primary beneficiary of this alliance in the 1936 mayoral contest, and the connection lasted over three decades. During Hartsfield's mayoralty (which lasted until 1961, except for a brief hiatus in the early 1940s), the city hired black policemen, integrated public transit, and encouraged black voter registration and participation.

Hartsfield heralded a new breed of urban mayor in the postwar South that eschewed overt racial appeals as distractions from the main business of local government—economic development. Though privately they may have expressed reservations about segregation, their strategy was to avoid the race issue altogether. Indifference rather than advocacy characterized their outlook. This represented an advance, albeit limited, over their early-twentieth-century booster predecessors who had supported and advocated white supremacy. In addition, they tacitly acknowledged the blacks' presence in urban society through their willingness to trade votes for jobs and services.

Even in such Deep South cities as Montgomery, the growing black political voice altered urban politics. Montgomery's black voters were successful in electing a white liberal, Dave Birmingham, to one of three positions on the commission that governed the city. The commission in turn appointed four black policemen and sought to improve drainage in low-lying black residential areas. In Houston, a small group of business leaders had controlled political affairs since the 1920s, convening periodically in Room 8F of the Lamar Hotel to socialize and devise policy. As the city grew rapidly after World War II, this exclusivity proved inefficient and frustrating. By the mid-1950s, new business leaders emerged and put up one of their own, Lewis Cutrer, to run against the candidate of the "8F Crowd," Oscar Holcombe. The black vote played a significant role in Cutrer's upset victory. In fact, in Texas, where the *Smith* case originated, black political power grew to the extent that venerable Democrats such as Congressman Wright Patman (who vowed in the wake of the *Smith* ruling that blacks would vote in his district "over my dead body") took care to attend black church picnics and make known their espousal of black interests in Washington. And in Alabama, fifty thousand blacks swelled the voting ranks in the 1954 Democratic primary to keep progressive John Sparkman in the U.S. Senate and elect populist James Folsom to a second term as governor.

But black voting in the postwar South was primarily an urban phenomenon. From 80 to 85 percent of registered black voters in the South resided in cities. Though black voter registration approached 20 percent regionwide by the late 1950s, it was considerably lower in the rural southern states. In Mississippi, for example, less than 5 percent of the eligible black electorate was registered to vote. Yet these statistics were not greatly discouraging to the Negro Voters Leagues throughout the region. Blacks were moving to southern cities in increasing numbers—more than 750,000 blacks migrated from the countryside to the urban South in the decade and a half after 1940—and the cities themselves were coming to occupy a greater importance in the regional economy and polity. It even happened that in a few scattered places where black concentrations had reached significant proportions blacks were able to elect one of their own to public office for the first time in generations. Oliver Hill, a black political leader from Rich-

mond, narrowly missed election to the Virginia House of Delegates in
1947 but became the city's first black councilman the following year.
Two blacks were elected to the Nashville city council in 1948.

There was cause for optimism among blacks even at the state level.
Just as a new elite was poised to take control of southern cities, new
political leaders emerged in several southern states. Though these
leaders may have hailed from small towns or even farms, they advocated, according to historian Numan V. Bartley, "a metropolitan ideology that stresse[d] economic expansion, businesslike administration,
and free market individualism." They too discarded the rhetoric of
white supremacy, and some recognized that poverty, illiteracy, and
disease were sapping the contributions of all constituents, black and
white. Their programs often recalled the Populist insurgency of the
1890s, but they sought to work within the Democratic party and generally avoided radical rhetoric. Their simultaneous appearance over
various parts of the South during the half decade after 1945 heralded a
southern political spring of fresh ideas and an expanded electorate.

Veteran political observers scarcely gave James E. ("Big Jim") Folsom
a chance in the 1946 Alabama Democratic gubernatorial primary. The
six-foot eight-inch Folsom had his roots in southeastern Alabama,
though he had sold insurance in the northern part of the state and
served with the Civil Works Administration in Marshall County during the New Deal years. If his background was not exceptional, his
personality was. He undertook a whirlwind, shoestring campaign
throughout the state carting around a country band, the Strawberry
Pickers, and a mop and washbucket that he promised to use to clean
out the moguls in Montgomery and install a government of the plain
folk. He constructed a "People's Platform" that included road building, pensions for the elderly, improved public education, higher corporate taxes, and industrial development. He also promised to lower the
poll tax and ease voter-registration requirements for both blacks and
whites. For those who were concerned about the appearance of racial
equanimity, Folsom replied that "as long as the Negroes are held down
by deprivation and lack of opportunity, the other poor people will be
held down alongside them." Folsom won and joined Alabama's two
United States senators, John Sparkman and Lister Hill, as the state's
contributions to a new progressive political era for Dixie.

Other states also experienced a political thaw. In Arkansas, Marine
Corps veteran Sid McMath became governor in 1948 on a platform
similar to Folsom's. Earl and Russell Long led the resurgent Long dy-

nasty in Louisiana and instituted a range of public health, education, and welfare services for both races. In Tennessee, a trio of progressive politicians emerged by the early 1950s—Senators Albert Gore and Estes Kefauver, and a young governor, Frank Clement, who introduced reforms in health and education. Kefauver became widely known as a consumer advocate and as a watchdog against monopolistic restraints of trade in major industries. The election of Ellis Arnall as governor of Georgia in 1943 and the appointment of former University of North Carolina president Frank Porter Graham to the U.S. Senate in 1949 to fill an unexpired term, as well as the continued liberal presence of Florida senator Claude Pepper, rounded out an impressive array of postwar southern political leaders. These men not only discarded the convenient cry of "nigger" but began to address the glaring social inequities in southern society. Though they did not direct their policies at blacks per se, they subscribed to the progressive doctrine that education and improved public services would help both races. In addition, they believed that the improved situation of the region's poor whites would eliminate their need to employ racial distinction as the sole measure of their worth. Atlanta journalist Ralph McGill, writing in the *Saturday Evening Post* in 1950, rejoiced that "the South is freer of ranters and demagogues than it has been for a generation or more."

It seemed as if the war had functioned as a hurricane, clearing dank, fetid air and replacing it with fresh breezes that soothed rather than agitated the regional mind. The wind awakened the southern liberal from his despairing retirement and revived the hope of an internal solution to the racial dilemma. Liberals hurried to catch up to prevailing public sentiment by working with blacks to form new regionwide interracial organizations designed to promote civil rights from within.

Organizing for a "Full Share of Dignity and Self-Respect"

The Atlanta-based Southern Regional Council (SRC) was probably the most prominent postwar interracial group. Under the leadership of Chapel Hill sociologists Howard W. Odum and Guy Johnson, as well as prominent black educator Benjamin Mays, the council began operation in 1944 and attracted businessmen and professionals of both races, indicating the growing desire to remove white supremacy as a burden on regional development. Northern philanthropic agencies such as the Rosenwald Fund and the General Education Board provided financial

support for the council to conduct research and to carry on an educational campaign informing returning black GI's of their rights. Odum
proposed that the research should also be used to educate whites on the
efficacy of civil rights for blacks. As he argued, "I don't see why one
who has been entrusted with the opportunity to do research . . . should
give back to the people only the things that they believed a hundred
years ago."

The council initially steered clear of endorsing an assault on segregation. However, the heady postwar political atmosphere as well as the
restlessness of some council members, black and white, pushed the
leadership toward an integrationist position. In 1949, through its publication *New South*, the council issued an unequivocal statement that
segregation "in and of itself constitutes discrimination and inequality
of treatment." The following year, the council came out with a more
forceful document on its visions for an interracial South:

> The South of the future . . . is a South freed of stultifying inheritances from
> the past. It is a South where the measure of a man will be his ability, not his
> race; . . . where all who labor will be rewarded in proportion to their skill and
> achievement; where there will exist no double standard in housing, health,
> education or other public services; where segregation will be recognized as a
> cruel and needless penalty of the human spirit, and will no longer be im-
> posed; where, above all, every individual will enjoy a full share of dignity
> and self-respect, in recognition of his creations in the image of God.

This ringing declaration appeared only seven years after council
member Virginius Dabney's modest proposal to end segregation on
Richmond's public transit facilities had incurred a regionwide rebuke.
The barrier of segregation now seemed more vulnerable. The SRC was
not necessarily far in advance of white thought in the South; the
Southern Conference Education Fund (SCEF), for example, presented a
comprehensive integrationist program several years before the SRC's
statement. The fund grew out of another interracial organization, the
Southern Conference for Human Welfare (SCHW), that had been active since the 1930s in promoting interracial causes. The fund's objective, similar to that of the SRC, was "to improve the educational and
cultural standards of the Southern People." The leadership, individuals such as former New Dealer Aubrey Williams, ex-seminarian
James Dombrowski, Frank Porter Graham, and black educators Benjamin Mays and Mary McLeod Bethune, reflected the faith of black and
white southern progressives in the power of education to effect social
change. The fund's journal, *Southern Patriot*, devoted considerable

space to documenting the evils of segregation. The high point of the fund's activities occurred in 1948, two years after its founding, when Williams convened an interracial gathering of southern ministers, writers, educators, and attorneys in Charlottesville, Virginia. The Declaratory Conference on Civil Rights called upon churches and professional associations to take the lead by integrating their memberships and meetings.

Dorothy Tilly, an Atlanta churchwoman, answered the call and in 1949 formed the Fellowship of the Concerned, an organization of women from churches and synagogues in the Southeast. Women's reform organizations affiliated with religious denominations were nothing new in the South; since the antebellum era, middle-class white women had taken the lead in espousing a variety of causes, including prohibition, prison reform, public education, and city planning. Capitalizing on this tradition and the network that accompanied it, the fellowship sponsored interracial meetings designed to break down the barriers between women of both races and promote an understanding that would ease the transition to racial equality. Tilly—who had long been involved in the reform activities of Jessie Daniel Ames's Association of Southern Women for the Prevention of Lynching, participated in the regional political renaissance as a supporter of Georgia governor Ellis Arnall, and was a charter member of the Southern Regional Council—believed that integration was inevitable and that southern churchwomen could and should play a leading role in this process.

The region's largest denomination, the Southern Baptists, did not respond to the new postwar climate as readily as the churchwomen who belonged to other, primarily Methodist, congregations. The Baptists' atomized church polity and lengthy tradition of avoiding controversial social issues limited their participation. Nevertheless, the Southern Baptist Convention (SBC), the closest apparatus to a governing body for the denomination, began to acknowledge the appropriateness of attending to the needs of southern blacks. The SBC expenditure for ministry to blacks jumped from $33,000 in 1944 to $109,000 in 1945. The convention's Home Mission Board, in order to educate and sensitize its members on the conditions of southern blacks, published a series of study books on race in 1946. T. B. Maston, the author of the volume for adults, *Of One*, noted with approval that "there is a stirring in the hearts and consciousness of Southern Baptists. There are signs of a new day and a new attitude. Many Southern Baptists, individuals and groups, are overcoming their racial prejudice." That same year, the annual meeting of the convention passed a "Statement of Principles" regarding civil rights, including the right to vote, to serve on juries, to receive equal treatment under the law, to participate equally in public-education expenditures, and to receive equal service on public carriers. The convention was careful not to challenge segregation outright, but the tenor of its statement was obvious enough for the North Carolina Baptist Convention to pass a companion resolution declaring that "segregation of believers holding the same tenets of faith because of color or social status into racial or class churches is a denial of the New Testament affirmation of the equality of all believers."

The advocacy of the new interracial organizations and the professions of religious bodies and their members did not readily translate into public policy. Most of these efforts placed great faith in education and direction by a "talented tenth" of both races to effect the necessary gradual change, and all except the most radical members of these groups believed that pushing for an abrupt, across-the-board alteration in race relations would be counterproductive. Progressives akin to Faulkner's Gavin Stevens looked forward to a day when the black man would be able to vote "anywhen and anywhere a white can and send his children to the same school anywhere the white man's children go and travel anywhere the white man travels. . . . But it won't be next Tuesday."

Though Stevens and his like-minded colleagues were often vague as to how many Tuesdays would pass before racial equality would be a reality, the very openness of the debate, the moderate and occasionally bold rhetoric emanating from the political arena, and the gains at the polls were important beginning points in a region that had historically recoiled from any suggestion that could possibly undermine white supremacy. But we shall never know how quickly this gradualism might have spread its roots through the hard ground of racism, because, ironically, just as the South appeared to be making good on its oft-repeated promise of solving its own problems, the federal government renewed its quest for racial justice in the region.

"To Secure These Rights": Federal Initiatives

It may have been that renewed liberal and organizational activity in the South after World War II on behalf of racial accommodation resulted, to some extent, from a desire to forestall inevitable federal initiatives as much as from the postwar optimism and political climate. All three branches of the federal government had become involved in civil rights by 1945: the judiciary had already taken up segregation and voting-rights cases; Congress had debated antilynching laws and poll-tax amendments and had passed fair-employment legislation; and the president had issued various executive orders pertaining to voting rights and job discrimination. Admittedly, most of these efforts fell short of their objectives, but there was ample recent precedent for federal involvement in civil rights to suggest continued interest after the war.

Within a few weeks of the victory over Germany and two months before the end of the war with Japan in August, 1945, President Harry S. Truman rebuked the House Appropriations Committee for cutting off funds for the FEPC and ordered them restored. Truman, as a border-state senator, had not compiled a notable civil-rights voting record, and when the Missourian became President Roosevelt's running-mate in the 1944 election, blacks generally opposed the nomination and expected little when Roosevelt's death in April, 1945, elevated Truman to the presidency. But, beginning with his FEPC message, Truman confounded erstwhile friends and enemies alike with his support and initiative in the field of civil rights. Whether it was his innate sense of fairness (he termed his domestic program the "Fair Deal"), or whether he self-consciously sought to transcend his geography, or whether he calculatingly understood that the new Democratic coalition rendered such positions necessary, Truman brought the issue of civil rights into full public view.

Truman's next major civil rights effort occurred the following year when he appointed the first President's Committee on Civil Rights. The immediate impetus behind his decision was a rash of racial violence that had erupted in the South since the end of the war as some southern whites, unwilling to participate in the season of hope, sought swiftly to reassert their dominance before contrary ideas motivated returning black GI's. Whites assaulted and blinded a black veteran who allegedly failed to follow the prescribed etiquette on a bus in South Carolina; the lynching of four black men and women in Monroe, Georgia, and a random attack on blacks in Columbia, Tennessee, were other examples of heightened racial tensions in the South. Truman charged the committee to prepare recommendations to improve race relations throughout the region. Among the committee members, he appointed two southerners, Frank Porter Graham and Dorothy Tilly.

The committee issued its report, *To Secure These Rights*, in 1947. It included a sweeping agenda for transforming race relations not only in the South, but in the nation: an antilynching law; the abolition of the poll tax; laws to prevent voter-registration discrimination; desegregation of the armed forces; an end to segregation in Washington, D.C., and in interstate public transportation; the establishment of a permanent civil rights section within the Justice Department; and the withdrawal of federal funds to institutions practicing segregation. Both Graham and Tilly endorsed all of these proposals, except the last, fearing a strong backlash among southern whites as well as damage to the South's struggling educational institutions.

Though such national civil rights organizations as the NAACP and the Congress of Racial Equality (CORE) had advocated these measures in the past, this was the first time in the twentieth century that the federal government had associated itself with such a comprehensive civil rights agenda. Truman may have received more than he bargained for in the report, but he incorporated the recommendations (except for the funding-withdrawal provision) into the first civil rights package introduced to Congress in eighty years.

When Truman presented the proposal to Congress in February, 1948, he understood that its passage was remote. The one-party political system in the South and low voter turnout produced a long list of veteran southern lawmakers, and the seniority system had elevated them to key positions in both houses. Senators James O. Eastland of Mississippi and Richard Russell of Georgia not only occupied important committee chairmanships but wielded power beyond their committees. Eastland, as head of the Senate Judiciary Committee, was the southern sentry for every piece of legislation. Truman also recognized that the introduction of any civil rights legislation, regardless of the gesture's futility, was bound to alienate southern Democrats, an integral and faithful component in the Democratic coalition.

Truman may have simply felt that this was the right thing to do at this particular time, especially since an ideological war was escalating with the Soviets, but in November, 1947, presidential adviser Clark Clifford, a southerner, prepared a report on strategy for the 1948 presidential campaign indicating that Truman could win the election without the Solid South. More than 1.7 million blacks had migrated from the South since 1940, many settling in the cities of four major northern swing states—Illinois, Ohio, Pennsylvania, and California. If Truman won these states, southern support was less important. Northern blacks recognized their potential political clout as well and pressed Truman for something more concrete than a doomed legislative package. The president responded with two executive orders in the summer of 1948: one abolishing segregation in the armed forces, and the other prohibiting discrimination in federal employment and at facilities operating under government contract.

Although these orders benefited southern blacks only marginally, the general direction and tenor of the president's policies generated considerable hope among blacks, since they represented a trend at the federal level that could not help but influence race relations in the South in the near future. Also encouraging was the slower-paced but just as evident direction of the U.S. Supreme Court. The white-primary case in 1944 was a signal victory, of course, but the Court was preparing to issue precedent-shattering decisions on other civil rights fronts as well, particularly in the realm of education.

Schools for Scandal: Separate and Unequal

Since 1938 at least, the Court had been chipping away at the *Plessy* v. *Ferguson* precedent established in 1896 that gave judicial sanction to segregated facilities so long as they were of equal quality. The separate-but-equal ruling was a farce from its inception, since black facilities were invariably inferior, and in some cases comparable arrangements were lacking entirely. This was especially so with respect to education.

Southern states were traditionally parsimonious with respect to public services, but expenditures for educating blacks lagged far behind the low standards set for white education: in 1930, for example, for every seven dollars spent for a white child in the South, black children received two dollars. Wide discrepancies existed, even in the larger cities of the South. In Birmingham, white teachers earned, on the average, $1,466 in 1930, compared with $682 for black teachers. In Atlanta, annual per-pupil expenditures varied from $95.20 for white students to only $30.55 for black schoolchildren.

The physical facilities and the quality of education for blacks reflected the divergence in public funding. Classrooms, buildings, and equipment were seriously deficient in black school districts, and some rural school boards made no provisions at all for black school buildings. Black residents of such areas either held classes in churches or initiated a building fund to erect their own school. In the late 1930s, Gunnar Myrdal visited a black school built not with local money, but with funds from the Rosenwald Foundation. Despite the outside funding source, the one-room, one-teacher facility near Atlanta schooled children from six years of age up to seventeen. Myrdal noticed the presence of a twenty-year-old mentally retarded black man, a not-uncommon sight in black schools, since there were few public institutions available for blacks with learning or mental disabilities. The teacher was a frail twenty-year-old black woman who had some high-school education; in some black schools, it was not unusual to have teachers who had not completed formal education beyond the eighth grade. There were relatively few secondary schools for blacks in the rural South in the 1930s. Whereas one out of four southern white adults had a high-school education in 1940, only 5 percent of black adults in the South had obtained their diplomas. Myrdal was most appalled at the lack of basic knowledge among the students—"No one could tell who was President of the United States or even what the President was," nor had they heard of any black leaders, such as Booker T. Washington, W. E. B. Du Bois, or John Hope. A few could identify Joe Louis and Ella Fitzgerald. When Myrdal asked what the Constitution of the United States was, the students greeted him with silence, until one boy piped up and said that it was a "newspaper in Atlanta."

Black schools remained open as much as seven months of the year and as little as three months in rural areas where local landowners determined the school-year calendar. White schools had sessions ranging from eight to nine months a year. Attendance at black schools was poor. Black children often had long walks to school; white children generally had the convenience of school buses. Some parents "solved" the transportation problem by paying for private bus service or boarding their children in town. Black parents often had to supplement teachers' salaries and pay for materials that white children received through public funding. Hard-pressed sharecroppers or tenants held children out of school to help with field work or out of shame because of inadequate clothing. Poor health or merely ignorance were other reasons for low attendance. Communities rarely enforced truancy laws against blacks.

Though some blacks, especially in urban schools, learned something of their history in an off-the-cuff manner, school officials designed curricula for blacks that reinforced their place in southern society. Black children received training in "character building" or, as Myrdal put it, in "courtesy, humility, self-control, satisfaction with the poorer things of life, and all the traits which mark a 'good nigger' in the eyes of the Southern whites." The curricula generally avoided civics and social studies. Vocational training comprised a major component of black education, schooling blacks in the basics of menial occupations from domestic service to waiting on tables. There was a concerted effort to discourage blacks from learning or thinking about "the duties and privileges of citizenship." The black child came out of the public-school system handicapped for life in the twentieth century but generally suited to assume his position in the American South.

White perceptions of black intellectual capabilities justified the separate and unequal education system, and the system produced blacks of limited abilities that reinforced white perceptions. A Gallup Poll taken in 1940 indicated that 98 percent of white southerners supported segregated education. With such widespread approbation, political leaders felt little compulsion to fund improvements for black schools. In fact, many agreed with Mississippi's James K. Vardaman, who declared earlier in the century that "money spent today for the maintenance of public schools for negroes is robbery of the white man, and a waste upon the negro . . . you rob the white child of the advantages it would afford him, and you spend it upon the negro in an effort to make of the negro what god Almighty never intended should be made."

Southern education was another institutional support for white supremacy, but unlike the political or economic systems, the schools reinforced the generational continuity of race relations by initiating black children into their respective places in southern society. It was not simply a matter of curriculum; the environment also left black children with the indelible mark of inferiority. The physical surroundings, the long walks, the inadequate or absent materials, and the frequent interruptions in attendance were early lessons internalized by black pupils. Lewis Harvie Blair, a rare white critic of separate education, succinctly summarized its impact upon black youngsters in 1887: "Separate schools are a public proclamation to all of African or mixed blood that they are an inferior caste, fundamentally inferior and totally unfit to mingle on terms of equality with the superior caste." As with all elements of white supremacy, separation took its toll on whites as well. White children, Harvie continued, learned that "superiority consists in a white skin[.] [T]hey will naturally be satisfied with that kind of superiority, and they will not willingly undergo the tedious, painful and patient ordeal requisite to prepare them for superiority in science, art, literature."

The impact of separation was most evident in the lower grades of the public-school system, but it existed through all educational institutions in the region. For the few blacks who could manage to overcome the deficiencies of public education in the South, frustration confronted them at the college and particularly at the graduate-school level. At that point, the system provided less segregation than exclusion and inhibited the development of an indigenously trained black professional class. Of course, from the perspective of the white South, a black professional was incongruent with the assigned role of blacks in southern society, and since whites rarely came into contact with these blacks, their relative absence further confirmed black inferiority. As black author James Weldon Johnson noted in *Autobiography of an Ex-Coloured Man* (1912), "if a coloured man wanted to separate himself from his white neighbours, he had but to acquire some money, education, and culture." This isolation was still the case a generation later, as Gunnar Myrdal commented: "There are Negro doctors, dentists, teachers, preachers, morticians, and druggists in the South who might as well be living in a foreign country." If the southern black was invisible, the black professional was the most transparent of all; accordingly, white officials were not going to provide for a class that could not and did not exist. If some of the more enlightened whites recognized a need for professional services in the black community, the attempt at providing appropriate training was apt to be perfunctory.

The U.S. Supreme Court thought otherwise. In 1938, the Court heard *Missouri ex rel. Gaines* v. *Canada*, a case involving a black applicant to the University of Missouri Law School. The state had denied Lloyd Gaines admission to the all-white school, recommending that he instead apply for an out-of-state scholarship to attend a law school of his choice in any adjacent state. The Court ruled that Missouri had violated the "equal" provision of the *Plessy* precedent. Chief Justice Charles Evans Hughes wrote that admission to Missouri's law school was the only "appropriate remedy consistent with the constitutional standard of equality . . . in the absence of other and proper provisions for his legal training within the state." The implication was that if Missouri had provided a separate law school for blacks, the Court would likely have upheld the state.

In the hopeful era immediately following the end of World War II, attorneys for the NAACP asked the Supreme Court to expand the application of *Plessy*. One case involved George McLaurin, a sixty-eight-year-old black doctoral student in education at the University of Oklahoma. In 1948, a federal district court ordered the university to admit McLaurin because none of the state's black colleges offered the doctoral degree in education. The university administration, determined to enforce segregation in some form and perhaps hoping to discourage McLaurin and other blacks from challenging the system again, forced McLaurin to sit at a desk in an anteroom outside his classroom, provided a segregated desk in a dingy corner of the library, and allowed him to use the cafeteria only at odd hours and to eat only at a specific table. McLaurin returned to court, where the judge rejected his petition for relief. While the Supreme Court was reviewing the case on appeal, the university, sensing an adverse ruling, modified its position and permitted McLaurin to sit in the classroom, but only in a seat that was railed off and marked "Reserved for Colored." McLaurin could also enter the library's main floor and eat in the cafeteria at regular mealtimes, though still separate from whites.

White fellow graduate students, however, upset the university's bizarre compromise by ripping down the railing and by joining McLaurin for meals. The Supreme Court delivered the next blow in *McLaurin* v. *Oklahoma Board of Regents*. Ruling for a unanimous Court in June, 1950, Chief Justice Fred M. Vinson stated that "the restrictions placed upon him [McLaurin] were such that he had been handicapped in his pursuit of effective graduate instruction. . . . Those who will come under his guidance and influence . . . will necessarily suffer to the extent that his training is unequal to that of his classmates. State-imposed restrictions which produce such inequalities cannot be sustained." While the *Plessy* precedent remained intact, the Court had broadened the definition of what constituted inequality.

That same day, the Court handed down its decision in a companion case, *Sweatt* v. *Painter*. The University of Texas Law School had refused the admission of black applicant Heman Sweatt, contending that all-black Texas Southern University possessed a law school that complied with the separate-but-equal standard. In another unanimous decision, the justices acknowledged the existence of the black law school but noted significant disparities in faculty and facilities between the two law schools. In addition, the Court noted some intangible distinctions: "The University of Texas Law School possesses to a far greater degree those qualities which are incapable of objective measurement but which make for greatness in a law school." The Court cited the school's prestige, the network of influential alumni, and the quality of the faculty. Excluding Sweatt from such perquisites would place him in an "academic vacuum" and at a singular disadvantage in the practice of law. Again, the Court did not toss out *Plessy*, but it was merely a short step further to declaring that segregation itself was inequality.

In fact, by 1950 a few judges in the lower federal-court system were prepared to reach that conclusion. As in other cases, a courageous black plaintiff stepped forward to push history a bit closer to a new reality, even if that was not his initial intent. The major difference from the earlier litigation, however, was that this case involved a local public-school system in the Lower South.

Harry Briggs was a navy veteran who, returning to his Summerton, South Carolina, home at the end of World War II, hoped for a better future for himself and his children. Like many other southern blacks in that rare postwar season, Briggs believed in the possibilities of hope. His children went to school in a dilapidated structure surrounded by a dirt yard that was either dust or mud, depending on the weather. The school served grades one through twelve, and more than one hundred children crowded into a single classroom with the hallways jammed with desks. A potbellied stove provided heat in the winter; the toilet facilities were outdoors. The local white elementary school had none of these encumbrances; it was a relatively new brick structure with modern fixtures and sufficient space for youngsters' education and recreation. By any reading of *Plessy*, this was unconstitutional. Briggs, however, was not prepared to press his case along those lines—this was, after all, rural South Carolina, and he had a family to feed on his salary as a gas-station attendant. He merely wanted a school bus so his children would not need to walk nine miles around a lake or else row across it to get to school. Clarendon County's white schoolchildren had thirty buses at their disposal; black pupils had none. Briggs took his request to the county school board in 1947. The chairman, lumber merchant R. W. Elliott, responded succinctly: "We ain't got no money to buy a bus for your nigger children."

With the assistance of the local NAACP director, the Reverend J. A. DeLaine, Briggs took Elliott to court to get that school bus. Then, encouraged by national NAACP counsel Thurgood Marshall and federal district-court judge J. Waties Waring, the navy veteran altered the suit to challenge the precedent of *Plessy*: whether segregation under any circumstances could be equal. It was unlikely that Briggs would receive satisfaction in the lower courts, staffed as they were by local judges, and the hearing before the district court in Charleston in the spring of 1951, presided over by a three-judge panel—including Waring—concluded predictably when the panel refused to uphold Briggs's petition.

Judge Waring, however, in a strong dissent presaged the language that was to become part of the U.S. Supreme Court's *Brown* v. *Board of*

Education opinion three years later. Waring was a judicial iconoclast of the first order and, by 1951, had earned the opprobrium of his high-toned neighbors in Charleston's historic district. Not only had the aristocratic Waring rejected South Carolina's attempt to bypass the *Smith* v. *Allwright* ruling, but he had divorced his wife of many years to marry a Yankee woman. In Charleston society, the latter offense was more grievous than the former. Waring had assumed his district-court judgeship in 1941 perceived as a staunch, if genteel, exponent of white supremacy, but as he gradually abandoned that perspective he became an outcast. If Waring was not a gracious neighbor, he was a prophetic judge. His dissent in the Briggs case was unequivocal: "Segregation in education can never produce equality and . . . is an evil that must be eradicated. . . . [A]ll of the legal guideposts, expert testimony, common sense and reason point unerringly to the conclusion that the system of segregation in education adopted and practiced in the state of South Carolina must go and must go now. Segregation is per se inequality."

"Segregation is per se inequality" were prescient words. The drift of the court cases, the activities of the interracial organizations, the growing political and legal pressure applied by blacks, and the efforts of the federal government pointed to a trend that segregation, if not the etiquette of race in its entirety, would be undergoing significant changes in the near future. A few newspaper editors forewarned their readers. C. A. "Pete" McKnight of the Charlotte *News* penned an editorial titled "Handwriting on the Wall," which recounted recent legal history on the subject of segregation. He added, for good measure, that "segregation as an abstract moral principle cannot be defended by any intellectually or spiritually honorable person."

Four other cases besides *Briggs* were progressing through the federal judiciary at roughly the same time. The Supreme Court merged these five cases together under the heading of one of them, *Brown* v. *Board of Education of Topeka, Kansas*. The Court's new chief justice, former governor of California Earl Warren, appointed by the recently elected Republican Dwight D. Eisenhower in 1953, delivered the opinion for a unanimous Court. The justices employed the arguments that had accumulated since the 1930s and emphasized particularly the intangible attributes of an integrated education, drawing on evidence from academics that separation of black children "solely because of their race generates a feeling of inferiority as to their status in the community that may affect their hearts and minds in a way unlikely ever to be undone." Chief Justice Warren, echoing Judge Waring's dissent three years earlier, declared that separate educational facilities were "inherently unequal." *Plessy* and the "separate-but-equal" charade were dead.

But segregation was not merely a sorting-out of the races that could be reshuffled like a deck of cards; racial etiquette was not a custom that could be argued away through legalisms; and the political system that nurtured the biracial society was not as malleable as the election returns made it seem. It was true that some white southerners were flirting with the brighter side of their regional culture, seeking a new understanding of their faith, past, and place. But an older order depended on the darker interpretation, and it would soon transform this season of hope into a time of turbulence and despair.

IV / Flight from Reality: The Rise of White Resistance, 1945–1956

By the time of the *Brown* decision in 1954, southern white leaders had already drawn the battle lines, so the decision was more a last straw than a preeminent cause of what followed. National events were obviously important to southerners, especially after 1940, but what was happening at the county courthouse, on the floor of the state legislature, and in the governor's mansion was of more imminent concern to the leadership. Challenges to traditional politics multiplied like kudzu in the immediate postwar years and threatened to strangle the old-line leaders, and the new wave of governors, congressmen, and senators promoted policies that signaled an end to traditional parsimony and oligarchy. Government spending implied new taxes, new businesses coming in, new bureaucracies created, and ultimately a new power structure perhaps not more inclusive than the old, but certainly different. Political and economic change implied social change, and that meant not only an alteration in the etiquette of race but also the eruption of class divisions among whites. For the heirs of the Redeemers, these were frightening prospects. The specter of chaos and disorder loomed, not to mention their own fall from power. Add to this the initiatives of the federal government and its various branches as well as the increasing boldness of southern blacks and white liberals, and their alarm was understandable.

It was all of one piece: politics could not be changed without altering the economy without upsetting the precarious class and racial balances in the region without toppling the heirs. White supremacy was the infernal glue that held this structure together, the mechanism that would restore white solidarity and black subservience, fend off challenges from within and without, and repel new ideas and economic opportunities that could broaden the base of power. The defenders undertook a second redemption and, in the process, employed many of the tactics of the first. The major difference was that their crusade of reaction and resistance would ultimately fail.

The Second Redemption: Witch Burning and Hell Raising

The crusade, in a sense, preached to the converted. Virginia Durr, referring to white supremacy, noted that it was something "you take for granted." The white southerner was also susceptible to arguments that outsiders were threatening a cherished way of life. The way of life need not be defined; the mere presence of an external threat was enough to stimulate the blood of history that ran through the southerners' hearts.

The activity in the Alabama legislature following the surprise electoral victories of Governor James E. Folsom and Senator John Sparkman in 1946 indicated how swiftly the old-liners, or "Old Guard stalwarts," as Numan V. Bartley called them, moved to reassert their leadership. They thwarted Folsom's plans to repeal the poll tax, reapportion the legislature, and increase funding for a range of social programs. Folsom's idiosyncratic style and personal impecunities did not help his program. The legislature also passed the Boswell Amendment to the state constitution, empowering registrars to determine whether prospective voters could "read and write, understand and explain any article of the Constitution of the United States, [were of] good character, and [understood] the duties and obligations of good citizenship under a republican form of government."

The amendment's proponents launched a virulent but successful campaign to convince Alabama's white voters that such suffrage restrictions were in their best interests. Registrar boards, composed of political appointees—some of whom were barely literate—could now not only eliminate blacks but suspect whites as well. Reports from Birmingham indicated that registrars frequently turned away whites wearing overalls but accepted business-attired individuals with little difficulty. After the federal courts declared the Boswell Amendment unconstitutional in 1954, the Alabama electorate swelled by 200,000 new voters, three-quarters of whom were white women and poor white men, and the rest of whom were blacks. They were instrumental in returning Folsom to office (he was defeated in a 1950 re-election bid) as well as re-electing John Sparkman to the U.S. Senate.

Though the Boswell Amendment failed, its supporters witnessed again the powerful attraction of race in uniting white voters, even for a cause detrimental to the political status of many of them. After 1946, the old-line leaders chipped away at progressive politics by excavating the race issue. The exploitation of race reflected, in part, the cynicism

of Redeemer leadership. As one Deep South senator informed economist William Nicholls in the mid-1950s: "Give me another issue I can
run and be sure of winning out in the counties, and I'll drop the nigger
question."

But race-baiting by itself was insufficient to wean the rising urban
managers and entrepreneurs from progressive politics. In order to attract urban leaders, the old-liners stressed regressive taxes (like the
sales tax), moderate expenditures (on roads in particular), and vigorous
industrial recruitment. There emerged a tacit understanding that
race-baiting was a tactic for the provinces and not a philosophy of
governance.

Georgia governor Eugene Talmadge, for example, who prided himself on his rural background and constituency, successfully, though
quietly, courted Atlanta's business elite. After a brief flirtation with
reform under Ellis Arnall, Georgia voters returned to the Talmadge
clan in 1948 by electing son Herman as governor. Though he hollered
"nigger" as loud as his father, he was also effective in the staid boardrooms in Atlanta, where he invited business leaders to develop a regressive package of consumer taxes to finance economic development.
George Smathers, who used race-baiting to unseat veteran New Deal
progressive senator Claude Pepper of Florida in 1950, also advocated a
vigorous laissez-faire economic program. As political analyst Robert
Sherrill noted, Smathers was "the perfect case of the southern politician who, having treated his constituents to the public orgy of a witch-
burning, is thereafter left alone to the private orgies of serving special
interests and himself."

The old-liners used the Truman administration and the federal judiciary as foils to forge white solidarity and obstruct reform efforts. "The
race question is applied to nearly every political issue," noted one
discouraged South Carolina progressive in the early 1950s, "either
openly or covertly, and all-out attempts have been . . . made to discredit any proposal or policy that would alter the status quo." Those
who otherwise might have dismissed the political retreads began to
realize, as Gunnar Myrdal suggested, that "social equality *will* be promoted in a society remade by social reform." If blacks became com-
petitors for jobs, services, and office, what then? If the federal government was allowed to dictate social relations, where would it end?

The response to President Truman's 1948 civil rights package reflected the broadening base of white solidarity in the South. Editorials
accused Truman of "a stab in the back" and of "ingratitude to the

South." Texas congressman Ed Lee Gossett charged that groveling urban liberals were guiding Democratic party policy. Virginia senator Harry F. Byrd contended that Truman had delivered a "devastating broadside at the dignity of southern traditions and institutions." Even such moderate journals as the Nashville *Banner* scored the "vicious planks" in the president's package.

The letters Truman received from white southerners indicated that public opinion in the region was aroused and turning against the administration. A Tennessee voter admonished the president that "when you asked Congress to pass your Civil Rights Legislation, and press down the Crown of Thorns on the South's brow and crisify [*sic*] the South's people on a Communistic Cross disguised in Negro Equality, that was the straw that broke the camel's back." Another writer reminded the president that "multiplied thousands of Negro men in the South have almost an insane desire to rape a white woman and despoil her body and reduce her to his own level." And one southerner acknowledged in Faulknerian terms, "I am for civil rights, but not at this time." To be sure, the president also received some supportive correspondence from the South, but the wave of protest greeting his civil rights program indicated a shift in southern opinion. Southerners were clearly hurt by a man whom they had perceived as a friend. In the honor code of the region, Truman's betrayal was at least as important as the substantive elements in his package.

The extent and tone of southern reaction reflected other factors in addition to the violation of etiquette. It indicated an accelerated campaign by old-liners who recognized that the postwar political thaw was not a temporary phenomenon. Not only were blacks voting in record numbers, but whites were going to the polls as well. Also, organizations such as the NAACP were becoming more active in the region, encouraging blacks (such as Harry Briggs) to attack the racial status quo through the courts. If these challenges were successful and the rulings implemented, then white supremacy could crumble. Finally, southern white leaders understood national demographics and their declining influence within the Democratic party; they faced the loss of patronage and ultimately of congressional leadership. The latter particularly would bring the social upheaval closer to reality.

Southern leaders issued an ultimatum to Truman and the Democratic party at the national convention in July, 1948, when they demanded that the delegates repudiate the president's civil rights package. Truman sought a compromise, but the civil rights issue had become such a political boon for northern urban Democrats that the delegates rejected any modification to the program. As *Time* magazine reported, "the South had been kicked in the pants, turned around and kicked in the stomach." Their bluff called, most of the southern delegates stomped out of the convention and reassembled in Birmingham a few weeks later to nominate South Carolina governor Strom Thurmond and Mississippi governor Fielding L. Wright for president and vice president respectively on the States' Rights Democratic party ticket.

The Dixiecrats, as they were popularly called, fizzled in the November election. Despite President Truman's continued high profile on civil rights—establishing a fair-employment board within the Civil Service Commission and becoming the first president to address a rally in Harlem—the Dixiecrats carried only those states (South Carolina, Alabama, Mississippi, and Louisiana) where they ran under the regular Democratic party emblem. The white South was not ready for revolt. As Virginia attorney general J. Lindsay Almond explained, "the only sane and constructive course to follow is to remain in the house of our fathers—even though the roof leaks, and there be bats in the belfry, rats in the pantry, a cockroach waltz in the kitchen and skunks in the parlor."

Although the Dixiecrats failed to loosen party loyalty, the focus on race slowed racial progress. There was a noticeable retreat from conciliatory racial rhetoric among progressive politicians in the South and a studied avoidance of racial issues in general. Along the way, there were numerous casualties. Lister Hill, Alabama's promising progressive senator, resigned from his position as Democratic whip in order to avoid an inevitable confrontation with the president on civil rights. Hill was also concerned that his entanglement with race would destroy his effectiveness as a fighter for "the cause"—securing educational, health, and social programs for his constituents while restricting the rapacity of absentee industry that plagued his state. He was well aware of the attempts of his political enemies back home to forge the connection between reform and race, so Hill stunted a promising political career by adhering to racial orthodoxy. His colleague John Sparkman resigned himself to a similar compromise, as did Arkansas senator J. William Fulbright.

Frank Porter Graham was another casualty of the growing orthodoxy on race, though in a different way than Lister Hill. Graham was one of the South's leading progressives by the mid-1940s, having served as one of two southerners on President Truman's Commission on Civil

Rights. Prior to his service for the Truman administration, "Dr. Frank" had distinguished himself first as a history professor and then as president of the University of North Carolina, where he fought vigorously for academic freedom, developed a quality faculty, and molded the institution into one of the major state universities in the South. In 1949, Governor W. Kerr Scott appointed Graham to fill the unexpired U.S. Senate term of recently deceased J. Melville Broughton.

The seat came up for election in 1950, and Graham decided to seek a full term. Although he was noticeably in advance of his colleagues and many of his constituents on racial and economic issues, his national reputation and his leadership at Chapel Hill earned him widespread respect. He emerged from the Democratic primary with 49.1 percent of the vote and a 53,000-vote lead over his nearest competitor, former president of the American Bar Association and chairman of the Duke University Board of Trustees Willis Smith. North Carolina, like most other southern states, required a runoff primary if no candidate received a clear majority (50 percent or higher) in the first primary. The runoff primary, an electoral device instituted by the Democratic party in the South during the early years of the twentieth century to dilute the effect of bloc voting for minority (race or class) candidates who might be able to muster a plurality in a large field, was another mechanism to deflect democratic challenges to the political status quo.

Graham's substantial lead over Smith in the first primary made him the odds-on favorite in the runoff, and as the campaign entered the final two weeks, he continued to maintain a comfortable advantage in the polls. At that time, anonymous handbills mysteriously appeared in the newspaper boxes or inside screened doors of voters across the state imploring, "WHITE PEOPLE WAKE UP!" The paragraph below the headline declared that "Frank Graham Favors Mingling of the Races" and predicted race warfare if he won. In rapid succession, newspaper ads appeared exposing Graham's secret agenda: "End of Racial Segregation Proposed" and "The South Under Attack." Another wave of handbills followed with a doctored photograph depicting Graham's wife dancing with a black man. Allegations spread that "Dr. Frank" had appointed a black youngster to the U.S. Military Academy at West Point. When Graham responded to this accusation by bringing the white teenager whom he had actually appointed to a political rally, some remained unconvinced. A reporter sampling crowd response at the rally concluded that the sentiment was, "Why didn't he bring the nigger he appointed? Who was he trying to fool, showing us that white boy?"

The campaign coincided with the height of the Cold War, and Graham's opponents threw in the loyalty issue for good measure. They did not accuse him of being a Communist, but they linked his positions on issues, as well as some of his acquaintances, to communism. The charge haunted Graham for years after the election—in 1959, for example, the South Carolina senate banned him from speaking at a state college campus because of the campaign allegations nearly a decade earlier.

The charges threw the Graham campaign into confusion and dismay. Campaign workers left in droves, fearing for their reputations, even for their personal safety, and former supporters dumped Graham literature and snatched off bumper stickers. "My neighbors won't talk to me!" one erstwhile Graham worker complained. The campaign leadership faced a terrible quandary: responding to the charges legitimized them to some degree, and ignoring them appeared as a tacit admission of guilt. It was also difficult to mount a counteroffensive in the closing days of a campaign. Though Willis Smith did not participate in the race- or red-baiting, he never renounced its use. His staff, including a young journalist by the name of Jesse Helms, crafted an artful campaign of innuendo that proved irresistible to Tarheel voters. Smith captured the runoff with nearly 52 percent of the vote. There were two decisive voting elements in Smith's victory: eighteen eastern counties with heavy concentrations of black population and some of the poorest citizens in the state switched to Smith's column after supporting Graham in the first primary; and the urban middle classes, fiscally conservative and doubtless concerned about Graham's reputation as a New Dealer, swung overwhelmingly for Smith, solidifying the old-line coalition that was attempting a comeback throughout the South.

Graham lost not only the campaign but friends and prestige as well. The fire that destroyed the distinguished educator apparently could be stoked by old-line opponents with relative ease to suit the occasion the person. In addition, the anti-Communist hysteria provided a fortuitous companion issue that enabled old-liners to cloak their assaults in the mantle of patriotism. President Truman's civil rights initiatives represented a dangerous centralizing tendency in the federal government that corresponded to Soviet-style politics, critics argued. Just as black southerners had learned to expect the worst from whites, so white southerners assumed the worst of Washington. Southern whites, staunchly individualistic, were receptive to charges that pending federal legislation would force them to associate with blacks. The irony was that these arguments sought a conformity of another sort. The target of this offensive was not the administration or the Supreme Court, for its true objective was to regain control at home by restoring white solidarity.

The Liberals' Choice

Southern liberalism became a victim again after its brief revival in the late 1940s. The liberals had never been a uniform group to begin with, and for many, their years on the edge of public opinion had left them extremely sensitive and wary of falling off. Their organizations ranged from the moderate SRC, which subsumed race under a broad range of economic and social objectives, to the militant SCEF, which demanded immediate racial integration. There were Jim Crow liberals (*i.e.*, those who openly supported segregation) such as journalists Hodding Carter and Mark Ethridge, and militant integrationists such as Aubrey Williams and Lillian Smith. When the pressure for racial orthodoxy mounted in southern society, the liberal movement, such as it was, collapsed. Its leaders either went silent or left the region.

The increasing intensity of racial rhetoric forced the liberals to choose sides—a painful and ultimately destructive exercise. The SRC abandoned its Jim Crow liberalism with its 1950 credo and saw its membership drop by nearly one-half between that pronouncement and 1954. The National Committee to Abolish the Poll Tax disbanded for lack of support in 1948. That same year, the militant SCHW expired, a victim of race- and red-baiting. The SCEF struggled into the early 1950s. Its director, Aubrey Williams, received a subpoena to appear before the U.S. Senate Committee on Internal Security following a radio debate on school desegregation with Georgia governor Herman Talmadge early in 1954. Committee member Senator James O. Eastland succeeded in identifying the SCEF as an element in the "Communist conspiracy," although he found nothing incriminating on Williams. The charge had its desired effect, however, because it drove off funding and some members, such as black educator Benjamin Mays, and it ruined Williams' publishing career.

Other liberals retreated and alternated between professions of regional loyalty (*i.e.*, support for segregation) and attacks on other liberals for carelessly consorting with alleged Communists or their sympathizers. As early as 1947, Ralph McGill denounced the SCHW as being "Communist-infiltrated." The civil rights offensive by the Truman administration also came under liberal criticism. Hodding Carter, in his book *Southern Legacy* (1950), warned that "any abrupt Federal effort to end segregation" would not only fail but would "dangerously impair the present progressive adjustments between the races." The rhetoric was reminiscent of the liberal pessimism during World War II, though with the important difference that fear and concern had turned to defense. North Carolina journalist Gerald W. Johnson expressed surprise at the attack on southern racial customs from "uninformed" outsiders. He lectured:

> If you compare the rise of the American Negro since 1865 with the rise of any other dominated race, you will find in the record of the white South a magnanimity, wisdom, and charity, never approached by any other dominant race in the history of mankind. Compared with any similar episode, the treatment of the American Negro is not the disgrace, but the supreme glory of America. It is ironical that the greatest thing we ever did is now used against us because it was not the perfect work of archangels instead of the merely creditable work of men.

In a region where posturing and form were essential accompaniments to public influence, these statements should not be taken at face value. When progressive Georgia governor Ellis Arnall was running for re-election against race-baiting Eugene Talmadge in 1946, Arnall's fealty to race became an issue. Arnall supporter Ralph McGill reassured the electorate, "there will be no mixing of the races in the schools. There will be no social equality measures. Now or later." The objective was to secure Arnall's election (he lost) in order to promote a progressive program for a struggling state, and—much as Lister Hill and John Sparkman saluted the flag of white supremacy, though distasteful to them—McGill swallowed his principles for what he believed to be greater ends. The difficulty, of course, was that when these men abandoned the moderate position there were no responsible leaders to enter a plea on behalf of southern blacks, or to prepare the South generally for an alteration in race relations. The result was that the extremists prevailed.

Those few who continued to speak out, like Aubrey Williams, suffered the consequences of isolation, exile, or worse. Judge Waring became anathema to Charleston society, and his house on Meeting Street was the target of periodic cross burnings, garbage dumping, and sniper fire. When lightning struck a house next to the judge's vacation cottage near Charleston, the owner erected a sign: "Dear God, he lives next door." By the early 1950s, the Warings fled Charleston for exile in New

York City. The judge directed his parting shot at the Jim Crow liberals whose espousal of the "dangerous and insidious doctrine . . . of gradualism" was a greater obstacle to racial accommodation than the rhetoric and policies of avowed racists. (Martin Luther King, Jr., was to say much the same thing less than a decade later.) Waring died on January 11, 1968, and was interred in Charleston. Even at that late date, his neighbors and former colleagues were unforgiving. Out of more than two hundred mourners at his funeral, only twelve were white. As one of the whites rationalized to reporter Carl Rowan, "We all can't do like him. We can't all be crucified."

Dorothy Tilly was another white liberal who braved the consequences of dissent and suffered accordingly. Her activities with the Fellowship of the Concerned removed the cloak of protection typically afforded to southern white women. Obscene calls harassed her day and night, and she eventually moved a record player near her phone and whenever a caller launched into a diatribe she would play the Lord's Prayer. Atlanta mayor Hartsfield ordered a plainclothesman to follow Tilly and a police car to cruise her street during the night; he went so far as to have a streetlight installed in front of her house. Columnists held her up to ridicule, one denouncing her as "a parasite who while living upon funds furnished by the Methodist Church had rendered much of her service to the cause of Socialism and Communism."

The examples of Williams, Waring, and Tilly, as well as the political demise of Pepper and Graham, demonstrated the consequences of dissent and accounted in part for the retreat and for the professions of regional loyalty by liberals. Southern communities were built upon an intricate web of social relations involving family, church, and club. In a rural and small-town society—and even the larger cities maintained the intimacy of the lesser centers—lives revolved around and drew sustenance and identity from these contacts. The increasing emphasis on white solidarity deprived dissenters of this fellowship, isolated them and their families, and subjected them to public snubs. The pressure for conformity effectively minimized dissent.

Soap Bubbles for Blacks

The constricting environment ultimately squeezed blacks the most. Lynchings accelerated after the war. Harry Briggs's lawsuit resulted in his dismissal from work, and his wife lost her job as a cleaning woman in a local motel. Briggs's co-petitioner, farmer Levi Pearson, could no longer obtain credit from any Clarendon County bank, and the local sawmill, run by school board chairman R. W. Elliott, refused to cut his timber, leaving it to rot on the ground. J. A. DeLaine, the local NAACP director who took up the Briggs case, was fired from his position as principal of one of the county's black schools; his wife, two of his sisters, and a niece also lost their jobs. Vandals burned his house to the ground while the fire department watched the blaze. One night he fled the county in a hail of gunfire, never to return.

Though the electoral process was more open to blacks than at any time since the Reconstruction era, outside of cities and especially in the Deep South exercising the suffrage was dangerous. In 1946, black army veteran Etoy Fletcher was publicly whipped in Brandon, Mississippi, for attempting to register. Mississippi senator Theodore G. Bilbo had a strategy for ensuring low black voter turnout: "The best way to keep a nigger away from a white primary is to see him the night before." The Jackson (Miss.) *Daily News* warned prospective black voters (only 1,500 out of 500,000 potential black participants): "Don't attempt to participate in the Democratic primary anywhere in Mississippi . . . staying away from the polls will be the best way to prevent unhealthy and unhappy results." For those few blacks courageous (or foolhardy) enough to attempt to register, Mississippi registrars had a list of nonsensical questions to test the literacy of potential black registrants, including "How many bubbles in a bar of soap?" Registrars, especially in rural areas of the South, possessed wide latitude in interpreting suffrage statutes: they were sole arbiters of literacy competence; they set hours and locations for registration designed to maximize inconvenience for blacks; they occasionally "ran out" of registration forms or were deliberately slow in processing applications; and they arbitrarily removed voters from the rolls. In Sunflower County, Mississippi (Senator Eastland's home), black voter registration in 1955 plummeted from 114 to zero. In fourteen Mississippi counties—most with large black populations—not one black was registered to vote.

But even in cities such as Atlanta, where blacks enjoyed suffrage rights and modest political power, the accommodating white leadership was uneasy. As early as 1943, Mayor William B. Hartsfield, the major beneficiary of black votes, sought to dilute their influence through a vigorous annexation program. As he explained privately, "this annexation movement . . . is a movement for better government. We want voters, not money. . . . Our negro population is growing by leaps and bounds. They stay right in the city limits . . . the time is not far distant when they will become a potent political force in Atlanta.

. . . [D]o you want to hand them political control of Atlanta?" Under the 1952 Plan of Improvement, the city annexed the white suburb of Buckhead; the few blacks who had resided there occupied an area called Bagley Park until the county evicted them and turned the area into a park at the request of Buckhead's white residents.

The restriction, dilution, or outright elimination of black suffrage was essential for restoring the old order. These were responses both to increased black political mobilization after World War II and to the growing independence of the white electorate. Voting had been a symbol of white solidarity and supremacy for a half century or more— Reconstruction lore included numerous elements, but few evoked more powerful images than the depiction of blacks marching to the polls en masse and holding public office. In a region where such display related directly to status, voting was public behavior, and for most whites, voting had become another symbol of superiority. The franchise question seemed more pressing after 1945 because the war experience and educational opportunities had rendered blacks more demanding of their political rights. As one Alabama legislator admitted during the debate over the Boswell Amendment, "if it was necessary to eliminate the Negro in 1901 because of certain inherent characteristics, it is even more necessary now because some intellectual progress makes the Negroes more dangerous to our political structure now than in 1901."

The old-liners had succeeded in stirring white reaction and in precipitating a retreat among political and intellectual progressives. In the process, they had begun to restore the limited government and political participation, grounded on white supremacy, that had characterized the prewar order. However, their success was by no means secure. Demographics were working against them: blacks and whites were moving to southern cities; the Black Belt and other rural strongholds, long the rotten boroughs of southern politics, might not sustain the challenge from an urban South that contained the region's economic future. It was also more difficult to apply the subtle pressures of caste and class in a larger urban environment; and, although old-liners had found political friends among the urban economic elite, it was an alliance of convenience, not one of ideology. The loyalty of such partners might not extend beyond the ledger line.

There was also a complacency in the white South. Although it was possible to rouse the white electorate to a fury on specific issues or candidates, it could prove difficult to sustain that attitude. Things were going well for the South; money and jobs were coming in. Whites were also secure in their racial supremacy; their leaders' own rhetoric had stressed the indestructibility of racial etiquette and segregation. And empirical evidence seemed to support this view. Blacks remained invisible as individuals to most whites and inferior as a group. Shut away in "nigger towns," segregated in schools, excluded from parks, restaurants, clubs, and most occupations, deferential in the few points of public contact, blacks for the most part remained in their designated place. The few concessions to black political power in the cities were also mostly unseen by whites: a paved street, more systematic trash collection, and black policemen stationed in black districts empowered only to arrest black offenders. The South had also weathered the Truman civil rights offensive easily. The Eisenhower administration seemed little inclined to embark on a similar crusade and, in fact, was making overtures to crack the solid Democratic South. For all these reasons, white solidarity, and hence the position of the old-liners, was uncertain. But then the *Brown* decision appeared in May, 1954.

Reaction to *Brown*: The Failure of Leadership

Ironically, the immediate reaction to *Brown* was relatively mild, indicating perhaps both complacency and resignation. The decision could not have surprised southerners aware of the Court's earlier rulings on segregated education; also, there were untold numbers of southern whites who, beneath the façade of etiquette, regretted the charade and would have thrown off the burden had their place in white fellowship been assured. The Supreme Court had provided them with an "out" that allowed the white southerner to turn to his brethren with practiced resignation and sigh that, regardless of his personal feelings, he would follow the law of the land. But the Court's decision conjured up liabilities as well: it was an outside agency, and its ruling was a federal provocation that might give encouragement to blacks beyond school desegregation. Defiance rather than compliance had historically won out in the South, a region frequently living on the edge of its emotions, steeped in romanticism and lore. Such was the case after 1954.

There were some predictable reactions to the *Brown* decision, such as Senator Eastland's assessment that "the Supreme Court of the United States in the false name of law and justice has perpetrated a monstrous crime." The decision inspired Mississippi judge Tom Brady to write a book-length rebuke of the Court, entitled *Black Monday*

(1954) (the Court announced its decision on a Monday). Brady admonished the justices that they had "arrested and retarded the economic and political and, yes, the social status of the Negro in the South for at least one hundred years." But his interest in black welfare was fleeting; Brady soon went to the heart of the matter in a peroration that would strike the uninitiated as a non sequitur but that followed logically from the illogic of white supremacy: "When a law transgresses . . . moral and ethical sanctions and standards . . . invariably strife, bloodshed, and revolution follow in the wake of its attempted enforcement. The loveliest and the purest of God's creatures, the nearest thing to an angelic being that treads this terrestrial ball is a well-bred, cultured Southern white woman or her blue-eyed, golden-haired little girl."

But the threat against racial purity, not to mention white womanhood, did not cause all or even most Mississippians to mount the barricades. Governor James P. Coleman appealed for "cool thinking" in his state and warned against troublemakers who would carry the state "beyond the point of no return." Obviously drawing a different conclusion from judicial events than Eastland, Coleman allowed that "riding the niggers is no longer a political asset in Mississippi." Duncan Gray, an Episcopal priest in Cleveland, Mississippi, confirmed Coleman's judgment by noting that school boards around the state were discussing desegregation plans and foresaw a smooth transition to an integrated educational system, albeit not in the immediate future.

White church leaders, if they took sides at all, were similarly divided. Some, such as Henry E. Egger, rector of St. Peter's Episcopal Church in Charlotte, were concerned that race mixing was inspired by the political left: "Unadulterated socialism is behind this social leveling, and, if we do not have the courage or the energy to stop it, we will lose what freedom we have left." Jerry Falwell, a young preacher at the modest Thomas Road Baptist Church in Lynchburg, Virginia, held theological reservations about *Brown*: "If Chief Justice Warren and his associates had known God's Word, I am confident that the . . . decision would never have been made." And what was God's word on school desegregation? Falwell dredged up the biblical arguments used by antebellum clerics to justify slavery: God put a curse on Ham, the alleged progenitor of Africans, so "they were cursed to be the servants of the Jews and Gentiles." The irony, Falwell explained, was that "the true Negro does not want integration." Who, then, was behind the litigation? "[W]e see the hand of Moscow in the background," he concluded.

On the other hand, the SBC passed a resolution just ten days after the *Brown* judgment, stating, "we recognize the fact that this Supreme Court decision is in harmony with the constitutional guarantee of equal freedom to all citizens, and with the Christian principles of equal justice and love for all men."

In fact, it was difficult to discern a trend in public opinion after the *Brown* decision. The lines drawn were apparently no different from the other postwar controversies over race. There was Georgia's Herman Talmadge predicting that interracial marriage was the ultimate objective of the Court and the NAACP, while Alabama governor James E. Folsom said simply, "when the Supreme Court speaks, that's the law." The chief justice of Florida's Supreme Court, notorious for his racial views, offered science as a rebuttal to the Court: "Fish in the sea segregate in schools of their kind," so it was reasonable to assume that different races would prefer separate schools as well. But Arkansas governor Francis Cherry announced to citizens that "Arkansas will obey the law."

Shortly after the *Brown* ruling, the New York *Times* surveyed southern school officials and found that the general feeling was that desegregation would proceed peacefully, if painfully. By the fall of 1956, several school districts in Kentucky, Tennessee, Arkansas, and Texas implemented desegregation plans. Though scattered outbreaks of violence occurred in Kentucky and Tennessee, Governors Frank Clement and A. B. ("Happy") Chandler, respectively, maintained order with state police and National Guardsmen. By the 1956–57 school year, desegregation affecting three hundred thousand black youngsters was underway in 723 school districts, mainly in the Upper South where black populations were not heavily concentrated.

But the sanguine reports emanating from various parts of the South may have been, in retrospect, whistling in the dark. In the small towns and cities across the region, schools were much more than educational facilities. They were extensions of family life, of community and individual values. The boundaries between public and private in the South were never clear; one was often the extension of the other. School buildings functioned as community landmarks; athletic teams infused pride in the town and within individuals. Club meetings, voting, and recreational activities frequently occurred on school grounds in both the black and white communities. School desegregation, especially in those cities and rural areas where blacks comprised sizable minorities or a majority of the population, was akin to opening one's home to strangers—and uninvited strangers at that. It was a violation of privacy; it contradicted conventional perceptions of the role of blacks in southern society; and it aroused deep-seated fears that propinquity would ultimately become intimacy.

Few leaders stepped forward to calm those fears and offer alternative visions to the dire depictions conjured up by those who had a personal stake in maintaining racial separation and antagonism. During the months following the *Brown* decision, a leadership vacuum characterized much of the South; local, state, and federal officials seemed wary or unwilling to endorse the ruling unequivocally, or at least to prepare their citizens to implement the Court's wishes. More common was the regional leader who perceived political capital in opposing the decision and whose field of operation was uncluttered by contrary voices. In Washington, though President Eisenhower acted quickly in outlawing, by executive order, segregation in the District of Columbia's public schools, he had serious reservations about either the advisability or legality of federal power over local school boards. Privately, the president expressed concern that the *Brown* decision would *"set back* progress in the South *at least fifteen years,"* even though he felt the Court's ruling was correct.

Frank E. Smith was a congressman from Mississippi who had attempted to fill part of that vacuum by urging compliance. He paid with the destruction of his political career. In his memoir of those troubled years, *Look Away from Dixie* (1965), Smith averred that "the central theme from the . . . decision of the Supreme Court is the failure of those in positions of responsibility to meet the challenge to secure peaceably rapid, and orderly compliance with the decision." In this absence, Smith contended, other elements in southern society stepped forth.

Respectable Resistance: Deliberate and Speedy

The resistance that emerged was a far cry from the one-gallused exhorters of an earlier era, their contorted faces spewing tobacco juice and rhetoric dipped in fire. This was the postwar South, a cooler time with a more sophisticated electorate that had experienced war, travel, employment, and education, and the resistance rarely resorted to metaphoric rebel yells or blood-curdling appeals to violence. This is not to say that they disavowed the fringe elements in the resistance. The resisters not only tolerated, but encouraged these elements, because, by contrast, respectable opponents would then be perceived not as nullifiers in three-piece suits, but as advocating preferable alternatives to race war.

James J. Kilpatrick, editor of the Richmond *News-Leader*, was among the leaders of this respectable resistance. Kilpatrick and his fellow anticompliance journalists pointed out the different intellectual capacities of blacks as reflected by their poor performance in school and their menial occupations. (Of course, that was one of the maddening features of the biracial society: the shortcomings in black economic status and education, which were consequences of that society, became arguments for perpetuating it.) Since most whites saw few if any blacks in prominent positions in the South, the assumption was that this reflected black inferiority. Kilpatrick summarized this argument in a 1955 editorial:

> . . . white and Negro children in the South have many quite different educational requirements. . . . For years to come in the South, the practice of law and medicine, the handling of banking and finance, the sale of stocks and bonds, the management of large retail and wholesale enterprises, and the administration of commerce and government will continue to be overwhelmingly restricted to white persons. . . . All this has to be considered practically in terms of curriculum planning, guidance, teaching, emphasis, and the like. Nothing very significant is accomplished really, in offering physics or calculus to Negro boys who intend to drop out at the ninth grade level and go to work farming or cutting pulpwood.

Kilpatrick, in addition to his expertise on curriculum matters, fashioned complex, often arcane legalistic arguments to prove the invalidity of the Court decision and the correctness of dual school systems. He also encouraged state legislatures to adopt these arguments in the form of legislation. In the three years following the *Brown* decision, southern lawmakers passed 450 laws designed to circumvent that ruling. These measures included closing schools faced with desegregation orders, firing teachers who taught mixed classes, allowing white children to transfer from integrated schools, and state funding for private education. State legislatures also targeted the NAACP, the organization most likely to file suit against their maneuvers, by forcing the group to reveal its membership, dismissing public employees who belonged to the organization, and barring it from challenging local segregation ordinances in court.

Kilpatrick and others who advocated the legislative course to circumvention understood that those measures were probably unconstitutional. But that was beside the point. The objectives were to tie up and deplete NAACP energies and resources, and to delay indefinitely the implementation of *Brown*. An example of this cynical use of state power occurred in the Louisiana legislature early in 1956. On this occasion, it passed a measure requiring black applicants to white public schools to present a "certificate of good moral character" signed by their principal and the district superintendent before they could be admitted. The lawmakers passed a companion measure providing for the dismissal of anyone signing such a certificate. As Kilpatrick advised, the best way to defeat *Brown* was "to take lawful advantage of every moment of the law's delays. . . . Litigate? Let us pledge ourselves to litigate this thing for fifty years. If one remedial law is ruled invalid, then let us try another; and if the second is ruled invalid, then let us enact a third." This orgy of law making led one observer to remark that "the Court's decision was the greatest thing that has happened to the legal profession since the invention of the ambulance."

The school boards devised their own respectable strategies for delaying implementation. Their major weapon was the so-called "freedom-of-choice" plan that enabled children of both races to select schools of their choice. In practice, however, black candidates faced lengthy application procedures, interviews, occasional harassment, and high rates of rejection. In New Orleans, black applicants were put through a humiliating battery of tests to determine psychological stability and physical fitness. White pupils, on the other hand, could be assured of automatic reassignment if they would rather not attend classes with blacks. When the NAACP finally became frustrated with the machinations of the school board in Greensboro, North Carolina—a board that had been among the first in the South to declare its intentions to comply with *Brown*—board members produced a unique evasion. In 1959, four black students applied to an all-white school and were rejected. After the NAACP filed suit, the board, sensing an unfavorable ruling, merged the white school to which the students had applied with a black school and transferred the white students to another school. The court ruled that the issue was moot since the black students were now enrolled in the school to which they had applied.

Evasion was becoming a community effort, and there were no counterpoints in the white community offering an alternative, and no encouragement out of Washington to do so. The Eisenhower administration had become even more circumspect in its lukewarm endorsement of *Brown*. The president was especially fearful that outside pressure on the insular South would result in massive and violent defiance of the law and place him in the uncomfortable position of enforcement. The Supreme Court itself provided indirect encouragement to respectable resistance through its implementation ruling in May, 1955. The 1954 *Brown* decision, while throwing out the separate-but-equal formula, did not provide a timetable for desegregation. That came in the so-called *Brown* II ruling a year later.

To the dismay of the NAACP and its supporters, the Court required only a "prompt and reasonable start toward full compliance," and that desegregation should proceed "with all deliberate speed." The NAACP warned that without a specific timetable, the proclivity of school boards to delay would become endemic. There was some speculation that in exchange for a unanimous opinion in the first *Brown* decision, the justices agreed to give the South the benefit of doubt on implementation. More likely, the Court, by 1955, was isolated, receiving little support from the other branches of government. Also, recent public opinion polls revealed that more than 80 percent of white southerners were opposed to school desegregation. The growing list of southern leaders who opposed any implementation, as well as the warnings of violence if desegregation proceeded too quickly, convinced the justices that the integrity of the judicial system depended on developing a position that would not alienate a strong majority of the South's population. So the responsibility for desegregating the region's schools fell upon local boards and courts whose members comprised a cross-section of white leadership in the tight-knit communities over the South.

Among the readings the Court received on desegregation sentiment in the South was that active resistance was not confined to the usual political and journalistic race-baiters but had permeated a good portion of the white population. Respectable resistance had the benefit of appearing to be the moderate position while it advocated defiance of the law of the land. The White Citizens' Councils became the epitome of the organized effort at conservative lawbreaking, especially in the Deep South. The rise of the councils also reflected the collective commitment to defiance and the intolerance of contrary views that came to characterize the South by 1956.

The Citizens' Councils

Late in 1954, the Montgomery *Advertiser* informed its readers of a danger in their midst, greater perhaps than a meddling Supreme Court: "The manicured Kluxism of these White Citizens' Councils is rash, indecent and vicious. . . . The night-riding and lash of the 1920s have become an abomination in the eyes of public opinion. So the bigots have resorted to a more decorous, tidy and less conspicuous method—economic thuggery." The *Advertiser* was referring to an organization founded in the summer of 1954 by Mississippi farmer and World War II veteran Robert Patterson, whose purpose was to gather leading citizens to resist integration through legal measures. Patterson boasted that the councils were "channelling . . . popular resistance to integration into lawful, coherent and proper modes, and prevent[ing] . . . violence or racial tension." But, as the *Advertiser* editorial indicated, their actions belied their rhetoric.

The councils applied systematic economic pressure on the parents of black children who sought to attend white schools. Composed of merchants, bankers, farmers, and politicians, these bodies controlled the economic (and hence political) life of the numerous small towns and cities of the Deep South. These leaders denied credit, provisions, employment, and services to blacks, and their purview extended far beyond school desegregation to include every aspect of racial etiquette, including suffrage. A Mississippi registrar explained the councils' strategy with respect to voter registration: "The Council obtains names of Negroes registered from the circuit court clerks. If those who are working for someone sympathetic to the Council's view are found objectionable, their employer tells them to take a vacation. Then, if they remove their names from the registration books, they are told that the vacation is over and they can return to work."

In order to work most effectively, the councils were dependent on the white community not only for acquiescence to their activities but for membership as well. Once a council organized, peer pressure to join mounted. Former president Jimmy Carter was one of the few residents of Sumter County, Georgia, in the mid-1950s who refused to join the local council. The council threatened to boycott his peanut business, though nothing came of it. In many areas of the Deep South, it became impossible for political candidates to run successfully for office without council endorsements, and this extended to statewide candidates as well. In Mississippi, the state treasury subsidized council activities, and one of their own, Ross Barnett, became governor in 1959.

The mass rally, a device that adhered to the region's evangelical tradition, was the main recruitment vehicle for council organizers. The rally was a form of entertainment and excitement for a population still tied to the dull rhythms of agricultural or basic industrial work. As in religious revivals, the crowd reinforced individual faith and imparted courage to those who might have been too timid to participate if approached alone. The mass rally, featuring speakers from out of state who spouted invective at Washington, sociologists, jurists, Communists, and race-mixers, also enabled provincial whites to feel that they were important, that they were taking part in a grand crusade, and that their leaders cared enough about them to invite their participation in defense of their homeland. It gave them purpose, a cause, and, not incidentally, helped to forge a bond between white elite and white masses.

Journalist John Bartlow Martin attended a council rally at the Montgomery Coliseum in February, 1956. More than fifteen thousand people jammed into the arena. Thirty Alabama political luminaries adorned the platform and warmed up the crowd with defiant rhetoric as they awaited the arrival of the main attraction, Senator James O. Eastland. Suddenly, a highway patrol car careened into the coliseum, screeched to a halt, and disgorged the guest of honor to a tumultuous ovation accompanied by a stirring rendition of "Dixie" and the fervent waving of Confederate flags. The crowd cheered every word of defiance. A woman in the audience blurted to Martin, "God bless 'em. God bless 'em. God, give us more of 'em—men like those men. God, give us more of 'em."

Although the councils employed extreme rhetoric to galvanize public sentiment and attract members, they disclaimed extremism; but by openly advocating defiance of the law, they set a precedent for lawlessness. Despite their protests to the contrary, their work and words encouraged violent elements to carry council objectives to their logical conclusion. Such violence provided two benefits for the councils: it promoted their image as the conservative alternative to mob rule, and it underscored their warnings that altering race relations would provoke violence. Council leaders understood that the color bond was not fast and that deep-seated class antagonisms existed between whites; violence and animosity directed at blacks would, they hoped, deflect attention from the vast differences between white fortunes in the South.

Patterson warned repeatedly that if integration occurred, "we'll have violence and you know it," as if hoping his words would become a self-fulfilling prophecy. A speaker at a council rally in Selma, Alabama, in December, 1954, vowed that "we intend to maintain segregation and do so without violence," and added, "but I know the first time a Negro tries to enter Parrish High School at Selma, or any other white school, blood will be spilled on the campus." As James McBride Dabbs noted about such double-talk, "The part about violence is always said publicly . . . so that the lower-class whites know what is expected of them." Council leaders may have worn Brooks Brothers suits, displayed aristocratic manners, and belonged to the right clubs, but so far as Lillian Smith was concerned, "they are a mob nevertheless. For they not only protect the rabble, and tolerate its violence, they *think in the same primitive* mode, they share the same irrational anxieties, they are *just as lawless in their own quiet way*, and they are dominated by the same 'holy idea' of white supremacy."

Council membership did not everywhere become *de rigueur* for aspiring and established white southern businessmen. Councils were relatively weak in the Upper South, but their successful resistance in the Deep South made an impression on white leaders elsewhere. They not only stimulated the electorate but organized them as well, and they drove out what remained of moderate positions in their areas. As Mississippi's Reverend Duncan Gray lamented, the council "was creating a climate and atmosphere in which it was virtually impossible to question those who were fighting to preserve the status quo." And if anyone doubted that by early 1956 the councils did not represent the viewpoint of regional leadership generally, 101 southern congressmen and senators demonstrated otherwise. By then it was apparent not only that respectable resistance would provoke no penalties from the courts or Congress, but that it held distinct political advantages as well.

The "Southern Manifesto": Deepening the Trench

North Carolina senator Sam Ervin, who was hardly a race-baiter but who shared the social class and economic conservatism of the old-liners, was already known for his sharp wit and constitutional acumen. Early in 1956, Ervin turned his legal genius to aid the cause of resistance as he drafted a "Declaration of Constitutional Principles" that circulated in both houses of Congress and drew the signatures of nearly all southerners. The "Declaration," which came to be known as the "Southern Manifesto," condemned the *Brown* decision as "contrary to the constitution" by usurping the states' control over public education. The 101 signatories (out of 128 southern congressmen and senators) pledged to employ "all lawful means to bring about a reversal of this decision," and to ensure that the federal government would not use force to implement desegregation.

Some writers have contended that the Southern Manifesto marked the beginning of "massive resistance" in the South, a period of open and willful defiance of the Supreme Court. New York *Times* columnist Anthony Lewis noted that "the true meaning of the Manifesto was to make defiance of the Supreme Court and the Constitution socially acceptable in the South—to give resistance to the law the approval of the Southern Establishment." Actually, respectable resistance was already well established in the South by the time of the Manifesto, and the southern congressmen and senators who signed it were merely reinforcing and expanding what had become a regional pattern. School boards, legislatures, churches, White Citizens' Councils, and the press had already demonstrated the efficacy of respectable resistance and its consequence-free espousal. While congressmen were signing the Manifesto, school desegregation was already a dead issue in the Deep South. In response to a question on when desegregation would eventually come to the Deep South, an observer noted unequivocally, "never. . . . It looks utterly impossible." A liberal editor tried to be more hopeful: "Never? Never is a long time. But for so long that I can't see when." In the Upper South desegregation came to a standstill.

The Southern Manifesto did not draw the battle line; it deepened the trench. The diversity that white southerners had demonstrated on the race issue in the immediate postwar years—a heterodoxy that belied the myth of white solidarity—was ending. To maintain difference in the years after 1956 was to fall into the trench and into isolation, exile, or injury. Just as the mounting debate over slavery had stifled freedom of thought and expression a century earlier, so now a new generation of white southerners fell back behind the line of white supremacy and conformity, killing the same freedoms in their retreat. The Montgomery *Advertiser* no longer printed unfavorable editorials about the White Citizens' Councils, and, indeed, few newspapers had anything to say about integration except to pronounce it dead—"I don't know anybody that's demanding integration," Ralph McGill wrote early in 1957. The churches, which had taken some small steps toward supporting the Supreme Court decision, returned to the position James Joyce had reserved for God in his novel *Portrait of the Artist as a Young Man*: "Within or behind or beyond his handiwork, invisible, refined out of existence, indifferent, paring his fingernails." Billy Graham, emerging as one of the South's most respected young evangelists in the mid-1950s, counseled that "the church should not answer questions the people aren't asking. We've become advisers, social engineers, foreign policy experts when we should be answering the questions of the Soul."

This was the flight from reality, a movement not only behind the line but beyond civilization. It was a customary retreat for the South, shielding itself from the unpleasant burdens of its history—defeat, occupation, poverty, illiteracy, disease, and alienation from humanity in its midst—only to have those burdens grow ever more onerous, inducing a deeper flight in a vicious cycle that strangled both black and white. In a front-page editorial during the summer of 1956, the Jackson (Miss.) *Daily News* explained the ground rules for the coming conflict. The editors warned that "guts . . . and ramrod backbones is what we must have if we hope to win," and they praised the example set by the state's political leaders and citizens' councils: "It is to their voices we should listen, and not the twaddle being talked by wishy-washy people who prate about 'academic freedom,' and 'freedom of thought and of speech,' and similar nonsense. Puny parsons who prattle imbecilic propaganda in pulpits about obedience to the Supreme Court segregation decision being a 'manifestation of the Christian spirit' ought to have their pulpits kicked from under them. . . . In this fight you are either for us or against us. There is no middle ground."

By the time of the *News* editorial a new factor had entered into the South's struggle to preserve white supremacy. To some degree this new element accounted for the no-holds-barred stridency of the editorial. The fight was to be joined not only against the federal government and wavering southern whites, but against southern blacks as well, who were no longer mainly victims and occasional protesters of regional race relations but were becoming active participants in the struggle. This was an event that conjured up, for whites, a world turned on its head in much the same manner as their ancestors had perceived slave rebellions. But white southerners would soon learn, to their great benefit, the limits of their flight from reality. As Aeschylus observed long ago, "Against our will and in our own despite wisdom comes to us by the awful grace of God."

V / The Limits of Endurance: Buses, Books, and Balance Sheets, 1954–1960

Extinguishing the Light of Reason: Reliving History

On the face of it, blacks seemed to be unlikely candidates to secure their own liberation. By the mid-1950s, most parts of the South were becoming fortified battlegrounds of the mind and spirit. C. Vann Woodward observed of this period that "all over the South the light of reason and tolerance and moderation began to go out under the demand for conformity." The press, political leaders, schools, and churches conspired to defend or at least tolerate white supremacy. White southerners came to perceive segregation and integration as polar opposites, that one could not exist in the presence of the other, regardless of experiences to the contrary. Whereas integration meant access to dignity for blacks, it signified a threat to identity for whites, and even those sympathetic to black demands drew back, not yet able or willing to break the chains of history. William Faulkner admitted that "the Negroes are right . . . the [white] Southerners are wrong and . . . their position is untenable." But, he added, "if I have to make the same choice Robert E. Lee made then I'll make it." And Faulkner would have considerable company over the next several years as whites abandoned their sense of justice for their sense of history.

Words and symbols took on new meanings, and censorship harassed films, television, and libraries. A peculiar attempt to protect the public from the hint of racial accommodation occurred in Alabama in 1959. A state legislator vigorously objected to a children's book, *The Rabbit's Wedding*, in which a white rabbit married a black rabbit. The lawmaker convinced the legislature not only to ban the "bunny book" from the state's libraries as "subversive" but to burn it as well. Common sense and the Constitution were consumed in the process; as the Nashville *Tennessean* reported, "some legislators objected privately to the restriction, and one even ridiculed it. But they declined to be quoted by name because . . . their position might be misconstrued as pro-integration."

87

There was a fear abroad in the white South that to discuss race in terms other than staunch support for white supremacy would lead to ostracism or worse—fear among working-class whites of being "de-classed," unemployed, powerless; and fear among white leaders of losing their monopoly to Washington or to other whites. The energy generated by this fear found a convenient target in the region's blacks, whose penchant for equality had, after all, started and fueled the crisis in the first place.

A noticeable acceleration of white violence against blacks occurred after 1955, though the extent of such incidents may never be known. Blacks who disappeared under mysterious circumstances were not news to the southern press, and the relatively few reports that emerged often resulted from careless planning—bodies suddenly surfacing in rivers, too many witnesses, or especially grisly facts coming to light. The purported motives behind the various acts of violence varied and in many cases seemed contrived and flimsy to an outsider, almost as if groups of whites had gotten together and decided to "get a nigger" then concoct a reason afterwards. The case of Edward Aaron, a thirty-four-year-old black veteran from Union Springs, Alabama, highlights this point. On Labor Day, 1957, six white men kidnapped Aaron. In a cinderblock cabin on the outskirts of Birmingham, they sliced off his testicles and scrotum with a razor blade, poured turpentine on the wound, locked him in the trunk of a car, drove to a secluded area, and threw him out on the side of the road where he bled to death. Two Birmingham policemen investigating the case traveled to Union Springs to determine what in Aaron's background had provoked such an act. After numerous interviews, they found that Aaron was "a high-type individual that was a good citizen," although he was black and poor. Their report concluded that Aaron was a "white folk's nigger."

Two years earlier, an even more celebrated lynching occurred in Money, Mississippi, though the motive was clearer than in the Aaron case. Emmett Till was a fourteen-year-old black from Chicago visiting relatives in Money. As a city boy, he enjoyed impressing his cousins and their friends with how different life was in Chicago. To support his boast, he entered a store one morning and, contrary to the racial etiquette of the South, he addressed a white woman in a familiar manner, saying "Bye, baby," or words to that effect. That night, the woman's husband, Roy Bryant, and her brother-in-law, J. W. Milam, visited the home of Till's uncle, took Till at gunpoint, and eventually shot and beat him to death. Till's battered and mutilated body was discovered the next day floating in the Tallahatchie River, attached to a cotton gin fan. Bryant and Milam stood trial. A jury of twelve white men deliberated one hour and acquitted both.

While such incidents shocked the nation temporarily, their randomness and brutality struck southern blacks the most. In earlier times when race relations deteriorated, blacks were able to call upon white elites, appealing to their sense of paternalism, however one-sided, or they sought to ease tensions through existing interracial organizations. By the mid-1950s, however, such intercession was unlikely. The demise of traditional agricultural labor patterns and the exodus of millions of blacks off southern farms since the 1930s removed the last vestiges of paternalism, and events since 1945, especially the *Brown* decision and blacks' persistence in fulfilling its promise, hardly lessened the estrangement. Virginius Dabney noted in a *U.S. News & World Report* article in 1957 that "the tragic fact today in the South is that hardly any liaison remains between the white leadership and the Negro leadership. . . . The two races have been driven apart by the rancorous arguments over segregation, with the result that hardly any of the avenues of communication exist in most areas." Not that southern blacks mourned these developments. As James McBride Dabbs explained, "the Negroes . . . don't feel too keenly the ending of a peace that had been forced upon them."

What remained were raw emotions scraped clean of civility and conscience. The veneer of gentility that had covered the disorder of southern society had dissolved, and the tensions that lay beneath were exposed. Southern blacks confronted their proposed liberation alone. And the black community, as ever, was divided not only on tactics, but on even whether to proceed against such difficult odds at all. The odds encouraged inertia, as they did among some whites. As one Charlotte black woman recalled a generation later, "after awhile you get used to [segregation]. Things go along so long." And it was questionable whether blacks could generate sustained leadership to rouse them from their resignation and dispel the prevailing fear.

The Black Community: Searching for Leaders and Followers

The black church would have been an obvious locus of leadership, but the prevailing theology and the nature of the clergy made that prospect less certain. In the 1930s, Benjamin Mays surveyed more than one hundred ministers' sermons from a like number of urban black churches in the South. He discovered that only twenty-six sermons touched upon practical problems; the rest dealt with "other-worldly" topics. Most of the sermons, Mays found, were characterized more by pyrotechnics than by logic and intellect. He concluded that black clergy "encourage Negroes to feel that God will see to it that things work out all right; if not in this world, certainly in the world to come. They make God influential chiefly in the beyond, in preparing a home . . . where His suffering servants will be free of the trials and tribulations which beset them on earth." A decade later, Gunnar Myrdal found that Savannah's black ministers were actively discouraging a black voter-registration drive. As one pastor explained, "all we preachers is supposed to do is to preach the Lord and Saviour Jesus Christ and Him Crucified, and that's all." This was generally the view of many of the white evangelical churches in the South, but it was scarcely a perspective calculated to position the black church in a leadership role.

Historians have noted that whatever the theological bent of a particular black church, at the least it was one of the few black institutions independent of white control. However, the need for small mortgage loans and white contributions often restricted the independence of black urban churches, and in rural areas black preachers often worked at other jobs and were otherwise highly visible and therefore susceptible to white authority. The cloth afforded no protection from a relentless orthodoxy.

Other sectors of the black community indicated even less leadership potential. The most numerous of the small black professional class were the school principals and teachers, but they usually depended on white school boards for their positions. Black businessmen frequently enjoyed "protected markets" resulting from segregation. Most southern cities had black business districts (Auburn in Atlanta and East Hargett in Raleigh, for example) that catered to a predominantly black clientele. The more successful black entrepreneurs—morticians, hotel and restaurant operators, realtors, and publishers—benefited financially from the segregated society, as well as from bank loans, supplies, and advertising purchased from the white community. Black physicians and attorneys also based their practices on black clients.

A few of these black professionals nurtured ties with the white elite and by that association enhanced their status within the black community. They most often served on interracial panels, and white leaders designated them as "spokesmen" for the black community. Whatever these whites knew about the "pulse" of blacks usually came from these interlocutors, who were, of course, circumspect in the type of news they delivered. The black spokesmen, Myrdal explained, "labor under the risk of losing the good-will and protection of the influential whites." Opposition to white supremacy would have jeopardized both their position with whites and their status with blacks.

The mass of southern blacks were cognizant of these shortcomings in their purported betters. Myrdal noted that black leaders "are under constant suspicions from the Negro community that they are dishonest, venal and self-seeking." The younger, postwar generation of blacks who would form the shock troops for any assault on white supremacy were not only suspicious but also turned away by a leadership style that was frequently imperious (especially in academic settings). In the churches, the bombastic sermons lacking in social substance also distressed younger blacks hoping for guidance in solving this-worldly problems. By the mid-1950s, fear, poverty, illiteracy, and cynicism characterized the condition and outlook of many of these veterans. An assault hardly seemed likely, especially with the white South giving every indication that casualties would be extensive.

But there had always been floating about the black South another tendency, even if muted at times. The tendency had appeared in the runaway slave, in the faithful field hand who fired a tobacco barn, in the trusted house servant who secretly learned to read and write, and in countless others from slavery times to the days of Harry Briggs who knew well the dire personal consequences of their actions yet risked the security of slavery or segregation for freedom and justice. They were aware, even if subconsciously through their experience, of Frederick Douglass' dictum: "Find out just what people will submit to, and you have found out the exact amount of injustice and wrong which will be imposed upon them; and these will continue until they are resisted with either words or blows, or with both. The limits of tyrants are prescribed by the endurance of those whom they oppress." There were enough blacks in the South—and revolutions do not require large numbers—who had attained their limits of endurance. They only sought a catalyst and a leader who would transcend the obstacles implanted by white and black southerners too long accommodated to white supremacy.

The idea of rebellion was already well advanced among some blacks in the postwar South, but the white reaction and the divisiveness and inertia within the black community impeded open expression of that idea. However, the *Brown* decision raised black awareness. Harvey

Gantt recalled his insular boyhood in Charleston, South Carolina, and how the *Brown* decision touched his world as an eleven-year-old in 1954: "I started to get curious about the whole thing about segregation and why it was unconstitutional. And then I started to see our society in a different light; blacks, whites, and why we do things. . . . I never questioned it before and then I started." Gantt went on to become the first black to enroll at Clemson University, a successful architect, and Charlotte's first black mayor. For many other blacks besides Gantt, *Brown* implied that survival was not enough. As black novelist Alice Walker put it, "to survive *whole*" now became an option. The *Brown* decision galvanized resistance among southern whites, but it strengthened resolve among southern blacks to take control of their destiny.

Demographic trends enhanced this resolve as blacks continued to move to southern cities during the 1950s, so that the typical black southerner was no longer a Black Belt sharecropper. The city provided employment options, however limited, and cash wages, however meager. The dependence that marked country life was less evident in the city. Though still relatively powerless, black migrants now had connections to black institutions and black professionals. Numbers did not necessarily afford safety, but they did create possibility—and the *Brown* decision provided opportunity.

The legal process, however, was a tedious and uncertain vehicle with which to pursue civil rights. As blacks soon learned, the court system cut two ways. The legal system was not only time-consuming but expensive as well, and it was difficult to sustain interest, generate protest, and maintain support over the lengthy period of time required to see a case through. Even such relatively well-off national organizations as the NAACP had to choose their cases carefully; individual litigants, of course, had much greater financial burdens. Since legal challenges often involved individuals or small groups—easy targets for the white economic and political leadership—the publicity of legal action was a deterrent for aggrieved blacks. Even if a case concluded successfully, whites could engage in delay or evasion to render decisions more symbolic than real. A specific incident or confrontation was necessary, more to rally blacks than to impress whites.

The First Crusade: The Montgomery Bus Boycott

That opportunity arose in Montgomery, an unlikely venue for the beginning of a struggle for civil rights that would grow into a movement. The city was typical in many ways of the urban South: medium-sized (population 90,000); historically devoted to the marketing of cotton, though some processing industries appeared after the war; and possessed of the requisite amount of crepe myrtle and mimosa to lend a languid air to the place. But Montgomery was more than a place; it was a symbol. In this modest river town, only recently removed from the frontier, the Confederate States of America was born and Jefferson Davis inaugurated as its first and last president. Davis' house still stands, and the spot where he took his oath of office is appropriately marked with a star. Somehow, the fried okra and the pecan pie at the Elite (pronounced EE-light) Café, near the Capitol, taste more authentic than in most other places in the South. In a region that dotes on symbols, Montgomery was a shrine.

This is not to say that Montgomery's mind remained fixed at 1861, even if its heart was. Blacks could vote in the city and wielded enough political power for white politicians to take notice. The repressive and violent racial atmosphere of Birmingham was not evident in a town that had earned a reputation of gentlemanly, if restricted, race relations since the 1920s. In 1949, Jo Ann Robinson, a black professor at Alabama State College in Montgomery, emboldened by the Folsom-era political thaw, formed the Women's Political Council. The group ostensibly promoted the voter registration of black women, but over the next half decade the council evolved into the city's most effective and militant black political voice. Black women were less vulnerable to white economic pressure and less likely to be the target of violence than black men, so they could afford to be bolder. Among the most noteworthy accomplishments of the council was its successful support of white liberal Dave Birmingham for a seat on the three-member commission that administered city government in Montgomery. No sooner had the voters elected Birmingham in 1953 than he presented his fellow commissioners with an agenda of black demands. By May, 1954, the commission responded partially by hiring four black policemen—a significant achievement for a Deep South city.

Robinson and her council continued to lobby the commission to address other issues, such as the inadequate park and recreational facilities in black districts and the situation on city buses. The bus issue was a particularly sore point in the black community. The bus company practiced a system of "rolling segregation" on its vehicles. Black passengers took seats behind the white rider farthest back in the bus. If a white passenger boarded the bus and found all seats taken in the white section, the black behind the last white would be required to vacate his seat and locate another farther back, or stand. The bus drivers controlled the situation, and some were abusive in their directives to black passengers. The constant shifting of seats by blacks was humiliating, a never-ending game of musical chairs with the driver calling the tune. This public acknowledgment of inferiority irked the blacks, as did the practice of requiring them to pay their fares at the front of the bus, get off, and reboard through the rear doors. Occasionally, bus drivers took the fare and then drove off before the passenger could reboard.

Inspired by the *Brown* decision and frustrated by the unwillingness of the bus company to compromise, Robinson fired off a letter to Mayor W. A. ("Tacky") Gayle on May 21, 1954, on behalf of the Women's Political Council. Robinson's demands were modest: she wanted a law that would end "rolling segregation" in favor of a system where blacks would fill the bus from the back forward, and whites from the front back, until all seats were taken; additional passengers, regardless of race, would stand. To bolster the request, Robinson cited the cities of Atlanta, Macon, Savannah, and Mobile, where this seating pattern existed without incident. This first-come-first-served arrangement maintained segregation but eliminated the embarrassment of "rolling segregation" as well as limited the opportunity for bus drivers to exercise their authority in an abusive manner.

The petition and subsequent negotiations between Robinson, city officials, and bus-company representatives proved fruitless. As the citywide election campaign approached in the early spring of 1955, blacks were determined to make the bus situation a campaign issue. E. D. Nixon, a black union official and local NAACP head, inaugurated the lobbying effort by distributing a questionnaire to the three commission candidates—incumbent Dave Birmingham, James Stearns, and Clyde Sellers—requesting their positions on a number of issues important to black Montgomerians. The bus situation headed the list.

Birmingham and Stearns announced that they would consider the black program. Sellers, however, perceiving that his two opponents would likely split the black vote and that his best chance at victory lay with the city's white electorate, denounced his rivals' deference to black demands. Sellers was aware of a demographic transformation underway in Montgomery since World War II: attracted by a diversifying and industrializing economy as well as discouraged by prospects on the farm, rural whites were migrating to the city to take advantage of employers' preferences for white labor. At the end of the war, Montgomery's white-black ratio had been 55 percent to 45 percent; by 1955, the white portion of the population had increased to 63 percent. Although the newcomers, typically poor and low-skilled, rallied to Birmingham's populist rhetoric in the early 1950s, Sellers believed they were susceptible to racial appeals. He felt that he could secure enough white votes in his affluent South Montgomery district to combine with a large working-class white vote on his behalf to win the election.

The strategy worked. Though Birmingham received enough votes in the late March primary to force a runoff against front-runner Sellers, ill health forced him to withdraw prior to the general election. In the meantime, the bus issue simmered through the summer and early fall: a federal circuit court ruled Columbia, South Carolina's bus segregation statute unconstitutional; reports appeared in the local press of blacks in other cities defying segregated seating arrangements; and, in October, a black teen-aged girl in Montgomery refused to yield her seat to a white passenger. Though she pleaded guilty and paid a five-dollar fine, the political situation and increasing black assertiveness heightened racial tensions in the city.

On December 1, Rosa Parks, a forty-two-year-old seamstress at the Montgomery Fair department store, boarded the Cleveland Avenue bus bound for the housing project where she lived with her disabled husband. It had been an especially tiring day for Mrs. Parks: the Christmas rush had just begun, and the heavy pressing irons in her small, stifling workroom aggravated her bursitis. She gratefully took her seat on the bus and relaxed. The bus began to fill up, mostly with blacks heading for the housing project. When a few white men boarded the bus, the driver, James F. Blake, turned around and shouted, "Niggers, move back!" Parks, seated in the first row of blacks, refused to move. The driver stopped the bus and came over to the seamstress: "Y'all make it nice on yourself and let me have those seats." Parks remained in her seat. Blake, following procedure, called the police, who arrested and jailed her.

The incident might have ended there, as it had in October, and indeed the Montgomery *Advertiser* the following morning made light of the incident in a small column headlined, "Negro Jailed Here for 'Overlooking' Bus Segregation." Had the reporter known Parks, he would have realized that this was no random protest by a tired black woman supporting a household on twenty-three dollars a week. The seamstress was well-suited to carry off her civil disobedience and, in fact, had been contemplating it for some time. Nor was this the first occasion on which she had defied bus segregation. During the war, Parks joined the local NAACP chapter. She was one of the few blacks in Montgomery who had achieved a high school diploma, yet she had drifted from one menial job to another, well below her intellect and skill, channeling her frustration through the NAACP and through Jo Ann Robinson's group. But the crucial event in her progression to action occurred during the summer of 1955 when, with the help of E. D. Nixon and Virginia Durr, she received a scholarship to attend the Highlander Folk School in Monteagle, Tennessee.

The Highlander School, run by Miles Horton, provided a unique experience in interracial living for southern blacks and whites (in open violation of Tennessee's segregation statutes, incidentally). The purpose of the encounter was to inspire the "students" to return home and work for improved race relations by breaking down the barriers of segregation. The atmosphere at the school was relaxed and informal, reflecting Horton's personality. When a skeptical reporter asked him how he managed to get blacks and whites to eat together, he replied: "First, the food is prepared. Second, it's put on the table. Third, we ring the bell."

The two-week experiment at Highlander impressed Parks with the possibilities of interracial living. The barriers separating black and white, she learned, resulted not from basic differences between the races, but rather from artificial distinctions promoted by those with a heavy stake in the maintenance of white supremacy. When Parks returned to the dull humiliation of life in Montgomery, the contrast with her exhilarating experience in Tennessee was marked, and she fought not to resume her tacit acquiescence in the city's biracial society. Her polite but firm refusal to move on the bus enabled her to redeem her self-respect. Though she could not know it, her decision was the catalyst for the black civil rights crusade.

Jo Ann Robinson understood that Parks's arrest provided the city's black community with an opportunity both to make a statement on bus grievances and to slow the erosion of their political influence. The day after the incident, Robinson ran off forty thousand handbills calling for a boycott of the city's bus lines. But a boycott, to be effective, required organization, leadership, and resolve among the city's black residents, many of whom would be fearful or skeptical of a boycott. Neither Robinson's political group nor Nixon's NAACP chapter involved the mass of the city's blacks; they were primarily middle-class organizations. Robinson, Nixon, and black attorney Fred D. Gray, in an effort to broaden their base, convinced the city's often timid and bickering black ministers to support a bus boycott on Monday, December 5. The ministers conveyed the message from their pulpits on Sunday, and the boycott the following day was successful.

In order to sustain the effort, however, a leader and a mass organization were necessary. Robinson and Nixon were too militant to attract a large following, and the ministers were either reluctant to step forward or jealous to choose one of their own. At a mass meeting on the evening of December 5, the city's black leaders selected Martin Luther King, Jr., a recently arrived minister at the Dexter Avenue Baptist Church, to lead the boycott.

King seemed ill-suited to the role thrust upon him. His greatest credential, it appeared, was that during his brief time in Montgomery, he had not made any enemies among the intensely competitive black ministers. King had arrived in the city the previous year, a twenty-five-year-old doctoral student from Boston University's School of Theology. He had sought out the Dexter Avenue pastorate because he wanted a relatively quiet post at which he could complete his doctoral dissertation. Montgomery would be a pleasant, uneventful way station to more prestigious pastorates and cities. King's background indicated as much. He had grown up in a rambling, thirteen-room house in an affluent black district in Atlanta, where his father was among the leading preachers of his day and held forth at one of the most prominent black churches in the South, the Ebenezer Baptist Church. But the elder King, along with young Martin's maternal grandfather, the Reverend A. D. Williams, differed from most of the black ministers of that era in their involvement in civil rights activities. Rev. Williams was an early leader of Georgia's NAACP, and Martin Luther King, Sr., fought for equal salaries for black teachers and the abolition of segregated elevators in Atlanta's courthouse.

King grew up in a protected middle-class environment, though aware of the injustice of the biracial society. He enrolled in Morehouse College at age fifteen and thought about becoming a doctor or a lawyer. Eventually, however, his interest turned to theology, and he attended Crozer Theological Seminary in Chester, Pennsylvania, before beginning his doctoral studies at Boston University. He was an avid and eclectic reader, with Gandhi, Reinhold Niebuhr, and his Boston University mentor, Edgar S. Brightman, among his favorites. His reading and training were sufficiently broad to prevent the development of a doctrinaire theology. Aside from his well-known commitment to non-violence, King was convinced that the evangelical church had a mission of social justice to complement its emphasis upon individual salvation. Although King admired Gandhi's efforts to redeem the British in India through love and appeals to conscience, he was also aware, through Niebuhr, that some Old Testament justice was necessary on occasion to separate the sin from the sinner. King was not a pacifist, but he believed in the destructiveness of hate. His father had admonished that "hate is like sin. When it is finished it brings death."

These comprised King's basic theological tenets when he arrived in Montgomery; they were flexible enough to fit specific situations, yet sufficiently substantive to provide the young minister with a philosophical framework to guide his endeavors in the coming years. His theology differed from that of his ministerial colleagues in terms of intellectual depth, complexity, and social commitment, though not in its fervor for liberation and redemption. Growing up in comfort in an activist environment and attending schools in the North, King was certain that interracial living was neither unnatural nor millennia away; it was the way things ought to be.

King's selection to lead the boycott caught some of his colleagues by surprise. Fellow clergyman Wyatt Tee Walker had pegged the young minister as "a thoroughgoing intellectual, born wealthy, . . . I simply did not expect to see him leading a movement." Another minister, Andrew Young, depicted King as a reluctant leader: "I'm convinced that Martin never wanted to be a leader . . . he wanted a nice quiet town where he could finish his doctoral dissertation and not even have the responsibility of a big church and got trapped." However backhanded his anointment and whatever his own reservations, King proved more than equal to the difficult task of uniting a disparate and dispirited community to carry out an uncertain and even dangerous assignment.

On the evening of December 5 at the Holt Street Baptist Church, Montgomery's black citizens crowded into pews and more than four thousand stood patiently outside, ears trained toward loudspeakers. They had assembled to determine whether or not to continue the boycott, begun successfully that day. The atmosphere was electric. Joe Azbell, a white reporter for the Montgomery *Advertiser*, described the meeting as "an old fashioned revival with . . . military discipline." The congregation opened with a rousing rendition of "Onward Christian Soldiers," and with each succeeding hymn, the assembled gathered strength, it seemed, and fear of their unprecedented action dissipated. By the time King took the pulpit, the continuation of the boycott was a foregone conclusion. King's words assured that it would work.

The congregation quieted as King approached the microphone to deliver his first address as a civil rights leader. He recounted the background of the bus boycott in an even, conversational tone, his audience waiting for some inspirational word or command. Then his tone changed: "We are here this evening to say to those who have mistreated us so long that we are tired—tired of being segregated and humiliated, tired of being kicked about by the brutal feet of oppression. We have no alternative but to protest. . . . We come here tonight to be saved from that patience that makes us patient with anything less than freedom and justice." In carrying out this protest, King disavowed violence and repeated Booker T. Washington's advice, "Let no man pull you so low as to make you hate him." But while he urged his listeners to "protest with love," he also noted that "there is another side called justice. . . . Not only are we using the tools of persuasion, but we've got to use the tools of coercion." If Montgomery's blacks could maintain this delicate balance between love and justice, between persuasion and coercion, and maintain it with nonviolence, then King promised, "when the history books are written in future generations, the historians will have to pause and say, 'There lived a great people—a black people—who injected new meaning and dignity into the veins of civilization.' This is our challenge and our overwhelming responsibility."

The oration charged his listeners like a lightning bolt. The speech also previewed the major themes of King's rhetorical strategy, both during the boycott and in the ensuing years. He had issued a startling warning to the white community that the days of racial business-as-usual were over; the notice served for blacks as well—that patience and endurance, regardless of their biblical virtues, were no longer appropriate. At the same time, he reassured whites that blacks would appeal to their consciences, not their fears. His pledge also enabled blacks to assume the high moral road and encouraged them to consider themselves as a race of destiny. Without extended quotes from the Bible, King was able to strike a Christian pose, to make the act of protest a religious crusade. Whether or not black and white southerners would accept King's rhetoric, at least they would understand it.

The boycott proceeded. Blacks walked Montgomery's streets, or they crowded into cars, station wagons, and pick-up trucks that, as time passed, made regularly scheduled runs to and from the city's black districts. White women inadvertently assisted the boycott by chauffeuring their domestics. When Mayor Gayle complained of this practice, one white woman offered him an invitation: "If the mayor wants to do my washing and ironing and cooking and cleaning and raise my children, let him come out here and do it." By February, 1956, the boycott was attracting nationwide attention, and as King's stature grew, the city's black population grew in pride and determination. Donations of money and vehicles poured in from across the country. By the summer, more than three hundred private conveyances were providing blacks with a regular, if somewhat unorthodox, transportation system. Though white officials harassed blacks participating in these arrangements and sought to outlaw car pools, blacks persisted.

In the meantime, King and his associates had formed the Montgomery Improvement Association (MIA), which served as an umbrella organization for black groups in the city and as the distribution point for volunteers and donations. The MIA also functioned as a liaison to the white community to negotiate a settlement. King believed, as did most blacks in the city, that the boycott would be short-lived. The boycotters were not demanding an end to segregated buses, merely the institution of a first-come, first-served system already in place in several other Deep South cities. But the political climate in Montgomery during the winter of 1955–56 was not conducive to a compromise.

As the boycott continued and drew national attention, white resistance in Montgomery stiffened. Clyde Sellers' political stock soared, as did the growth of the local White Citizens' Council chapter. The appearance and strength of the council rendered accession, even to modest demands, imprudent for political leaders. For those whites who thought about a compromise, council leader and state senator Sam Engelhardt offered this warning: "In the last few years we have had quite a number of backsliders . . . for political reasons . . . who've been trying to garner the Negro vote. . . . The Council is trying to destroy them." By the end of January, the mayor, the commissioners, and several lesser officials had joined the council, which had already enrolled twelve thousand white Montgomerians. A prominent attorney boasted that blacks would never again wield political influence in the city by "dangling their bloc votes" before candidates. The city government ostentatiously broke off negotiations with the MIA early in the new year.

By the end of January, King was discouraged. The possibility for compromise had vanished, police harassment of boycotters was increasing, and threats against his life and the lives of his wife and children mounted. He sat down in the kitchen of his home one night, drained of confidence and unable to sleep. He began to pray: "Lord, I'm down here trying to do what's right. I think I'm right. I think the cause that we represent is right. But Lord, I must confess that I'm weak now. I'm faltering. I'm losing my courage. And I can't let the people see me like this because if they see me weak and losing my courage, they will begin to get weak." At that moment, King recalled, "I could hear an inner voice saying to me, 'Martin Luther, stand up for righteousness. Stand up for justice. Stand up for truth. And lo I will be with you, even until the end of the world.'. . . I heard the voice of Jesus saying still to fight on. He promised never to leave me, never to leave me alone."

The kitchen revelation strengthened King's resolve. "Almost at once my fears began to go. My uncertainty disappeared." His renewed evangelical faith infused the boycott and eventually inspired a movement. The struggle for redeeming white men's souls and black men's dignity became a moral drama played to a people who understood the awful and wonderful implications of evangelical Christianity. Of the many twists and turns the struggle would take on the road from Montgomery, it would always remain foremost a religious movement.

As if to test his faith, three nights later, on January 30, a Klansman tossed a stick of dynamite from a passing car onto the porch of King's house. The explosion narrowly missed injuring King's wife and a friend. The incident and the climate that encouraged it convinced MIA leadership of something they were coming to realize anyway—that Montgomery's white leadership would not compromise, boycott or no. Another tactic was necessary, not to abandon the boycott, but to complement it with another action. On February 1, attorney Fred D. Gray filed suit challenging the constitutionality of segregated buses in Montgomery.

The boycott dragged on through the spring and summer, and media attention waned. The makeshift caravans still wound their way through black Montgomery mornings and evenings, the city continued to place obstacles in their way, and the yellow buses lurched through the streets mostly empty. By the fall, city officials sought to trump the MIA by seeking an injunction to halt the boycott. If successful, the action would defeat the boycott and black Montgomery, for the boycott had come to loom as a major symbol for both blacks and whites in the city, a surrogate for the status and condition of both races in

Montgomery and in the South. On the brink of failure, King urged his followers to maintain their faith: "We stand in life at midnight, we are always on the threshold of a new dawn."

Dawn arrived on November 13, 1956, when the U.S. Supreme Court, in *Gayle et al.* v. *Browder*, ruled that bus segregation in Montgomery was unconstitutional. A black Montgomerian rejoiced: "Praise the Lord. God has spoken from Washington, D.C." The boycott officially ended just before 6 A.M. on December 21, when King and his aides boarded a bus and sat in the front row, black next to white.

The Moral of Montgomery

The Montgomery bus boycott was significant not because of its immediate achievement, for in truth it achieved nothing: the court decision, not the boycott, desegregated the city's buses. It was not surprising that few blacks in southern cities followed the boycott strategy to end segregation on public conveyances. Most black communities lacked the cohesiveness, leadership, and resources that Montgomery came to possess. Also, a 381-day boycott that ended not with its resolution, but as a result of a court ruling, was not a positive advertisement for potential boycotters elsewhere. The importance of the boycott lay in what it meant for King and his followers as they embarked on the long and tortuous journey of racial redemption.

The boycott participants had broken from the stereotype and challenged whites' notions that blacks' acquiescence in segregation or racial etiquette meant approval or preference. The boycott may have had a bus as its focal point, but the stone cast many ripples and enabled blacks to air an array of grievances about the biracial society, from poor services to separate water fountains. The entire catalogue of racial etiquette was now on the table, and blacks were reading it back to startled whites. If nothing else—and whites seemed prepared to relinquish their racial perquisites only so far as the federal courts forced them to—the process instilled pride and confidence in Montgomery's blacks.

On the night of the *Gayle* decision, a fully robed contingent of the Ku Klux Klan in a procession of forty vehicles staged a "parade" through Montgomery's black neighborhoods. The visitation was an obvious warning to blacks that they should not presume that a ruling from Washington would affect the racial status quo in the Deep South. Ordinarily, such a scene would have at least stirred uneasiness in the black community, but on this happy night, blacks greeted the Hooded

Empire with applause and derisive laughter. The bewildered Klansmen sped off into the night. As King noted, "a once fear-ridden people had been transformed." Though premature, the pronouncement accurately reflected that, at this particular time and place, the gnawing fear that accompanied the struggle for survival in the shadow of white supremacy had dissipated. Perhaps an elderly woman expressed the feeling of black Montgomery best. She had walked through the cold, damp winter and the steamy summer. Despite her infirmity and despite the suggestion by King that she ought to take the bus, that she had earned that exemption, she persisted. "Yes, my feets is tired," she admitted, "but my soul is rested."

The boycott also demonstrated that, under proper circumstances, it was possible to organize and galvanize a black community, possible—given the proper message—for a preacher to interest young blacks in the cause of civil rights. Yancey Martin, a student at Alabama State, recalled that King was different from the other ministers; he did not merely quote the Scriptures and thump the tub: "He was talking about what we oughta have, and what we oughta be, and what the situation oughta be in the South." Heaven could wait; in the meantime, it was important to infuse the morality and beauty of southern religion into the righteous cause of ridding the region of sin.

King's leadership meant that the process of exorcism could leave both white and black—and the South—intact. Not only was King careful to distinguish the sin from the sinner, but he avoided portraying the issue as a black-white struggle. As he explained during the boycott, "this is not a war between the white and the Negro but a conflict between justice and injustice." That position not only elevated the struggle to a higher plane but left open the opportunity for a reconciliation once the battle was won. In addition, it framed black hopes in terms that whites understood as southerners, even if they found it difficult to listen. King's message not only fell within the evangelical tradition, but spoke to the shared history of southerners—a people who had experienced injustice, second-class citizenship, and numerous indignities inflicted by a powerful oppressor. His gospel was directed not at divesting the white southerner of his religion and history, but rather at fostering a closer, more inclusive connection with that culture.

But the boycott, and the reaction of white Montgomerians to it, had also impressed upon King that this revelation would come slowly. As he observed some years later, "freedom is never voluntarily given by the oppressor; it must be demanded by the oppressed." King and the MIA had demanded little of the city's white leaders, yet had seen their modest proposals rejected. The leaders seemed intent on proving that integration and segregation could not coexist, that pulling one thread would eventually unravel the entire fabric of white supremacy. Whether the stance was a political ploy, a deep-felt philosophy, or a combination of the two is beside the point. It shaped black tactics for the future and presaged white reaction in other circumstances.

This situation underscored a sad reality. As historian J. Mills Thornton III has argued, the bus boycott demonstrated that "the South did not possess within itself the capacity to save itself." From resisters to liberals, white southerners had begged outsiders to desist from meddling in the South's racial business, maintaining that southerners understood the problem best and would deal with it in the best interests of blacks and whites. The boycott indicated otherwise. From then on, as Thornton concluded, only "internal pressure sufficient to compel intervention from outside the South" would secure a racial accommodation.

So King went forth from Montgomery with an education he scarcely could have received in the quiet pursuit of his doctoral degree. His next step was to build an organization to channel and exercise the energy generated by the victory in Montgomery, while at the same time ensuring that the resulting strategies fell within the framework of the southern values held by both blacks and whites.

Three weeks after King rode at the front of a Montgomery bus, he met in Atlanta with a group of like-minded black clergymen and veteran civil rights activists such as Bayard Rustin of CORE and Ella Baker from the NAACP. Rustin in particular believed that a new civil rights organization was in order since CORE had failed to interest the black masses in the South and the NAACP remained wary of boycotts and demonstrations. King, fresh from his Montgomery experience, required little persuasion. The group of about sixty agreed to establish the Southern Leadership Conference on Transportation and Nonviolent Integration and resolved to meet again the following month at an expanded gathering to launch the new organization.

More than one hundred delegates, mainly clergymen, assembled at the Reverend A. L. Davis' Baptist Church in New Orleans on February 14, 1957. They shortened the name of the organization to the Southern Leadership Conference and elected King as president. At the first annual convention in August, the delegates inserted the word *Christian* to make it the Southern Christian Leadership Conference and adopted as its official motto, "To Redeem the Soul of America." The new name and motto reflected well the SCLC's membership and purpose. The organization's leadership consisted of ministers, most of them Baptists. Typically, they led substantial urban congregations; they held college degrees, and many had attended graduate school or seminary; and they had risen to the top of the black social elite in their communities. They differed, in short, from the other-worldly exhorters whom Benjamin Mays and Gunnar Myrdal found in the black church during the 1930s and early 1940s. Their training and position suited them well for leadership roles.

The SCLC was a distinctly southern organization, the first civil rights group with an exclusively regional cast, and a demonstrably Christian movement. In practical terms, such emphasis would deflect charges of radicalism or communism. On another level, the Christian identification was a label that all southerners, black and white, understood, a label that transcended religion and implied a way of life. It was a statement that no matter how radical SCLC strategy might appear, at base the organization's principles were firmly grounded in regional values. The cause was not to destroy, but to redeem, and southerners knew about redemption in both religious and political terms.

The SCLC, finally, signaled a shift in civil rights leadership not only from the North to the South, but also from educators, attorneys, and businessmen to the clergy. Some historians have claimed that the SCLC was little more than a personal vehicle for Martin Luther King, and the difficulties of the organization after his death tend to support that view. But, as Aldon Morris observed, the SCLC "functioned as the decentralized arm of the mass-based black church." Most of its good works were carried on at the local level, apart from King and beyond the glare of publicity. The SCLC established freedom schools across the South, training individuals in nonviolent protest and preparing them for the conflicts of the 1960s. Because of its clerical orientation, it drew upon and could organize the black masses. The black political clubs in Montgomery, for example, mustered, at most, two thousand adherents, while on any given Sunday, the black churches drew more than fifty thousand worshipers. Their pastors could turn their other-worldly emphasis to this-worldly advantage—as they did for slaves a century earlier when, in dimly lit cabins, they sang "Steal Away to Jesus" or recounted the story of the Hebrews' flight from Egypt—and the better-educated urban clergy of the 1950s forged a similar connection between theology and social justice.

In the meantime, black parents across the South, taking heart from

Brown and courage from Montgomery, chipped away at a much more sturdy structure than a city bus—the biracial system of education. Amid the lawsuits and countersuits, delaying tactics, humiliating application procedures, nullification edicts, and outright intimidation, blacks persisted. The battleground shifted from the streets to the courts and back to the streets again. In the process, blacks drew the federal government into the fray, a government that at last had reached the limits of *its* endurance.

Going to School: Little Rock, New Orleans, and Atlanta

The response to black efforts to desegregate schools in three cities ran the gamut from compliance (Atlanta) to resistance (New Orleans and Little Rock). In these and other cities, three general principles emerged. First, the legal system, despite the integrationist leanings of federal district courts, produced limited results. Second, though desegregation efforts exposed fissures in the white social structure, disaffected whites targeted resentment toward blacks, underscoring the efficacy of race in maintaining white solidarity. Finally, as in the Montgomery bus boycott, blacks found themselves alone; white leadership, if it responded at all, usually did so belatedly, primarily to hold down losses (economic and political) rather than to facilitate meaningful change.

Little Rock became synonymous with the extreme consequences of resistance to school desegregation. After the debacle there in the fall of 1957, civic leaders in many parts of the South used Little Rock as the example of how not to respond to a school crisis. For the Arkansas capital, its renown as a national spectacle of ignominy was ironic. The city enjoyed a reputation for racial moderation, and school superintendent Virgil Blossom had prepared for the inevitable desegregation ruling since he assumed the post in 1953. Within months of the *Brown* decision, he unveiled a desegregation plan that would be implemented beginning with the September, 1957, school year. The plan called for integration of the city's schools over a number of years starting with Central High School and working down through the elementary grades. Though the city's blacks had hoped for a more expeditious timetable, the plan received the general approbation of the community. Moreover, by the fall of 1957, the climate of opinion in the state had softened toward integrated schools. Arkansas led the South in the number of desegregated school districts by that time, and five of the six state-supported white colleges and universities had admitted black students. Black publisher L. C. Bates of the *Arkansas Free Press* predicted that Little Rock "will take school integration as just another going to school."

The statewide movement toward compliance with the *Brown* decision had the tacit approval of Governor Orval Faubus. The governor had spent most of his political life as a champion of the underdog, Arkansas' poor white and black population. He hailed from the hill country, the son of a poor farmer who traveled the depressed neighborhoods in and around Madison County delivering speeches espousing socialist doctrines. The father's political beliefs rubbed off on the boy, who grew up to be a liberal editorial writer for a hill country weekly before casting his fortunes with popular postwar governor Sid McMath. In 1954, Faubus ran for governor as McMath's political heir. Though opponents attempted to tag him as a Communist sympathizer—a popular epithet of the era—he won the Democratic primary (and hence the election). As governor, Faubus instituted a wide range of reforms eclipsing even the record of the progressive McMath. One of his first acts was to expand the state's Democratic party central committee by six members and to appoint six blacks to the positions. Subsequently, he secured a $22-million tax increase to improve the state's lagging educational system, and he established the Children's Colony, a model facility for the mentally retarded. Faubus also inaugurated an aggressive industrial development program, assisted by millionaire newcomer Winthrop Rockefeller. And he oversaw the gradual desegregation of the state's school systems.

As he ran for re-election in 1956, there was nothing in Faubus' background to indicate that he would not be supportive of Little Rock's forthcoming efforts to desegregate its schools. He repeated often during the campaign that "desegregation [was] an issue that should be left to local choice." By localizing the issue, Faubus hoped that the state legislature would concentrate on passing his populist program, especially a tax increase to support public education. The primary results, however, jolted Faubus. He barely fended off the challenge of former state senator Jim Johnson, who charged that the governor was "soft" on integration. Fearing increased opposition to his legislative program as well as for his political future (Arkansas governors serve two-year terms), Faubus began to reassess his position on integration during the early months of 1957.

In the meantime, Little Rock began to gear up for the integration of

Central High School on September 3, 1957. The choice of Central to receive nine black students was unpopular among the city's working-class white residents. Aside from the fact that there were among them numerous recent arrivals from the countryside who had brought their Negrophobic views to the city (as in Montgomery), the Blossom Plan seemed to single out their neighborhoods and children for the experiment in interracial education. Blossom "sold" his plan to the city's leadership by noting that the construction of another all-white high school on the fashionable west side of town would be completed by the time the plan went into effect in the fall of 1957, which meant that the children of the city's elite could attend a high school segregated by both class and race. Tension increased as September approached.

Winthrop Rockefeller understood that the situation was tailor-made for exploitation by a political opportunist. Though Faubus had not previously fit that description, there were indications in the weeks preceding the opening of school that the governor was contemplating intervention. Fearing for the fledgling economic development program and the adverse impact that could result from state-sponsored disruption, Rockefeller visited the governor at the end of August. As he recalled the meeting, "I reasoned with him, argued with him, almost pled with him" not to intervene, that "the local situation was none of his business." Faubus looked out of his office window and without turning to face his visitor explained, "I'm sorry, but I'm already committed. I'm going to run for a third term and if I don't do this, Jim Johnson and Bruce Bennett [another segregationist candidate] will tear me to shreds."

Thus resolved, Faubus set in motion a series of events that, as in a Greek tragedy, inexorably proceeded to a predictable, fateful end as the main characters played out their ordained roles. In the process, a promising political reputation was sullied for all time, a city and a state received an undeserved reputation for violence and racial extremism, and nine black children suffered the trauma of fear and humiliation brought upon them by the leaders of their city and state.

The day before school opened, Faubus deployed the Arkansas National Guard around Central High School. At the time, it was unclear whether the maneuver was to protect the black children and discourage violence or to obstruct the desegregation process, thereby imparting official sanction to more severe demonstrations of defiance. By the following morning, it was clear that the governor had thrown down the gauntlet and taken his stand with the segregationists. Faubus predicated his action on the grounds that "blood will run in the streets" if black pupils were to enter Central High, and he later compared his decision to the choice forced upon Robert E. Lee—whether to serve his country or protect his home. But Faubus' actions had little in common with the moral agony and sense of duty that characterized Lee; rather, his was a crude, cool calculation of the measure of political profit to be gained from championing a cause in which his belief was shallow at best.

Elizabeth Eckford was one of the nine black students to be admitted to Central High that day. She had scarcely slept the night before, excited about her first day of school. She rose early the next morning and pressed the dress that she had made for this occasion. The reports she heard of a crowd gathering around the school caused concern in the Eckford household, and before Elizabeth left her mother called the family together for a brief prayer. Her bus dropped her off one block from Central, and she walked toward the school and saw the soldiers guarding the entrance. Some in the crowd followed, taunting her as she walked up to the entrance. A guard raised his bayonet, barring her way, and other guards with bayonets fixed surrounded her. Somebody in the crowd yelled, "Lynch her! Lynch her!" As they closed in on her, she looked desperately for a friendly face and suddenly saw a kind-looking elderly woman. The woman leaned forward and spat on Elizabeth: "No nigger bitch is going to get in our school. Get out of here!"

She retreated down the steps and down the block toward a bench by a bus stop, all the while trailed by the mob hurling threats and obscenities. She made it to the bench and sat down to wait for the bus. A white man sat down beside her, patted her shoulder, and said, "Don't let them see you cry." A white woman came over and escorted Elizabeth to her bus while the mob continued their taunts. Her first school day was over.

Over the next three weeks Faubus attained celebrity status, earning an audience with President Eisenhower at Newport, Rhode Island. The president attempted to dissuade him from his reckless course. It played well in Arkansas. The game seemed over when federal district-court judge Ronald Davies enjoined the governor from interfering with the integration process, so Faubus dutifully removed the National Guard on September 20 and replaced them with city police. But the passions that the governor had encouraged could not be stifled by court order. Little Rock had become a mecca for rabid segregationists since the first day of school, and their ranks strengthened with each passing day.

When the nine black students reappeared on Monday, September 23, the angry crowd outside Central High turned into a raging mob. For the next two days they seemed to have the run of the city, carrying out Faubus' self-fulfilling prophecy that integration would trigger violence.

At this point, President Eisenhower, who had assumed that he had persuaded Faubus to back down from his defiant posture, dispatched the "Screaming Eagles" of the 101st Airborne Division to restore order in Little Rock. The president did not relish the specter of federal troops—the first invasion of the South since the Civil War—lumbering in to occupy an American city. Although he had not offered his moral support for the *Brown* decision, he had abolished segregation in those areas under direct federal control. He had also recently signed the 1957 Civil Rights Act, a mild measure offering some federal protection for black voter registration in the South (though the Justice Department rarely enforced any of its provisions). Finally, though Eisenhower believed that police power was reserved first for local authorities, the open violation of a federal court order—Faubus' inability or unwillingness to maintain order and allow desegregation to proceed as ordered by federal judge Davies—left him no option but to send in the troops.

The "Screaming Eagles" quelled the disturbance, and the black students entered Central High. But the appearance of federal forces silenced opposition to Faubus' strategy. Invoking the memory of the Lost Cause, the governor strutted the stage in the garb of a folk hero. The theater of the absurd continued as Faubus persisted in his claim that he opposed desegregation primarily because it threatened the public order; he cited the riot on September 23 as validating that fear and challenged the desegregation order on that basis. But in September, 1958, one year after the drama began, the U.S. Supreme Court in *Cooper* v. *Aaron* ruled that community opposition was no excuse for delaying integration and ordered the school board to proceed with the plan.

Faubus, his legal options played out, closed the city's high schools as the state legislature had empowered him to do. At this point, the long-silent business leadership was roused to action. As one businessman explained: "Of course their pride was hurt when the troops came . . . but not very deeply felt. But when you close a school and your number one son doesn't have a place to go to school, and all your hopes and dreams have rested on him, it's a very deep hurt." Despite the "deep hurt" in the business community, the first white citizen in Little Rock to protest the closings publicly was Adolphine Fletcher Terry, who quickly formed the Women's Emergency Committee to Open Our Schools. The economic leadership followed, and the governor rescinded his order.

The New Orleans crisis in the fall of 1960, which also precipitated a violent confrontation, was all the more remarkable because officials there had the benefit of hindsight in the Little Rock example. They ignored the Little Rock precedent mainly because they believed that integrated schools would never become a reality in the Crescent City, and in the six years since *Brown*, state leaders had promised that. But litigation by black parents resulted in a court order to desegregate the city's schools. The plan adopted reflected the same class-consciousness as the one implemented by the Little Rock school board. The New Orleans school board decided to integrate those schools whose median achievement test scores matched the scores of black applicants, which meant that schools in poor white districts became the front line for desegregation. Initially, the board chose two schools—McDonogh 19 and Frantz—both located in the Ninth Ward, which included working-class white families and two public housing projects, Desire for whites and Florida for blacks.

As the November, 1960, date for the integration of these two schools approached, local political and business leaders did little to prepare the public for the difficult transition. Progressive mayor de Lesseps Morrison was serving his third term and preening for statewide office; an appearance of compliance with the court order could jeopardize that ambition. Local segregationists filled the void with provocative rhetoric. At a rally on the evening of November 14—the day black children attended McDonogh 19 and Frantz schools for the first time—Leander Perez, political boss from nearby Plaquemines Parish, informed the crowd of five thousand assembled at the municipal auditorium that the day's events had resulted from a conspiracy of "zionist Jews" and the NAACP. As for confounding this cabal, Perez offered the following advice: "Don't wait for your daughter to be raped by these Congolese. Don't wait until the burr-heads are forced into your schools. Do something about it now!" The next day, a mob of three thousand rampaged through the downtown area throwing bottles and stones at passing blacks. That evening, black teenagers retaliated by shooting at and beating whites.

A different drama was unfolding in the Ninth Ward. On the morning of November 14, three black children integrated McDonogh 19 and one black child enrolled at Frantz. Within a few days the population at McDonogh consisted of only the principal, the secretary, the custodian, eighteen teachers, and the three black children. The white boycott of Frantz was less complete, and the white enrollment fluctuated from three to ten children. Pressure from neighbors, however, reduced that number to three—the children of Margaret and Jim Conner.

Twenty years later, the bewilderment remained in Margaret Conner's voice: "I never understood everybody's excitement about one little girl." Mrs. Conner stated that she "wasn't a crusader," but Frantz was her neighborhood school. Though she waded daily through a hostile crowd of neighbors who showered her with epithets as she escorted her children, she persisted. She was pregnant at the time and recalled one woman in the crowd asking, "Is it going to be black or white?" Mrs. Conner sought solace in her parish priest, but he turned her away. Fortunately, she had a good friend, her husband had an understanding employer (the Lykes Brothers Shipbuilding Company, the first major firm in the city to integrate its work force), and she received the support of a middle-class parents' group called Save Our Schools.

The black children endured a similar gauntlet on the way to school and learned their lessons in the eeriness of schools abandoned by their classmates. Mrs. Conner offered a cogent analysis of the events in and about Frantz school: "I always felt one of the reasons that they got out in the streets and did what they did was because they didn't have too many people below them. Sometimes you've got to feel like you're top dog, and they didn't have too much. So they wanted to say 'You can't do this to my school—I'll walk out.'" Poorly served by a political system and its leaders, and exploited by the economy, the city's poor whites channeled their frustrations to the streets and toward the blacks and their allies, with the approval of their social superiors.

The publicity was bad business. The New York *Times* ran a front-page story, "New Orleans Rift Takes Trade Toll," that detailed the decline in the tourist trade and in downtown retail sales. By the end of December, a group of businessmen and professionals (only a few of whom were among the city's leadership) called for public support of the school board and for integration.

When Atlanta's turn came in August, 1961, the city's leadership, perhaps the epitome of New South boosterism, was determined to avoid the mistakes of Little Rock and New Orleans. The city's economic and political elite was traditionally close-knit. Mayor William B. Hartsfield once boasted that he never made a decision without first consulting the management at Coca-Cola. The image-conscious leaders were also proud of their reputation for racial moderation, which they promoted vigorously even as they sought to delay any concession to the *Brown* ruling for seven years. Little Rock and New Orleans frightened them, however. Mayor Hartsfield vowed, "What happened in Little Rock won't happen here." To support his pledge he dispatched police officials to Little Rock and New Orleans to learn how to avoid their mistakes.

Violence was not the only concern of Atlanta's elite; by 1960, several southern states had simply closed schools rather than integrate. A padlocked school door was not the image Atlantans sought to promote among outside investors, conventions, and tourists. In November, 1959, *Life* magazine ran stories in consecutive weeks on "The Lost Class of '59," depicting the impact of school closings under Virginia law in Norfolk. The pictures of boys hanging out in a drugstore, of cheerleaders practicing on a sidewalk for a football season that would never be, and of student leaders praying for a resolution of the crisis spoke volumes to Atlanta leaders. Though Norfolk's schools reopened two months later after suddenly aroused white public opinion and a lawsuit initiated by black parents, schools in rural Prince Edward County, Virginia, remained closed for five years. Defiant white parents established a separate private school system while black children were locked out of the public schools and received little or no education until the U.S. Supreme Court ordered the schools reopened in 1964.

In January, 1960, the Atlanta Chamber of Commerce pledged itself to "open schools." Unlike their counterparts in Virginia, Arkansas, and Louisiana, Atlanta leaders received assistance from an unexpected source, Governor Ernest Vandiver. The Georgia legislature had passed a school-closing law and the governor had pledged to enforce it, but when one thousand Georgia businessmen called on the governor to set aside his pledge, he softened his position, at least privately. By a quirk of timing, the first test came not in an elementary or secondary school system but at the University of Georgia. Neither Vandiver nor the legislators were eager to uphold principle and lose a football season, so the university remained open, establishing a precedent for desegregation elsewhere.

The Atlanta community proceeded to erect an elaborate apparatus designed to ensure the successful integration of its schools at the beginning of the 1961–62 academic year. Several religious, civic, and service groups formed an umbrella body, Organizations Assisting Schools in September (OASIS), to inform Atlantans through meetings, speeches, and plays. The city declared a "Law and Order Weekend," churches and synagogues held prayer meetings as opening day approached, and the Chamber of Commerce took out a full-page ad in the Atlanta *Journal* inquiring, "How Great is Atlanta?" implying that greatness meant obeying the law. Reporters from around the country, lured to the city by this unique community process, received a handbook on the city and its schools prepared by OASIS and enjoyed a hospitality in sharp contrast to their experiences elsewhere in the South.

On August 30, 1961, nine black children integrated four Atlanta high schools. As one leader boasted, "it was the silence heard around the world." *Newsweek* extolled "a proud city," and the Kennedy administration, grateful at averting another embarrassing civil rights confrontation, wired its congratulations. Seldom had a city or a group of leaders received so much acclaim for merely abiding by the Constitution—and belatedly at that. The display underscored the rarity of peaceful compliance in the South's major cities; it was an era when torchbearers at noon could be hailed as illuminators of the darkness.

The Southern Report Card

In the South, public display was an end in itself. Atlanta promoted itself as "the city too busy to hate," and the fact that only nine black children attended white schools after seven years was quickly lost. Indeed, the results of these confrontations, violent or peaceful, were meager. By 1960, less than 1 percent of the South's black pupils attended integrated schools. In South Carolina, Alabama, and Mississippi, not a single public school was integrated. In the latter two states, segregation remained unperturbed, and any suggestion to the contrary summoned a swift remonstrance. In 1962, black student James Meredith attempted to enroll at the University of Mississippi. Before U.S. Army and federalized National Guard troops could restore order, 160 federal marshals had been injured and two bystanders were dead from gunshot wounds. Mississippi governor Ross Barnett had rallied the white citizens of the state, vowing, "we will not surrender to the evil and illegal forces of tyranny. . . . We must either submit to the unlawful dictates of the federal government or stand up like men and tell them 'NEVER!'" Meredith enrolled, but that was almost beside the point. Barnett had played his role to the public; he was now a hero—results were secondary.

Governor George C. Wallace of Alabama followed Barnett's example the next year as he attempted to prevent the enrollment of black students Vivian Malone and Jimmy Hood at the University of Alabama. This was not the first try to desegregate the university. Autherine Lucy entered the Tuscaloosa campus in February, 1956, accompanied by chants of "Two-four-six-eight, We Don't Want to Integrate!" On the night of her enrollment, students rioted and the university administration suspended her "for her own safety." When she challenged that order, the administration expelled her for insubordination.

By the time of the second attempt in June, 1963, Wallace had emerged as the region's leading segregationist politician. Ironically, he had been a disciple of "Big Jim" Folsom during the early 1950s. Like Faubus, Wallace had championed populist causes in his youth, but a bitter defeat in the 1958 Democratic gubernatorial primary convinced him that race politics was the only road to elective office in Alabama. Wallace exuded excitement with his jet black hair, jutting chin, and confident swagger of the pugilist he had been during his military service. A spellbinding orator, he captured the frustrations and fears of the little man, the state's poor whites so long exploited by the Birmingham industrialists and the Black Belt planters. In his inaugural address in January, 1963, he proclaimed, "In the name of the greatest people that have ever trod the earth, I draw the line in the dust and toss the gauntlet before the feet of tyranny, and I say: 'Segregation now—segregation tomorrow—segregation forever.'"

True to his vow, on June 11, 1963, Wallace stood before the door of Foster Auditorium on the University of Alabama campus. Alabama National Guardsmen flanked the governor and a tense quiet descended on the campus. President Kennedy had sent Nicholas Katzenbach from the Justice Department to ensure that Wallace would not obstruct the federal court order to admit Hood and Malone. Katzenbach accompanied the students to the auditorium door where he attempted to read the president's order. "We don't need your speech," Wallace interrupted, and proceeded to read a five-page statement of his own expressing his determination to "forbid this illegal act." Katzenbach retreated with the students to the dormitories. Within a few hours, Kennedy federalized 17,000 Alabama National Guardsmen, thus removing them from Wallace's control. The governor stepped aside, and the students registered. Again, it was the show that mattered most to

Wallace and his supporters. The university's integration sparked no new protest. Honor had been preserved.

Whether accompanied by defiance and violence or by compliance and order, school desegregation proceeded at an excruciatingly slow pace at all educational levels. At the rate the South was progressing by the early 1960s, it would take the region 7,288 years to integrate its schools, a timetable that imparted novel meaning to the phrase "all deliberate speed." Only when the economic balance sheet could not withstand further disruption did white leaders seek a compromise. Ralph McGill looked around the South and wondered, "where have the 'best people,' the 'good people' been?" Perhaps at one time in the crisis they had attempted to reach out and exert an ameliorative influence, as had Columbus, Georgia, Reverend Robert Blakely McNeill, who authored an article in *Look* magazine in May, 1957, urging "creative contact" between the races to promote racial harmony and discharge Christian duty. The Southeast Georgia Presbytery stripped McNeill of his pastorate, and a leader in his congregation informed members, "now we must find a preacher with the right kind of religion." Three days later, the forty-four-year-old McNeill suffered a near-fatal heart attack, prompting a member of the congregation to remark that the Lord finally had "taken care of him." Another, fearing a wave of sympathy for the minister, declared, "it's a fake attack."

Blacks recognized, though, that their loneliness was primarily a local phenomenon. The federal court system, especially judges appointed at the district level during the Eisenhower administration, such as J. Skelly Wright in New Orleans, Frank M. Johnson in Montgomery, and Elbert Tuttle in Atlanta, provided a sympathetic counterweight to the region's silent or obstructive political and economic leadership. Many of the advances attained by black southerners by 1960 emanated from the courts of these justices. But litigation was a tedious, expensive process, as noted earlier, and the victories scarcely dented the armor of white supremacy. Something more was necessary, something direct and startling.

Twenty years earlier, W. E. B. Du Bois in his autobiography, *Dusk of Dawn* (1940), depicted the southern black caught behind the impenetrable wall of white supremacy:

> It gradually penetrates the minds of the prisoners that the people passing do not hear; that some thick sheet of invisible but horribly tangible plate glass is between them and the world. They get excited; they talk louder; they gesticulate. Some of the passing world stop in curiosity; these gesticulations

seem so pointless; they laugh and pass on. . . . Then the people within may become hysterical. They may scream and hurl themselves against the barriers, hardly realizing in their bewilderment that they are screaming in a vacuum unheard. . . . They may even, here and there, break through in blood and disfigurement, and find themselves faced by a horrified, implacable, and . . . overwhelming mob of people frightened for their own very existence.

Southern blacks, for the most part, remained invisible to southern whites in the half decade following the *Brown* decision. Whites had tried to ignore black protests, had relented grudgingly and minimally when forced to do so, but had maintained both the barrier and white solidarity—or "consensus" as urban leaders would have it. Blacks had drawn together, too, taking courage, gaining self-respect, training leaders, and securing small victories. These were important formative years. But the barrier remained. And the danger loomed that an attempted breakthrough would generate the kind of bloody conflict Du Bois implied.

VI / The Crusade Against
Segregation, 1960–1964

The shrines of southern history had a heroic quality about them: a mansion, a monument, a capitol, a battleground. These artifacts commemorated great deeds and great men. The physical symbolism of a rewritten southern history emerging in the 1950s and sixties was more pedestrian: a yellow bus, a spartan courtroom, a dormitory, a lunch counter, and a voting booth. Future generations would make few pilgrimages to these new regional shrines, but perhaps they should. For what happened in these modest places helped southerners—black and white—to redefine themselves and their region, much as an earlier era and its symbols defined another South.

"Gonna Sit at the Welcome Table": The Sit-Ins

The four freshmen sitting in a dormitory room at all-black North Carolina A&T College in Greensboro on a cool, clear January evening could not have known that they were about to launch a moral revolution that was both American and southern. Much as the embattled colonists harked back to a constitutional regime they had enjoyed prior to 1763, and much as the Confederates depicted themselves as the true heirs of 1787, these teenagers were preservationists: they sought to extend the law of the land to themselves and their region. In doing so, their objective was to educate the white southerner, to reveal to him the liberating side of his culture. Though northerners found it difficult to grasp, these students and their colleagues loved their region, had settled there for generations, and had suffered along with if not alongside their white neighbors; their roots lay in the red clay of Carolina or the black loam of Mississippi, and their ancestors called to them from unmarked graves near the rivers and streams. The events that followed the late-night discussion among Franklin McCain, Ezell Blair, Jr., David Richmond, and Joseph McNeill would be distinctively southern in their character.

Earlier that day, January 31, Joseph McNeill had been denied counter service at the Greyhound bus terminal in Greensboro. The rebuff was typical in the South of that era, but McNeill, looking for sympathy and support, took up the issue with his friends that evening. As Franklin McCain recalled, the discussion eventually centered around the question of "at what point does the moral man act against injustice?" Once they agreed that they had reached that point, the question became what to do about it. In fixing on a sit-in at the Woolworth lunch counter in downtown Greensboro the next day, the students would stress the justice of their cause in an orderly, prayerful manner. As McCain noted, "the most powerful and potent weapon that people have literally no defense for is love [and] kindness." Theirs would be a "nonviolent" and a "Christian" action. The students had read Gandhi and knew about King and Montgomery, but this was mostly a spontaneous act emanating more from their religious backgrounds and how their existence in the South contradicted Christian tenets. They were unaware that CORE had employed the tactic of the sit-in in Chicago twenty years earlier and that as recently as 1958 and 1959 students had successfully desegregated some lunch counters in Tulsa and Miami.

The lunch counter was an obvious target because it highlighted the preposterous and humiliating nature of segregation. Blacks could purchase toothpaste and underwear at Woolworth's, but not a soft drink. In the elaborate etiquette that defined southern culture, eating with someone held particular connotations. As one white southerner informed Gunnar Myrdal, "in the South, the table . . . possesses the sanctity of an intimate social institution." To break bread together implied a rough equality. Slaves and later servants, regardless of their length of service or extent of their intimacy with white family members during childhood, never ate at the same place as whites. Southerners were appalled, for example, when President Theodore Roosevelt invited Booker T. Washington to join him for dinner at the White House, and stunned when Jim Folsom and black congressman Adam Clayton Powell, Jr., had drinks together in Montgomery.

But the students recognized that it was precisely this etiquette that must be attacked; it was a barrier inhibiting their visibility and ultimately their equality. They entered Woolworth's the following day, sat down with their school books, and ordered. The waitress refused to serve them. The students remained seated. Soon a policeman entered the store. He had been trained to react to violence and overt illegal action. Here, nothing was happening; it was a still life. He paced up and down the aisle, nervously slapping his nightstick into the palm of his hand. Some whites approached the four students who were settling into their reading material. A few condemned their behavior; others, surprisingly, offered encouragement. Forty-five minutes after they had sat down, the students left. As McNeill recalled, "we were scared as hell."

Yet they returned the next day, Tuesday, accompanied by twenty-three additional students, and on Wednesday with sixty-six, occupying almost all of the places at the lunch counter. By Thursday, the group had grown to over one hundred, including, for the first time, some white students from the North Carolina Women's College in Greensboro (now the University of North Carolina at Greensboro). Also by Thursday, white youths began to heckle the demonstrators, one setting fire to a black student's coat. On Friday, the sit-in spilled over into the streets of downtown Greensboro, as one thousand students demanded an end to segregated eating facilities. Within two weeks the sit-in spread to fifteen other southern cities. By April, demonstrations were occurring in fifty-four cities in nine southern states. By the end of the year, seventy thousand students had sat in at lunch counters in one hundred southern cities.

Unlike the bus boycott and school desegregation suits, the results of the sit-ins were immediate. By July, the Woolworth lunch counter in Greensboro accommodated blacks. Lunch counters in twenty-eight other cities were also integrated. In a few cities, other downtown facilities such as theaters and restaurants opened to blacks. The color line was at last beginning to fade. True, subsequent victories over segregation in public accommodations would not come so swiftly nor unaccompanied by violence, especially in the Deep South. It took federal legislation—the 1964 Civil Rights Act—to demolish public segregation completely. Nevertheless, the initial victories attained by the sit-in demonstrations were sufficient to convince the protesters that civil war was not a prerequisite for civil rights, that the quality of tactics and the demonstrators themselves were effective weapons in attacking an important element of white supremacy. They had proceeded in an orderly, almost ritualistic manner; they were polite and observed the manners of the region up to a point; and they were well-dressed and well-groomed, reflecting their middle-class backgrounds and aspirations. The contrast between their actions and the look and tone of white hecklers was significant enough for massive resister James J. Kilpatrick to comment in the Richmond *News-Leader*: "Here were the colored students, in coats, white shirts, ties, and one of them was reading Goethe and one was taking notes from a biology text. And here, on the sidewalk outside, was a gang of white boys come to heckle, a ragtail rabble, slack-jawed, black-jacketed, grinning fit to kill. . . . Eheu! It gives one pause."

Since southerners attached a great deal of importance to public behavior and appearance, such distinctions were important in impressing white opinion. Indeed, for the first time since the early days of the *Brown* decision, journalists, citizens, and even political leaders ventured out to support the demonstrations. The Greensboro *Daily News* editorialized, "there are many white people in the South who recognize the injustice of the lunch counter system. It is based on circumstances which may have made sense 100 years ago; today it has a touch of medievalism. It smacks of Indian 'untouchables' or Hitlerian Germany's Master Race Theories." Florida governor LeRoy Collins focused on the illogic of the situation that the demonstrators had illuminated so well: "I don't mind saying that if a man has a department store and he invites the public generally to come . . . I think then it is unfair and morally wrong for him to single out one department . . . and say he does not want or will not allow Negroes to patronize that one department."

Both Collins and the Greensboro editor pointed to another significant aspect of sit-in demeanor. In using words such as "injustice" and "morally wrong" to describe the lunch counter system, the governor and the editor indicated that a moral issue was involved. White southerners, once they recognized it as such, must either reconcile their deep religious faith to a new social order or live with and explain away the increasingly glaring contradiction between faith and reality. The sit-ins' great contribution to the region was in forcing this confrontation. As theologian James Sellers noted in 1961, the sit-in demonstrations provided a swift "updating into reality" for many white southerners. Buried in the courts or on buses that whites rarely patronized, civil rights could remain an abstract concept. Whites could be indifferent to such protests. But with the sit-ins some moral squirming had to occur. When Fisk University student and Nashville sit-in leader Diane Nash confronted Mayor Ben West with the question, "Do you feel it's wrong to discriminate against a person solely on the basis of race or color?" the moral absurdity of the proposition forced West from behind the barrier of tradition: "I couldn't agree it was morally right to sell them merchandise and refuse them service. . . . It was a moral question." Three weeks after West's confession on the steps of city hall, downtown lunch counters were serving blacks. It was difficult to dismiss these earnest young people (black *and* white) with their appeals to the regional conscience. James McBride Dabbs called the sit-in "the great creative moment of Southern culture," because of its moral dimension and its intrusion into white consciousness.

The sit-ins scored other breakthroughs to white consciousness. White southerners came into contact with blacks almost exclusively in subservient, menial positions, so the blacks encountered by most whites merely reinforced the latter's conception of an inferior race as well as the justice and wisdom of segregation. But the sit-in demonstrators, with their books, polished manners and shoes, and business attire, presented an unaccustomed picture. They presented the white southerner with another anomaly: the preconceived notion of what blacks ought to look and behave like, and the reality of the demonstrators. In addition, the sit-ins blasted the notion that blacks were content with the system of segregation. James A. Rogers, editor of the Florence (S.C.) *Morning News*, considered himself a moderate, even a liberal on racial issues in the late 1950s and early sixties. He supported segregation, as he explained, not "because I was against the black, but because I was for him . . . ; not because I wished to keep him in his place, but because I wished for him to have every opportunity that I had to make a place for himself." That place was behind the color line where, Rogers believed, there existed "no social tension" that would retard the blacks' development. The sit-ins taught Rogers otherwise: that segregation generated considerable tension by perpetuating a permanent second-class citizenship.

In other words, the sit-ins initiated the process of lifting the veil of anonymity from blacks. By stepping out of stereotype and appealing to southern culture, they had achieved notice. The demonstrators jarred the preconceptions of southern whites, and even if such jarring provoked rage, blacks had scored an important point. As Leslie Dunbar of the SRC observed in 1961, "at least Negroes are not regarded as instruments and tools, but as antagonists. That, in itself, is a higher status."

Blacks rejoiced in their sudden materialization. As invisibles and subservients, their self-respect and confidence suffered. Franklin Mc-Cain recalled his feeling after the initial sit-in: "I probably felt better that day than I've ever felt in my life. I felt as though I had gained my manhood, so to speak, and not only gained it, but had developed quite a lot of respect for it." Southern blacks had assumed a new character, had dropped the old role and demanded a greater part in regional life. Their actions not only forced a moral conflict on whites, but altered blacks' self-perceptions as well. Discussing the impact of the sit-ins on blacks, *Ebony* magazine analyzed the transformation: "The Negro has lost some of his former virtues and a good many illusions. Gone is his celebrated patience, his childlike obedience, and his colossal fear. He has waited ninety-eight years. . . . The day he stopped being a good old Negro was the day he became a man."

But *Ebony* was premature in heralding the regeneration of the southern black psyche. The demonstrators hardly represented a cross-section of the black community and, in fact, their initial efforts received little support and even some antagonism from traditional black leaders. These were youngsters mainly, who faced few of the economic burdens of their elders. A few days in jail or a name or picture in the newspaper did not spell financial ruin. They usually had no families to support. Because they could accept the consequences of their actions, they could act boldly even in a nonviolent framework. During the next few years, students would increasingly supply the shock troops for the army of redemption.

In the meantime, the sit-in demonstrators helped to form a new civil rights organization that would engage and represent this constituency. Ella Baker, an SCLC founder, felt that neither her group nor the NAACP could effectively harness the militant and potentially volatile power of the youthful, urbanized sit-in demonstrators. She gathered about two hundred youth leaders from across the South at a Youth Leadership meeting in Raleigh in April, 1960, just as the sit-ins were gathering momentum. Baker's keynote address, "More Than a Hamburger," stressed the importance of going beyond the lunch counter to strike down every vestige of segregation in the South. Martin Luther King, Jr., special guest at the meeting, then took the platform. In the years since Montgomery, King had largely failed to shake "the apathy and complacency of adults in the Negro community." He recommended to the gathering "some type of continuing organization" to coordinate student protest in a nonviolent manner. His emphasis on nonviolence chafed some of the delegates who believed that it was an expendable tactic and had in mind a more confrontational organization. One month later in Atlanta, Baker met with the more strident faction to form the Student Nonviolent Coordinating Committee (SNCC) with Nashville's Marion Barry (now mayor of Washington, D.C.) as chairman. The bow to nonviolence, evident in the new organization's name, did not signify a commitment to passive resistance. Even King recognized that white supremacy was inherently violent and that once it drew blacks into its vortex, the fine line separating nonviolent confrontation from violent encounter would become less clear.

Bound for Glory: The Freedom Rides

Ironically, the first example of how fine this line was occurred not as a result of a SNCC-sponsored action but from the resurrection of an old tactic by James Farmer's Chicago-based CORE. In 1947, CORE had engineered the Journey of Reconciliation, a successful experiment in integrated bus travel through more than two dozen cities of the Upper South. The Journey was ahead of its time, however. The Interstate Commerce Commission (ICC) declined to issue an order forcing the bus companies to abide by the 1946 Supreme Court decision *Morgan* v. *Virginia*, which banned segregated seating on interstate bus routes. The matter rested there until 1961. Encouraged by the success of the sit-ins as well as by renewed evidence of white support, Farmer felt the time was right for an action encompassing the entire region rather than the separate, local demonstrations that characterized the sit-ins. In addition, in December, 1960, the U.S. Supreme Court had extended its *Morgan* ruling to include segregated terminal facilities (*Boynton* v. *Virginia*). Farmer believed that the only way to convince the federal government to enforce that decision was to test terminal facilities all over the South, hoping to provoke a reaction in the form of arrests or even violence. As Farmer recalled the strategy, "we were counting on the bigots in the South to do our work for us."

The strategy entailed considerable danger. The Deep South, especially Alabama and Mississippi, remained a proud fortress of segregation. Both states were in the vise of political reaction, and support for the White Citizens' Councils and the Ku Klux Klan ran high. But, Farmer reasoned, if the bus riders provoked a violent response, the federal government would be certain to intervene; if the authorities in either or both states acquiesced in integration, that would be a victory in segregation's heartland.

On May 4, 1961, seven blacks and six whites—youthful sit-in demonstrators and veterans who had participated in the Journey of Reconciliation—divided into two interracial groups and boarded a Greyhound and a Trailways bus respectively, heading south from Washington, D.C. The previous evening, the thirteen riders had enjoyed a farewell Chinese dinner in the city. John Lewis, one of the young riders (now a congressman from Atlanta), called it "The Last Supper."

> Yes, we are the Freedom Riders
> And we ride a long Greyhound;
> White or black, we know no difference,
> Lord, for we are Glory bound.

The road to Glory turned out to be uneventful as the buses crossed Virginia and entered the Carolinas. The welcome mat had, in fact, been set out in the Old Dominion and in North Carolina as officials from both bus companies removed the "For Colored" and "For Whites" signs from terminal facilities. The first violence occurred at a stop in Rock Hill, South Carolina, just over the state line from North Carolina. John Lewis attempted to enter the white waiting room and several white youths forcibly intervened to prevent his passage. Police rescued Lewis and a colleague and hustled them back on the bus. There were no further incidents in South Carolina, nor in Georgia. The two teams arrived safely in Atlanta on May 13. They were heartened by their reception thus far, but the most difficult part of the journey lay ahead—through Alabama to their destination at Jackson, Mississippi.

Leaving Atlanta, the two buses split, the Greyhound heading for Anniston, Alabama, and the Trailways bus going on to Birmingham. Anniston was a small industrial city that benefited from defense contracts during the war and maintained a diverse industrial base afterward. The city's population included hundreds of new white arrivals from the surrounding poor hill country. As the Greyhound bus pulled into the Anniston terminal, a mob of whites surrounded it and smashed windows and slashed tires before the police arrived to quell the vandalism. The bus limped out of the city on its way to meet the Trailways group in Birmingham.

Six miles outside of Anniston, however, the tires went flat, and groups of whites who had stalked the stricken vehicle since it left the corporate limits resumed their attack on the bus. The riders huddled inside until a fire bomb broke through one of the windows and filled the bus with smoke. As the bus burst into flames the passengers exited quickly, only to run into a gauntlet of clubs and blackjacks. The timely arrival of a caravan from Birmingham led by a King aide, the Reverend Fred L. Shuttlesworth, who had been alerted about possible violence, managed to spirit the riders to safety.

In the meantime, the Trailways contingent made its way to Birmingham. By 1961, Birmingham had earned a reputation as one of the South's toughest cities, and its most segregated. It was a raw city, hewed out of the north Alabama woods in 1870, a creation of coal and iron and railroads, and untouched by the moonlight-and-magnolia mystique that softened other urban places in the region. Its white citizens seemed intent on proving their southernness in an environment without lineage. In this migrant town where black and white competed for jobs in the steel mills and coal mines, racial tensions frequently bubbled to the surface, and bombs, police brutality, and lynchings were common fare.

In 1956, after the Alabama legislature had outlawed the NAACP, Fred L. Shuttlesworth and several other black ministers formed the Alabama Christian Movement for Human Rights (ACMHR). Over the next five years, the Klan and the local police (membership overlapped) orchestrated a systematic campaign of terror against the group and its members. Ministers received death threats over the telephone and through the mail, and in December, 1956, Shuttlesworth's house was bombed, though he escaped serious injury. Police harassed visitors to his house, and the Klan abducted an ACMHR member, the Reverend Charles Billups, tied him to a tree, and beat him. Whites assaulted Shuttlesworth in 1957 as he attempted to enroll his children in an all-white school. John Bartlow Martin remarked that year, "Birmingham is the worst city for race relations in the South." This was a standard that white Birminghamians sought to maintain during the ensuing years.

The Trailways bus pulled into the eerie quiet of the Birmingham terminal on Mother's Day, May 14. Approximately forty whites, including a few newsmen, lined the terminal bay. There were no policemen in sight. The whites, mostly Klansmen, descended on the riders and beat them severely (only two of the nine passengers seriously injured were Freedom Riders). After twenty minutes, the police arrived and the mob retreated unmolested. When reporters later questioned Public Safety Commissioner Eugene "Bull" Connor as to why there were no policemen at the terminal, he replied that they were visiting their mothers.

At this point, the Kennedy administration began to take a greater interest in the proceedings. Burke Marshall, assistant attorney general for civil rights, had earlier advised the president that he lacked the the constitutional authority to protect the Freedom Riders. Protection was the responsibility of local law enforcement agencies. FBI agents formed the only federal connection with the Freedom Riders as they monitored their progress from state offices in the Deep South. The role of the FBI, however, was strictly informational. They shared material with the Justice Department and with the local police, who often passed along the information to colleagues in the Klan. But the incidents outside Anniston and in Birmingham made front-page headlines and caused international embarrassment. Privately, Attorney General Robert F. Kennedy moved to secure a pledge of cooperation from Alabama governor John Patterson. The governor replied that "we can't act as nursemaids to agitators. . . . You can't guarantee the safety of fools." The attorney general, wary of a constitutional and political confrontation, did not press the matter. The Freedom Riders, though determined to continue their pilgrimage to Montgomery, could find no bus willing to take them, nor could they be certain of their own safety. The only realistic alternative was to abandon the protest and accept the Justice Department's offer of a flight to New Orleans from Birmingham.

The matter did not end there, however. Though CORE had reluctantly halted the Ride, SNCC was prepared to resume it regardless of the danger. SNCC hurriedly assembled twenty-one volunteers, and on May 20 the group set out from Birmingham for Montgomery. President Kennedy, hoping to avoid the debacle that occurred in Birmingham, sent several emissaries from the Justice Department, including two high-ranking officials in the Civil Rights Division, John Doar and John Seigenthaler. The president believed that the federal presence would prompt state officials to initiate security measures. Seigenthaler succeeded in extracting a pledge from Colonel Floyd Mann, director of Alabama public safety, to protect the riders en route to Montgomery.

Initially, it appeared that the administration's strategy was working. An armada of buses, helicopters, and police cruisers escorted the riders for the two-hour journey to the state capital. When the bus neared the city, however, the escort vanished. A sickeningly familiar quiet descended as the bus made its way to the downtown terminal. It was Saturday, a day when residents from the surrounding towns and countryside came to Montgomery to shop or merely to loiter and socialize. People milled about the downtown, but the usual casualness was absent. There was an air of expectancy, as if the crowds had come to witness an event.

Virginia Durr had gone downtown to shop. When she arrived in the area of the bus terminal, a noisy crowd was milling about. As she pressed closer she discovered the cause for the commotion. A mob had surrounded the riders as they debarked from the bus and begun to pummel them. The sight appalled her, not so much the violence but the onlookers' faces contorted with hate. Many were familiar to her. Neighbors were holding up their children to "see the niggers run." These were people with whom she had attended church, shared meals, and visited in times of joy and sorrow. "These were my people," she recalled. "These were the people I was living among and they were really crazy."

John Doar, from his vantage point across the street from the bus terminal, hurriedly placed a long-distance call to the attorney general to describe the scene: "A bunch of men led by a guy with a bleeding face are beating them [the passengers]. There are no cops. It's terrible. There's not a cop in sight. People are yelling, 'Get 'em, get 'em.' It's awful." Doar's colleague John Seigenthaler had gone out into the street to assist two women knocked to the ground by the mob. As he tried to help them to his car, a group of whites grabbed him and beat him into unconsciousness. He lay on the pavement for twenty-five minutes before an ambulance arrived. Montgomery commissioner of public safety Lester B. Sullivan explained the delay in coming to Seigenthaler's aid: "Every white ambulance in town reported their vehicles had broken down."

The nation was shocked. The Atlanta *Constitution*, which had previously criticized the Freedom Riders, led a chorus of southern journals condemning the violence in Alabama: "If the police, representing the people, refuse to intervene when a man—any man—is being beaten to the pavement of an American city, then this is not a noble land at all. It is a jungle." The Kennedy administration no longer placed faith in phone calls and monitors to secure the peace, and the attorney general dispatched four hundred U.S. marshals to Montgomery to ensure the safety of the Freedom Riders as they began the final leg of their troubled journey to Jackson, Mississippi. Six Alabama National Guardsmen with fixed bayonets accompanied the riders; police cars and helicopters provided an additional escort. At the Mississippi state line, National Guardsmen flanked the road, their guns pointing into the woods. As the bus approached Jackson a woman broke into an impromptu song, and soon the other riders joined her in a collective release of tension: "Hallelujah, I'm a-travelin'; Hallelujah, ain't it fine; Hallelujah, I'm a-travelin' down freedom's main line." When the group arrived in Jackson, police arrested them, but there was no violence—part of an arrangement between the attorney general and Senator Eastland. The Freedom Ride was over.

Four months later, the ICC issued an order integrating interstate carriers and terminal facilities. The Freedom Riders had achieved their goal. But just as the sit-ins held implications beyond the immediate objective, the journey through the Deep South changed perceptions and responses as well. The rides had demonstrated to a national audience that beneath the gentility of southern society lay the raw edge of violence. The rides captured national attention and by doing so drew the Kennedy administration into a more active participation in the civil rights struggle.

It was a reluctant entrance, to be sure. President Kennedy had won a narrow victory the previous November. Without an electoral mandate, he faced a Congress more likely to be independent, and he needed the assistance of powerful southerners who controlled key committees. He relied heavily, for example, on the advice of Senate Judiciary Committee head Eastland for appointment recommendations to the federal judiciary. The result was a series of disastrous nominations early in the administration that clogged the civil rights process at the district court level for at least the next half decade. One such appointment, W. Harold Cox of Mississippi's Southern District, referred to black litigants as "niggers" or "chimpanzees." Another Mississippi judicial appointee, Ben Cameron, offered this rationale: "It is the universal conviction of the people . . . that the judges who function in this circuit should render justice in individual cases against a background of, and as interpreters of, the ethos of the people whose servants they are." But as the political fallout from the violence in Alabama descended on the White House, the administration's economic and foreign policy initiatives suddenly diminished in importance and with them the courting of key southern legislators. Though the administration would not assume the activist role that civil rights leaders hoped for, it would use its prestige and weight more often on behalf of their cause over the next two years.

The Freedom Rides had internal as well as external consequences for the growing civil rights movement. Specifically, it thrust SNCC into the forefront of the civil rights organizations operating in the South. The doctrines of love and nonviolence seemed less relevant alongside the pictures of violence and terror that accompanied the Freedom Rides. Though the stoicism and courage of the victims heightened national revulsion, some of SNCC's members questioned the wisdom of continuing to turn the other cheek. A confrontation was brewing between the younger and more militant members of SNCC, and the SCLC, CORE, and the NAACP.

Finally, because the Freedom Rides were a region-wide protest, they touched more white southerners than did previous demonstrations. The extensive national news coverage and the actions of the White House seemed to place the South under a magnifying glass. The view was not an attractive one and etched itself in the minds of some white leaders as blacks in their own communities began to press for more than token integration. For other whites, the rides conjured up the specter of outside invaders in a way that the sit-ins did not. For those southerners, the invasion was a new call to battle.

Mind over Matter: The Albany Movement

With growing support from Washington, the increasing willingness of whites to speak out on the more egregious examples of white supremacy, and the growing confidence of blacks, Martin Luther King believed it was important to expand the objectives of the demonstrations. With this in mind, he accepted an invitation from a coalition of black organizations in Albany, Georgia, in November, 1961. Albany was becoming an important commercial center for southern Georgia, and its population had grown 15 percent during the previous decade to 56,000. Prosperity had not softened the rigid segregation that characterized race relations in the community, however. Local officials, for example, had defied an ICC order to desegregate all train stations and bus terminals and that autumn had arrested black students who tested that resolve. The arrests mobilized the black community. SNCC, which had been in the area conducting voter registration drives since the summer, organized students for additional protests. Eventually adults joined their demonstrations and helped to form the Albany Movement. It was at this point that King arrived.

But Albany was ready for King. Police Chief Laurie Pritchett had studied King's philosophy and had learned about the national impact of violence from the Freedom Rides. He was determined to avoid such a spectacle in Albany. As Pritchett put it, Albany "can't tolerate the NAACP or any other 'nigger' organization to take over this town with mass demonstrations." To this end, he intended to respond to King's pressure by not responding at all, or by responding in such a way as to deflate any impact of that pressure beyond the borders of the city.

Pritchett contacted county officials within a one-hundred-mile radius of Albany and secured their cooperation in using their jails to house the thousands of protesters that the demonstrations would draw. In addition, he insisted on fair treatment for the prisoners and promised to send deputies along to ensure their safety. In this way, Pritchett could resort to mass arrests without fear of overextending his facilities, and the polite handling of the demonstrators would defuse adverse publicity. As a final precaution, the chief gave a course on nonviolence for his officers.

The strategy worked. Demonstrators went to prison by the thousands and suffered lost time, expense, and occasionally loss of employment. Pritchett was careful to charge them with breach of the peace and unlawful assembly rather than with violation of the city's segregation ordinances, which could have invited litigation. Black and white informants kept the police chief aware of protest plans, and political leaders gave him free rein to command the situation. The demonstrations lasted from November, 1961, to the summer of 1963 and accomplished nothing while the city persisted in its refusal to negotiate. "[We thought] we could fill up the jails," SNCC worker Bill Hansen explained in a post-mortem. "We ran out of people before [Chief Pritchett] ran out of jails."

In the meantime, Pritchett had attained the status of a celebrity. The attorney general wired his congratulations for maintaining the peace (and thus, incidentally, enabling the administration to avoid intervention). An Atlanta newspaper declared that Albany's police chief was now "widely known—not only in the South, but throughout the world—as a stalwart exponent of the nonviolent method of quelling integrationist uprisings." And Pritchett became a sought-after consultant to police departments in other southern cities. But SCLC official Wyatt Tee Walker had a different appraisal of Pritchett's conduct: "Pritchett was non-brutal, not non-violent . . . segregation is not non-violent." Underneath his calm, disciplined exterior, Chief Pritchett was as staunch a defender of white supremacy as the most violent Klansman. As he stated matter-of-factly to SNCC leader Charles Sherrod, "It's just a matter of mind over matter. I don't mind, and you don't matter."

King's failure in Albany resulted from a number of factors. The city was located in a predominantly rural area of Georgia little influenced by the currents of black protest, and white residents were not inclined to negotiate. They saw the fact that King brought numerous protesters and funds from outside the area as another challenge to their efforts to maintain the status quo. Also, the black community remained divided throughout the protest—some of the younger demonstrators affiliated with SNCC disdained King's philosophy and tactics; some older leaders felt that any agitation in the current racial environment was unwise; and there were many who resented outside advice and influence. The attempt to attack all aspects of public segregation in the city was a diffuse and overly ambitious strategy. Most important, the actions of Police Chief Pritchett were crucial in limiting the impact of the demonstrations, generating frustration and discouragement in the black community, and removing the threat of federal intervention.

The Business of Desegregation

Strangely enough, few southern cities followed Pritchett's example over the next three years. The business communities, which usually controlled or greatly influenced the decision-making process in their cities, were wary of handing over too much authority to local police forces. The average police officer came from the lower economic strata, and his selection was rarely by examination. In smaller cities, as sociologist Arthur Raper noted, "almost anyone on the outside of the penitentiary who weighs enough and is not blind or crippled can be considered as a police candidate." These were individuals who were primed by economic circumstance and political rhetoric to be most hostile to blacks and less controlled in a tense situation.

In several southern cities, especially those in the Upper South, the white leadership eventually opted for accommodation with the black community rather than relying on police strategy to wear down the demonstrators. A survey of business leaders in five southern cities in 1963 indicated that they were no more inclined to support integration than other white southerners, but they feared the potential damage to economic development programs caused by violent reactions to peaceful protest. Most could recite the costs of Little Rock, where Governor Faubus' indulgence was responsible for a decline in new investment in Arkansas from $131 million in 1956 to $25.4 million in 1958. The adverse publicity generated by the Freedom Rides sent new shock waves through business communities across the urban South. Either on an ad-hoc basis or through formal associations, business leaders sought to exercise a moderating role in the escalating racial confrontation.

Atlanta was a case in point. In 1961, along with the pressure to desegregate the public school system, blacks protested the segregation of public facilities in the downtown area. Fearful of the potential for violence, Robert W. Woodruff, powerful chairman of Atlanta-based Coca-Cola, and Mayor Ivan Allen, Jr., called a meeting of business leaders to persuade them that desegregation of public accommodations was in their best interests. The meeting produced the desired agreement, and Allen returned to his office to remove the "Colored Only" signs from city hall as the first step in the desegregation of the city.

Though most southern cities that reached an agreement with blacks prior to the 1964 Civil Rights Act were not as prompt as Atlanta, the scenario was similar. In Charlotte, for example, business leaders waited until 1963 to acquiesce to black demands for the desegregation of public accommodations. The Charlotte Chamber of Commerce and Mayor Stanford Brookshire took the lead following an informal discussion at church one Sunday morning. The Chamber was proud of the fact that it had brought fifty new companies to Charlotte in 1962, including a major computer center for Eastern Airlines. As one Chamber leader put it, "this [is] too good a town to have it ruined." The first step was to integrate the Chamber and have each member take a black businessman to lunch, thus integrating downtown restaurants. Charlotte *Observer* editor "Pete" McKnight rallied the rest of the community with supportive editorials, and soon integration was achieved at most downtown facilities.

The Atlanta and Charlotte examples indicated that at least two prerequisites were necessary to integrate public accommodations. First, economic development, especially that based on securing outside investment and commerce, had to be a top priority among the business leadership. When businessmen were content with the economic status quo they were not likely to take the initiative for integration. In St. Augustine, Florida, for instance, business leaders were members of the ultra-conservative John Birch Society and were more concerned with maintaining the color line than with development issues; accordingly, integration did not occur there until the 1964 Civil Rights Act (and even then there were attempts to circumvent the law). Second, without continued pressure from the black community, especially in the form of demonstrations and boycotts, it was unlikely that white leaders would act on their own to eliminate segregation. These leaders most feared the impact of disorder and violence, not the maintenance of segregation.

By the spring of 1963, most cities in the Upper South had reached at least a partial accommodation to black demands. The cities of the Deep South, however, remained unbroken. In these locations, state leaders and local institutions such as churches and the press created an environment that precluded white initiatives for integration. If the war for southern redemption was to be won, a region half-bound and half-free would not do. But these were closed societies, girded against intrusion (as the Freedom Rides demonstrated), and successful in maintaining the solidarity of white opinion and action. Robert Zellner, a white civil rights worker from Mobile who was expelled from college in Montgomery because of his views, put it this way: "they gave no white southerner . . . any choice. If you bucked the system at all you had two choices: you either capitulated absolutely and completely, or you became a rebel, a complete outlaw." It was unlikely that segregation would fall from within.

The Battle for Birmingham

"We've got to have a crisis to bargain with," SCLC official Wyatt Tee Walker advised Martin Luther King, Jr., late in 1962. The Albany experience had weakened the SCLC as well as King's credibility as a leader. King was wrestling with another bout of uncertainty, and when the Reverend Fred L. Shuttlesworth asked him to come to Birmingham, he hesitated. If Albany would not yield, could Birmingham be broken? Shuttlesworth persisted, and King relented, half-joking with colleague Andy Young, "You better let me know what kind of eulogy you want." He understood, as did everyone else in the SCLC, that Birmingham's Public Safety commissioner Eugene "Bull" Connor was not likely to effect the intellectual approach to black demonstrators adopted by Laurie Pritchett.

But Connor's intransigence could also provide an opportunity for the SCLC. If he reprised his Freedom Ride role and created a national spectacle, Birmingham's blacks would have a national audience for their moral drama. Appropriately, the SCLC called its Birmingham campaign "Project C" (C for *Confrontation*). King planned a series of demonstrations for the city beginning in early April to coincide with the Easter shopping season. The objectives were not only to integrate all public facilities in Birmingham, but also to guarantee employment opportunities for blacks in downtown businesses, desegregate the schools, improve the quality and level of services in black neighborhoods, and provide low-income housing. The wide-ranging goals were calculated to elicit a sharp response from the South's most impenetrable fortress of segregation.

The climate in Birmingham had changed since the Freedom Rides of May, 1961, however. The violence of that episode and the ensuing national embarrassment had roused the business leadership to action. In order to generate interracial dialogue and prevent further violence, businessmen formed the biracial Committee of 100 in the fall of 1961 and discussed a modest plan for school desegregation as well as the integration of city parks. When the businessmen presented the latter proposal to the city commission (the main governing body in Birmingham consisting of three elected commissioners), the commissioners angrily rejected it and in January, 1962, closed the parks. Business leaders felt that their only remaining option in settling black demands without disrupting economic development objectives was to elect more conciliatory public officials. To this end, they succeeded in putting a referendum on the ballot to change the city's form of government to a mayor-council system. The referendum won by a narrow margin, and an election to choose a new government was set for the end of March, 1963. In that election, Albert Boutwell, a racial moderate, won out over Eugene "Bull" Connor for mayor. A new political era seemed imminent in Birmingham.

The election board scarcely had time to certify the results when King launched his demonstrations on April 3. Black and white leaders in the community, as well as the Kennedy administration, had urged the SCLC to postpone its campaign, at least until the new government was installed on April 15. Guided by the feeling that no time was a "good time" for these protests, King proceeded. In the meantime, the former city government challenged the legality of the election and refused to vacate its offices. So Birmingham had two city governments, two mayors, and massive civil rights demonstrations as the Easter shopping season approached. Connor remained in charge of the police and fire departments until the government tangle could be resolved. The business leaders, fearing a public backlash that would dash their political plans, were not in a position to reach an agreement with King. On April 11, the city secured an injunction against further demonstrations. King ignored the court order and was arrested on Good Friday, April 12. Just as in Montgomery, local politics was playing a significant role in deciding the nature and the outcome of an unfolding civil rights drama.

King's arrest was not particularly noteworthy; it had happened many times before. While in prison over that Easter weekend, however, King found the time to respond to an open letter from Birmingham's white clergy that chided and criticized him for the demonstrations. The clergymen had charged that King was an outsider who had no business in the city. In addition, his demonstrations were untimely, demanding too much too soon. The clergymen were also concerned that King was encouraging the breaking of laws and that his so-called nonviolent tactics would lead to considerable violence. Accordingly, they felt that King was an extremist who was disrupting the orderly evolution of race relations in the city.

Writing with a stubby pencil along the margins of the New York *Times* page on which the letter appeared, King's reply was a remarkable document that encapsulated the essence of his nonviolent philosophy. To the charge of being an "outside agitator," he wrote, "I am in Birmingham because injustice is here. Just as the prophets of the eighth century B.C. left their villages and carried their 'thus saith the Lord' far beyond the boundaries of their home towns, . . . so am I compelled to carry the gospel of freedom beyond my own home town." When the clergymen counseled patience, King replied:

> We have waited for more than 340 years for our constitutional and God-given rights. . . . Perhaps it is easy for those who have never felt the stinging darts of segregation to say, "Wait." But when you have seen vicious mobs lynch your mothers and fathers at will and drown your sisters and brothers at whim; when you have seen hate-filled policemen curse, kick, and even kill your black brothers and sisters; when you see the vast majority of your twenty million Negro brothers smothering in an airtight cage of poverty in the midst of an affluent society; when you suddenly find your tongue twisted and your speech stammering as you seek to explain to your six-year-old daughter why she can't go to the public amusement park . . . and see tears welling up in her eyes . . . ; when you take a cross-country drive and find it necessary to sleep night after night in the uncomfortable corners of your automobile because no motel will accept you; . . . when your first name becomes "nigger," your middle name becomes "boy" . . . and your last name becomes "John," and your wife and mother are never given the respected title "Mrs."; . . . when you are forever fighting a degenerating sense of "nobodiness"—then you will understand why we find it difficult to wait.

This catalogue of life under segregation was remarkable for both its articulation of that life and its sharp tone. King believed strongly in the educative function of his work, and his reply to the clergymen was a lecture in many respects. Though some younger blacks questioned King's intensity, he was never fearful of asserting his demands forcefully. Persistent pressure was a key principle of nonviolence.

In addressing the charge that he engaged in illegal actions, King made the distinction between just laws and unjust laws, and labeled segregation an unjust law because it was sinful. He quoted theologian Paul Tillich that "sin was separation." King asked, "Is not segregation an existential expression of man's tragic separation, his awful estrangement, his terrible sinfulness?" As for the related question that his illegal demonstrations were directed at provoking violence, King again phrased his response with a question: "Isn't this like condemning Jesus because his unique God-consciousness and never-ceasing devotion to God's will precipitated the evil act of crucifixion?" By framing his replies within a Christian context, King hoped not only to convince the clergymen of the righteousness of his cause, but to demonstrate that their perspective was outside that context.

This latter objective was evident in King's response to the charge of extremism. First, he reminded the clergymen that he stood "in the middle of two opposing forces in the Negro community. One is a force of complacency. . . . The other force is one of bitterness and hatred, and it comes perilously close to advocating violence." King presented himself as the best alternative for peaceful change, but he did not shun the label "extremist" altogether. The question for King was not "whether we will be extremists, but what kind of extremists we will be. Will we be extremists for hate or for love?" He added that "Jesus Christ . . . was an extremist for love, truth, and goodness, and thereby rose above his environment. Perhaps the South, the nation, and the world are in dire need of creative extremists."

King expressed deep disappointment in the role of the white church in the South during the nine years since the *Brown* decision. The absence of the white church as a positive moral force during this difficult era had, of course, troubled some whites as well. The Reverend Carlyle Marney of Myers Park Baptist Church in Charlotte lamented that "there's a social revolution under way, and Baptists in God's white hand have had precious little to do with it except when run over from the rear." The problem was not, as novelist Walker Percy noted, one of "putting into practice the Judeo-Christian ethic [because] Christendom of a sort has already won." The problem was to expose the church and its congregants to a more expansive view of that ethic that did not "canonize the existing social and political structure." But who would make that exposure? "I have heard numerous southern religious leaders admonish their worshipers to comply with a desegregation decision because it is the law," King wrote, "but I have longed to hear white ministers declare: 'Follow this decree because integration is morally right and because the Negro is your brother.'

In the midst of blatant injustices inflicted upon the Negro, I have watched white churchmen stand on the sideline and mouth pious irrelevancies and sanctimonious trivialities. In the midst of a mighty struggle to rid our nation of racial and economic injustice, I have heard many ministers say: 'Those are social issues with which the gospel has no real concern.'" King warned that "if today's church does not recapture the sacrificial spirit of the early church, it will lose its authenticity, forfeit the loyalty of millions, and be dismissed as an irrelevant social club with no meaning for the twentieth century."

But even if the white church remained on the sidelines, King was optimistic that the objectives of his crusade would be fulfilled. He invited the clergymen to be a part of that future, to look beyond the confrontation of the moment to see the emergence of a new South. "One day," King concluded, "the South will know that when these disinherited children of God sat down at lunch counters, they were in reality standing up for what is best in the American dream and for the most sacred values in our Judeo-Christian heritage, thereby bringing our nation back to those great wells of democracy which were dug deep by the founding fathers in their formulation of the Constitution and the Declaration of Independence." If, as King implied, we need as a region and a nation to be reminded of our founding constitutional and religious principles, then the recognition of black civil rights would be the fulfillment of that reminder.

As King walked out of prison a week later on April 20, he understood the arduous task confronting him and his people. His "Letter from Birmingham Jail," eloquent as it was, would not open the restaurants, theaters, parks, playgrounds, and city hall for blacks. That victory had to be won in the streets. The demonstrations resumed, but city leaders remained unperturbed, and Birmingham disappeared as a major story in the national media. "Bull" Connor's police force was showing remarkable restraint—perhaps Albany's Laurie Pritchett had taught him something. If so, then another failure was in the offing, and King and black southerners could not afford that.

It would be necessary to lure the police into violence. For all of King's advocacy of nonviolence, he recognized the value and efficacy of a violent response of the type seen in Little Rock, New Orleans, and the Freedom Rides. Open conflict would bring in the federal government and thus ensure the fulfillment of the protest's objectives. Violence was also cleansing, a means to grace and hence to individual and regional redemption. As writer Flannery O'Connor noted in 1963, "I have found that violence is strangely capable of returning my characters to reality and preparing them to accept their moment of grace. Their heads are so hard that almost nothing else will do the work." O'Connor considered this a "Christian view of the world," and, indeed, Jacob's night-long wrestling match in the Old Testament results in his reconciliation with God. King concurred in this view as well. "There can be no remission of sin," he wrote, "without the shedding of blood."

Violence was cleansing for blacks as well. As victims, they would be the redeemers. For those who understandably feared the consequences of violence, King admonished, "if a man hasn't found something to die for, he isn't fit to live." Although this seemed like small solace in the face of the reality of injury and even death, southern blacks were deeply religious and, as King reminded them,

> We are gravely mistaken to think that religion protects us from the pain and agony of mortal existence. Life is not a euphoria of unalloyed comfort and untroubled ease. Christianity has always insisted that the cross we bear precedes the crown we wear. To be a Christian one must take up his cross, with all of its difficulties and agonizing and tension-packed content, and carry it until that very cross leaves its mark upon us and redeems us to that more excellent way which comes only through suffering.

Bearing the cross placed blacks and their cause on a high moral ground in the evangelical South. They were the army of God seeking to redeem a people and a region.

There was an earlier army of God that had sought redemption as well. The Confederates faced equally long odds as they entered battle. Charging twenty deep at Cold Harbor, they pinned their addresses on their backs so they could be identified after the Union artillery tore them to shreds. So it was a century later, only this time with black children entering the maelstrom in the battle of Birmingham and for the South. It was a calculated risk by King to use schoolchildren to capture the imagination of the nation and, hoping against hope, the wrath of "Bull" Connor. On Thursday, May 2, seven hundred black youngsters gathered at the Sixteenth Street Baptist Church preparing to march out to meet Connor's men. They exited the church as if on a holiday, singing freedom songs and chanting slogans. As they knelt to pray, Connor's men, obviously unsure of what was happening, gingerly waded in and arrested the marchers, who laughed and sang their way to the waiting patrol wagons.

Though the children's crusade was the lead story on the six o'clock news and in newspapers across the country, King realized that the continued restraint shown by the police would eventually cause public interest to wane. The following day, another one thousand school-children gathered at the church and again marched out into the down-town area. This time, Connor was prepared with a strategy of his own. His men barred the exits from the church, trapping roughly one-half of the demonstrators inside. Another contingent of police pursued those who had left the church across the street to Kelly Ingram Park, where they loosed their German shepherd dogs on the children and beat dem-onstrators and onlookers alike. When adults in the park tried to ward off the attacking police with bricks and bottles, Connor ordered the firemen to turn their high-pressure hoses on the crowd. The sudden thrust of water knocked people to the ground, ripped off their clothes, and sent children skittering down the street. King had his spectacle.

Responding to an aroused public opinion, the Kennedy administra-tion urged a negotiated settlement. Business leaders announced that they were prepared to compromise, but in fact the new, urgent negotia-tions went nowhere. On May 6, King took to the streets with his children again, and Connor obliged by repeating the scene of May 3. An even more extensive demonstration occurred the following day, com-pletely disrupting downtown rush-hour traffic and business. Again, Connor turned loose his dogs and hoses. But blacks were no longer resisting passively. The Reverend James Bevel, a King aide, had to grab a police bullhorn to dissuade angered blacks from retaliating during one of Connor's assaults the previous week. By the 6th, Bevel could no longer contain black frustration, and sporadic fighting erupted throughout the downtown area between whites and blacks. Con-fronted with the possibility of race war on their doorstep, business leaders resumed negotiations on May 7 and reached an accord with the SCLC three days later. The settlement included the removal of segre-gation signs, the desegregation of lunch counters, promises to employ blacks in downtown stores, and a sixty-day moratorium on demonstra-tions.

But Connor and state political leaders denounced the agreement. Robert Shelton, Grand Dragon of the Ku Klux Klan, declared that the businessmen had no authority to reach an agreement. He warned that "Martin Luther King's epitaph is written here in Birmingham." A few hours later, two dynamite bombs severely damaged the home of King's brother, the Reverend A. D. King, though there were no injuries, and a bomb exploded at SCLC headquarters in the city. Blacks streamed into the streets to attack police and firemen arriving at the scene. King hurriedly returned from Atlanta to ensure that order was restored. The accord held. Birmingham had fallen.

For southern blacks, the Birmingham victory was inspirational. They were no longer content with token gains; they went after segregation with a new resolve. Within three months of the Birmingham agreement, eight hundred boycotts, marches, and sit-ins occurred in two hundred cities and towns across the South. Within five months, fifty southern communities had desegregated their public accommodations. As historian Harvard Sitkoff observed, "more racial change came in these few months than had occurred in three-quarters of a century." In addition, Birmingham had enlarged the corps of black participants. Both King and the sit-in movement had appealed primarily to middle-class blacks. The brutality of Birmingham and the success there drew in the cynical or apolitical black underclass. This development both ensured fresh troops for the coming battles and threatened the concept of nonviolence as the foundation of black protest.

In the meantime, King sought to reap the benefits of his victory in Birmingham at the federal level. Recently released White House tapes indicate that President Kennedy took a more active role in local demonstrations after Birmingham. For example, in June, 1963, he telephoned the mayor of Jackson, Mississippi, to secure an agreement from the mayor to hire blacks for city jobs, including the police force. That same month, the president addressed a national television audience on the civil rights issue: "We are confronted primarily with a moral issue . . . as old as the scriptures and . . . as clear as the American Constitution." By using the rhetoric of the movement and by elevating the issue to more than a question of integration, Kennedy helped to set a national tone that would spur federal civil rights legislation. The president was convinced that his ad-hoc approach to dealing with civil rights was both time-consuming and fraught with political danger. Federal legislation mandating the integration of public accommodations in all southern cities would lighten his burden considerably.

Let Freedom Ring:
The March on Washington

In order to hasten that legislation, King began to prepare for a massive march on Washington in August, 1963. King's objective was to stage a peaceful lobbying event that would capture the imagination of the

American people and their leaders by appealing to basic national ideals. The sporadic violence of blacks in Birmingham, though provoked, had concerned congressmen and whites outside the South—two groups whose support was essential for the passage of civil rights legislation. King took care to instruct southern blacks on proper behavior in the nation's capital—not to litter, not to be loud and boisterous, and to dress comfortably but properly. The SCLC leader also secured the participation of predominantly white labor unions to guarantee an interracial audience. He urged prospective speakers to soft-pedal economic grievances. The march would be a conservative demonstration for the application of constitutional rights to blacks.

The crowd that assembled in front of the Lincoln Memorial on August 28, 1963, exceeded the most optimistic hopes of the organizers. More than two hundred thousand people gathered in the sweltering summer heat of Washington to petition Congress to enact civil rights legislation. Even after several hours of listening to Peter, Paul, and Mary, Bob Dylan, and black gospel singer Mahalia Jackson, as well as to numerous speeches and introductions, the crowd remained good-natured, if increasingly less attentive. Then it was King's turn.

His brief (fifteen minutes) comments were drawn from speeches he had delivered earlier in his career but tailored for this event. He reviewed briefly and in general terms the second-class nature of black life in America. But he believed that in the near future, Americans in all regions and of all colors would recognize the justice of the black protest and that all citizens would live together in interracial harmony. In his deliberate southern preacher's cadence, he declared, "I have a dream today! I have a dream that one day down in Alabama—with its vicious racists . . . one day right there in Alabama, little black boys and black girls will be able to join hands with little white boys and white girls as sisters and brothers." And placing that theme in a familiar religious context: "I have a dream today! I have a dream that one day 'every valley shall be exalted and every hill and mountain shall be made low . . . and the glory of the Lord shall be revealed, and all flesh shall see it together.'" He concluded with a stirring declaration: "And when we allow freedom to ring, when we let it ring from every village and every hamlet, from every state and every city, we will be able to speed up that day when all God's children, black men and white men, Jews and gentiles, Protestants and Catholics, will be able to join hands and sing in the words of the old Negro spiritual: 'Free at last. Free at last. Thank God Almighty, we are free at last.'"

The speech accomplished its purpose. It won the approbation of white America, including some southern whites. The rhetoric was not threatening, it mentioned only fleetingly specific instances of discrimination, and it conjured up symbols and ideals that white Americans liked to believe they cherished. But for some southern blacks with memories of Birmingham still fresh in their minds, or who were working in great personal danger in small towns throughout the Deep South, King's words were disappointing. March leaders had barely averted a split when A. Philip Randolph talked SNCC's John Lewis out of delivering a speech that condemned the proposed civil rights legislation as inadequate. Other young blacks who attended the Washington march were freer to express their frustration. "Fuck that dream, Martin," a young black man exclaimed, "Now goddamit, NOW!" Anne Moody, a young civil rights worker from Canton, Mississippi, sat on the grass listening to King and thought, "in Canton we never had time to sleep, much less dream."

Unmerited Suffering: A Reprise in Birmingham

The frustration of some younger blacks proved prophetic. Scarcely had the echoes of King's rhetorical dream quieted when another tragedy visited Birmingham. On Sunday, September 15, four junior-high-school girls—Cynthia Wesley, Denise McNair, Addie Mae Collins, and Carol Robertson—excitedly made their way to the basement restroom of the Sixteenth Street Baptist Church. The church had been the focal point for the Children's Crusade, but this morning such events were far from the girls' minds as they primped for the ten o'clock service. This was to be their first participation in an adult service at the church. Suddenly, an explosion ripped through the basement. Civil defense volunteers, police, and firemen converged on the church. Pastor John H. Cross was first on the scene, and he frantically cleared away the rubble, assisted by the adult worshippers. Denise McNair's grandfather uncovered a patent leather shoe. It belonged to his granddaughter. The awful reality dawned that the struggle for regional redemption had claimed four more lives.

That evening, Birmingham's white leaders, including the police chief, went on television to appeal for calm and express regret over the incident. At least one white citizen of Birmingham sensed the hypocrisy of the show. Attorney Chuck Morgan felt that the tone was less one of regret than of "Oh, God, why did it happen here? It will hurt the community's image." The following day, Morgan spoke before the all-white Young Men's Business Club. Barely containing his anger and shame, he admonished the members not to waste their energy wondering who did it. That was the simple part. "The 'who,'" Morgan offered, "is every little individual who talks about the 'niggers' and spreads the seeds of his hate to his neighbor and his son. . . . The 'who' is every governor who ever shouted for lawlessness and became a law violator. . . . Who is really guilty? Each of us. Each citizen who has not consciously attempted to bring about peaceful compliance . . . ; each citizen who has ever said, 'They ought to kill that nigger.' Every person in this community who has in any way contributed to the popularity of hatred is at least as guilty, or more so, as the demented fool who threw that bomb."

Federal legislation would not absolve such collective complicity in the tragedy of white supremacy, but at least it would remove the burden from both whites and blacks of having to maintain a degrading component of that system, segregation. In his eulogy for the four girls, King promised that "unmerited suffering is redemptive." He called on the mourners "not to lose faith in our white brothers. Somehow we must believe that even the most misguided among them can learn to respect the dignity and worth of all human personalities." To many blacks this seemed to be a one-sided appeal. The taking of victims, especially victims so young and in a church as well, was a test almost beyond endurance. Yet the peace held. And King used the forbearance and the church bombing to warn President Kennedy that unless legislation moved forward, "there is a danger we will face the worst race riot we've ever seen."

Segregation Falls: The South Lives On

Ironically, the assassination of Kennedy sped that legislation. His successor in the White House, Lyndon B. Johnson, had become one of the most influential senators during his years in that body. He knew the legislative process well and, as a southerner, he had a better chance of modifying the obstreperous behavior of powerful southern senators. In addition, Johnson sought to reassure the supporters of the martyred president that he would not abandon Kennedy's legislative agenda regardless of his own regional affiliation. Just five days after he took office, Johnson declared to the nation, "no memorial oration or eulogy could more eloquently honor President Kennedy's memory than the earliest possible passage of the civil rights bill for which he fought. We have talked long enough in this country about equal rights. We have talked for 100 years or more. It is now time to write the next chapter—and to write it in the books of law."

The Senate responded and voted for the first time in its history to impose cloture—a procedure that cuts off debate on a measure before the body. With the southern filibuster thus ended, the Senate passed the 1964 Civil Rights Act, which the president signed into law on July 2. Johnson hoped that the measure would "close the springs of racial poison." The major features of the act prohibited segregation in public accommodations (hotels, restaurants, theaters, and parks, for example) and discriminatory application of voter-registration procedures. It created an Equal Employment Opportunity Commission to ensure equal treatment in hiring, and authorized the government to withhdraw or withhold federal funds from public programs practicing discrimination. Critics of the act complained that it did not go far enough, that it did not require employers to redress racial imbalances in their firms, and that it would not change the attitudes of southern whites in any case.

Yet the law's impact on the South was remarkably swift. Overnight, segregated facilities opened to blacks. Andrew Young recalled returning to a St. Augustine motel five days after the act's passage. Just the previous week, a waitress had poured hot coffee over Young and his group, who were seeking service in the motel restaurant, and the manager had laced the swimming pool with hydrochloric acid just as Young prepared to wade in. "We went back to that same restaurant," Young related, "and those people were just wonderful. They were apologetic. They said, 'we were just afraid of losing our business. We didn't want to be the only ones to be integrated. But if everybody's got to do it, we've been ready for it a long time. We're so glad the president signed this law and now we can be through these troubles.'" While some may question whether this about-face represented a revelation or merely an attempt to avoid prison, the practice of integration was more important for the time being than the attitudes of southern whites. Segregation and the demeaning and inferior condition in which it placed blacks reinforced white perceptions of black inferiority. The removal of segregation—more positively, the practice of integration—undercut a major justification for that perception. Attitudes would follow. As Ralph McGill argued, "there was . . . a great prejudice against women being allowed to vote. . . . Legislation at last succeeded. The end of this discrimination saw the decline of the prejudice." By the

1960s, few thought twice about or commented on a woman entering a polling booth. Eventually, it would be that way with integration. Novelty would become habit, and habit would become the natural order of things.

What was significant in the short run was that in the weeks following July, 1964, compliance was widespread and defiance was minimal. To be sure, some restaurants closed and reopened as private clubs, and political leaders such as George Wallace condemned the federal intrusion. But for the most part, the fortress of segregation, that seeming linchpin of white supremacy, crumbled easily. In accounting for this easy transition, it is important to recognize that, however sturdy the edifice of segregation appeared to outsiders, the events of the early 1960s had weakened its foundation considerably. In a region where public behavior and appearance counted for a great deal, the importance of openly defending honor and principle transcended private reservations about those principles and even about the result of that defense. In 1961, Leslie Dunbar predicted that "once the fight is decisively lost, the typical white Southerner will shrug his shoulders, resume his stride and go on. . . . There is now one fewer fight which history requires of him. He has done his ancestral duty. He is free of part of his load, he can relax a bit more."

There was also some truth in the motel manager's remark to Andrew Young that "we've been ready for it a long time." When not mentally fleeing from reality or drugged by political rhetoric, the white southerner recognized the inevitability of an integrated society. A Gallup poll conducted in January, 1961, indicated that 76 percent of white southerners thought that desegregation of public facilities was inevitable. Already by that date communities, especially in the Upper South, were readying plans for school integration; the sit-ins the previous summer had opened up some facilities downtown; and urban businessmen, though cautious, were becoming more prominent as voices of reason. Finally, a younger generation of white southerners was in the midst of a rebellion of its own, setting its feelings about segregation to music.

Southern music has historically been a blend of black and white, but not until the 1950s was this mixture made so evident, especially by southern white performers. Country music star Hank Williams probably initiated this exposure in the 1940s and early 1950s with his raw blues style in songs such as "Cold, Cold Heart," "Lovesick Blues," and "The Blues Come Around." Williams' battles with drugs and alcohol, his gyrations on stage, and his hard-hitting lyrics and music exuded a "raw, sexual primitivism," as one critic put it. The style and the themes were black, a fact even more apparent by the mid-1950s with the emergence of Elvis Presley from Tupelo, Mississippi, and Buddy Holly from Lubbock, Texas. As Presley described his music to Charlotte *Observer* columnist Kays Gary in 1956, "the Colored folks been singing it and playing it just like I'm doin' now, . . . for more years than I know. They played it like that in the shanties and in their juke joints, and nobody paid it no mind 'til I goose it up. I got it from them."

The success of Presley and Holly opened up white markets and airwaves to southern black performers. Chuck Berry, Fats Domino, and Richard Penniman (Little Richard) led the integration of southern music. Like Presley, they were openly defiant on stage; their movements, their attire (Little Richard favored zoot suits, white shoes, and a six-inch-high pompadour), and their music shocked white adults as they delighted white teenagers. It was not surprising that segregationist groups tried to ban such music from the radio and the concert stage, and cited the NAACP "as the evil force behind rock 'n' roll." The Alabama White Citizens' Councils went so far as to set up a committee "to do away with this vulgar, animalistic, nigger rock & roll bop." Needless to say, they received little cooperation from the state's white teenagers.

In addition, the excesses engendered by the Freedom Rides and the Birmingham demonstrations revulsed most white southerners, regardless of their feelings of the moment on the appropriateness of demonstrations. As Walker Percy observed, "after a while the ordinary citizen gets sick and tired of the climate of violence and of the odor of disgrace which hangs over his region." Most important, the rhetoric of black leaders, especially of Martin Luther King, and the actions of the black demonstrators not only forced whites to recognize the visibility of blacks, but touched their consciences as well. It brought to the surface feelings they may have harbored for quite some time. As Ralph McGill noted in 1961, "all Southerners, save the most obtuse and insensitive, have long carried a private weight of guilt about the inequities of segregation." The religious framework of the movement and its appeal to constitutional ideals pushed that private weight to the surface.

McGill was saying what King and his colleagues had been articulating since Montgomery: that the southern white was not inherently evil, but rather bound by a culture that had constrained his natural instincts for good. The civil rights demonstrations loosened those cultural shackles by revealing that southernness—religious faith, place, past, and manners—was not identical with white supremacy or at least with segregation. Southern blacks used these cultural elements not cynically but because they were southerners, and they touched white souls as a result. Even if whites could not bring themselves to embrace integration mentally, their awareness and guilt over seeing a mirror image of themselves in the black protesters minimized resistance to the law. Eventually they would come to feel good about integration, not necessarily because they had participated in a heroic resistance, but because it was the right thing, the *southern* thing to do.

But even as the barriers of segregation were falling, blacks were dying in Mississippi and Alabama. The small towns and rural areas of those states remained beyond the redemptive touch of the movement. They would become the last great battlegrounds of the civil rights crusade.

VII / The Last Crusade: Voting Rights, 1962–1965

For years, blacks bravely climbed county courthouse steps to register to vote. The registrars, if they were there, would sometimes smile and say, "Who you work for, boy?" and the courage would be gone. On occasion, the voting official would go through the motions, administer a literacy test or inquire about character. But it would be a charade, a way to pass the time of day, material for amusing dinner-table conversation. Once in a while, when things were slow, a few courthouse regulars would teach the prospective voter an indelible lesson in racial etiquette. There were even a few times when a lucky applicant would be registered, though there was no guarantee that his poll tax receipt would not be lost before election day or that his name would not be purged from the voting rolls.

For white southerners, voting was an important part of the regional racial etiquette. Voting, like segregation, was a form of public behavior that reflected the status of both black and white. To admit blacks into the polling booth was to admit political equality, and the carefully tended myths of the Reconstruction era had taught whites that the electoral participation of blacks was an invitation to corruption, disorder, and oppression. It meant that whites could find themselves on the other side of the color line. White political leaders had a significant stake in maintaining this fiction. As New South prophet Henry W. Grady explained candidly in the 1880s, "let the whites divide, what happens? Here is this dangerous and alien influence that holds the balance of power. It cannot be won by argument, for it is without information, understanding, or traditions. It must be bought by race privileges." So the leaders disfranchised blacks, congratulated whites on their regained status, and continued to holler "nigger" at the appropriate times to maintain white solidarity.

White leaders also had long memories. The specter of a poor white and black political alliance, dangerously close in the 1890s, loomed large. Such a merger would not only upset the political balance but could lead to economic changes—tax reforms, educational and social service measures, and regulatory agencies—that would erode or threaten economic privilege in the region. In short, black suffrage could substantially alter the political and economic landscape of southern localities and states.

Voting was such a fundamental American right that the plight of black applicants generated considerable notice in many parts of the country after World War II. It was possible to argue that a lunch counter or a theater was a private enterprise and that the rights of property extended to patron selection, but elections were unmistakably public activities, the foundations of representative government. At a time when the American system and communism were being constantly compared in the forum of world opinion, it would not do for so basic a right to be denied to a segment of the American citizenry.

The Limits of Federalism

The federal government moved to correct the embarrassment. The Eisenhower administration, heartened by its showing among black voters in the 1956 presidential election, supported a voting-rights bill in Congress. After passage in the House, Democratic senator and majority leader Lyndon B. Johnson successfully maneuvered a weakened version through the upper chamber. Johnson, a Texan, had not compiled a notable record on civil rights prior to 1957, but he had presidential ambitions and sought to build a constituency with northern Democrats and blacks. The final version of the bill, which President Eisenhower signed into law in August, 1957, authorized the Justice Department to issue injunctions against voting officials who interfered with a citizen's right to register or vote. The bill also established a Commission on Civil Rights to investigate voting-rights violations and a Civil Rights Division within the Justice Department to initiate litigation when violations were uncovered.

The fact that southern lawmakers made only a half-hearted attempt at a filibuster indicated that the Civil Rights Act of 1957 was not perceived as a threat to Dixie's political culture. Only a formal complaint from a locality would set the machinery of the act in motion. Many blacks were unaware of the new law, and those who knew about it feared the inevitable reprisals that would accompany such action. If a black citizen screwed up enough courage to file a complaint, the law provided that the FBI would investigate. The federal agents were accustomed to working closely with local officials, so it was unlikely that they would jeopardize those relationships. In the improbable event that the FBI would certify a complaint and litigation were initiated, there was a good possibility that the case would be tried before a federal district-court judge in sympathy with the defendants.

By 1960, the act had added few blacks to the registration lists, despite the widespread abuses documented by the Civil Rights Commission. The NAACP continued to press for a stronger law, and in 1960, on the eve of a presidential election, Congress passed another voting-rights act. The 1960 Civil Rights Act only marginally strengthened the earlier statute by giving the Civil Rights Division access to local registrar records in order to build a case for litigation.

The access provision assumed that federal district-court judges would direct registrars to turn over their records to Justice Department attorneys. Judge Harold Cox demonstrated the fallacy of that assumption in *U.S.* v. *Lynd*. In August, 1960, the Justice Department requested Forrest County, Mississippi, registrar Theron Lynd to turn over his records in order to prepare a discrimination suit against him for violating the 1960 Civil Rights Act. Lynd refused, and federal attorneys petitioned Judge Cox in January, 1961, to order Lynd to comply with their request. Cox did nothing. In July, the Justice Department filed its request again. Seven months later, in February, 1962, Judge Cox dismissed the January, 1961, petition on the grounds that the July request superseded it. One month later, Cox called the case for trial. The Justice Department still had not received the registrar's records. Without that evidence, Cox ruled against the department.

Black registration figures reflected the ineffectiveness of federal initiatives. In 1958, the Civil Rights Commission discovered forty-four counties in the Deep South where not a single black was registered to vote, although blacks formed a majority or a strong minority of eligible voters in these districts. Altogether in the South, black voter registration had increased by only 3 percent between 1957 and 1960, but even that modest figure was misleading, since almost all of that gain occurred in the cities. Rural blacks, especially in the Deep South, remained disfranchised.

The persistence of voting-rights abuses embarrassed not only the federal government but a number of white southerners as well. The blatant nature of black disfranchisement became too obvious to ignore. In 1959, the Greensboro *Daily News* declared that "if a Negro is a citizen he should be treated as any other citizen in his right to the franchise." The Lee County (Ala.) *Bulletin* concurred a year later, stating that "states have failed to act honorably. [Alabama] officials ought to act in good faith in this matter of registering voter applicants regardless of race or color."

The newly installed Kennedy administration, impressed with such indigenous support for voting rights and rhetorically committed to furthering those rights, resumed the federal initiative. There was evidence that Deep South jurisdictions were tightening suffrage qualifications, despite federal law to the contrary. The Georgia legislature, for example, stiffened its literacy qualification in 1957. A political science professor at the University of Georgia conceded that even he might have difficulty passing the test. The Mississippi state legislature considered a constitutional amendment to prohibit citizens convicted of vagrancy, perjury, child desertion, adultery, fornication, larceny, and gambling from voting. When some lawmakers suggested adding habitual drunkenness to the list, objections were raised that such a provision "might even get some of us."

Finally, there was concern within the Kennedy administration that the sit-ins, which began during the president's first full month in office and soon spread throughout much of the South, could trigger violence. This might force federal action that could jeopardize the administration's legislative agenda. By shifting attention to voting rights and redirecting black protest into that channel, the administration hoped to avoid a volatile situation. Registering individual blacks seemed much less threatening than the massing of hundreds of demonstrators in the streets of southern cities. A longer-range consideration was that a growing black electorate in the South could liberalize Democratic party politics in that region, facilitating a better working relationship with the national administration.

Accordingly, Assistant Attorney General Burke Marshall and civil rights adviser Harris Wofford served as intermediaries to introduce SNCC leaders to several philanthropic foundations with the objective of financing a voting-rights drive in the South. Eventually SCLC, CORE, the NAACP, and the Urban League joined SNCC to form the Voter Education Project (VEP), to be administered through Atlanta by the Southern Regional Council. The civil rights conglomerate received grants from the Taconic and Field Foundations as well as from the Edgar Stern Family Fund totaling $870,000. Each organization within the VEP would choose a state and launch a voter-registration drive with the blessings of the Justice Department. The assumption among

VEP workers was that the federal government would be behind them if trouble arose.

The Delta Campaign: A Prison of Fear

SNCC drew Alabama and Mississippi primarily because, as one member recalled, "nobody else wanted 'em." SNCC began its campaign during the spring of 1962 in the Mississippi Delta. The Delta is an unflinchingly flat expanse of fertile land nourished (and occasionally overrun) by the Mississippi River, extending from the northwest quarter of the state up to Memphis, Tennessee. A few weather-beaten shacks dotted the landscape, but mostly it was cotton and soybeans for as far as the eye could see. Blacks still chopped (weeded) the crops by hand and lived under a racial regime that had changed little since the Civil War. They were the poorest of that state's impoverished population, subsisting on a level equal to one-fifth of the federal poverty standard, or $600 per year.

The campaign focused on Greenwood and its environs in Leflore County, the gateway to the Delta. Both Greenwood and Leflore took their names from a wealthy antebellum planter, Greenwood Leflore, who fashioned his plantation house after the Empress Josephine's palace, Malmaison. Leflore maintained his allegiance to the Union during the Civil War and died on his front porch framed by four grandchildren holding American flags over him. A century later, defiance of a different sort marked the area. No sooner had SNCC begun its activity than its workers were arrested and jailed. Though the Justice Department intervened to secure their release, it was only the beginning of SNCC's difficulties. The county cut off welfare to those blacks who had attempted to register, and SNCC soon became more a provider of social services than a civil rights organization.

The economic pressure failed to deter either SNCC or Leflore's blacks. When attempts to register blacks persisted, violence erupted. SNCC leader Bob Moses, a native New Yorker with a master's degree in philosophy from Harvard, received a vicious beating from some whites after attempting to register blacks in Liberty, Mississippi. The whites warned him and a colleague to "get the hell out of town" or they would be killed. In nearby Amite County, a white state legislator shot and killed a black farmer for no other apparent reason than that the farmer had attempted to register to vote. In Winona, SNCC worker Lawrence Guyot, who had gone to the sheriff's office to check on the arrest of some of his colleagues, was worked over for four hours and then charged with attempted murder. In Clinton, twelve blacks who had petitioned the mayor to establish a biracial committee to discuss the community's problems were arrested on the charge of intimidating a public official. Within the year, SNCC, its resources and nerves depleted, abandoned the Delta campaign.

While the other VEP organizations achieved some modest success in other southern states, enfranchising a majority of eligible black voters in Tennessee, Florida, and Texas, only a few blacks were able to register in Alabama and Mississippi. The implied protection from the federal government never materialized—a bitter disappointment to SNCC. But even when the administration attempted to investigate the situation under existing law, Judge W. Harold Cox continued to obstruct Justice Department access to registrars' files.

SNCC workers faced a situation similar to what had confronted Martin Luther King, Jr., and the SCLC after the Albany demonstrations. Not only had the Delta campaign failed, but the national media, after initial interest, generally ignored the voting-rights drive. It was difficult in a rural state to generate a critical mass of people to provoke a headline-grabbing confrontation. Ambushing individual blacks was not a drama; it was commonplace.

Equally important, the strong white reaction had frightened prospective black voters. Mississippi, the "closed society," as exiled university professor James Silver termed it, was shut tight. A rigorous censorship prevailed, blacking out national news broadcasts that depicted the state unfavorably, harassing editors who reported official violence against blacks, banning films that hinted at racial or ethnic brotherhood, deposing ministers who offered contrary interpretations, and corrupting the language to the point where the truth became whatever the newspapers and political leaders declared, regardless of its correspondence to reality. Thus when black leader Medgar Evers was murdered in June, 1963, the Jackson *Daily News* announced that police had arrested a Californian in connection with the crime. It turned out that the suspect was a native Mississippian who had spent a brief portion of his childhood out west. So too, Senator James O. Eastland assured his constituents that "there is no discrimination in Mississippi," and that "all who are qualified to vote, black or white, exercise the right of suffrage." In the senator's native Sunflower County, 161 blacks were registered to vote out of a black population of 31,020 in 1964. When the senator and his colleagues sought to explain the situation to uninformed outsiders, they adopted the following explanatory syllogism, according to native son Walker Percy: "a. There is no ill-feeling in Mississippi between the races; the Negroes like things the way they are; if you don't believe it, I'll call my cook out of the kitchen and you can ask her; b. The trouble is caused by outside agitators who are communist-inspired; c. Therefore, the real issue is between atheistic communism and patriotic God-fearing Mississippians." All of this reflected, Percy noted sadly, "a condition which can only be described . . . as insane."

With internal dissent thus effectively stifled and with external pressure deflected and increasingly weaker, it was not surprising that Delta blacks drew back from participation. Examples of the risks involved in even the appearance of civil rights activity abounded. Rumors of murders and beatings circulated constantly in the black communities. Police placed suspected activists under surveillance, opened mail, and warned family members to stay away from kin involved with voter registration. Anne Moody, who worked in the Delta town of Canton, recalled that her grandmother refused to let her stay at her house and that her sister begged her to give up her registration work because the police were harassing family members. When Moody recruited teenagers to canvass the area, a group of whites peppered them with buckshot to persuade their parents to keep the children at home. The fear wore down even dedicated workers. "It was always there," activist Cleveland Sellers wrote of the fear, "always stretched like a tight steel wire between the pit of the stomach and the center of the brain." The wire would snap on occasion, and the worker would be furloughed. With good reason, SNCC field worker Fannie Lou Hamer of Sunflower County called her native state "the land of the tree and the home of the grave."

But Bob Moses and other SNCC leaders were reluctant to abandon Mississippi and the blacks with whom they had worked and lived. Voting rights would succeed in the state, they believed, only if Mississippi blacks organized and assumed leadership roles. National or even regional civil rights organizations could not superimpose their structures or leaders on local blacks, nor could local black institutions effect change. As Moses explained, "there were very few agencies available in the Negro community that could act as a vehicle for any sort of campaign. The Negro churches could not in general be counted on; the Negro business leaders could also not in general be counted on. . . . Therefore, . . . the only way to run this campaign was to begin to

build a group of young people who wouldn't be responsible economically to any sector of the white community." And building required
education and above all the dissipation of fear that hung over black
Mississippi like a clinging shroud.

Despite the collapse of the campaign, SNCC began this building
process. At least they raised the political consciousness of Delta
blacks. As Hamer noted, "I had never heard until 1962 that black
people could register to vote . . . I didn't know we had that right."
There were also indications by the fall of 1963, however slight, that
some white Mississippians, painfully aware of what Walker Percy
called the "rift . . . between a genuine kindliness and a highly developed individual moral consciousness on the one hand, and on the other
a purely political and amoral view of 'states' rights' at the expense of
human rights," were seeking to close that "rift." Hundreds of women
organized during the summer to smooth the way for the integration of
a few school districts. Also, 650 white men in McComb issued a joint
statement affirming their belief in law and order and opposing the use
of coercion on voting-rights workers. It was likely that many more
white Mississippians felt that way but were still afraid to speak out.
Like the blacks, they were victims of fear as well.

SNCC leaders also took heart from events in Birmingham. The once-
impregnable fortress of segregation had fallen that summer. Perhaps a
dramatic confrontation would facilitate the enfranchisement of blacks
in Mississippi. To that end, Moses contacted the other civil rights
organizations for the purpose of reassembling the Council of Federated
Organizations (COFO), which had formed during the Freedom Rides in
the spring of 1961. The NAACP, CORE, and the SCLC responded
favorably. Together with SNCC, they resolved to implement a strategy
for black voter registration in the state. It was clear to COFO leaders
that, as in Birmingham, their efforts depended on attracting media
coverage that would, in turn, move the federal government to action.

Since blacks were barred from registering or voting in the upcoming
state gubernatorial election, COFO leaders decided to hold a parallel
"election" to demonstrate the eagerness of Mississippi's black population to participate in the political process. The so-called "Freedom
Election" had the additional attraction of avoiding the official electoral machinery, thus reducing the hazards of participation for wary
blacks. COFO presented a slate of "Freedom Candidates" headed by
state NAACP chairman Aaron Henry. Though white officials caught
on to the campaign and tried to intimidate "voters," the election was a

great success as eighty thousand "votes" were cast. The event did indeed generate media attention, though what struck Bob Moses was that some of the coverage focused on the one hundred or so white college students, mostly from Stanford or Yale, who came down to assist in the canvass. During their two-week stay, the students had drawn FBI protection for all of the campaign workers. Perhaps in the future, these students could be as useful for COFO objectives as the black schoolchildren were to Martin Luther King in Birmingham.

By the end of 1963, COFO had become mostly a SNCC operation. The support of the other civil rights groups had not been enthusiastic; there were too many dangers and too few chances for success to commit workers and resources beyond the "Freedom Election." Then, too, efforts focused on lobbying the civil rights bill through Congress, and the battle against segregation in public accommodations was not yet won. Even some SNCC members questioned the high priority given to voting rights. As Clarence Robinson argued, "this house-to-house activity is fine, but people are afraid of what they can't grasp. They never *have* voted, they don't know what it's all about. But they know they can't go to that movie." Bob Moses disagreed, believing that the ability to sit down and eat with whites at lunch counters (the action that, ironically, had produced SNCC) was meaningless unless you could afford to eat in the first place. And without the ballot, white leaders would be under no compulsion to improve service levels and job opportunities for black citizens.

Freedom Summer: How Many Roads?

Bob Moses and his field director, David Dennis, planned a voter-registration drive for the summer of 1964 in Mississippi. On the face of it, this was nothing more than the resurrection of the failed VEP effort. SNCC leaders, however, proposed to invite hundreds of white college students to the state to assist in registering blacks. They knew that few blacks would actually be registered that summer, but they hoped that the presence of white college students would provoke the kind of reaction to make voting rights a national priority and to create a moral drama. Both Moses and Dennis understood that the likely response of some white Mississippians to the "invasion" of their state by northern college students would be violent. As Dennis calculated, "we knew that if we had brought in a thousand blacks, the country would have watched them slaughtered without doing anything about it. Bring a thousand whites and the country is going to react to that." Indeed, another SNCC worker, Lawrence Guyot, estimated that prior to 1964 sixty-three blacks had been murdered in Mississippi as a result of voter-registration campaigns, and the media had generally ignored the killings.

By mid-June, hundreds of student-volunteers had gathered in Oxford, Ohio, for a briefing prior to their descent into Mississippi. The sessions covered the type of work expected of the volunteers as well as an overview of Mississippi society and politics. The time was too short for reflection on why the state's white population behaved that way, on the generations of poverty and cynical leadership, or on the nature of regional culture. As Stephen Mitchell Bingham, a volunteer from Connecticut, complained, "we had, unfortunately, no fair idea of the white southerner." Perhaps it would have made no difference, considering the students' short stay in the Deep South and the confrontational character of their work, but, as Bingham noted, the absence of this perspective meant that the volunteers went south "hating what the staff hated, believing what others believed *because* others believed it." The moral foundation of the struggle and the ability to separate the sin from the sinner were missing.

The volunteers had time enough to learn fear, however. Discussion leaders such as Bob Moses told of earlier voter-registration drives and the fates of other workers. He recalled for the students a song Fannie Lou Hamer sang: "If you miss me from the freedom fight, / You can't find me nowhere, / Come on over to the graveyard, / I'll be buried over there."

The buses and cars crowded with the forewarned crusaders headed south and dropped off their passengers at small-town depots or weather-beaten stores stuck in the middle of a soybean field. June was "Hospitality Month" in Mississippi, and blacks opened their homes to the young visitors and with polite amusement listened to their optimism. The volunteers quickly fell into a routine, waking up at dawn, washing at the cold water pump (90 percent of black households in Mississippi lacked indoor plumbing), and taking a breakfast of pancakes before heading off in several cars to predetermined areas in order to canvass. At times they noticed patrol cars monitoring their movements. Even when law enforcement officials were not about, the volunteers found it difficult to break through the fear of the rural and small-town blacks. Rural blacks, well schooled in racial etiquette and mindful of the danger involved in even talking with these outsiders, politely agreed with everything the white workers said, but as one white college student noted in frustration, "we knew we were not getting across . . . we were a danger to them." The workers tried mass meetings at local churches to overcome this problem; the blacks sang freedom songs and signed lists promising to visit the courthouse, but few ever undertook that dangerous journey.

The Freedom Summer was less than a week old when news spread that three COFO workers were missing near Philadelphia, Mississippi, in Neshoba County. Michael Schwerner was a twenty-four-year-old social worker from New York City who had been in the state since January running a COFO community center in Meridian, Mississippi, with his wife, Rita. Andrew Goodman, twenty-one years old, was a student at Queens College in New York. James Chaney, also twenty-one, was a black Mississippian who had been working as a CORE volunteer. The three had come to Neshoba County to inspect the ruins of a black church recently burned by night riders and to reassure blacks in the area that the voter-registration drive would continue. On their way back to Meridian, they passed through Philadelphia, and just outside of that town deputy sheriff Cecil Price arrested them. They were never seen alive again.

Six weeks later, the FBI uncovered three bodies from an earthen dam near Philadelphia. Long before then, the Freedom Summer workers had known the fate of Schwerner, Chaney, and Goodman despite fervent denials by Neshoba County sheriff Lawrence Rainey. The fear that had immobilized much of the black community now accompanied the white volunteers on every canvass. As Bingham related, "we lived in a perpetual state, not of fear so much as rational apprehension." Whatever it was called, it constrained the workers' movements and caused many workers to go about their rounds armed. It was not until December that the FBI arrested twenty-one men, including the sheriff and deputy sheriff, for carrying out a Klan-inspired plot to murder the three workers. Three years later, an all-white jury returned a guilty verdict against seven of the defendants. Judge W. Harold Cox meted out sentences, the most severe being a ten-year prison term.

COFO leaders now had the incident that would purportedly galvanize the nation for the cause of voting rights. The nation was indeed shocked by the wanton brutality of the Mississippi murders, but as the college students filtered back north in August, the spotlight on voting rights dimmed. The country was immersed in a presidential campaign, and registration drives became a sideshow. Alone now, COFO counted the results of the Freedom Summer: 35 shooting incidents; 30 homes and other buildings bombed; 80 persons beaten; 6 murders; and 1,200 blacks registered to vote across the state.

Freedom Summer was more a casualty list than a moral drama. In particular, the murders of the three volunteers early in the campaign altered the tone of the effort from an idealistic crusade against injustice to an embittered fight for survival. At James Chaney's funeral, David Dennis cried out in anguish, "I've got vengeance in my heart tonight. Don't just look at me and go back and tell folks you've been to a nice service. . . . If you go back home and sit down and take what these white men in Mississippi are doing to us . . . if you take it and don't do something about it . . . then God damn your souls!" Dennis' grief was understandable. By expressing it in such a manner, however, he risked losing the moral imperative. Throughout the Birmingham drama—the water hoses on helpless schoolchildren and the bombing of the Sixteenth Street Baptist Church—King had struck a deliberate pose of nonviolence, focusing on the redemptive nature of suffering. This as much as the events themselves stirred white southerners and the nation. Despite the obvious justice of the voting-rights cause, COFO leaders failed to frame it in a rhetoric appropriate to the regional culture or for a national policy initiative. The solution to voting rights awaited another crusade.

In the fall of 1964, Martin Luther King and his SCLC staff met to develop a strategy to focus national attention on black suffrage in the South. Another Birmingham-type confrontation would be necessary in order to fulfill that objective. As King explained in an article in the *New Republic* early in 1965, the strategy was relatively straightforward. It consisted of four components: "a. Nonviolent demonstrators go into the streets to exercise their constitutional rights; b. Racists resist by unleashing violence against them; c. Americans of conscience in the name of decency demand federal intervention and legislation; d. The Administration, under mass pressure, initiates measures of immediate intervention and remedial legislation."

King's candid admission that the success of his program depended in great part on provoking violence might have shocked some readers more accustomed to softer rhetoric from the prophet of nonviolence, but it was merely a simple statement of the strategy that King and his aides had followed with varied success since the beginning of the decade. The difficult feature of the plan was to find a suitable target. Mississippi was a likely choice: it was to voting rights what Birmingham had been to segregation. But the Freedom Summer had demonstrated that a statewide campaign covering mostly rural districts was not likely to produce the type of focused event implied by King's strategy. Instead, King chose Dallas County, Alabama, and its county seat, Selma.

Selma: "Marchin' On to Freedom Land"

Selma was a lovely southern town nestled gently above the Alabama River, a place of front porches, generous shade trees, white frame houses, and iced tea. Selma was at its loveliest in the spring, in March, when the residential streets of the well-tended white neighborhoods came alive with color and fragrance, where muffled voices mixed with gentle breezes in an expectant air of renewed life. Tree-lined Broad Street concealed the town's business activities, prosperous yet even-paced. At the foot of Broad, the Edmund Pettus Bridge, named for a Confederate brigadier general, arched gracefully above the river, an appropriate denouement to the community's graceful way of life.

Hidden away from the consciousness of lovely Selma lay another town off Broad, down Jeff Davis Avenue. There, Selma's blacks lived in shanties and drab rows of federal housing streaked with diesel soot from the passing engines of the L&N Railroad, whose tracks skirted the district. Soon these two disparate worlds would collide. Though the physical and psychological distances would persist, the two Selmas would henceforth be cognizant of each other.

Since the spring of 1962, black Selma had attempted to make this introduction by mounting a voter-registration drive. In two years, the effort netted a total of 93 new registrants. All told, 2.1 percent of eligible black voters were on the registration lists of Dallas County by that time. King quipped that, at this rate, "it would take about 103 years to register the adult Negroes." Nor were prospects good that the situation would change for the better. Dallas County officials, responding to the pressure from the black community, stiffened registration requirements in February, 1964, reducing the registrars' schedule to two days per month and lengthening the application procedure by presenting prospective voters with a list of sixty-eight difficult questions about the state constitution and government. These requirements were additions to the already extensive stipulations asking applicants to read, write, and interpret any article of the federal constitution and to present testimonials of good character from registered voters (read white voters).

Despite these restrictive regulations, King felt that he had an unwitting ally in the person of Dallas County sheriff Jim Clark. The sheriff, almost a caricature of the Hollywood-inspired image of a Deep South lawman, was a tall, beer-bellied man who sported mirror sunglasses and a lapel button proclaiming "NEVER!" He wore an Eisenhower jacket and a helmet, and carried a swagger stick. Julian Bond said that he looked like General Patton. Clark's racial views were straightforward: when a reporter asked him if a particular woman defendant was married, the sheriff replied, "She's a nigger woman and she hasn't got a Miss or a Mrs. in front of her name." Public and private law enforcement had traditionally blended together in the South, especially in rural areas, and Clark was perhaps most notable in the vicinity for the personal posse that he had raised and led to racial trouble spots around the state. In defense of white supremacy, he had ridden to Montgomery during the bus boycott, to Tuscaloosa where he supported Governor Wallace's last stand for segregation at the university, and had offered to take his men to Birmingham. He had a reputation for a quick temper, and blacks perceived him as a "Bull" Connor of the Black Belt.

Selma's other public officials represented the newer breed of educated, business-oriented leadership that was becoming common throughout the urban South. Newly elected mayor Joe Smitherman, a small man in his late twenties with short black hair and large ears, had succeeded Chris Heinz, a vocal segregationist. The new mayor hired Wilson Baker, an old adversary of Clark, to serve as public safety director. After losing the sheriff's race to Clark in 1958, Baker left Selma to take a faculty position at the University of Alabama, teaching law enforcement. Though Smitherman had assured white residents that "I am a segregationist," his main objective was to build the economic base of the community, and Baker was merely one symbol of the reorientation at city hall. Smitherman was in the midst of negotiating with the Hammermill Paper Company to build a major facility in Selma when the Dallas County Voters' League, a coalition of black groups, invited Martin Luther King, Jr., and the SCLC to come to Selma and launch a voter-registration drive.

King arrived in early January, 1965, and immediately organized the black community for marches to the Dallas County Courthouse in Selma. By the end of the month, Sheriff Clark had arrested nearly two thousand demonstrators and had held his temper. King decided to increase the pressure on February 1 by gathering seven hundred supporters, many of them children, and marching on the courthouse. They were arrested without incident. King continued the pressure of these mass pilgrimages to the courthouse throughout the month, and he succeeded in mobilizing middle-class blacks for their first protest marches, despite the danger of losing their jobs. Though Clark and his men occasionally lost control and began to shove and kick some of the demonstrators, they avoided the type of excessive violence that would create a national audience.

During the last week in February, King's dilemma heightened. A state trooper in nearby Marion, Alabama, had seriously wounded a black teenager, Jimmie Lee Jackson. The youngster and his mother were fleeing police who had forcibly dispersed a voting-rights demonstration. He died eight days later, but the incident failed to generate much national publicity about the ongoing repression in Alabama's Black Belt. Disillusionment and impatience were surging through the black community. King felt that something dramatic had to occur or the Dallas County campaign would collapse and with it the opportunity for black suffrage in the Deep South.

King and his SCLC aides discussed the possibility of a march from Marion to Montgomery to protest Jackson's death and to present voting-rights petitions to Governor Wallace, but King felt that the proposed route was too lengthy, so the starting point was changed to Selma, fifty-four miles from the state capital. The SCLC leadership set March 7, one week after Jackson's funeral, as the date for the march to Montgomery. King returned to SCLC headquarters in Atlanta and left his lieutenant Hosea Williams in charge. King's absence probably resulted from his desire to avoid a confrontation with President Johnson, who requested that King not lead the march, fearing his arrest or worse. King was also aware that the president was in the process of preparing voting-rights legislation.

On Sunday morning, March 7, white Selma was in a festive mood. Confederate flags decked parts of the town, and sales in firecrackers were brisk. Some families prepared picnic lunches to take to Pettus Bridge, which the demonstrators had to cross on the road to Montgomery. A different mood prevailed inside Brown's Chapel AME Church on Sylvan Street in the black section of town. As the March wind rattled against the windows, Hosea Williams addressed the two thousand marchers and supporters squeezed into the church. "I believe in the resurrection," he intoned. "But if you read your Bible carefully, you will notice that resurrection comes *after* crucifixion. If it is necessary to bring out the Southern white man's hatred by letting him beat us, then that is what we must do." Williams impressed upon the marchers the importance of provoking violence while not participating in it. "We must pray that we are attacked, for if the sheriff does nothing to stop us, if the state troopers help us accomplish our long walk, if the governor meets us on the steps of the Capitol, . . . then we have lost. . . . We must pray, in God's name, for the white man to commit violence, and *we must not fight back!*"

The congregation prayed silently, interrupted by a single, thin soprano voice singing, "Be not dismayed whate'er betide, / God will take care of you," and soon all were lifting their voices: "Beneath His wings of love abide, / God will take care of you." Six hundred marchers walked double-file from the church with the hymn on their lips. They marched down Sylvan Street, some clutching tiny American flags, then turned onto Water Avenue and eventually onto Broad Street toward Pettus Bridge. They began to climb the bridge, still singing, looking straight ahead, trying not to think about Jim Clark and his posse who had watched the procession pass down Broad.

Deployed across the four-lane expanse of Highway 80 on the opposite side of the bridge stood Major John Cloud and fifty Alabama state troopers in their black uniforms and black helmets, backed up by thirty of Sheriff Clark's mounted possemen. The troopers had goggles and tin-can snouts covering their faces. Governor Wallace had dispatched Major Cloud and his men to preserve public safety and enforce his order forbidding the march. When the marchers passed the midpoint high above the Alabama River, Major Cloud stepped forward and announced, "I am Major Cloud. This is an unlawful march. It will not be allowed to continue. You have three minutes to disperse." Hosea Williams attempted to have a word with the major, who only repeated his order. Some of the demonstrators knelt to pray, others stood in frozen, fearful silence. Scarcely a minute had passed when the major raised his black-gloved hand and ordered, "Troopers, advance!" On the signal, his men charged toward the demonstrators, accompanied by shrieking rebel yells. Hosea Williams ordered a retreat back across the bridge as the troopers, flailing away with bullwhips and nightsticks, descended on them. Tear gas filled the air, blinding and choking the retreating marchers.

Up to this time, Sheriff Clark and his men on Broad Street were spectators. John Nixon, an observer from the Justice Department, had extracted a pledge from Clark not to pursue the marchers once they had left the bridge. But when the fleeing marchers entered the business district, Clark and the posse converged on them, twirling lassos of rubber tubing wrapped with barbed wire. They pursued the bloodied demonstrators into the black section of town, stopping only when the marchers made it to the sanctuary of Brown's Chapel.

The ABC television network interrupted its popular "Sunday Night at the Movies" (the film was *Judgment at Nuremburg*) to bring viewers the scenes from Selma. They provoked a reaction not heard since the violence in Birmingham. King in Atlanta sought to capitalize on the national attention by ordering another demonstration on March 9. The SCLC sent out a national call for "people of good will" to join the march. As Andrew Young explained, "we didn't think they'd send out the National Guard to protect black people." Among the new recruits were 450 white clergymen. The atmosphere in the Brown's Chapel headquarters soon changed from despair to inspiration. The Johnson administration, fearing an even worse spectacle, sent former Florida governor Leroy Collins to work out a deal with King. The compromise called for King to lead a group across the bridge. Then, according to the scenario, Major Cloud would order the procession to halt. The marchers would stop and pray briefly, then retreat in an orderly fashion, unmolested by Cloud or Clark.

The script worked until King and his two thousand followers knelt on the bridge to pray. At that point, Major Cloud ordered his troopers to stand aside, and suddenly the road to Montgomery lay open. It was clearly a maneuver to embarrass King, who could do nothing but ask his bewildered followers to turn around and return to Selma. During the next several days, SNCC leaders and young Selma blacks expressed their anger and disappointment at the "Tuesday turnaround." Indeed, the compromise, even prior to Major Cloud's script change, seemed one-sided. The reason for King's strict adherence to the agreement, however, became evident on March 15 when President Johnson addressed a joint session of Congress on the subject of voting rights. Actually, the president had placed the ballot high on his legislative agenda soon after his November election victory. He received more than 90 percent of the black vote nationwide, and black voters were crucial in holding the Upper South for the Democrats. He had directed Attorney General Katzenbach to draft "the next civil rights bill—legislation to secure, once and for all, equal voting rights."

In his March 15 address to the joint session of Congress—the first such personal appearance by a president on a domestic issue since 1946—Johnson adopted the rhetoric of the movement: "Their cause must be our cause too. Because it is not just Negroes, but really it is all of us who must overcome the crippling legacy of bigotry and injustice. And we *shall* overcome." Those last words, Joe Smitherman recalled, were "like a dagger in your heart." King, who watched the speech on television, wept. Two days later, the president dispatched a voting-rights bill to Congress. In addition, he persuaded a sympathetic federal district-court judge, Frank M. Johnson, to expedite his ruling to lift the state's injunction against the march to Montgomery. The president also notified Governor Wallace that he intended to protect the demonstrators with 1,800 federalized Alabama National Guardsmen and would not tolerate interference with the procession.

President Johnson's concern about the potential for violence was well founded. Even prior to his voting-rights address, a gang of white youths had attacked three Unitarian ministers on a Selma street. One of them, the Reverend James J. Reeb of Boston, died from his injuries. The tense week culminated on Sunday, March 21, the scheduled date for the march. A sullenness had settled on Selma, at least among the white community. The holiday atmosphere of two weeks before was gone. Inside Brown's Chapel, the mood was still tense, though the omnipresent fear had receded, and Martin Luther King seized the moment to galvanize the marchers, whose ranks had now swelled to three thousand. "You will be the people that will light a new chapter in the history books of our nation," he promised. "Walk together, children, don't you get weary, and it will lead us to the Promised Land. And Alabama will be a new Alabama and America will be a new America." Flanked by Guardsmen, the marchers followed the familiar path from Sylvan Street, over to Water, onto Broad, and finally across the Edmund Pettus Bridge on the road to Montgomery, singing as they went, "We're marchin' on to Freedom Land."

Four days later, the caravan, joined along the way by an interracial contingent of twenty-five thousand additional demonstrators, marched into Montgomery. If not exactly the "Promised Land," at least it was the satisfying culmination of a particularly difficult campaign. The fact that Governor Wallace refused to meet with the march leaders scarcely surprised or even interested the marchers. They had played for a national audience and had succeeded in drawing its attention. King mounted the Capitol steps, just as Jefferson Davis had little more than a century earlier, and proclaimed the coming of another sort of victory. "I know some of you are asking today, 'How long will it take?' I come to say to you this afternoon," he declared from the very spot where Davis had taken his oath of office as president of the Confederacy, "however difficult the moment, however frustrating the hour, it will not be long because truth pressed to earth will rise again." His rhythmic cadence reached a crescendo as he asked again, "how long? Not long, because no lie can live forever. How long? Not long, because the arm of the moral universe is long but it bends toward justice." King concluded with a ringing declaration that connected the cause of justice both to that conflict a century earlier and to the religious foundation of his crusade. "How long? Not long. Because mine eyes have seen the glory of the coming of the Lord. . . . His truth is marching on! Glory hallelujah! Glory hallelujah! Glory hallelujah!"

Viola Liuzzo, a white housewife from Detroit, was driving down Highway 80 between Montgomery and Selma that night. She had just ferried a carload of marchers back to Selma and was returning to the capital to pick up another group. A car containing four Ku Klux Klansmen pulled alongside her vehicle, shot her in the head, and killed her. An all-white jury in nearby Hayneville eventually acquitted the Klansmen despite the eyewitness testimony of an FBI informant. It seemed as if tragedy had to accompany triumph, as if unmitigated joy was inappropriate until the last vestige of white supremacy crumbled.

On August 6, 1965, President Johnson signed the Voting Rights Act into law. The act applied specifically to Alabama, Georgia, Louisiana, Mississippi, South Carolina, Virginia, and twenty-six counties in North Carolina which, according to congressional formula, had evidenced significant voter discrimination. Aside from suspending literacy tests and other registration subterfuges, the act provided for federal registrars and poll watchers in those districts where blacks had complained about registration abuses. Within two months of the arrival of a federal registrar in Selma, black voter registration had increased from 10 to 60 percent. And the following spring black voters helped to elect Wilson Baker over Jim Clark for sheriff of Dallas County.

After Selma: Not an End, But a Beginning

Although King could not have known it at the time, his address at the Alabama state capitol and the subsequent passage of the Voting Rights Act marked the culmination of a phase in the continuing struggle for racial equality in the South. Some observers have referred to the period ending with the voting-rights legislation as the "Second Reconstruction." The implied connection with the first Reconstruction immediately after the Civil War is misleading, as historian Howard Rabinowitz has argued. The major thrust of the earlier movement was for equal access. The freedmen accepted, even welcomed, segregation as an improvement over their exclusion from southern institutions. The epiphany from Montgomery to Montgomery a century later represented broader aims of full integration and participation in southern life. This included not only institutional involvement but the sharing of jobs and housing as well. As Rabinowitz noted, "there is a world of difference between the call for equal opportunity that dominated the First Reconstruction and the demand for equality of condition which threatened to control the Second."

Scholars have also tended to agree that the 1965 Voting Rights Act marked the end of the civil rights movement. They have argued that the disintegration of the interracial coalition, the internal dissension among the various civil rights groups, the difficulty of focusing strategies and objectives, the distraction of the war in Vietnam, the white backlash against black rights in the aftermath of northern urban riots, and the pursuit of a "southern strategy" by a Republican administration all served to deaden the moral intensity and policy momentum generated by the movement in the early 1960s. While these events slowed the advance of blacks in the South, they did not end the civil rights movement in the region.

For one thing, writers have overemphasized the national dimensions of the movement. While the legislation and court rulings as well as the major events such as Birmingham and Selma deserve a center-stage role in any account of the period, it is important not to lose sight of the fact that the civil rights movement was comprised of many smaller movements. The tributaries of local activity flowed together to form the mainstream of the movement. Most of this activity occurred away from the national spotlight and away from the strategies of national or even of regional organizations. Black communities throughout the South reached deeply into their institutional heritage, or with the help of the outside groups formed new alliances to fashion an attack on the racial status quo. Churches, black schools, political clubs, and local branches of national civil rights or labor organizations formed the foundation of the movement at the local level. These institutions and the people who emerged to leadership and participation from them persisted after 1965, ready to pursue new goals for local blacks. These were the individuals and organizations that would put into practice the legal and legislative gains of the early 1960s. In this view, the 1965 Voting Rights Act represented not so much an end as the beginning of a maturation process for southern blacks. Leadership and participation had left them well armed with self-respect, identity, and visibility to continue the pressure against the vestiges of white supremacy.

Thus fortified, southern blacks, even in smaller communities, were able to strike down the demeaning racial etiquette that had governed contact between the races since the days of the Old South. The averted eyes, the shuffling response, the deferential tone, the careful choice of conversation topics, and the acknowledgment of "boy," "auntie," or "uncle" as proper names receded from public behavior and consequently as a reminder and definer of inferior status. This was especially so for younger blacks schooled in the movement. The readjustment in public behavior was as crucial, if much less publicized, as the ability to eat at lunch counters or even to cast a vote. Southern culture placed considerable emphasis on etiquette, not only because it made human interaction more pleasant, but also because it served to place people. At the least, the new etiquette placed blacks as persons.

Civil Rights and White Southerners: The Fruits of Liberation

This is not to say that the civil rights movement continued on only as a legacy among its black participants, for one of the most important characteristics of the movement was that it engaged southern whites as well, sometimes unwittingly and often unwillingly. The movement offered whites an education about the blacks in their midst. The events of the fifties and sixties supplied whites with numerous examples of how their preconceptions concerning blacks were erroneous, as events transported southern whites beyond their maids and shoeshine boys to ministers, professionals, and students—a class of blacks previously beyond their comprehension because it jarred the image of inferiority. The movement, in short, enabled whites to close a personal gap between reality and myth. The oft-heard rationale about contented blacks living in good environments could no longer be maintained when those same blacks were marching in the streets. As eyewitnesses, television watchers, or newspaper readers, whites found it difficult to escape the import of the events on the front lines. Whereas prior to the 1960s it was relatively easy for a white southerner to conjure up the image of inferiority in his daily encounters with blacks, other contradictory and often painful images surfaced when whites met blacks after 1965.

On occasion, the education became a revelatory experience for white southerners. South Carolina senator Ernest F. Hollings recalled that moment in his life when the verities of his culture suddenly disappeared to reveal a different truth. It came to him when he read Martin Luther King's "Letter from Birmingham Jail." Hollings admitted that "as governor, for four years I enforced those Jim Crow laws. I did not understand, I did not appreciate what King had in mind . . . until he wrote that letter. He opened my eyes and he set me free." True enough, such awareness and repentance may not have been general among white southerners, but numbers were not that important. What was important, especially for the continuation of racial reconciliation, was that at least a few whites attained enlightenment. Referring to God's pledge in Genesis not to destroy Sodom if only ten righteous people could be found there, German theologian Dietrich Bonhoeffer observed that God "is able to see the whole people in a few, just as he saw and reconciled in One the whole of humanity."

Whatever the number of the redeemed, in the long run the experience of the movement would permeate southern culture. Perhaps the most signal aspect of the battle against white supremacy was its restorative impact on that culture. In terms of the important religious element of southern culture, the extirpation of white supremacy facilitated a reconciliation with God since, as Will Campbell noted, the classification and judging of groups denied "the sovereignty of God." In addition, by removing the public obsession with race, southern blacks enabled whites to regain contact with other cultural elements such as past, place, and manners. As theologian James Sellers noted, that obsession had diverted southerners from the enjoyment and learning derived from their land and history. The "domain of superior status" was a great temptation to the white southerner, but now he had the opportunity, courtesy of his black neighbors, to pursue his true destiny. The South could leaven "the nation with its sense of the land, personal relations, [and] the past." The movement had taught that white supremacy was not synonymous with southern culture; in fact, it was inhibiting the exercise of that culture.

This inhibition was especially evident with respect to the white southerner's sense of past, his perspective on history. The belief in the inferiority of the black man was at the center of that perspective, but the events of the sixties demonstrated, as James McBride Dabbs argued, that blacks and whites had been "fused by the fires of history." They had shared the same land, defeat, poverty, ignorance, and exploitation. And now blacks were imparting the lessons of that past to whites in order to remove the burdens from both races. With blacks as partners instead of objects, whites could allow their historical perspective to gain a maturity and an understanding that would liberate the future. The movement, by debunking one important myth of that perspective—black inferiority—called into question the meaning of other historical myths such as the Lost Cause, the Old South, and southern society after the Civil War. The movement did not necessarily degrade these myths so much as allow for varying interpretations. It was no coincidence, for example, that white southern historians launched major revisions on these themes in the fifties and sixties.

The liberation of southern history reflected the waning of the fortress mentality that had guarded regional culture prior to the 1960s. The victories in school desegregation, public accommodations, and voting rights dissipated the southern obsession with race. Race was the topic that colored all other aspects of regional life. It intruded heavily into politics; it limited economic development; it restricted the free flow of ideas and hence the education process for both races; and it prevented the cooperation of the races to build a better South for both. "By accepting the legal direction to obey the Constitution and do what was morally right," Ralph McGill observed in 1968, "the Southern white man was freed to advance his economy, to remove his political system from bondage, and to begin improving the quality of his education so that it would give Southern children equal opportunity . . . with children in the rest of the nation." It was no coincidence that the Sunbelt and racial reconciliation emerged in tandem in the mid-1960s.

Above all, the movement enabled the white southerner to be himself. By removing the false pride of racial superiority and the etiquette that accompanied it, black southerners allowed whites to exercise the gentility and love that derived from their rural-based culture. Black writer C. V. Roman reported in 1916 that he had visited a southern city and witnessed "a modest-appearing, well-dressed, but frail colored woman with a child in her arms attempt to board a street-car. She was about to fall. The conductor started to help her, then looked at the other passengers and desisted." Nearly a half century later, Pat Watters related the story of a white teacher in a Black Belt town who had one black boy in her second-grade class. On the last day of school, it was the custom for the students to come by her desk for a good-bye hug. "And do you know," the teacher explained to Watters, "that little colored boy came too, holding his arms out to me, just like the rest. And I just had to push him away. All the other children were there watching. I just had to." The movement, by removing the stamp of inferiority and routing the orthodoxies of race relations, proffered a choice to whites. They could now act on their good instincts. As Martin Luther King had noted many times, it was the sin, not the sinner, that was the problem with the South.

But whether or not the southern white would accept the choice and assume the new perspective on his culture was another matter. Southern blacks had altered regional race relations less through moral suasion and the promise of redemption than through the compulsion of law. Instead of interpreting events of the sixties as liberating experiences, whites could very well perceive a massive defeat. As historian Joel Williamson argued, "the Southern white psyche in 1965 had reached a new low." The reason for this depression, Williamson concluded, was that "the Southern psyche was long driven to seek respect from the North and love from the Negro. Southerners might survive a lack of respect from the North, but they could not survive continuing manifestations of hate from black people." In short, the victory could produce a massive backlash, a persistent guerrilla war to maintain traditional race relations that would destroy blacks' accomplishments for themselves and their region.

But that was unlikely. In the rural areas of the Deep South, especially in Black Belt areas with relatively significant black populations, the new order doubtless generated hostility, fear, and even depression. But this was a passing South, physically and economically; the future of the region lay elsewhere. In the Piedmont cities and the prosperous farm areas of the Tennessee Valley, quite a different mentality prevailed. It was, as Walker Percy termed it in 1966, "an almost invincible happiness." That "happiness" stemmed from whites' having the region's most tragic problem behind them and believing (however erroneously and self-servingly) that they played a role in its relatively peaceful solution—compared with the conflagrations erupting in northern urban ghettos. Southerners were also happy because they were prosperous and because the North loved them still, despite the self-righteousness hurled in their direction over the previous decade. Indeed, things southern attained a high currency in the North—music, food, life-style, tourist attractions—in direct proportion to the deterioration of the quality of life above the Mason-Dixon Line. And this reversal of feeling occurred relatively quickly: the Watts riot in Los

Angeles followed the signing of the 1965 Voting Rights Act by only five days. The urban crisis was upon us, and the racial dilemma had migrated out of the South.

But there was another reason for the regional good mood of the mid-1960s. The major change in race relations had occurred without destroying southern culture. The demonstrations were not "manifestations of hate," though for some blacks they were; rather, they were witnesses for redemption. Southern blacks sought not to overturn the South or to conquer whites. They sought reconciliation, not annihilation; participation, not domination. "To change," historian George B. Tindall wrote, "is not necessarily to lose one's identity; to change, sometimes, is to find it." And that was the blacks' greatest gift to their region.

Happiness, however, can readily induce forgetfulness or indifference. Black southerners could not count on a general conversion among whites just yet. In the succeeding years, blacks would draw upon their experience and organization to secure their hard-fought victories and forge new ones. To be sure, the last crusade was over. But the fruit of that triumph—the ballot—would play a major role in future challenges. And, as always, the moral imperative, the ground in southern culture, would be the straightest path to the fulfillment of Martin Luther King's dream.

First black student in a Fort Smith, Arkansas, elementary school, September, 1957. Numerous school districts in Arkansas, Texas, Kentucky, and Tennessee began to integrate their classrooms relatively quickly after the 1954 *Brown* decision.

A white girl responds to the integration of Central High School in Little Rock, Arkansas: "They came right into my classroom and sat down!" October, 1957.

Turned away from church, *ca.* 1963.

"It's Nice to Have You in Birmingham," September, 1963.

Sit-in at Woolworth's lunch counter, Birmingham, 1961.

Selling flowers rather than serving hamburgers: Woolworth's response to sit-ins in Birmingham, June, 1963.

Injured Freedom Rider "welcomed" to Birmingham, May, 1961. Birmingham *News*

The children's crusade begins. Birmingham public safety commissioner Eugene "Bull" Connor (the man on the right with his back to the camera) marches schoolchildren off to jail, May, 1963. Birmingham *News*

Dogs and hoses, Birmingham, May, 1963.

Birmingham *News*

Saying grace. Religious values were paramount for Dr. King and the movement he led.

National Archives

Rev. Martin Luther King, Jr., Rev. Fred L. Shuttlesworth, and Rev. Ralph David Abernathy note progress in discussions with white businessmen over the desegregation of public facilities and the employment of blacks in downtown Alabama, May 8, 1963.

Birmingham *News*

One result of the negotiations: the bombing of the home of Rev. A. D. King, Martin Luther King, Jr.'s brother, May 12, 1963. King and the six members of his family escaped injury.

Birmingham *News*

The battle site: Kelly Ingram Park in Birmingham, with the 16th Street Baptist Church in the background, June, 1963.

Library of Congress

State police clean their weapons in Kelly Ingram Park, June, 1963.   Library of Congress

Police and the FBI sift through debris at the bombed 16th Street Baptist Church, September 16, 1963.   From the Archives Collection, Birmingham Public Library, Birmingham, Alabama

"This Do in Remembrance of Me": the damaged interior of the 16th Street Baptist Church, September 15, 1963.   From the Archives Collection, Birmingham Public Library, Birmingham, Alabama

Standing in the schoolhouse door: Governor George C. Wallace confronts U.S. Deputy Attorney General Nicholas Katzenbach at the University of Alabama, Tuscaloosa, June 11, 1963.

Pickets in front of a Chattanooga swimming pool, *ca.* 1963.

The first organized effort to desegregate a municipal facility, Birmingham Public Library. Later that day, the library voted to desegregate. 1963.

VIII / The First Hurrah: Black Ballots

The scene was chillingly familiar. Blacks and whites marched down Broad Street with Pettus Bridge looming in the distance. Freedom songs filled the spring morning air. Alabama state troopers flanked the bridge and the highway to Montgomery beyond. Television crews and reporters watched expectantly.

But this was ten years later, and the five thousand marchers walked in commemoration, not apprehension. The state troopers were there to provide an escort, not to engage in combat, and the media were there to record a solemn though happy ritual, not to depict a sacrifice. A few months later, Congress would almost routinely approve the extension of the Voting Rights Act by lopsided majorities in both houses and with a majority of southern lawmakers supporting the measure. Still later, a diminished and crippled George Wallace, the governor who refused to meet with the voting-rights demonstrators, would seek them out at the Dexter Avenue Baptist Church. And at the Democratic National Convention in the summer of 1976, a panoply of southern leaders, black and white, Wallace and Coretta Scott King, and the Democratic presidential nominee, Jimmy Carter of Georgia, mounted the podium and led the delegates in a rousing rendition of "We Shall Overcome."

If the struggle for black freedom in the South was also about regional redemption, then these events were witness to the extirpation of race pride as a regional sin and burden. The events were also symbolic of how the battle for the soul of the South had shifted its locus from the streets to the ballot box in the decade after 1965. Atlanta mayor Maynard Jackson, a beneficiary of the new political consciousness among blacks, declared that "anyone looking for the civil-rights movement in the streets is fooling himself. Politics is the civil-rights movement of the 1970s. Politics is our first hurrah. It's where things are today."

The Magic Ballot: Black Political Power and Officeholding

Indeed, the prospects of the ballot for blacks seemed limitless after 1965. Unlike a lunch counter or a movie house, the voting booth was something all adult blacks, regardless of means or location, could enter. In addition, the southern political system had been one of the major props of white supremacy. Politicians had harangued their constituents on the importance of maintaining racial purity in public life, since the system depended upon white solidarity and black isolation. Now that blacks were no longer outcast, it was evident that the system itself would undergo basic change and that the lives of previously disfranchised blacks could only change for the better. Soon after passage of the Voting Rights Act, Martin Luther King predicted that the ballot for blacks "will help to achieve many far-ranging changes during our lifetime." Within a decade, southern white political leaders were confirming King's judgment approvingly. As Louisiana governor Edwin Edwards summarized, the act "provided the catalyst for . . . black power at the polls, not only in electing huge numbers of black legislators, local officials and even now some congressmen, but more important in making white politicians sensitive to their needs and desires." And Alabama senator John Sparkman, asked to assess the state of southern politics in 1974, responded that he was especially grateful for voting rights because it eliminated "the civil rights question as a political issue." For those leaders who feared the worst, Republican congressman John Buchanan from Birmingham reassured that black enfranchisement "has hurt our state approximately as much as black participation has hurt Bear Bryant's football team."

The widespread approbation of black electoral participation reflected a recast southern political system that was significantly more open than the exclusive and fear-ridden mechanism it replaced. No longer encrusted with the barnacles of racism and accompanying demagoguery, southern politics was perhaps more prosaic, but its leaders could attend to more immanent regional issues. The result was particularly rewarding for blacks because, lacking a ballot, they had lacked a voice, and political leaders could safely ignore their needs. Social and political invisibility had complemented each other. The ballot, however, opened up new possibilities.

Blacks sensed these opportunities immediately and proceeded to transform the Voting Rights Act from a vehicle to register voters to a means to attain political power. Voter registration proceeded briskly. In the nine Deep South counties chosen initially by the Justice Department to receive federal registrars, the number of blacks enrolled quadrupled from 1,764 to 6,998 within one week. Leflore County in Mississippi, a bloody voter-registration battleground where SNCC workers had succeeded in registering 33 black voters in four years, increased its black registration to 5,000 within two months after the appearance of federal registrars. Within four years, 59.8 percent of age-eligible blacks were registered in Mississippi, compared with only 6.7 percent prior to 1965. In the South generally by 1970, 60 percent of eligible blacks were registered, compared with a regionwide average of 65 percent for all races.

Registration figures soon translated into voting power. Most noticeably, there was a sharp rise in the number of black elected officials. There were fewer than 100 black officeholders in 1965, more than 500 in 1970, and over 1,600 by 1975. Mississippi had more black officeholders than any other state in the country by the latter date. Most of these officials held local offices in small communities with large black populations: over one-half of the black elected officials in 1975 were city councilmen in towns of less than 10,000 in population. Less than 5 percent held seats in state legislatures, and no black held a statewide elective office, though in 1972 Barbara Jordan of Houston and Atlanta's Andrew Young were elected to Congress. Young was the first black congressman from the Deep South since the nineteenth century.

Although black elected officials were concentrated in poor Black Belt counties with majority black populations, they were able to provide some new, if limited, benefits for fellow blacks. Local government in the South had not been particularly responsive to service needs, regardless of race. Inadequate financial resources—especially in the typical southern urban settlement, the small town—philosophical and traditional opposition to government spending, and class and racial perceptions served to limit local government expenditures (and revenues). Even in the larger metropolitan areas as late as 1975, governments did not spend more than one-half the national average in welfare expenditures, for example. Local governments were also wary of federal spending and especially of the requirements and restrictions attached to most grant-in-aid programs. Black officials, however, possessed no such qualms about federal assistance. For one thing, they owed their elective position in great part to federal legislation; for another, the poverty of their communities inhibited significant investments on infrastructure and social services. Black officials found ready allies in the Johnson administration for funding local capital projects. Foundations that had traditionally supported civil rights causes also provided some support. The Ford Foundation, for example, presented Charles Evers, the black mayor of Fayette, Mississippi, with a $4-million grant.

Aside from improved service levels, black elected officials were able to make a more direct contribution to black economic status and visibility through patronage. Black mayors and council members made key appointments in law enforcement and civil service agencies. Fannie Lou Hamer, a victim of local police brutality in Mississippi during the 1960s, remarked on the advent of a black administration in her hometown of Ruleville in the 1970s, "we've got a real change in the police officials. I don't think at this point they could be any better, because brutality is really not [here]."

Black officials in larger, more affluent communities had the opportunity to make more significant improvements in black life. Atlanta mayor Maynard Jackson exemplified the priorities of black political leadership. Blacks, of course, had voted in Atlanta throughout the twentieth century, though not in appreciable numbers until after World War II, but they were decided junior partners in the ruling business-oriented coalition built by William B. Hartsfield and continued in the 1960s by Ivan Allen, Jr. Despite loyal support, blacks lived and worked in a segregated city as late as 1961, and Hartsfield made only a few token black appointments to local government positions during his lengthy administration. As his police chief, Herbert Jenkins, recalled, "he [Hartsfield] was just as liberal as necessary to get the black vote." Finally, though Atlanta boasted perhaps the most affluent black community in the South, its influence in white business and social circles was minimal.

The Voting Rights Act energized the Atlanta black community and heightened its political consciousness. In addition, by the late 1960s blacks comprised 41 percent of the city's population. In the 1969 mayoral campaign, an outsider, Jewish businessman Sam Massell, won the election with a coalition of blacks and white liberals. Maynard Jackson became vice-mayor. By 1973, Massell had managed to alienate both of these constituencies and Jackson won the office, carrying 95 percent of the black vote and 17.5 percent of the white electorate. Though Jackson supported the economic-development objectives of his predecessors, particularly the expansion of Hartsfield International Airport, he was determined to enlist a greater role for blacks. Accordingly, he set aside 20 percent of city contracts on the airport expansion for minority firms. In addition, Jackson informed bank presidents that evidence of discrimination in loans and promotions to minorities would result in the removal of city funds to banks in Birmingham (an event that would have left Atlanta's bankers perpetually red-faced). Jackson also improved service levels in black neighborhoods and removed the white chief of police who had been a source of friction between blacks and city hall. Although business leaders chafed under what they considered the mayor's arrogance, voters of both races generally approved his administration. Blacks appreciated his forthrightness and the substantive gains in jobs and services, and whites, especially those in the revitalized inner-city neighborhoods such as Inman Park and Ansley Park, liked his emphasis on services rather than on the architectural aggrandizement and highway construction that marked previous administrations. Jackson won a landslide re-election victory in 1977.

A Political Spring Blooms Again: Farewell to the Demagogues

The benefits of suffrage were reflected not only in black officeholders and their policies but in major shifts among white political leaders as well. The Voting Rights Act opened the way for white moderates to ascend to power in a region where, prior to 1965, any position deviating from the orthodoxy of white supremacy was likely to doom a candidacy. By 1972, eleven of the twelve southern states had moderate governors who conspicuously avoided racial rhetoric and had advocated progressive policies in their campaigns. The era of race-mongering ended abruptly.

Jimmy Carter, for example, inaugurated a new political era in Georgia, taking over the statehouse from segregationist governor Lester Maddox in 1970. In the Democratic primary, Carter had opposed school busing and polled only 10 percent of the black vote. In his inauguration speech, however, he declared, "the time for racial discrimination is over. . . . No poor, rural, weak, or black person should ever have to bear the additional burden of being deprived of the opportunity of an education, a job, or simple justice." As governor, Carter appointed blacks to state administrative positions in unprecedented numbers, saw to it that blacks were added to the highway patrol force, and established a biracial commission to review complaints of discrimination. In an important symbolic gesture, he hung a portrait of Martin Luther King in the capitol.

Carter's success in Georgia helped to launch his presidential campaign in 1974, a campaign that no southern white politician could have waged realistically a decade earlier. The amelioration of race and, especially, black voting power made Carter a viable national candidate. His personal redemption reflected a regional renunciation of the sin of race pride. On election night, 1976, as the close presidential race unfolded, the heavy (90 percent) black vote for the former governor of Georgia in Ohio, Pennsylvania, and New York, as well as in southern states Alabama, Texas, and finally Mississippi, proved crucial in Carter's narrow electoral-college victory over Gerald Ford. As Andrew Young recalled the drama, "I heard that it may depend on how Mississippi went, and I thought, 'Lord have mercy.' But when I heard that Mississippi had gone our way, I knew that the hands that picked cotton finally picked the president."

Carter was not, of course, the only white political beneficiary of black ballots. A new generation of southern politicians was emerging. In 1970, Dale Bumpers became governor of Arkansas, handily defeating former governor Orval Faubus with a coalition of working-class whites and blacks. In Florida that same year, Reubin Askew and Lawton Chiles parlayed a similar coalition to victories as governor and senator respectively. The following year, William Waller, a former aide to segregationist governor Ross Barnett, won election as governor of Mississippi on a platform of racial moderation and populist legislation. Southern politicians were learning that hollering "class" was as effective as hollering "nigger" once had been. As Carter's successor in Georgia, George Busbee, noted, "the politics of race has gone with the wind."

Equally important, the composition of state legislatures, those traditional bastions of county courthouse rings, was changing. Reapportionment and black voters helped to elect not only black legislators (Julian Bond in Georgia was only one example) but a number of sympathetic whites as well. Though black representatives, because of their small numbers, found it difficult to initiate legislation that would directly benefit black constituents, they forged alliances with white liberals to block proposals on taxes and service expenditures that would have harmed blacks. On rare occasions, as in the Virginia House of Delegates where blacks pushed through a fair-housing law, their role could be more positive. At the least, the agenda of state government changed from its preoccupation with racial issues. William Winter noted the difference in the Mississippi legislature from the 1950s, when he served there, to 1971 when, as lieutenant governor, he presided over the senate. By the latter date, lawmakers were concerned with "bread-and-butter" issues, not with the protection of white supremacy. Winter attributed the change to the fact that "many legislators are here by virtue of [receiving] more black votes than somebody else did."

The influence of southern black votes extended to the federal level as well. The roll call on the voting-rights extension in 1975 revealed the impact of black enfranchisement on southern congressmen. In the House, the 1974 class of southern Democrats voted twelve to one in favor of extension; the 1972 group supported the measure by a ten to two margin. In the Senate, southern Democrats voted for the extension nine to six. Those Democratic senators elected after 1966 supported the bill by a vote of eight to one; those elected prior to 1966 opposed the extension by a margin of five to one. But the voting-rights extension was only the most obvious reflection of black political power. Black ballots not only elected sympathetic legislators but altered the voting record of those former segregationists who sought to remain in Washington. Walter Flowers, a Democratic congressman from an Alabama district with a black population of 38 percent, boosted his civil rights rating from zero to 44 percent by the early 1970s. As the Birmingham *News* noted, "black votes . . . are . . . a significant factor—and a force which exerts pressure on elected officials regardless of race to represent blacks fairly."

In a broader sense, black voters helped to reorient regional priorities. William Winter's comment about the change among Mississippi's lawmakers was valid for the entire region. Statewide candidates dusted off populist rhetoric, minus the race-baiting, and implied that the decades of hollering "nigger" had not served the white working class well. "Keeping the nigger down" had also left numerous whites in similar positions. More than that, it appeared that these whites were becoming more aware of the fraud behind the old-style southern politics. Atlanta attorney George Dean predicted that some of these whites were "going to start thinking . . . : 'It's time to roll up your sleeves and go after those banks and those corporations.'" Maynard Jackson, who received some modest support from poor white farmers in south Georgia in his quixotic 1968 senatorial campaign against Herman Talmadge, had the same observation in 1971: "The white guy who lives down in Ludowici or Cairo or even in the white ghetto of Atlanta is beginning to tell himself that it is not enough just to be white. When he feeds his children grits and grease for breakfast and sends them in rags and shoeless to an inferior school; when he gets up to go look for the job that has evaded him for five years; . . . you know he's telling himself it's not enough just to be white. . . . Too long have politicians made their money and power by separating black and white Southerners. We are one South, by blood and suffering, by horror and triumph."

The demonstrations and the ensuing federal legislation had opened up the possibility of a cultural reorientation in the South; that past, place, and religion could now advance a new order of race relations instead of reinforcing the old. The education of whites to realize that possibility began after 1965, and voting rights became a major element in that process. Black ballots could count not only *against* historical myths, but *for*, as Maynard Jackson implied, an appreciation of a common heritage.

New Politics and New Policies at the Local Level

At the same time that the new white leaders were seeking to build a coalition of blacks and working-class whites, they also pursued a vigorous policy of economic development. In fact, the two viewpoints complemented each other: the amelioration of race enhanced a state's or a locality's image to outside investors, and economic development provided employment and generated taxes for improved services. Though seemingly an odd couple, populism and development became a common tandem for prospective leaders, both black and white.

The dual focus implied an expanded role for government, local and state, whether as a provider of services or as an aggressive recruiter and promoter of economic activities. This marked a change for southern governments, particularly in the service sector, and local officials learned to become federal grantsmen to serve both purposes. Selma's repentant mayor, Joe Smitherman, coaxed millions of dollars from the federal government to improve black neighborhoods and, not incidentally, his city's infrastructure to make Selma more attractive to potential investors. In 1976, Smitherman received 75 percent of the black vote in his successful re-election campaign.

There was also a decided movement away from the grand but destructive urban renewal and downtown rehabilitation programs of the 1950s and sixties. Part of this shift resulted from a change in priorities and funding at the federal level, but the new emphasis on environmental and neighborhood issues also reflected the increased political presence of blacks and a changed perception of the factors that enhanced a city's image for growth.

Federal grants for urban renewal after World War II enabled southern urban leaders to accomplish two objectives. First, they demolished unsightly dwellings, occupied mainly by blacks near the city center. Second, in place of these structures civic leaders erected hotels, office buildings, civic centers, or highways to ease clogged downtown arteries. Aside from destroying existing black neighborhoods, such policies created a major housing crisis for blacks as remaining black districts became overcrowded with those displaced by the renewal process. In Atlanta between 1957 and 1967, urban renewal accomplished the demolition of 21,000 housing units occupied primarily by blacks; during this time, the city constructed only 5,000 public housing units. City officials reserved renewal land for a stadium, a civic center, and acres of parking lots. Charlotte officials tore down an average of 1,100 housing units per year between 1965 and 1968, replacing them with only 425 new units of public housing. New office buildings and a hotel sprouted on erstwhile residential land, and the result was the same as in Atlanta: increased segregation, low-cost housing shortages, and deterioration of existing housing in remaining black enclaves. Urban renewal followed a similar path in cities elsewhere in the country, but the shortfall between housing units destroyed and new public housing erected was greater in southern cities.

By the early 1970s, changes in federal housing policy as well as increased black political power sensitized local leaders to the benefits of residential preservation. The Voting Rights Act, through its Section 5 provision requiring prior clearance for changes in electoral procedures, encouraged district rather than at-large representation for city council elections, thereby enhancing the political clout of neighborhoods. White residents, particularly those in revitalized inner-city neighborhoods who were concerned about highway extensions, zoning changes, and service levels in the wake of aggressive annexation programs, joined blacks in moderating city hall's penchant for glitzy megaprojects and territorial aggrandizement. The growing presence of black and white neighborhood advocates in city government by the mid-1970s facilitated this change. The new coalition helped to elect Maynard Jackson in Atlanta, Henry L. Marsh III in Richmond, and Clarence Lightner in Raleigh—black mayors who combined racial issues with neighborhood concerns. Major changes in government composition and policy also occurred in San Antonio, Houston, and New Orleans.

Black voting power had changed the political landscape of the South. Black elected officials, the ascendance of white moderates and liberals, new policies, and the decline of race-baiting signaled a new political era for the region. The change in the Black Belt, the region's most conservative and repressive area, was especially significant. In 1973, a staff member of the Southern Regional Council's Voter Education Project recounted her pleasant surprise as she observed a black minister in a rural Mississippi county challenge a white registrar: "I *demand* that you open the doors to that courthouse. We are here to serve notice upon you that it belongs to us too, and you will run things no longer." Two years earlier, a VEP team had traveled through the state's Black Belt registering voters. Julian Bond, one of the leaders of that expedition, recalled the changes he and his staff encountered: "We received police escorts in towns where we might once have been arrested or harassed. . . . In one town where several black men had been killed for first attempting to register and vote, we were welcomed by the white mayor." The press secretary to Mississippi governor John Bell Williams explained the change in behavior: "Things wouldn't have changed one iota, but now these mayors know they'll be ex-mayors if they don't look after those votes."

It was understandable if some black leaders gloated over their new political prospects. Charles Evers, mayor of Fayette, wrote a "letter" to his martyred brother in 1969: "Remember, Medgar, when that old Bilbo warned that rabble if they weren't careful they'd wake up to find those two little nigger boys representing them? Well, he wasn't far wrong. We are representing them, quite a few of them." Evers' tone also reflected the rising self-confidence and self-respect of blacks who could now play some role in their communities and region. As Lawrence Guyot, who worked Mississippi for SNCC in the 1960s, noted, "the number of victories isn't as important as the fact that they symbolize a bit of black authority, a gradual return to respect for those accustomed to having their lives manipulated by white hands."

Holding Off Armageddon: Circumventing Black Suffrage

It would be a mistake to imply that whites graciously handed over their political power to blacks and to white outsiders. The South's white leaders had employed a variety of procedural and rhetorical subterfuges over the years to guard their power, and despite the irresistible combination of federal law and black persistence, some white officials were still prepared to subvert black voting rights. They were motivated not only by fear of losing their power, but by a concern over the policies that black officials would institute and the patronage they would wield. Having grown up with the perception that "black" and "power" were mutually exclusive terms, these whites had sustained the elaborate mechanisms designed to keep blacks powerless—segregation, exclusion, disfranchisement. Now that these trappings of white supremacy were gone, or mostly so, the adjustment to a new order, a new perception, was difficult. Jones Lane, a white representative to the Georgia legislature from Statesboro, referring to his new colleague Julian Bond in 1967, admitted, "I'm scared of him. I'm scared of all those people." When black registration passed white enrollment in Greene County, Alabama, in 1966, a white leader looked toward the upcoming election and cursed, "Goddamn, nothing could be worse than this, this is *Armageddon*."

It was not surprising, then, that some white officials sought to circumvent or undermine the intentions of the Voting Rights Act to keep blacks away from the polls. Since it was difficult to deny outright a black's right to register (such efforts would likely bring on federal registrars), whites resorted to more subtle means of limiting or diluting black voting, although the persistence of black leaders and the cooperation of the federal courts and the Justice Department with their liberal interpretation and enforcement of the provisions of the Voting Rights Act reduced the impact of these ploys.

White efforts to restrict black political power fell generally into two categories: those that discouraged blacks from voting, and those that reduced the impact of black ballots. In the former instance, some jurisdictions attempted to purge registration rolls periodically, alter the location of polling places on short notice or without any notice at all, and reduce the number of voting machines in black districts. The hope was that blacks confronted by one or more of these obstacles would become discouraged and not vote. If these efforts failed to deter them, whites could and did employ more traditional methods, such as threats and intimidation. Despite the improved climate in Mississippi, for example, the 1975 report of the U.S. Civil Rights Commission noted that "acts of violence against blacks involved in the political process still occur often enough in Mississippi that the atmosphere of intimidation and fear has not yet cleared." Voter-registration workers in the state confirmed that fear was still a major obstacle in persuading blacks to register. "Our biggest problem," a worker admitted, "is trying to encourage Negroes to go to the courthouse and register. They are still afraid, they're still frightened, and still fear that there will never be a change for them."

Vote dilution was a more subtle means of circumventing voting-rights legislation. At-large elections, especially at the local level, had traditionally served to maintain class and race exclusivity among elected officials. This method utilized city- or countywide boundaries to form one election district, diluting concentrations of black voters. Between 1964 and 1975, twenty county governments in Georgia, for example, switched from district to at-large elections. Where blacks were numerous, as in the Black Belt, gerrymandering—confining the black population to one electoral district by redrawing district lines— was another dilutionary device. The most celebrated example of gerry- mandering occurred in Tuskegee, Alabama. Anticipating future black participation in the electoral process, the town's all-white city council redrew city boundaries in the late 1950s to exclude most black resi- dents (who comprised the majority of the town's population) from the city. As Marshall Frady put it aptly, the resulting municipal map re- sembled "a Picasso abstract of a chicken." Buoyed by the Voting Rights Act, blacks took the city to court and in *Gomillion* v. *Lightfoot* (1969), the U.S. Supreme Court ruled the Tuskegee gerrymander unconstitu- tional under the act.

Another notorious gerrymander, this one in Mississippi, has sur- vived legal challenges mainly because it involved a uniform redrawing of district boundaries statewide. Prior to 1966, the Delta region of Mississippi, 66 percent of whose residents were black, formed one congressional district. Since few blacks voted, whites dominated the political structure of the area and controlled the congressional seat. In 1966, however, the state legislature redrew the five congressional dis- tricts horizontally across the state, splitting the heavily black Delta into four of the five new districts. All five districts now held a majority- white voting-age population.

Mississippi also pioneered other dilutionary mechanisms, including the open primary. After Charles Evers nearly captured a congressional seat as an independent candidate in 1968, the legislature passed a pri- mary law that abolished party primaries and required all candidates to compete in a nonpartisan or open primary. If no individual received a majority, a run-off primary would occur between the top two candi- dates, and the winner would be elected. The system effectively elimi- nated third-party candidacies and reduced the likelihood of a black victor. Though U.S. Attorney General John Mitchell initially approved the Open Primary Law, a federal district court in Jackson, Mississippi, overturned the procedure.

Perhaps the most subtle method of diluting black votes was annexa- tion, which made it difficult for complainants to prove the discriminatory intent necessary under the Voting Rights Act. Local officials could claim the lure of extra tax revenues or the protection of adjacent land from unregulated development—there were numerous examples of hostile suburbs ringing and strangling cities in the North and Midwest to make a good case for these arguments. In addition, the territorial and demographic accretions that accompanied annexation boosted the image of a growing and thriving metropolis, quite apart from racial considerations. Houston's voracious land appetite, for example, was part of its image as an aggressive, wide-open, prospering city, an investor's delight.

Regardless of motivation, annexation diluted black voting strength. Southern cities that could not annex adjacent territory because of either unfavorable state legislation or the mobilization of suburban jurisdictions experienced black majorities or nearly so by the early 1970s. Atlanta and New Orleans were two of the most prominent cities with black electorates substantial enough to take control of city administrations with only token white support. In 1970, the city of Richmond annexed twenty-three square miles of Chesterfield County that included 43,000 whites and 4,000 blacks. The annexation reduced the city's black population from 52 percent of the total to 42 percent. Black leaders challenged the annexation in court, with city officials maintaining that the additional territory reflected economic necessity rather than racial dilution. In *Richmond* v. *U.S.* (1975), the U.S. Supreme Court upheld the city's contention but required the city to replace its at-large system of voting with a ward (*i.e.*, district) procedure. Though Richmond blacks had lost on the annexation issue, the new voting system enabled them to attain a majority on the city council and elect the city's first black mayor, Henry L. Marsh III. In addition, the annexation and threats of more territorial imperialism led whites to move beyond—and in some cases, far beyond—existing city boundaries, thereby accelerating the decline of white population.

The very real threat of annexation alarmed suburbs in metropolitan areas across the South. Race was a major factor in raising this concern. The expansion of Atlanta's black west-side neighborhoods in the mid-1970s, for example, triggered a "Stop Atlanta" movement in adjacent Cobb County. Even earlier, suburbs around the Norfolk–Newport News area feared encroachment from those increasingly black cities. In the 1960s, two city-county consolidations occurred that effectively shut out Norfolk. The first involved the merger of the resort community of Virginia Beach with Princess Anne County, and the second encompassed semisuburban areas of Norfolk County to form the new town of Chesapeake.

The legal and practical difficulties in reversing annexation aside, blacks attained some notable successes in combating vote obstruction and vote-dilution tactics. Their major weapon was the Section 5 pre-clearance provision of the Voting Rights Act, which received a significant boost from the U.S. Supreme Court in the *Allen* case (1969), expanding the list of procedural alterations that required Justice Department approval. In addition, the ruling affirmed the right of individual citizens and not only the Justice Department to seek judicial enforcement of the pre-clearance provision. This was an important point, because it meant that the strength of pre-clearance did not depend on the willingness of a particular presidential administration to enforce it. Included among the procedures requiring review were redistricting, annexation, changes in polling places, re-registration procedures, filing fees, and at-large elections. Between 1965 and 1981, southern jurisdictions submitted some 35,000 changes for pre-clearance. Though the attorneys general filed objections to only 815 or 2.3 percent of these changes, the Justice Department's practice of negotiating and providing assistance and advice tended to minimize the number of interpositions. Also, the department's enforcement of the provision was strong enough to serve as a deterrent.

"This Ain't Civil Rights No More": The Limits of Black Political Power

Despite relative success in parrying challenges to voting rights, as well as the significant electoral and policy advances discussed earlier, there was growing disillusionment among black voters, especially younger voters, by the early 1970s. Perhaps the increasing skepticism was natural, given the high expectations that followed the passage of the Voting Rights Act in 1965, but also, the shift from the streets to the voting booth involved more than a change in venue. The democratic political process is inherently conservative, existing on compromise, checks and balances, and incremental advances. When blacks entered the process, they had to conform to the rules of existing institutions—political parties, electoral procedures, and the etiquette of legislative bodies—and they were sometimes unprepared for the political arena. John Cashin, a black political leader from Alabama, admitted that "people were not able to bridge the gap between confrontation politics and electoral politics." Mississippi's Charles Evers chided his followers that "this ain't civil rights no more. Y'all got your local candidates. They gotta buy placards, bumper stickers—that stuff ain't free. Prayer and marchin' ain't gonna get elected officials."

On numerous occasions, blacks were unable to turn strong voter-registration figures into votes. Fear, of course, played a role, especially in Black Belt jurisdictions, as did the machinations of local officials with respect to procedures. In rural areas with a high rate of illiteracy and poverty, blacks were susceptible to numerous ruses. Blacks would appear at a polling place and be told that someone already voted in their name or that their names were unaccountably missing from the voting rolls, or they would receive "assistance" in marking paper ballots that they could not read or understand. These were tactics very difficult to catch and prosecute. In addition, rural blacks sometimes found it difficult to obtain time off from their jobs or to secure transportation to polling places. These factors accounted for, to a large degree, the gap between black and white voter participation in rural areas of the South. In 1970, for example, 46 percent of eligible whites voted in non-metropolitan areas, compared with 32 percent of eligible blacks. In metropolitan areas, the figures were closer: 46 percent to 40 percent, respectively. The lower turnout reduced the likelihood of electing blacks or sympathetic whites, which in turn discouraged black participation in the next election.

But even when blacks voted in appreciable numbers there was no certainty that they would support candidates of their best interests. When blacks attained a registration majority in Greene County, Alabama, in 1966, most observers assumed the election of at least a few black candidates in the upcoming contest. When whites retained control of all offices, a puzzled reporter asked one black what happened. He responded, "Well, see, I been knowing Mr. Lee for almost forty years, and I used to foxhunt with his daddy, Mr. Frank. . . . Mr. Lee, he been a pretty fair man." The reporter passed this off as a vestige of the old-fashioned paternalism that had governed race relations in the Black Belt for decades, but although there was undoubtedly some truth in that interpretation, the comment exemplified the personalized politics of the rural South, where personal relations and loyalty counted for more than self-interest or were indistinguishable from it.

The fact that majority or near-majority registration was not tantamount to electoral victory for blacks also indicated that it was incorrect to assume that the black vote was a bloc vote. The Greene County case is at least one instance of this phenomenon, and there were others.

Blacks in the Mississippi Delta voted overwhelmingly for Charles Evers in his unsuccessful 1971 gubernatorial bid but split in support of local black candidates. This may have reflected the appeals of white candidates for black support, genuine or otherwise, or of vestigial paternalism, but it also indicated the presence of factions within the black community.

Given the nature of democratic politics, the emergence of factions among black voters was unsurprising. After all, divisions had existed within black communities long before the civil rights movement, but they frustrated those who sought to use black political power as a directed force for particular candidates and causes. In the view of some, factionalism was a form of self-dilution. Class divisions were a familiar point of conflict within the black community. The political process and its rewards tended to attract middle-class, middle-aged, and relatively well-educated urban blacks whose background and connections suited them to negotiate the financial and strategic obstacles of political campaigns and coalition-building. At the same time, they aroused resentment, especially among younger blacks, veterans of field work and mass protest, who distrusted the conservatism of their elders, suspected their roles in the movement, and were jealous that others who had not laid their lives on the line were reaping the rewards of office, elective or appointed.

The brief history of the Mississippi Freedom Democratic Party (FDP) provides some interesting insights into the generational and class conflicts that characterized black political life. The FDP evolved from the 1963 "Freedom Election" in Mississippi and took shape during the following summer in order to challenge the seating of the state's regular, all-white Democratic party delegation to the upcoming Democratic National Convention in Atlantic City. The FDP included a broad coalition of black leaders—SNCC officials such as David Dennis and Bob Moses; field directors such as Fannie Lou Hamer; and the more traditional black leaders in the state, Aaron Henry and Charles Evers of the NAACP. The FDP also had a few whites, including white college instructor Ed King. They hoped not only to unseat the regular delegation but also, in the process, to present to a national audience the extent of black disfranchisement in Mississippi.

President Johnson wanted to avoid a floor fight over the FDP challenge, so he and his aides pressed for a compromise. With Minnesota senator and vice-presidential hopeful Hubert H. Humphrey taking the lead, the administration offered to seat two FDP delegates—Aaron

Henry and Ed King—and to allow the rest onto the convention floor as "honored guests" without voting privileges. After a bitter debate, the FDP rejected the terms. As Bob Moses recalled with some acrimony, those delegates oriented toward the NAACP—"the more established people from the large cities"—favored the compromise, while the rural delegates, younger and poorer than the others, opposed the administration's terms. These delegates also felt betrayed by the white liberals, especially Senator Humphrey.

The bitterness of this internecine struggle lingered long after Atlantic City. The NAACP pulled out of COFO, Dennis left the state, and Moses assumed an increasingly radical black nationalist position. In the meantime, Charles Evers and Aaron Henry, among others, sought to build an interracial political coalition with white moderates and liberals in order to mount a challenge for the 1968 Democratic National Convention in Chicago. This time, the challenge was successful as the Credentials Committee voted to seat Mississippi's interracial "Loyalist" delegation. The coalition of what historian Neil R. McMillen called "young white moderates and old-line black stalwarts" thereafter became first in line for federal programs and political patronage, while the white "regulars" maintained control within the state. By 1976, however, the two groups had effected a merger, and the guest list for a testimonial dinner honoring Senator Eastland included Evers and Henry. In the process, the rural, more militant, younger blacks were for the most part closed out of political leadership.

Class and age were not the only factors, of course, in generating political divisions among blacks. The nature of politics itself—the spoils of office, government contracts and programs, and the prestige of power—contributed to factionalism as well. In New Orleans, for example, numerous black political organizations vied for black votes: the Southern Organization for Unified Leadership (SOUL) emerged in the late 1960s, primarily in the heavily black Ninth Ward; the Community Organization for Urban Politics (COUP) was based in the Seventh Ward; and splinter groups appeared and disappeared with regularity. White politicians courted these groups avidly. Congressman Gillis Long contributed more than $50,000 to SOUL in the 1971 gubernatorial primary, and $30,000 to COUP. SOUL endorsed segregationist Jamar Adcock for lieutenant governor because he was the favorite and would remember their support when it came time to give out appointments. The work of these organizations for political candidates also paid off in federal patronage. Nils Douglas, head of SOUL, received a

$20,000 legal retainer from the federally funded Family Health Foundation, and his colleague Don Hubbard became director of the agency at a salary of $39,500 in 1973. Black leaders quickly became acculturated to politics Louisiana-style, but such machinations were by no means confined to Louisiana. As one white Alabama politician noted ruefully in the early 1970s, "let's face it: our niggers are acting like white folks."

It was perhaps not surprising that the pace of black registration began to fall off by the early 1970s and that criticism by blacks against black elected officials began to mount at the same time. Virginia Durr recalled a visit she and her husband, Clifford Durr, made to Tuskegee College in 1971. She began talking with some students about the successful struggle for black voting rights when one student interrupted Durr and challenged her upbeat interpretation. "You don't believe that politics is going to do you any good?" Durr asked. The student replied, "No." Her view was that black officials in Tuskegee were no better than their white predecessors. Durr wondered whether the student felt the same way about the black officials in Greene County. "They're a bunch of crooks, too. They're no good." Durr was shocked to discover that no one in the classroom had bothered to register.

Black elected officials sensed the growing restiveness among their constituents and complained that black expectations were unrealistic, given the nature of the political process and the resources available to black leaders. Georgia state senator Leroy Johnson noted that "it's more difficult to be a black legislator than it is to be a white one. The reason is that black people expect more from their politicians than whites. They expect us to move the World." Atlanta's Andrew Young was more sympathetic to the disillusionment of black voters, offering an explanation for that cynicism: "For ten years we went around yelling 'Freedom Now'—and a lot of people translated that into having a black congressman, meaning we're going to have all of our freedom now, so on Monday morning they come to city hall and say, 'Where is it?'"

Black elected officials could not, in fact, deliver a new life to their black constituents. In order to be effective at all, they had to work with white political and business leaders, which inherently limited or proscribed distributionist policies even had they been so inclined. And many were not. Black politicians were recruited, generally, from the black middle class and held the same political objectives as their white colleagues. Although they might be more sensitive to service levels and social issues, they were also supportive of economic development schemes and, at the local level, conscious of their community's image for outside investors. Thus it was not unusual, for example, to see Atlanta's Maynard Jackson firing nine hundred mostly black garbage collectors in 1977 for striking against the city. Nor was it surprising that the policies of black elected officials did not depart significantly from those of their white predecessors. As Julian Bond complained in the mid-1970s, "many of the region's black elected officials have turned out to be only slightly better than the white officials whose places they took."

But Bond was unfair. The typical black officeholder presided in an impoverished rural setting that left little room for improved services and expanded employment opportunities, especially as federal funding receded in the 1970s. As a black politician in Lowndes County, Alabama, discovered, "if you're talking about the county putting up money for something, then forget it." In nearby Greene County, where almost all of the officeholders were black by the early 1970s, black leaders faced a similar circumstance. The county was one of the poorest in the nation: the unemployment rate was over 40 percent, and the median per capita income in 1972 was $400. The county's blacks owed creditors over $5 million. And this was the case in heavily black counties throughout the South. The proportion of families on welfare was five times greater in these counties than elsewhere in the South. Even had black officials in these jurisdictions been well trained and experienced (and most were not), the nature and extent of the problems they confronted were beyond their capabilities and resources to solve.

Even in more affluent locations, black officials found themselves locked into institutional frameworks and financial constraints. In Atlanta, for example, city administrations had neglected or shortchanged black neighborhoods for decades, and the quality and level of services there were significantly below those in white districts. Mayor Ivan Allen, Jr., posed the problem for himself and his successors in the mid-1960s:

> For one hundred years, metropolitan and city centers of the Southeast almost totally ignored anywhere from 25 to 40% of the population. . . . There were no building regulations. There was no code enforcement. There was no planning. There was no effort to provide any form of housing . . . , garbage was not picked up regularly, the streets were not paved. . . . Today in a rapidly expanding market, as millions more people move into urban centers, we find a great need of running fast in both directions. Not only are we

endeavoring to provide extended and better services for all the people who live in the city, but also we are trying to take up the slack of what has been the slums of the deteriorated areas of each city.

It was difficult to reverse planning decisions that cut highways through black neighborhoods or that loaded these districts with high-density, mixed-use zoning that devalued residential properties; difficult to generate sufficient revenues to rectify service inequities or reorder priorities at a time when cities everywhere were engaging in fierce competition for investment dollars; difficult to treat poverty, even in the Atlantas of the South, as the changing nature of the metro-politan economy created a vast disequilibrium in skills and location to the disadvantage of blacks. And it was difficult to govern at all without a modest amount of support from white business leaders, those men who had traditionally formulated policy in the urban South. To main-tain such support, black politicians could not initiate new property taxes or neglect economic development.

There were many examples in the early 1970s of stymied black administrations that had lost white support. White leaders were frac-tious at this time in any case, and the feeling of approaching "Arma-geddon" expressed by the white official in Greene County was shared in other jurisdictions as well, if more subtly. When blacks began to fill important elective positions in Petersburg, Virginia, in 1973, whites began to drop out. As one white leader informed a reporter, whites "just don't get involved in Petersburg. They have their golf games and their bridge games and that's the extent of their civic involvement. Their children are in private schools. . . . So long as they get their garbage picked up, they don't have a stake." An even more extreme withdrawal occurred in Prichard, Alabama, a working-class suburb of Mobile. In 1970, its population of 40,000 inhabitants was divided roughly equally between black and white. As blacks were elected to the town government, whites began to flee to other suburbs. By the end of the decade, Prichard was more than 75 percent black, with one-quarter of its citizens on food stamps, high unemployment, crime, and drug addiction.

Given these constraints, black elected officials probably did well to initiate modest improvement in services and open more public-sector jobs for blacks. Even so, disappointment among the rank and file was understandable. Martin Luther King had predicted in 1965 that "if Negroes could vote . . . there would be no more oppressive poverty."

Now Negroes voted, and poverty persisted. The novelty of having a black face at city hall or in the state legislature wore off quickly—pride dissipated before poverty.

If black voters became disillusioned with black officials, their cynicism grew even greater with the white moderates and liberals whom they had helped to leadership. These new leaders had risen to power espousing racial reconciliation and economic equity, but once in office, they were hardly promoters of incipient class warfare. Though they generally expanded black opportunities within state government and encouraged a climate of racial toleration, they suggested few innovative programs designed to relieve the social inequities that they noted during their campaigns. As Julian Bond commented, "my colleagues are very clever at ingratiating themselves with a few blacks and think that serves as adequate representation. But most of these people are indifferent to the needs of poor people." The suspicion was that populist rhetoric now performed the same function as the old race-baiting diatribes—an effective means of securing elective office rather than an agenda of action once elected. Indeed, the way some of the new leaders eagerly seized on investment and tax incentives and touted cheap, nonunion labor belied the intentions of their election campaigns.

The new breed of southern governors turned out to be a plodding group—competent, devoid of public prejudice, but more like economic-development officers than anything else. Leslie Dunbar of the SRC summarized the group as follows: "These men, even the best of them, have been strikingly empty of ideas. They have presented themselves as 'problem solvers,' as efficient managers, as honest men . . . a managerial class sprung so quickly into political prominence." Because of their "managerial" bent, it was unlikely that they would promote major social legislation, at least nothing that would increase taxes and government spending. As Roy Reed, southern correspondent for the New York *Times*, offered, "none of the new leaders has made real headway in providing industrial jobs for the multitudes of poor people who still live in the black belts. None has found the answers to newer problems such as urban blight and the growing concentration of economic power in fewer hands." Of course, no one else in the rest of the country had found these answers, either, but the point was that many of the new southern leaders might not have even been looking.

The caution of the new white leadership owed to more than their fondness for economic development. The Voting Rights Act had not only helped to thrust individuals such as Jimmy Carter, Dale Bumpers, and Reubin Askew into prominent public office; it had also triggered a major change in southern party politics. Specifically, by the time the new class of governors took office in 1970 and in the years immediately following, a new political force had appeared in the region that would limit the number of innovative policies they dared to put forward.

Hunting for Ducks: A Southern Strategy

Fealty to the Democratic party was a religious affiliation as much as a political preference in the South before World War II, but the national party was growing away from southern influence. This was becoming evident in the Roosevelt administration and would become even more striking during the Truman presidency. The Republicans declined the implied invitation and, in fact, sought to outperform the Democrats on civil rights issues from time to time. The GOP posted strong civil rights planks through the 1960 presidential election. Richard Nixon was a card-carrying member of the NAACP. And the relatively few blacks who could vote in the South favored Eisenhower in the 1956 election.

But the civil rights turmoil in the South during the early 1960s proved too tempting for some national Republican strategists. In 1961, Arizona Republican senator Barry Goldwater, speaking to a gathering in Atlanta, reasoned that "we're not going to get the Negro vote as a bloc in 1964 and 1968 so we ought to go hunting where the ducks are." The "ducks" were, of course, southern whites who were disaffected with the racial changes coming into their midst and who blamed such changes on the Democratic administration in Washington. This was not the first time, of course, that white southerners had been displeased with the national party. The nomination of New York Catholic Al Smith in 1928 and the Truman civil rights program that led to the Dixiecrat defection were earlier indications of revolt, but in these instances there were no realistic alternatives outside of the Democratic party. Senator Goldwater hoped to fill that breach.

Thus, the so-called "southern strategy" was born, though, in truth, Republican leaders from Rutherford Hayes in the nineteenth century to Herbert Hoover in the twentieth had actively explored appeals to southern whites, especially the bleaching of Republican organizations in the region. The 1964 presidential election provided the first major test of the strategy and, with Goldwater as the Republican nominee, the experiment was generally successful. For the first time in history, a

Republican candidate carried the five Deep South states of Louisiana, Mississippi, Alabama, Georgia, and South Carolina. As Walker Percy interpreted the vote in Mississippi, "it would not have mattered if Goldwater had advocated the collectivization of the plantations and open saloons in Jackson; he voted against the Civil Rights bill and that was that." Though Goldwater won only one other state (Arizona), the southern strategy had proved its mettle.

In fairness to Goldwater, his purpose was not to extend and exacerbate racial tensions in the South; he genuinely believed in limited government and felt that the actions of the federal courts and the Congress were beyond the intent of the Constitution. But the finer constitutional points were lost on his admirers in the South. As Ralph McGill reported, "to the rednecks and peckerwoods of the rural areas or to the disenchanted in the cities, the many phrases about individual rights, and the tyranny of the courts mean 'Nigger.'" On his campaign swings through the Deep South, the senator seemed genuinely surprised at times when his recondite discourses would suddenly be interrupted by vigorous applause and cheering. Regardless of motive, however, the southern strategy adopted by the Republican party ensured that the issue of race would remain a part of political campaigns in the region even after segregation and voting rights were ostensibly removed as issues.

There were at least two ironies connected with the southern strategy. First, the Republican pre-emption of racism forced state Democratic parties in the South to accept interracial organization and leadership. The party of white supremacy thus became the party of racial accommodation. Second, the strategy altered the composition and leadership of local Republican organizations. In 1968, successful Arkansas gubernatorial candidate Winthrop Rockefeller polled a whopping 88 percent of the black vote in that state. In 1969, Virginia Republican Linwood Holton received nearly one-half of that state's black vote in his successful bid for governor. Moderate Republicans such as Gil Carmichael in Mississippi, Winfield Dunn in Tennessee, and James Holshouser in North Carolina attracted significant numbers of black votes as well. But the Republicans' southern strategy brought new types into the party, quite different from its urban and mountain base of years past, forcing a sharp swing to the right and, in some cases, purging moderates. Blacks soon had nowhere to go but to the Democrats.

The southern strategy produced a new rhetorical genre in the South, or, more properly, a new variation on an old theme. The rhetoric of the new Republican candidates was blow-dried race-baiting, respectable enough to attract growing numbers of urban businessmen and transplants from the North, but also shrewdly employing veiled code words understandable to working-class whites. Phrases such as *forced busing, law and order, crime in the streets, neighborhood schools,* and *the welfare rolls,* innocuous by themselves, took on deeper meaning in the context of the 1970s. Less subtle were references to "bloc voting," projecting a Reconstruction-era image of hordes of duped blacks marching to the polls to cast ballots for carpetbaggers and scalawags. These latter unsavory individuals were now lumped together under the rubric *Democrat.* As a Leesburg, Virginia, bar patron commented in Willie Morris' *The Last of the Southern Girls* (1973), "there was a time when the only thing around here protecting Republicans was the game laws. Now I might be one of 'em. The niggers are takin' over the Democrats down here." And when the press wanted to exhibit a particularly outlandish quote from a southern politician—a great journalistic sport prior to the 1960s—they invariably chose a southern Republican like Virginia senator William L. Scott, who allegedly stated that "the only reason we need zip codes is because niggers can't read."

The Republican insurgency presented a dilemma for the new breed of southern Democratic leaders. They knew that, regardless of registration drives, black votes alone would not keep them in office. Also, at least as many new white voters, perhaps spurred by black registration and Republican rhetoric, had registered in the decade since 1965. They also realized, privately and never publicly, that the black–working-class white coalition was an ill fit. These groups were in direct competition with each other for jobs and housing. In addition, the whites had been saturated with decades of racial rhetoric that could not be drawn off so easily. Yet these whites had historically formed the backbone of the Democratic party. The trick was to play on that loyalty and tradition in a region where loyalty and tradition counted for much, and at the same time not alienate the black vote, a vote that could stay home or, on occasion, go over to the Republicans. A final twist to the strategic dilemma was that working-class whites, especially in rural areas, were a diminishing portion of the southern population. Sun Belt prosperity had elevated a good many of them into middle-class urban occupations or at least incomes. Added to increasing numbers of white-collar migrants from the North, they seemed especially susceptible to the Republican emphasis on race and fiscal conservatism.

So Democratic candidates and officeholders walked a tightrope to maintain their success. They perfected the straddle. New leaders, such as Dale Bumpers, Sam Nunn of Georgia, Dick Riley of South Carolina, William Winter of Mississippi, Chuck Robb of Virginia, and Robert Morgan of North Carolina, "took various stances on the issues," as political scientist Alexander Lamis noted, but "rarely did their positions form a coherent approach that allowed them to be easily labeled in recognizable partisan terms. And through this straddling process, they managed to remain acceptable to white traditional Democrats who preferred to stay with their party if it was at all possible." The straddle meant that social issues would be approached gingerly, if at all, and the economic problems of the black community would continue. This is not to imply that these Democrats provided do-nothing leadership. Their tenures as governors or United States senators were productive and beneficial for their constituents generally, but in terms of evolving black needs during the 1970s—economic needs—their impact was minimal.

Some blacks were understanding of this tightrope act by the progressive white Democrats, whom they viewed as their natural allies. Commenting on the veiled racial appeals Sam Nunn was making to Georgia's rural whites in the 1974 senatorial campaign, black state representative Bobby Hill explained, "it's obvious what kind of image [Nunn is] trying to portray. . . . But I have a different kind of insight. I served with him for four years . . . in the House. . . . When the chips are down on an issue, I think we can count on him." But most blacks were not in Bobby Hill's position. They were poor, perhaps unemployed, and no doubt wondering what had happened to the revolution that voting rights was supposedly going to generate. Things were just as bad for them, if not worse, in 1976 as they were in 1965, with the difference that they were hopeful in 1965. The political events in the intervening years justified the effusive praises of Maynard Jackson and Andrew Young, as well as of John Sparkman and William Waller. But black political scientist Mack Jones's comment in 1975 was also justified: "The keys to black liberation lie somewhere external to electoral politics." Just as there were now two political parties in the South, there were at least two black communities.

IX / The Rough Side of the Mountain: The Black Economy, 1965–1976

"Where the People?": Twilight on the Farm

Just before Thanksgiving Day, 1966, Charlie White, a poor black tenant farmer in Sumter County, Alabama, received the following letter from his landlord:

> Charlie:
>
> This letter is to advise you that the land which you have been renting from me for the past several years will no longer be available to you for rent. I have rented this land to———Paper Company, and they are going to grow timber on the lands.
>
> This is to give you notice that you will not be able to have the acreage formerly cultivated by you, for the years 1967 and thereafter, and you can make arrangements to get acreage elsewhere.
>
> If you wish to live in the house which you have occupied, you can continue to do so for a monthly rental of $15. The first rent payment will be due on or before the 5th day of January, 1967.
>
> Under my contract with the paper company, you will not be able to have a garden or any cultivable land, or have any pasture or run any livestock, nor will you be able to cut any wood from the woods.
>
> This is to advise you that if you do not wish to rent the house, then you must immediately make your arrangements to vacate the property before January 1, 1967, when the———Paper Company will take charge of the property.
>
> Yours very truly,
> Mrs. Deborah Calhoun

The letter, though brief and to-the-point, spoke volumes of what was occurring throughout the rural South in the mid- and late-1960s. The black farmer was disappearing, a victim of continued mechanization, federal farm programs, and, ironically, the civil rights movement. Whatever sense of noblesse oblige or paternalism that existed in the erstwhile plantation empires had vanished. Charlie White had less than six weeks to pack up a lifetime of farm work and living. The option of remaining on the land was in reality no choice at all; since he was barred from producing the crops that would sustain him, the modest rent might just as well have been a king's ransom. The suggestion "to get acreage elsewhere" was also disingenuous. Few farm owners in the Black Belt were in the market for tenants by the 1960s—whatever seasonal labor was necessary on the mechanized farms of the South could be obtained from nearby towns and cities at cheap wages.

Nor were there alternatives in "public work" (nonfarm employment). The industries that found nonunion, low-tax havens in rural southern counties after World War II were moving out or up to labor-saving machinery; in any case, the skill levels of black sharecroppers and tenants were usually inappropriate for industrial work. The towns and cities of the region offered few opportunities. The southern economy of the 1960s was undergoing a major transformation that would eventually parallel and, in some cases, surpass the national shift to a postindustrial economy that made low-skill, industrial employment obsolete.

The black farmer became a relic. Between 1950 and 1959, the number of black farmers was halved, and during the next decade, the number was cut by two-thirds. By 1969 there were ninety thousand black farmers, compared with nearly one million in 1920. More than half of these remaining farmers were tenants or croppers, compared with 19 percent of the white farmers, and their days on the land were numbered. Blacks invariably cultivated small farms, which were made increasingly inefficient by mechanization, marketing, and institutional improvements on large corporate farms. In addition, landowners like Mrs. Calhoun found that they could make more money by putting their land into timber or soybeans than by maintaining labor-intensive crops such as cotton. Since the federal government continued to take land out of cotton production (with landlords frequently pocketing the checks meant for tenants or croppers), owners found additional incentives to change cultivation patterns.

The institutional supports that might have carried inefficient black tenants or owners through difficult times were lacking. When a group of black farmers asked the Federal Extension Service in Georgia to show them and their wives how to raise vegetables and chickens, the service gave them only perfunctory assistance. There was also reported discrimination in cotton acreage allotments. A black Burke County, Georgia, farmer complained that the Agricultural Stabilization and Conservation Service (ASCS) committee had reduced his acreage, while increasing that of his white neighbor. The manager of the ASCS office in Waynesboro, Georgia, explained to a reporter from *Fortune* magazine that "these minority people who live in these shacks don't want to work. They'd rather go off somewhere and get on relief."

Finally, the civil rights movement provided landlords an additional incentive to modernize their operations. To the extent that the movement penetrated the South's rural areas, blacks were emboldened to demand better terms from farm owners, higher wages, more cooperation from government agencies, and better living conditions. The increased militancy, mild though it was, encouraged landlords to displace their black tenants and sharecroppers. As one black farmer in Alabama noted ruefully in 1967, "them white folks got a lot more interested in machinery after the civil rights bill was passed."

So the black farmer moved to town, obtained odd jobs, and commuted during peak times back to the farm to work for below-subsistence wages, or he may have remained on the land, commuting to town for work. In 1964, the proportion of black farmers working more than one hundred days off the farm was 20 percent; by 1969, that figure had climbed to 40 percent. Those able to find public work, however sporadic, were fortunate in a sense. The typical black farmer caught in displacement during the 1960s was over fifty years old; his health, color, and age were obstacles to even the scraps of work available in the changing southern urban economy.

Something else was lost besides the land and work. Though life on the farm was difficult, a community existed amid the scrub fields and tar-paper shacks. Croppers shared their meager returns, built churches, married, experienced the laughter and tears of children, and of themselves, and rejoiced during holidays. Now the aged remnants of an agrarian people survived in advancing isolation or moved to town to be with relatives. Their hands were their tools, but the economy required other machinery. They spent their days gazing out of cheap-curtained windows, getting by on welfare, if at all, thinking of friends mostly dead and of a life mostly gone. The community was scattered, and the land that had figured so prominently in southern black culture faded from experience, though it lingered in memory. "Y'all remember how it used to be?" Johnny Paul asked wistfully in Ernest Gaines's novel of racial and economic change in rural Louisiana, *A Gathering of Old Men* (1982),

> Thirty, forty of us going out in the field with cane knives, hoes, plows— name it. Sunup to sundown, hard, miserable work, but we managed to get it done. We stuck together, shared what little we had, and loved and respected each other. But just look at things today. Where the people? Where the roses? Where the four-o'clocks? The palm-of-Christians? Where the people used to sing and pray in the church? I'll tell you. Under them trees back there, that's where. And where they used to stay, the weeds got it now, just waiting for the tractor to come plow it up.

Rural Poverty: Denial and Discovery

For those blacks who remained behind, life in the rural South took on a desperate character. Housing, usually inadequate, became more so. Black writer Don Anderson, touring the Black Belt in the mid-1970s, reported that the typical black dwelling had cardboard walls and a tin roof. Some families lived in converted stables or former chicken coops. Indoor plumbing and running water remained luxuries. Health care was nonexistent, even for pregnant women. Cries of hunger from infants pierced the night air, pacified by sugar and water—sometimes the sustenance of an entire household for days. A 1968 housing survey conducted in the Alabama Black Belt found that 95 percent of blacks' housing was dilapidated. Near Americus, Georgia, one enterprising white landlord converted chicken sheds into a five-unit apartment "complex" with the backyard serving as the only toilet facility. When tenants failed to keep up with their rent, the landlord would remove the front door of the offending tenant. One winter, a child was discovered frozen to death in a doorless unit.

Such housing conditions were reflections of the general poverty among rural blacks. In 1969, nearly two of every three blacks in the rural South lived below the poverty line. In Mississippi, the death rate for black infants between one month and one year was five times that of white infants. Life expectancy for rural black men and women was as much as ten years below that of whites. And medical care consisted primarily of home remedies.

These conditions may have existed relatively unchanged for decades, but the general chronic poverty of the South masked the poverty of rural blacks. Few people within or from outside the South, save a scattering of photographers and writers, took note of such living conditions in any case. Even when civil rights workers moved into these areas during the early 1960s, poverty and the circumstances generated by it did not become major concerns. As Don Anderson explained, "the all-black world forced upon us by the color bar caused us to believe that that was the whole problem for black people in the South. All of our thoughts were directed toward ridding ourselves of bars to our legal rights." But as demonstrations and legislation eradicated the color line, "I began to see the more trying problem confronted by a large part of the black race. . . . This was the problem of poverty."

As a handful of people began to investigate this phenomenon in the rural South, they were struck not only by the abjectness of the poverty they encountered but also by the fact that it persisted, if not worsened, amid increasing regional and national affluence. Beginning in the late 1960s, a few white physicians uncovered shocking living conditions among the black poor of the rural South. Dr. Raymond Wheeler of Charlotte journeyed into the Mississippi Delta and discovered bright-eyed black children with "their shriveled arms and swollen bellies, their sickness and pain and the fear and misery of their parents." A South Carolina state health officer, Dr. E. Kenneth Aycock, uncovered similar conditions in the rural areas of his state, where he estimated that over 11 percent of the population, or 300,000 people, went hungry. Southern politicians scoffed at such reports, attributing them to radical political beliefs or to the basic laziness of rural blacks.

South Carolina senator Ernest F. Hollings was one such skeptic, but the reports piqued his curiosity, and he undertook some research on his own. His "poverty tours" in 1969 uncovered widespread hunger, poverty, and health problems in his home state. Equally distressing to a public servant, few county governments in the state were willing to acknowledge the problem, let alone expend funds to deal with it. Only thirteen of South Carolina's forty-six counties had food-stamp programs, for example. Hollings attributed this parsimony to what he called "hunger myopia." As he wrote in his book, *The Case Against Hunger* (1970), "within a forty-mile radius of Timmonsville, SC, there are forty farmers who each received last year over $40,000 from the US government—for not working. This doesn't affect the character of the farmer. He's still as red-blooded, capitalistic, free enterprising, and patriotic as ever before. But give the poor, little hungry child a forty-cent breakfast and you've destroyed his character. You've ruined his incentive."

And Shame in the Cities

Hollings went beyond the work of the physicians by pointing out that poverty was not merely a condition of rural blacks but extended into cities and towns as well—and in some instances blacks were worse off in these locales than they had been decades earlier. In the years following World War II, the typical southern black became an urban dweller. In 1940, 35 percent of the South's black population resided in cities; by 1970, that figure had climbed to 67 percent. Though most blacks migrated to southern cities to improve their economic circumstances, they usually fell into menial occupations, men as day laborers or service workers (shoeshiners, busboys, waiters, and janitors), and women as domestics. In Augusta, Georgia, in 1970, for example, over 90 percent of black employees held menial positions.

There was some hope that the employment situation would change after a combination of executive orders in the Kennedy and Johnson administrations and the 1964 Civil Rights Act charged employers to practice affirmative action (actively to seek and hire black workers) and end discrimination on the job and exclusion in hiring. These measures opened up the predominantly white textile industry to blacks. In South Carolina, for example, less than 5 percent of mill employees were black in 1964; by 1976, nearly one in three textile workers in the state was black. In addition, blacks in other industries who had consistently been passed over for promotions now had legal recourse to ensure fair treatment. Historian Robert J. Norrell recounted the story of Clarence Dean, a worker at the Sloss-Sheffield Steel and Iron Company in Birmingham, who had sought the job of "iron pourer" unsuccessfully for years. Pressing his case again in 1961, in the wake of President Kennedy's Executive Order 10925, which directed companies holding federal contracts to end discriminatory labor practices, Dean received his promotion.

But urban blacks were entering industries that, by the late 1960s and early 1970s, were already in decline. Norrell noted the irony of the steel industry in Birmingham: "Most of the jobs to which they [black workers] had just gained access now disappeared." The Sloss-Sheffield furnace closed down in 1971. Textiles began to suffer from foreign competition and inefficient production methods by the mid-1970s, and a combination of mill closings and mechanization reduced work forces in that industry, which typically followed the "last-hired-first-fired" dictum of labor relations. The situation was scarcely better in other southern industries. No industry, in fact, employed more than 2.6 percent of its black workers in white-collar occupations by 1970. Black women were at a greater disadvantage, concentrated in paper, lumber, and tobacco industries that were in the process of either closing down or mechanizing. More than one-half of the black women in these industries were engaged in the cleaning and maintenance of the factory buildings rather than in the production process itself.

Urban living conditions reflected the blacks' low economic status. During the late 1970s, Joel Garreau, touring glitzy Houston, noticed that "literally in the shadow of the tall buildings . . . are black slums straight out of the heart of Mississippi. They are so antiquely southern, they're not even urban." Garreau was looking at so-called "shotgun shacks," the rural contribution to southern vernacular architecture—structures often propped up on blocks, of flimsy wooden construction, scarcely bigger than two-car garages. In most instances, there was a high correlation in a city between poor drainage areas and black neighborhoods. Though black political power had helped alleviate the service backlog in these districts, the vast extent of necessary repairs to streets, sewer and water connections, trash pick-up, and building inspections necessary to improve living conditions were beyond the means of most city governments to handle.

The decline in black business districts reflected in part the deterioration of residential areas. These districts became victims of urban renewal as well, but more particularly—and ironically—of integration as better-stocked and -priced white establishments welcomed blacks on an equal basis. By the mid-1970s, Birmingham's once-thriving Fourth Avenue North was littered with sleazy pool halls, barbecue parlors, and vacant stores and theaters. "Sweet Auburn," a stretch of blocks west of downtown Atlanta, took on a similar aspect, boarded up and desolate. As one long-time resident explained, "the truth is that integration killed 'Sweet Auburn.'" For those black businesses, such as funeral homes, that managed to survive integration, the decline, if not disappearance, of neighboring black residential areas and the movement of affluent blacks to the urban periphery or to the suburbs further undercut black capital. Black businesses, which had not only serviced the black community but functioned as meeting places, training grounds for leadership, founts of charity, and examples of success, were gone, and with them a part of community life. Although some black businessmen had profited handsomely from segregation and inequality, nothing replaced their establishments as focal points for the black community.

The same community-splintering process that affected rural blacks occurred in black urban neighborhoods. Urban renewal, neglect, migration, and integration gutted families and institutions. Black writer James McPherson returned to his old Savannah neighborhood in the early 1980s and wrote: "There is not one house where I lived as a child still standing. My family is scattered." Though southern blacks were historically among the most mobile Americans, they often retained a home place with a group of kin. Perhaps now they became like everyone else, drawn by affluence or its promise, or merely drifting, seeking things rather than people or places.

Race Relations and the Black Economy:
Short Memories and Long Traditions

The general impotence of the black economy adversely affected race relations. Initially, as noted earlier, there was a general optimism among black leaders that voting rights would ameliorate economic problems. When Bayard Rustin called for a redistributionist policy for black southerners in 1964, he asked, "How are these radical objectives to be achieved? The answer is simple, . . . *through political power.*" No less a realist than Stokely Carmichael agreed. In 1966, he predicted that "if a black man is elected tax assessor, he can collect and channel funds for the building of better roads and schools serving black people—thus advancing the move from political power into the economic arena."

The close link between political and economic power never materialized, for reasons explored in the previous chapter, and the result was to sustain certain patterns of behavior between the races that had existed prior to the 1960s. These patterns were especially evident in rural areas and small towns, where black economic power was notoriously weak. It was not that the civil rights movement bypassed these places, but rather that whites assimilated the new rules, ignoring some, following others, and mostly molding the rest to suit local traditions. Blacks, for their part, knew instinctively when not to challenge custom, prevailing law to the contrary. In most instances, blacks were long-time residents of small towns and rural districts; they had attained a compromise, however one-sided, and lived in relative peace. Few elderly blacks had actively participated in the movement anyway. The chance to register and vote, to go to the local movie theater, or to eat at a restaurant in town often paled before the grinding poverty experienced by many rural blacks, but even those who could afford the time and money required to take advantage of newly won rights weighed carefully the consequences of availing themselves of these opportunities. A black sharecropper's wife in Franklin County, North Carolina, explained the situation to journalist Fred Powledge in the mid-1970s: "The KKK is still here . . . we don't go out places to eat because he [her husband] don't know whether blacks are allowed . . . he is so uncertain of it, that he just doesn't want to be bothered with it."

For those who thought of taking that trouble, there was the example of Sammy Younge to consider. Following his discharge from the navy at age twenty-two, Younge went to work for SNCC in Alabama and Mississippi during the early 1960s. On January 3, 1966, Younge was sponsoring a voter-registration drive in Macon County, Alabama, when the local registrar threatened him and his colleagues with a knife. Younge escaped injury. That evening he pulled into a gas station to use the rest room; an argument ensued, and the attendant shot and killed Younge.

Though segregation and discrimination were no longer open and official in the rural, small-town South, the sensitivity of both races to patterns of etiquette and custom built up over the decades enabled a subtle, unofficial residue to continue. Blacks in Terrell County, Georgia, for example, knew to be off the streets of Dawson, the county seat, by sundown, just as blacks in a rural parish in southwestern Louisiana knew that Jacques Thibeaux, owner of a crossroads grocery-liquor store, would not allow them to consume their alcoholic purchases on the premises. In the rural Piedmont of North Carolina, de facto segregated seating patterns persisted in courtrooms and political meetings, and certain street corners in county seats were reserved for one race or the other, not for both. Wariness rather than accommodation characterized race relations in these places, and when contact occurred, it was often strained and unpleasant, as if both black and white had been betrayed—the white from his comfortable position of superiority, and the black from his hope that things would get better.

In Selma during the mid-1970s, for all the talk of reconciliation during the tenth anniversary celebration of the march to Montgomery, a growing cynicism was evident among younger blacks stuck without jobs in the town's black district. James Walker, an unemployed black in his late twenties, vented his frustration to a journalist. "Black man's losin' ground again. My momma's afraid to talk to a white, and my grandmomma don't care." As for him, "Last week I went to get my driver's license. . . . Lunchtime. Sign on the door says they open again at one. I wanted to wait inside. . . . Trooper comes out and says, 'What's wrong, fool? . . . Get off that door less you want me next time comin' out shootin'.'" Walker noted wryly that the trooper's behavior had represented a change of sorts from an earlier era: "Ten years ago he woulda come out shootin' the first time."

Walker's companions in the run-down federal housing project offered similar stories to the reporter. For the few who held jobs, employment was a weapon to keep the black man silent. Because of the blacks' poor economic prospects, any sort of civil rights activity would doom a prospective worker's chances for a job or would leave someone already employed out on the street. When the journalist noted that federal laws prohibited such discrimination, a young black explained, "they don't fire him—ain't that clean. They hassle him. Get him thinkin' new ideas ain't worth it." If a black persisted in his activist role, "they goan frame you. Goan plant some dope in your ride or your house. Put a white bitch on you and pay her to yell rape. They come up with somethin'."

The continued economic dependence and impotence of rural and small-town blacks rendered them vulnerable; for these people, the civil rights movement was becoming irrelevant. As journalist Paul Schrag noted, for whites in small towns across the South "the time is always vaguely 1945 or 1950, a time between times, the Old South with the promise of Northern prosperity, the New South without integration or social ambivalence."

It could be argued, however, that the conditions confronting rural and small-town blacks were temporary phenomena. The trend of black demography was toward the cities, and large cities at that; black migrants concentrated in those cities, with more than 500,000 inhabitants in 1970. Coupled with the elderly nature of the rural population, migration patterns would leave a constantly smaller group of blacks in the countryside and small communities to endure the vestiges of old-style race relations. Unfortunately, the economic conditions of the majority of urban blacks left this population vulnerable to discrimination and exclusion as well.

A good deal of the problem related to black life in the South's metropolitan areas resulted from the planning and zoning decisions of the 1950s and 1960s. The increased residential segregation, the rapid expansion of the metropolitan area facilitated by freeway construction, and the erection of secure glass-and-steel skyscrapers that ignored street activity created a hermetic environment for the white middle class. Leaving all- or mostly white suburban communities, traveling on limited-access roads that shielded them from unpleasant living conditions, and entering environmentally controlled buildings and offices that through architecture, siting, and security kept the black underclass out of view, the white middle class could see few, if any, problems. Blacks were once again rendered invisible, not by racial etiquette this time, but rather through the metropolitan topography.

This is not to say that whites had less contact with blacks in the modern southern metropolis. Blacks appeared in corporate offices, in banks, in law offices, on the bench, and at city hall. Affirmative action, better education, the rapid growth of the postindustrial economy in general, had opened up civil-service, white-collar, and professional positions for blacks. In Jackson, Mississippi, for example, by the mid-1970s it was routine for whites to see black clerks at downtown and suburban retail stores, to see black police officers patrolling white neighborhoods, to see black reporters and announcers on local television stations, and to see blacks on the school board and on the city council. One white Jackson official boasted that his city was "the most integrated place in America." Indeed, after being pilloried throughout most of the sixties, southern whites were happy to view these scenes of racial progress and read about racial disorders elsewhere.

The combination of perceived racial progress and peace in the South and its absence elsewhere prompted a barrage of missionary statements and conclusions by southern white liberals, who took as fact that the cultural reorientation of white and black southerners was complete or nearly so. Anniston, Alabama, journalist H. Brandt Ayers proclaimed a "postracial South" in 1971. Former North Carolina governor (now U.S. senator) Terry Sanford, referring to improved race relations in 1970, declared that "now is the time, and the South can lead the way. . . . The South's time has come after a century of being the whipping boy and the backward child." Writer and publisher Willie Morris noted that the South could offer "more than a few crucial lessons to other Americans." The enthusiasm of these liberal leaders is understandable. They and the South had just emerged from a wrenching time; just a few years earlier, segregation and black disfranchisement were givens, now they were gone. Who could blame them for a bit of celebrating and for not looking a little deeper into what they really saw around them?

However understandable, these statements and the interpretation by other whites of growing numbers of blacks in the mainstream encouraged no one to look further. The black underclass remained invisible and forgotten; if its members entered white consciousness at all, they could be readily dismissed as beyond hope anyway, considering how many of their brothers and sisters had taken advantage of the new order in the South. This attitude filtered into the North as well, in a scenario reminiscent of the Reconstruction era. The proclamations of southern whites and the highly publicized examples of black progress in the South lulled northerners. The South was "in" again; its music, folklore, literature, and political leaders attained national exposure and admiration. It was no longer the Old South; it was the Sun Belt.

Occasionally, blacks found it necessary to make their presence felt. Unlike the problems of the old days—segregation and voting rights— the new difficulties—housing, unemployment, intimidation through economic pressure—were more difficult to dramatize. As David Halberstam wrote in *Harper's* in August, 1967, "the slum lords are evil enough, but they will not be there by their homes waiting for King and the TV crews to show up, ready to split black heads open. . . . The jobs are bad, but the reasons Negroes aren't ready for decent jobs are complicated; there won't be one sinister hillbilly waiting outside the employment agency grinding cigarettes into the necks of King and his followers." Some blacks opted to dramatize their case through the channel of violence: Tampa in 1967, where a year earlier a biracial commission reported that "gains . . . are middle class advantages, the average Negro still remains untrained, unemployed, and unthought of"; and Augusta in 1970, where officials had ignored wretched living conditions in the "Terry," the city's black ghetto.

Though minor skirmishes occurred after 1970, it was not until the Miami riot of 1980 that blacks in a southern city engaged in general violence. As opposed to larger, more congested northern cities, the urban South made it easy for troops and police to deploy and maneuver. More important, the brutality of police in quashing the few uprisings discouraged other blacks. The five blacks killed in the Augusta riot were all shot in the back. Two years earlier in Orangeburg, South Carolina, black students at South Carolina State College were demonstrating against a segregated bowling alley when law enforcement officers opened fire, killing three students and wounding twenty-seven. In May, 1970, at mostly black Jackson State College in Mississippi, campus demonstrations more against college governance than against continued discrimination in the city ended when Mississippi highway-safety patrolmen and Jackson city police fired into a crowd of demonstrators, killing two students and wounding twelve others. The police defended their actions by claiming that they were aiming at a sniper on the upper floor of a nearby dormitory, but ballistics experts testified that the shots were aimed at the crowd, not above it. The report of the Hinds County grand jury investigating the shooting absolved the police, noting that "when people . . . engage in civil disorders and riots, they must expect to be injured or killed when law enforcement officers are required to reestablish order."

The national press scarcely reported the incidents at Orangeburg and at Jackson State, in significant contrast to the killing of white students at Kent State University a week before the shootings in Jackson, which became front-page, top-of-the-hour news. The nation slumbered on Lethe's wharf, and the white South was not about to jog its unconsciousness. Yet, thumbing through the file labeled "Race-Related Deaths, 1967," at the SRC in Atlanta, one finds sample entries like this one from the Okolona (Miss.) *Delta Democrat Times:* "A white Okolona policeman was freed by a three-man justice of the peace tribunal. He was charged with murder in the pistol slaying of Robert E. Townsend, who was handcuffed at the time of the shooting." Or like this one from the *Southern Courier*, a black newspaper in Birmingham:

> Robert Lacey, the father of six children, was shot to death last week by a Jefferson County sheriff's deputy while members of his family watched in horror. Lacey had been charged with failing to take his dog to a veterinarian. . . . "Please don't shoot again," I [his wife] said, and my little girl came running to see what was happening to her daddy, laying there, bleeding, and I said again, "Please don't," and that's when they shot him through the head.

Klan membership tripled during the 1970s, and its opposition to blacks turned particularly violent late in the decade. In May, 1979, Klansmen gunned down a black in Carbon Hill, Alabama, and in November of that year in Greensboro, North Carolina, seventy-five Klansmen and Nazis killed five people at a "Death-to-the-Klan" rally. Twelve lynchings occurred in Mississippi during 1980. In October, 1981, a black man from Eastover, Mississippi, was found dead with his ears and sex organs hacked off. Lynn Jackson, a black woman, was lynched in Social Circle, Georgia, a few months later, and the following year Frederick York, an Atlanta black, was hanged from a tree near downtown.

If blacks had become invisible again to middle-class whites, it was apparent that some other whites were taking note of them, especially whites who were likely caught in the same economic bind—those whose skill levels and schooling rendered them obsolete for the new postindustrial age; those who saw better times all around them and were unable to be part of them. The new political leaders, populist rhetoric or no, could not address this constituency any more than they could satisfy poor blacks, and the rumble of trouble from the lower economic orders seldom penetrated the office towers or suburban homes. Given the South's oligarchic traditions, it was perhaps just as well that working-class whites and blacks were at odds; occupied with each other, they would not challenge anyone else.

From Race to Class: The Drum Major's Final Journey

And what of the black leadership—those brave, savvy men and women of the fifties and sixties who helped to shape the moral tone and tactics of a successful movement? Could they broaden the net to capture equity and opportunity for the southern black masses, or had they run out of solutions, misunderstood the depths of the racial problem? Or, worse, had success in the legislature, in the courts, and in their bank accounts numbed their sensitivities? Historians have noted the disarray of black leadership after Selma, especially after Martin Luther King's death in 1968, and they have focused on the splintering of the major civil rights groups and the failure to provide a consensus on either programs or tactics for black economic problems. All of this is accurate, of course, but it ignores two things. First, black leaders, including King, were well aware of the deeper dilemmas that confronted blacks, and second, local black leaders and organizations were more significant determinants of the extent of black progress in the long run than their national counterparts.

Since the 1950s, Martin Luther King had recognized the importance of economic equality. He believed that the removal of segregation would lend a necessary confidence and dignity to blacks so they could attack the more difficult problem. He also understood that white southerners (and white northerners, too) would be more sympathetic to granting individual rights documented in the Constitution than to promoting group solutions for poverty. Economic status, according to widespread belief, was a matter of individual initiative. Although King announced his March on Washington in 1963 as a demonstration for "Jobs and Freedom," the former objective was barely audible in the platform rhetoric.

By the end of the Selma campaign, however, it was clear to most black leaders that a new agenda was necessary and that economic opportunity would be the dominant element in that agenda. Some white leaders recognized this as well. In a speech at the Howard University commencement exercises in June, 1965, President Johnson declared forcefully that "freedom is not enough. . . . You do not take a person who for years has been hobbled by chains and liberate him, bring him up to the starting line of a race and then say, 'You are free to compete with all the others.' . . . We seek not just freedom but opportunity—not just legal equity but human ability—not just equality as a right and a theory but equality as a fact and as a result." For King, a new era was dawning as well. Blacks had moved, King noted in a speech to his staff in May, 1967, "into a new era, an era of revolution. . . . We are engaged in a class struggle . . . dealing with the problem of the gulf between the haves and the have-nots."

Though both President Johnson and King agreed on the problem, their rhetoric underscored both the growing divergence between black and white that occurred after 1965 and the extent to which each group would be willing to go to rectify the situation. It also indicated the inaccurate perception of King's critics that his emphasis on non-violence had left him behind in the black struggle for justice, that he had become too conservative and out of touch with the black masses. King's disastrous visit to Harlem in 1964, where he was booed by hostile blacks in the wake of civil disturbances there, helped to fuel that perception. But his espousal of nonviolence as a tactic should not be confused with his advocacy of radical policy. As he put it in 1967, "we can't solve our problems now until there is a radical distribution of economic and political power." This is scarcely different from Stokely Carmichael's statement the previous year that "ultimately, the economic foundations of this country must be shaken if black people are to control their lives." The difference was that Carmichael condoned violence as an acceptable means to attaining that end.

King hoped to demonstrate that nonviolence could be a more effective strategy toward achieving economic equity than Carmichael's threatening "Black Power," which scared off potential white allies and was unrealistic, particularly for southern blacks. King, unlike the emerging black leaders of the mid-1960s, was a southerner, and his way would be the southern way. In the fall of 1967, King unveiled his plans for another march on Washington. This time, he would gather poor people, representing a cross-section of groups, and take them to Washington "to dramatize and call attention to the economic problem and the gulf between promise and fulfillment." For King, the problem now transcended race. He sensed, long before the policy-makers and academics of the 1980s, that poverty was not a race-specific issue. "The long journey ahead," he wrote, "requires that we emphasize the needs of all America's poor, for there is no way merely to find work, or adequate housing, or quality-integrated schools for Negroes alone. We shall eliminate unemployment for Negroes when we demand full and fair employment for *all*."

Just as King felt the need to transcend race, he saw the interconnectedness of problems on a global scale: the war in Vietnam, imperialism in Africa, and the arms race were all of one piece, each a threat to civil rights and to economic equality, and each a violation of religious sensibility. As he defended his expanded perspective on one occasion: "One cannot be just concerned with civil rights. It is very nice to drink milk at an unsegregated lunch counter—but not when there is Strontium 90 in it." Or, on Vietnam: "I knew that America would never invest the necessary funds or energies in the rehabilitation of its poor so long as Vietnam continued to draw men and skills and money."

King hoped to maintain the moral flame that had lighted the crusades of the early 1960s. The flame was fragile, however, and when it was brought to the larger arena of the North and employed to illuminate other issues, it flickered and died. Darkness prevailed on that part of the globe that remained untouched by King's Christian vision, and in those parts still blessed by the light, there was a dark presence in the wings.

Critics from the left buffeted King on his nonviolent philosophy, and more moderate blacks were concerned that he had alienated President Johnson and had run too far afield, or had become too fond of publicity. Nevertheless, King pushed ahead with his Poor People's Campaign. As he traveled the country during the early months of 1968, King failed to generate significant interest in his new crusade—the nation was torn over Vietnam, and a presidential election campaign was in the offing. Though he exuded confidence publicly, in private he succumbed to depression. Aside from the difficulty he experienced in gaining publicity for the nation's poor, divisions within the SCLC, criticism from other black leaders, and the open hostility of younger blacks toward his philosophy and leadership troubled him deeply. Although he had often talked freely about his own death with aides and on occasion in speeches, his preoccupation with the subject grew in these months. In a February sermon at the Ebenezer Baptist Church in Atlanta, King discussed his funeral at some length, asking the congregation to remember him as a "drum major for justice."

It was almost with relief that he accepted an invitation in mid-February from a long-time friend, the Reverend James Lawson of Memphis, to lend his support to a recently begun strike of black sanitation workers in that city. King believed that by speaking in behalf of the strikers, he could focus attention on the working poor, and Memphis would be a good showcase for his message. In terms of race relations, the city was an extension of the Mississippi Delta, which, observers said, ended in the lobby of the Peabody Hotel. The city and the hotel had settled into an uncomfortable dotage after the cotton trade and jazz that had given Memphis economic and cultural pre-eminence drifted away. Still, the city clung to some of its racial traditions. Blacks remained closed out of the economic and social life of the community, and when they obtained city work, it was invariably in menial positions and framed by discrimination.

The sanitation workers represented a good case in point. When it rained on January 31, the city sent black workers home with two hours' pay, whereas white workers received a full day's salary. When negotiations with the city broke down in early February, the black workers struck. As with so many other racial confrontations in the South, the Memphis conflict became embroiled in local politics. During the 1960s, younger blacks had grown increasingly restive with the slow pace of racial reform. At the same time, white voters, angered by both black militancy and the apparent willingness of the city's business elite to continue an interracial dialogue, supported conservative Republican candidates. By 1968, the race issue had thoroughly polarized Memphis politics. Mayor Henry Loeb, a member of the conservative faction, refused to concede to the workers' request for equal treatment and by the end of March had cut off food stamps to the strikers. King arrived into this charged atmosphere on March 18 to give a speech and lead a demonstration. Nearly seventeen thousand enthusiastic blacks greeted him at the Masonic Temple in what appeared to be a revival of the old civil rights spirit. However, the demonstration soon erupted into sporadic acts of vandalism as young blacks ignored King's counsel for nonviolence and broke away from the main line of marchers. King left the city further discredited, with his future as a black leader more in doubt.

The situation had not improved when, a few weeks later, on April 3, King returned to Memphis to address a small crowd of two thousand supporters at the Temple. His speech was less about the garbage strike in Memphis than it was a valedictory on the civil rights movement and his role in that crusade. He talked about Birmingham; he talked about his journey to the Holy Land; and he talked about how, some ten years earlier, he had escaped death in New York when a demented woman stabbed him as he was autographing copies of his first book, *Stride Toward Freedom* (1958). The blade had lodged so close to his aorta that, had he sneezed, it would have punctured that vital artery. By escaping death, King recounted, he was able to experience the lunch counters, Albany, Birmingham, and Selma. As if sensing that Memphis would be his final crusade, King declared that "it doesn't matter with me now. Because I've been to the mountaintop. . . . Like anybody, I would like to live a long life. . . . But I'm not concerned about that now. I just want to do God's will. And He's allowed me to go up to the mountain. And I've looked over. And I've seen the promised land. I may not get there with you. But I want you to know tonight, that we, as a people will get to the promised land. . . . I'm not fearing any man. Mine eyes have seen the glory of the coming of the Lord."

Around six o'clock the following evening, King and his staff were preparing to go out to dinner before another rally. He stepped out on the balcony of his motel and reminded Ben Branch, who was to sing that night, "Make sure you play 'Precious Lord, Take My Hand,' at the meeting tonight." The report of a Remington-30.06 shattered the quiet evening. As Andrew Young rushed over to the fallen figure on the balcony, he cried out, "Oh, my God, my God, it's all over!"

It was over before then. In national terms, the South was redeemed and forgotten. Interest in civil rights fled north after Selma, not because the southern agenda had been fulfilled but because of Watts, Detroit, and Newark. In regional terms, the enormity of dealing with the black economy as well as the exhaustion of a soul-wrenching and body-racking crusade thinned the ranks of field workers. As black writer Paul Delaney noted, "the victors turned and looked at each other and were amazed to find that after all their effort, they had only scratched the surface, merely to expose the most vulnerable and expendable layer of the skin of racism." The disillusionment was reflected in black-white estrangement, in the abandonment of field offices, and in the disintegration of SNCC. Warren Fortson, a white attorney from Americus, Georgia, who had been driven from his hometown for his liberal views, left this account of his travels in rural Mississippi in 1967: "The Movement as we used to know it just doesn't exist anymore. . . . All that's left of it here is a few scattered seedy students who never went back up North, cranking out leaflets on mimeograph machines in a few grubby back rooms. As for the Negroes, they're moving into themselves now. . . . They've quit the field." In 1965 COFO had a thousand workers in Mississippi. Two years later, the number had dropped to fewer than fifty.

It was little wonder that historians and the participants themselves viewed Selma and the Voting Rights Act as the movement's climax. The great civil rights organizations of the South—SCLC and SNCC—

devolved into bickering constituencies, the latter over tactics and philosophy, and the former, especially after King's death, rent by a power struggle between Ralph David Abernathy and the more militant Jesse Jackson. When the Poor People's Campaign, King's attempt to revive the interracial Christian crusade of the early 1960s, ended in the muck of the Mall in Washington with the few remaining inhabitants of the tent city carted off to jail with little fanfare, it seemed an appropriate metaphor for the movement in general. And when historians wrote about civil rights after Selma, they focused on the North. In 1974, C. Vann Woodward presented a new edition of his path-breaking study on the origins of segregation in the South, *The Strange Career of Jim Crow*. His new chapter outlining race relations since the mid-1960s dealt almost entirely with northern events.

Narrowing Institutions and an Expanding Middle Class: Growing Apart

Although looking away from Dixie was justified in terms of the headline events concerning race relations after 1965, the emphasis ignored the local foundations that preceded the national civil rights movement. Frustration over the southern black economy and its implications for race relations resulted more from the failures of local organizations and leaders to prepare and act upon an agenda for equal opportunity than from the breakdown of national organizations and their field staffs or the diversion of federal support and sympathy elsewhere. Whatever their national focus and significance, most of the major events of the late 1950s and early 1960s had local antecedents without which the success of the broader campaign would have been problematic.

When King and the SCLC chose Birmingham as their fateful target late in 1962, it was not only the city's reputation for racial violence that attracted them. Since the early 1950s, the Reverend Fred L. Shuttlesworth had provided leadership in Birmingham's black community, first through the NAACP and then, when the Alabama legislature outlawed the organization in May, 1956, through the Alabama Christian Movement for Human Rights. Its selective buying campaign against downtown stores in 1962 further turned the business community against the city administration. When King arrived in Birmingham in April, 1963, he had the benefit of a well-trained and well-led veteran organization that had succeeded in organizing local blacks and in forcing whites to choose sides.

The Selma campaign had a similar lineage. Since the late 1920s, a group of city and county blacks had gotten together to register voters. By the early 1960s, the Dallas County Voters' League (DCVL) and its two long-time leaders, Amelia and Samuel Boynton, had managed to register only 180 blacks, but in the process they had made the county's black residents aware of their voting rights through schools and clinics. In February, 1963—nearly two years before King went to Selma—SNCC field workers began to assist the DCVL in voter-registration drives. When black residents of Selma demonstrated little interest and great fear in going to the courthouse, SNCC took its operation out into the county, with some success. Bernard Lafayette, one of the first SNCC workers in Dallas County, recalled that he used the example of county blacks who risked life and property by attempting to register to shame city residents into doing the same. Between February and September, 1963, nearly 2,000 blacks went to the courthouse and about 600 succeeded in placing their names on the registration rolls. By the time King came to Selma, blacks there were well organized and thoroughly schooled in the procedures of voter registration.

This is not to denigrate the role of King and the SCLC. Without King's ability to dramatize the injustice of southern race relations in these communities and his talent for extracting the moral lessons of the struggle, the movement may not have touched the federal government, national opinion, and southern whites and blacks so deeply. "Alone among the major civil rights leaders of his time," Clayborne Carson explained, "King could not only articulate black concerns to white audiences, but could also mobilize blacks." As the corpses in Mississippi during the 1950s and early 1960s testified, local efforts, locally directed, were difficult to transmit to a national audience. Though conflicts inevitably developed between national and local organizations and their respective leaders, they complemented each other on most occasions, and when the national groups left, the local cadre remained behind to form a nucleus to consolidate gains and push ahead on new objectives. The roles of these local organizations and their leaders were unspectacular and usually unpublicized, just as their premovement activities were unheralded beyond their districts.

Their ultimate failure no doubt had a great deal to do with the problem itself: the condition of the southern black economy owed to historic debilities and to regional and national economic patterns that were beyond the scope of political solutions. Local activists faced other problems as well. Historian William Chafe's analysis of the origins of the civil rights movement in Greensboro implied that the very successes engineered and enjoyed by local blacks created an ambivalence that did not find a ready resolution after 1965. The attack against segregation obscured the positive aspects and strengths of all-black institutions, the church and the school in particular. Chafe noted that the teenagers who led Greensboro's sit-in movement attended all-black Shiloh Baptist Church, whose minister had obtained his civil rights baptism while a student at Shaw University, an all-black institution in Raleigh. Many of the students received their secondary education at segregated Dudley High School, where teachers who had gone through similarly segregated systems encouraged their pupils to address voter-registration envelopes during home-room period.

After 1965, the base of black institutions from which future leadership could be drawn narrowed. Although black churches remained intact, black-owned businesses, a major reservoir of black capital in southern cities, were early victims of integration, and the schools followed. Blacks were now the "new kids on the block" in integrated schools, in business offices, and in the professions. Learning to survive, let alone lead, in these new environments would take time, especially when both blacks and whites typically assumed that the black institutions were inferior—the U.S. Supreme Court had said as much, of course. Integration became its own reward.

If integration drained the vitality (as well as the inferiority) from some black institutions, the new standard of race relations also dulled the sense of urgency among local black leaders. Segregation and racial etiquette had been daily reminders of inferiority and invisibility; the moral, forceful nature of black protest removed the latter, and black protest combined with federal legislation brought down the former. But in many respects these were middle-class protests. Although it is true that students played critical roles in the sit-ins and in the voting-rights campaigns, a good deal of the leadership came from middle-class backgrounds. The victories enabled that leadership to participate more fully in regional life, and their objectives now were to work *within* the political and economic systems to attain power, not *against* them. As objectives changed, so did the nature of the leadership. Newly elected congressman Andrew Young told a reporter in 1973, "the black politician is replacing the civil rights leader as the spearpoint of black progress." And the black politician, as noted earlier, faced considerable constraints. The black economy remained largely untouched. New leaders included those college-educated blacks who took over federal programs at the local level—bureaucrats who now served as brokers for the black community, dispensing influence and federal funds to assist, yet still maintain, the impoverished black masses, regardless of anyone's best intentions.

When reporters sampled the opinions of southern black leaders in the early 1970s, the perspective was considerably different from that of the young black men hanging around the federal housing project in Selma. Maynard Jackson declared in 1973, "Atlanta is the best city in the country for black people." In Selma two years later, the Reverend Frederick Reese, a veteran local black leader, enthused, "We've come a long way. Whites who wouldn't tip their hats have learned to do it. People who wouldn't say 'Mister' or 'Miss' to a black have learned to say it mighty fine. We've got black policemen, black secretaries, and we can use the public restrooms. The word 'nigger' is almost out of existence." Andrew Young addressed a group of southern black mayors that same year and declared, "you know, we can't help but be people who believe in doing the impossible, because we've already done so much of it."

The black middle class could genuinely believe that. As sociologist John Shelton Reed observed, "people evaluate their situation not only in terms of how good or bad it is, but in light of how it is changing, and how rapidly." For these middle-class blacks, the heady mix of jobs and freedom was generally a reality that was virtually the total obverse of the situation a decade earlier. And this was true not only for the leaders, but for the new entries into the black middle class as well. Affirmative-action programs tended to favor those blacks who qualified for the expanding white-collar segment of the southern labor market. By 1975, nearly one in six black male employees in the South worked in professional and public administration occupations—the largest white-collar categories—compared with less than one in ten in 1960.

The attitudes of the blacks who found niches in the South's growing postindustrial economy differed markedly, of course, from those unemployed Selma blacks mentioned earlier. A black attorney in Atlanta noted that the only "ism" he was interested in was capitalism. Hugh Jackson, a black Mississippi Gulf Coast businessman, raved to a reporter about the "quality of life" in Mississippi and how it was a "decent environment" in which to raise children compared to New York City, where he had lived for a while. For the first time in more than a century, blacks began to relocate in or return to the South. Though some began returning in the late 1960s for family reasons, an increasing number during the 1970s came for the opportunities offered by a rejuvenated regional economy. Between 1970 and 1973, 247,000 blacks moved to the South—one-third of them for the first time—while 166,000 blacks left the region. Between 1975 and 1980, more than 500,000 blacks moved south, compared with 190,000 who went to other parts of the country. More significant, studies indicated that, whereas roughly one in five black migrants came south in the early 1970s to take employment, by the last half of the decade nearly one in two newcomers was motivated by job offers. Sociologist Carol Stack noted that these were successful blacks who had "made it" up north and were coming south to improve both their economic position and their life-style.

More pertinent to the persisting problems of the southern black poor, the advance experienced by middle-class blacks widened the gap between the two groups. In the era of white supremacy, all blacks had shared segregation and the demeaning etiquette of southern race relations; the virtual demise of those constraints broke the bond of suffering uniting all blacks, whatever their socioeconomic differences. Although there had always been divisions within the black community, most residents could agree on the importance of breaking down the barriers to integrity. Now that agreement would need to occur on an intellectual rather than an experiential level, and the experiential gap between the two groups was widening in the 1970s. As black sociologist William Julius Wilson predicted in 1978, "there are clear indications that the economic gap between the black underclass . . . and the higher-income blacks will very likely widen and solidify."

Aside from economic divisions, there were cultural distinctions as well. These had always existed within the black community, but with the well-publicized and visible expansion of the black middle class, such differences became more evident both to the new members of the affluent black population and to their white colleagues. Gunnar Myrdal noted in a 1966 address that the "Negro upper-middle class despise[s] . . . the lower-class Negro." Though an exaggeration, the statement held some accuracy. Southern culture placed great significance on public behavior, and affluent blacks sought to comport themselves in a manner that differentiated them from white stereotypes of blacks. Martin Luther King, for example, dressed with impeccable conservatism, rarely deviating from dark suits, and he urged his followers to avoid behavior that he associated with lower-class life. In messages to his congregations, he stressed the middle-class virtues of thrift and self-help. This is not to say that King had difficulty identifying with the problems of the black poor, but rather that his outlook and memories were probably typical of the differing perspectives that divided the black community then and would push the groups further apart after 1965. For King, behavior, appearance, and stability were important objectives; for the black poor, the goal was simply survival.

The increasing economic and cultural divisions within the black community hampered local organizations, because the distrust and frustration of the young and unemployed inhibited a consensus on policy and tactics. After the hostile reception she had received from students at Tuskegee, Virginia Durr noted that "those young blacks hated the big shots in the black community as much as they hated the ones in the white community." The growing economic gap coupled with the symbols and realities of the Sun Belt prosperity around them had thrust materialism to the forefront of the students' ambitions. As one student explained to Durr, "we want what the white folks have got." The moral-religious ideals that had permeated the earlier crusade were buried. Clearly disturbed, Durr felt that a historical perspective was missing, that these blacks were becoming as memoryless as southern whites. When she quizzed a young black in her employ—"Haven't you ever heard about the big struggle for desegregation of the buses?"— he responded, "Huh, Mrs. Durr, who wants to ride on a bus? I want a car of my own." Although this reflected, as Durr sensed, the need for some history lessons, it also indicated the new and inevitably frustrating materialist agenda of younger blacks.

From time to time after 1965, younger and poorer blacks in the South sought to revive the local impetus of the freedom struggle by forming organizations of their own. It was a matter of policy for SNCC to work through local groups frequently formed by their field directors. The groups included numerous students, but were generally short-lived as the youngsters left for school or moved away to find work elsewhere. The Meredith March Against Fear on June 5, 1966, provided a brief inspiration for radical black organization in the South.

James Meredith was a black Mississippian who had desegregated the University of Mississippi in 1962 amid violence and bloodshed, but he was proud to be a Mississippian nonetheless. As he noted on several occasions, "I am a Mississippian in all respects—even the bad ones." Despite his courage and his love for his native state, he was afraid. Fear was an imprisonment, and if he felt it, so must countless numbers of other blacks in the state; fear prevented them from testing their freedom, from registering to vote, from applying for a job, or seeking a promotion, or requesting a transfer to a white school. Meredith searched for a cure, and the one he found was one that blacks had employed on numerous occasions in the preceding years: he would walk through the state of Mississippi to conquer that fear and, by example, the fear of every other black in the state.

The walk would touch the major southern cultural traditions. Meredith's solitary dignity walking down a Mississippi highway would be a courageous, romantic gesture, carried off with civility and dignity. It would be a religious pilgrimage as well, guided by faith and love of the land of Mississippi. His walk would illuminate the importance of the individual in serving as witness for an entire people.

Not more than twenty-eight miles into his pilgrimage, a shot crackled through the stillness of a late spring morning, and Meredith fell, wounded by buckshot. State troopers and sheriff's deputies who were accompanying Meredith quickly rounded up his attacker, James Norvel. Meredith was taken to a Memphis hospital. The ambush temporarily revived SNCC and SCLC, and Martin Luther King, Jr., reluctantly agreed with SNCC's Stokely Carmichael and with Floyd McKissick of CORE to resume the march through Mississippi. The NAACP and the Urban League, concerned about the growing militancy of both SNCC and CORE (whose field workers had taken up the refrain, "Too much love / Too much love / Nothing kills a nigger like / Too much love," in obvious defiance of King and his philosophy) withdrew, but King hoped that he could limit the radical content of the demonstration through his presence.

The march itself proved uneventful as local and state officials treated the demonstrators with courtesy and accommodation. Mississippi was about to embark on an image-changing campaign to lure business and industry to the state, so officials were anxious to avoid negative publicity. They made considerable note of the rapid apprehension of the suspect and subsequently of the restraint and good nature of law-enforcement personnel. But during the march, SNCC official Willie Ricks circulated through the demonstrators and the black communities along the route promoting the slogan "Black Power." Richard Wright and New York congressman Adam Clayton Powell had used the slogan twenty-five years earlier, and it probably antedated them. King was concerned, however, that the slogan would be interpreted as antiwhite more than as an expression of black identity.

At a stop in Greenwood, Mississippi—the site of bloody voter-registration drives just a few years earlier—Stokely Carmichael defied the orders of state troopers and pitched a tent on the grounds of the black high school. He was promptly arrested, but then released. As he left the jail to the cheers of the marchers, he jumped up onto a flatbed truck, thrust his fist into the air, and declared, "this is the twenty-seventh time I have been arrested—and I ain't going to jail no more! The only way we gonna stop them white men from whippin' us is to take over." Then, in the familiar rhythmic preacher's cadence, Carmichael sang and his followers echoed, "We . . . want . . . Black . . . Power!" King tried to dilute Carmichael's meaning by telling reporters that "we must never seek power exclusively for the Negro, but the sharing of power with white people."

Regardless of King's benign interpretation, "Black Power" inspired the black community, especially poor blacks, and spread fear through the white community. It hastened the end of interracial cooperation, and its ambiguous connotations also served to further divide blacks. One division occurred between southern blacks and northern blacks. Julian Bond, a SNCC official and native Georgian, believed that "Black Power" meant political power, but for James Boggs, a black activist from Detroit, the slogan implied a "new revolutionary social force" against the middle classes. By 1972, President Richard M. Nixon had embraced the slogan as a synonym for black capitalism. This devaluation of "Black Power" reflected the powerlessness of the poor blacks whom Carmichael had primarily in mind.

But in a few scattered areas of the Deep South, "Black Power" provoked a militant response from young and poor blacks. There was already a paramilitary group in Bogalusa, Louisiana, called the Deacons for Defense, who served as Carmichael's bodyguards. After the Mississippi Freedom Summer in 1964, a group called the Lowndes County Freedom Organization formed in the Alabama Black Belt, reaching prominence later as the Black Panthers. Separatist groups appeared in greater numbers after 1966, sometimes taking on the character of farmers' cooperatives, heavy on ideology but short on specific programs. These groups fared poorly: they rarely had the support of the growing numbers of increasingly powerful black political leaders, and black professionals, bureaucrats, and managers were alienated by their leftist ideology. The separatist movement served primarily to widen the gap between middle- and lower-class blacks in the South.

There were many symbols by the mid-1970s that race relations in the South had undergone significant changes in the decade since President Johnson signed the Voting Rights Act, and symbols, again, were and are important to southerners, black and white. Mississippi was forging ahead with its "Rethink Mississippi" campaign, placing ads in the national media under various headings such as "Missinformed," "Missimpression," and "Missunderstood." When Fannie Lou Hamer, Mississippi's firebrand voting-rights activist, died in 1977, the state legislature unanimously passed a resolution praising her service to the state. By the time of the twentieth anniversary of the integration of Central High School in Little Rock, Arkansas, Ernest Green, who was among the first group of blacks to enter the school in 1957, was Assistant Secretary of Labor in the Carter administration; Orval Faubus was a bank teller in his hometown; and Central High had a black principal.

In Alabama, Governor George Wallace, confined to a wheelchair now, made an impromptu appearance, without reporters or television cameras, in Martin Luther King's old church in Montgomery, the Dexter Avenue Baptist Church, to give his personal witness. He talked movingly about his religious experiences, and he echoed King's words on the redemptive quality of human suffering. As his aide wheeled him slowly down the aisle to leave the church, the organ rang out with "The Battle Hymn of the Republic," and black hands reached out toward the pale figure in the wheelchair. Those present recalled King's words: "If you just keep on loving a man, ultimately you will get down to the God in him."

And sometimes when nothing happened, that also spoke volumes about the journey since 1965. Autherine Lucy had attempted to desegregate the University of Alabama in February, 1956. Admitted and then quickly expelled for suggesting that university officials were conspiring to bar her from classes, she moved to Texas, married a minister, and, in 1975, moved back to Birmingham. Two history professors at the university invited her to address their students, and she returned to the place where her appearance two decades earlier had provoked violence. Her remarks were reported matter-of-factly in the Tuscaloosa newspaper, but elsewhere her return passed without comment.

It was not surprising, then, to hear some southern blacks echo their white counterparts about the new order of race relations in the South. Jessie Campbell, a black store manager on Mississippi's Gulf Coast, told reporter Fred Powledge in 1976 that race "is almost nonexistent now. . . . There's been a new generation of people, black and white, here. And there's been a pretty big rise in the standard of living of the black people." Andrew Young two years earlier expounded on the missionary theme stressed by the South's new white political leadership: "I strangely think we're going to be able to deliver in the South . . . I think the direction of this nation is going to be determined by the direction that comes from the southern part of the United States."

Both Young and the young black men in Selma were right. The movement did not end with President Johnson's signature, but merely took different turns. A black middle class had emerged to consolidate its political and social victories, but a much larger black lower class remained confined by age, location, and above all economic circumstance. The black politicians, professionals, managers, and government bureaucrats in the South were near to the mountaintop; for the rest, in the words of Jesse Jackson, they faced "the rough side of the mountain."

X / No Broad Highways: Class and Race in the South Since 1976

If it is possible to divide a moral and cultural movement into discrete periods of time, then the result of the civil rights movement might look something like this: Confrontation (the years prior to 1965); Consolidation (1965–76); and Confusion (1976 to the present). By the mid-1970s, it was apparent that amid the very real gains following the Voting Rights Act, there remained some equally real problems that seemed impervious to legislation and protest. The situation had civil rights leaders like Joseph Lowery of the SCLC talking in riddles. "In the South," he stated, "everything has changed and nothing has changed." Others described this Dickensian situation in less cryptic but equally puzzled terms. North Carolina NAACP official Kelly Alexander, Sr., admitted in a 1981 interview that "these are confusing times, probably more confusing than any period in my lifetime."

The confusion expressed by black leaders resulted from the muddled picture of the political and economic status of southern blacks. The image projected on the regional screen was not only blurred, but there was no consensus on how to sharpen the focus.

Black Political Power: Coalitions and Repentant Sinners

In terms of black political power, there were unmistakable advances after 1976 in the numbers of black elected officials and in the growing sophistication of both officeholders and the electorate. These gains, in turn, had salutary results with respect to public policy from the local to the national levels of government. In addition, the strengthening of federal legislation and the increasing two-party competition in the South further enhanced black political prospects. On the other hand, economic weakness, bloc voting, increased white voter registration, subterfuge, and occasional lapses in federal support reduced black achievements in politics.

After a brief leveling off during the mid-1970s, black voter registration in the South accelerated. Between 1980 and 1984, nearly five hundred thousand blacks enrolled for the first time; better than two out of three eligible black voters were registered by the latter date. Mississippi blacks held first place in the South, with a registration rate of 75.8 percent. Twenty years earlier, that figure was below 6 percent.

The number of black elected officials increased accordingly during the 1980s, the biggest jump occurring between 1984 and 1986. Five southern states topped the national list for new black officeholders, with Alabama leading the way, showing an increase of sixty-one black elected officials. Although it was true that black officeholders comprised only 3 percent of the South's elected officials by 1986 (blacks accounted for 19 percent of the total population in the region), they fared relatively well compared with other sections of the country. In the Northeast, only one-half of 1 percent of elected officials were blacks; the figure was four-tenths of 1 percent in both the north-central and western states.

However impressive the aggregate statistics, it was the story of individual officeholders and specific localities that most reflected black political power in the modern South. Harvey Gantt moved to Charlotte after graduating from Clemson and eventually established his own architecture practice. Along with a number of other young black professionals, Gantt took an increasing interest in local politics during the 1970s. He ran for the city council successfully, benefiting from the modification of an at-large system to a combined process that included district representation. He lost the Democratic mayoral primary in 1981 but won it on a second try two years later and the general election as well, narrowly defeating his Republican opponent by receiving almost unanimous support from black voters and a surprising 25 percent of the white electorate. Gantt easily won re-election in 1985, garnering more than 40 percent of the white vote and a string of endorsements from the city's white retail and banking establishment.

Harvey Gantt's political career in Charlotte reflected some general themes about black chief executives in southern localities during the 1980s. First, they were invariably drawn from the upper strata of the black population. Gantt was a professional architect; Atlanta's mayor, Andrew Young, elected in 1981, had lengthy national and international experience in politics; and Richard Arrington, Birmingham's three-time mayor, was a prominent educator. Second, Gantt was successful in building a coalition of blacks and white elites and professionals—the old-style "Manhattan coalition" that had characterized politics in Atlanta and other southern cities for many years. In the new version of the coalition, blacks were no longer junior partners and had broadened their agenda. Gantt's commitment to downtown redevelopment was at least as important as his background as a neighborhood advocate in cementing this coalition. Andrew Young's support of economic development objectives has become legendary both within and beyond Atlanta. An *Esquire* magazine reporter termed the mayor's approach to public policy "Andynomics," adding with a touch of irony that Young is "making rich white people feel good again" through his philosophy that there "is salvation through free enterprise." Arrington, serving his third term as mayor, performs a similar though less publicized service in Birmingham. Though he received only 10 percent of the city's white vote in his 1987 re-election victory, he showed strength in the affluent districts of south Birmingham, where he won nearly one-third of the white vote.

Another common factor that Gantt shared with his colleagues in Atlanta and Birmingham was the persistence of virtually unanimous black electoral support and a steady increase in the white voting base. All three candidates exceeded their percentage of white support the second time around without losing black votes. White leaders discovered that black chief executives helped in recruiting outside investment, particularly from abroad, serving as a statement to corporations and investors of stable race relations and a progressive city. A black mayor was also insurance against a civil disturbance that could wreck a city's image. Miami, for example, had a difficult time selling itself after the violence in black neighborhoods in 1980 and 1989. The insurance issue also enabled black mayors to practice a version of affirmative action without running afoul of conservative white business sentiment. As Young explained in 1985, "we've given out 230 contracts worth $130 million to blacks in the last three years. That circulates to beauty parlors, barber shops, gets young people off the street. That's why we don't have black people jumping up and down . . . like black folks in Jamaica or Miami."

The new version of the Manhattan coalition reflected a trend in southern urban politics. In Durham, North Carolina, in 1983, for example, a coalition of three groups—the Durham Committee on the Affairs of Black People, the Durham Voters Alliance (a group of mostly young white professionals), and the Peoples' Alliance (a statewide, primarily white consumer-affairs organization)—captured local government. Though neighborhood preservation and environmental issues dominated the campaign, the new mayor and city council enacted the city's first fair housing ordinance and established a plan to contract with minority-owned businesses. In Selma, despite a black majority on the registration rolls, white mayor Joe Smitherman has managed to maintain his more-than-two-decade reign over the city by improving services in the black community and through appointments of blacks to local offices.

Since the black vote in the South tends to be concentrated in districts like the Black Belt or in the major cities, blacks have been less successful in translating the franchise to statewide political gains. The situation is changing, however, most notably in Virginia and Alabama. In 1985, Douglas Wilder, the grandson of a slave, became the first black to win election to a statewide executive position in the South since the Reconstruction era. As Wilder campaigned for the position of lieutenant governor of Virginia, he projected a conservative image bolstered by his sixteen years in the state senate and by his combat role during the Korean War. An effective television commercial (he committed 80 percent of his $700,000 campaign budget to television advertising) featured Joe Alder, a small-town police officer, endorsing Wilder. The message was that Wilder was a law-and-order candidate. Democrat Wilder's victory in the South's most Republican state, where the legacy of the arch-conservative Byrd regime survives, underscored another theme of the successful black candidate in the 1980s. Wilder did not present a racial agenda, nor did he run as a candidate of an aggrieved racial minority. His public agenda was little different from those of his moderate white running mates. It was also noteworthy that, although he received an impressive 46 percent of the white vote, most of that white support came from northern Virginia, an affluent, culturally diverse white-collar section of the state with a small black population. The vote was a statewide example of the Manhattan coalition.

A different and perhaps more remarkable coalition was emerging in Alabama, where black elected officials extended their domination over the Black Belt during the 1980s. In Lowndes County, which did not have a single black registered voter in 1965, black officeholders include the sheriff, the school superintendent, a majority of the school board, and a majority of the county commission. More than 80 percent of the registered voters in the county are black. So thorough is black power in rural Alabama that outnumbered whites are calling for federal examiners, while black leaders urge the federal government to stay out of local politics—a familiar refrain from an unfamiliar source. Sumter County black political activist Wendell Paris stated in 1982 that federal observers were "a hindrance," a feeling echoed by black

Lowndes County sheriff John Hulett, who advised that the observers might intimidate black voters and "do more harm than good."

Although Black Belt and urban political power in Alabama have yet to be translated into black executive officeholders at the state level, blacks are steadily increasing their influence in the Democratic party. In 1983, George Grayson of Huntsville was chosen by party delegates to run for the state senate, becoming the first black regular Democratic candidate for a state office from northern Alabama. The delegates cast aside a white conservative incumbent to nominate Grayson. Though part of the motivation was a redrawing of the electoral district to include a black majority, it also reflected the changing composition of the party. The state's leading Democrats are now more urban and dominated by a middle-class coalition of labor, trial lawyers, blacks, and the Alabama Education Association—and the new coalition had the blessing of Governor George Wallace.

It would probably be too much to state that George Wallace is a creation of black political power in Alabama. The images of the governor proclaiming "segregation forever," or standing at the schoolhouse door to prevent the integration of the University of Alabama, or disdainfully dismissing emissaries from the voting-rights march clash with more recent images of the repentant sinner painfully confined to a wheelchair. Yet the transformation of George Wallace is the great metaphor of black power in the South, certainly in a political sense, and—putting aside an understandable cynicism—in a moral sense as well.

In 1983, on the spot where he had vowed "segregation forever" twenty years earlier, George Wallace was sworn in for his final term as governor of Alabama. A black man led the governor's assembled supporters in the Pledge of Allegiance; a black minister pronounced the benediction; and a black man took the oath as a justice of the Alabama Supreme Court—the first black statewide elected official since Reconstruction. Blacks comprise 25 percent of the state's population, and, under Wallace, they make up 25.4 percent of the state's civil service positions, compared with less than 2 percent in 1970. His cabinet included a black revenue commissioner and a black welfare director. The state police force is integrated, and there are twenty-one blacks in the legislature. In March, 1985, Wallace received Jesse Jackson at the governor's mansion at the conclusion of the march from Selma to Montgomery commemorating the twentieth anniversary of that historic demonstration. Sitting comfortably on the balcony on that warm early spring day, sipping iced tea and eating cakes served on a silver tray, two of the major actors in the southern drama of the century, once on opposite sides of the stage but now drawn together in mutual respect and forgiveness, discussed the South and the movement. They were much like the old Confederate veterans who gathered on similar spring afternoons to recall their great adventure, but their conversation did not drift into a nostalgia over causes lost, but rather of wars won and of promises to be fulfilled. Jackson had looked into Wallace and had found a man of "sensitivity," a man "whose attitude has changed, whose behavior has changed."

And black Alabamians gave George Wallace what they had struggled and, some, died for—their votes. In the 1982 Democratic gubernatorial primary, a white Birmingham attorney, George McMillan, with a strong record on civil rights issues, challenged Wallace. His campaign drew Coretta Scott King and other movement leaders to Alabama, but despite this support, more than one-third of black voters supported Wallace, providing the crucial difference in his narrow (50.9 percent to 49.1 percent) victory over McMillan. In the general election, Wallace's black support was better than four to one over the Republican opponent, Montgomery mayor Emory Folmar. In both the primary and the general election, the strongest black support came from the Black Belt—the scene of bitter and violent voting-rights struggles of the 1960s.

There are several explanations as to why blacks, especially rural blacks in Alabama, would cast aside the evidence of history and the advice of their own leaders to support George Wallace. Some of the support may have come from the increasing political sophistication of blacks who recognized that, despite his obstreperous behavior in the 1960s, the Wallace of more recent vintage had significantly increased the black presence in state government. He had also created an extensive community college network that enabled blacks to attain educational and job-skill levels that offered the promise of a way out of Black Belt poverty. Also, it was not likely that the liberal McMillan would have won the general election, and regardless of the sincerity of Wallace's racial predilections, there was no ambiguity as to Folmar's racial posture. Blacks in Montgomery referred to him as the "Mayoratollah."

But that is imputing a Machiavellian bent that is mostly foreign to Alabama's rural blacks. More simply, the explanation probably lies in the deep religious roots of the southern black, the belief in conversion and redemption. Redemption of white souls, after all, was a major objective of the civil rights movement. Delores Pickett, a young black woman who served as Wallace's state coordinator for black support, explained her support and the forgiveness in the hearts of black Alabamians: "It's in our Christian upbringing, and it's something that Martin Luther King taught us, too." In a similar vein, Birmingham *News* reporter Frank Sikora visited a Black Belt county that had gone two to one for Wallace in the primary. He met Robert Strickland, who, in 1965, marched along U.S. Highway 80 between Selma and Montgomery singing his song, "Ain't gonna let George Wallace turn us around." Now, leaning against his pickup truck festooned with "Wallace" bumper stickers in front of the Lowndes County Courthouse, Strickland explained his political preference. Wallace, he noted, was "like Saul, who was struck down and then got up to do good. . . . He's said he regretted the past. And down here, the folks believe him. That's all." It was a simple statement of faith in mutual humanity and a particularly southern belief that personal relations, more than laws and doctrines, were what counted.

This is not to say that black voters responded positively to all white professions of repentance. Dallas County sheriff Jim Clark, despite reconciliatory gestures, became one of the earliest victims of black political power in the rural South. In 1980, black voters in Georgia turned on their erstwhile nemesis Herman Talmadge, who had also proffered the olive branch. The coolness of black voters to Talmadge's senatorial re-election campaign was one of the major factors in Republican Mack Mattingly's upset victory. Indeed, rhetoric was not enough to absolve old segregationists; Wallace not only professed a new faith but performed good works as well. Southern white politicians recognized the growing discernment among black voters and acted accordingly. Perhaps the most vivid example of white consciousness occurred in the debate over the Voting Rights Act extension in 1982.

In 1975, Congress had extended the Voting Rights Act for seven years. The act came up for renewal in 1982, in the midst of a national conservative tide and in the context of an administration that appeared to be, at best, indifferent to the concept of franchise protection. However, due primarily to the efforts of Republican senator Robert Dole, the Senate approved a twenty-five-year extension—the longest renewal period ever—by a resounding eighty-five to eight vote. Among those voting in the affirmative were Mississippi's John Stennis, who was facing a tough re-election campaign back home, and South Carolina's Republican senator Strom Thurmond, who supported a civil rights measure for the first time in his legislative career.

In addition to extending the act, the Senate also eased the burden of proof for plaintiffs bringing suit against discriminatory electoral practices. In 1980, the U.S. Supreme Court, in *City of Mobile* v. *Bolden*, had struck down a challenge to Mobile's at-large system of election by ruling that the plaintiff, civil rights leader Wiley Bolden, had presented only circumstantial evidence to demonstrate the discriminatory effect of the procedure. The Court stated that Bolden had failed to establish *intent*. The Senate overrode that difficult standard, restoring circumstantial factors as valid evidence for proving discrimination. The High Court reversed itself later that year, incidentally, bringing its precedent in line with the Congress.

The failure of Judge Robert Bork's nomination to the U.S. Supreme Court in October, 1987, is a more recent and equally impressive reflection of black electoral power in the South. Though numerous factors contributed to Judge Bork's defeat, columnist and North Carolina native Tom Wicker noted that "if any one factor seems more responsible than another . . . it is the new voting power of blacks in the conservative South." Sixteen southern Democratic senators aligned themselves with Bork's opponents. None of these senators had received a majority of the white vote in their respective states, but three of the sixteen—Richard Shelby and Howell Heflin of Alabama, and John Breaux of Louisiana—had won 75 percent of the black vote. Heflin played a major role in undermining the nomination.

The smooth extension of the Voting Rights Act and the defeat of Judge Bork's nomination reflected something more than raw black political power. It also indicated the growing sophistication and independence of the black electorate. Though there were examples of political acumen during the early 1970s, it did not become widespread until late in the decade, particularly after the major role that southern blacks played in electing President Jimmy Carter. Wallace aide Delores Pickett observed that black voters paid less attention to the governor's rhetoric in the late 1960s and early 1970s than to the things that "were happening that were good for black people. There were schools being built, junior colleges, jobs available." So when the rhetoric changed, blacks recalled the actions more than the words. In a similar vein, blacks were not adverse to voting for Republicans on occasion. Again, there were examples of such support prior to the late 1970s, but it became less of a novelty by the 1980s and more crucial in some instances to Republican success. Mack Mattingly's victorious 1980 senatorial campaign was one example, as was his subsequent defeat for reelection in 1986, when black voters returned to the Democratic fold to support the candidacy of Wyche Fowler.

There were also indications that blacks were not necessarily voting Republican in the 1980s merely as the lesser of two evils. In the 1984 U.S. Senate campaign in Mississippi, former governor William F. Winter, a liberal by that state's standards and a supporter of black agenda items during his term in the statehouse, was running against incumbent senator Thad Cochran, a Republican. Cochran counted himself among the conservative wing of his party, but he made a direct appeal for black votes during his campaign, standing on his record as senator. He targeted particularly the state's growing black urban middle class, or "Buppies" (Black Upwardly Mobile Professionals), a group that southern Republicans are courting increasingly. Though a majority of the state's blacks supported Winter, Cochran succeeded in siphoning off enough black votes to ensure a relatively easy victory.

It is likely that black support for Republican candidates will increase in the future; at the least, such behavior will keep Democratic hopefuls from assuming certain black support. Ironically, Jesse Jackson's presidential candidacies, though carried out under the Democratic party banner, loosened black party identification to some degree, encouraging independence among his southern black constituents. Jackson also noted the expanding black middle class as a new political base in the South whose interests could parallel the Republican philosophy. In fact, as far back as 1978, Jackson informed the Republican National Committee that such an alliance was possible in the South, that "blacks will vote for Republicans who appeal to their vested interest and engage in reciprocity."

Black support for Republican candidates was one indication of increasing independence among black voters. The black vote in the Alabama gubernatorial primary demonstrated that endorsements by national civil rights leaders did not ensure the black vote, nor would blacks automatically vote for a black candidate in a race against a white. In 1983, veteran black political leader Charles Evers made his third independent bid to be governor of Mississippi. He campaigned as a champion of the poor, contending that the "state is run by 11 percent of its people . . . mostly stuffy, redneck, old white men." Black voters did not respond to his appeal, giving Evers only 3.9 percent of the vote in a contest won by Attorney General Bill Allain of Natchez. The feeling among the state's black voters was that Evers could not win and a move to support him would fracture the Democratic party, enabling an undesirable Republican candidate to attain victory.

Black political styles are also changing—the era of the single-note candidacy is over. Southern blacks rarely campaign exclusively on a racial agenda now, and once they are in office, they are attuned to the shifting alliances of political survival. Maynard Jackson's strong push for minority rights, even to the point of holding up millions of dollars in construction, softened during his second term, and his successor, Andrew Young, some critics complain, scarcely has a racial agenda. Richard Arrington practiced confrontational politics on minority issues during his first term as mayor of Birmingham, but he acknowledged his "mistakes," softened his rhetoric, and became a successful administrator who broadened his support during his second term. In Richmond, black councilman Roy West replaced the city's first black mayor, Henry L. Marsh III, in 1982. Observers note that West, a school administrator, brought to the office an easy-going, accommodating style more attuned to the city's "slow-moving, genteel ways," as journalist Neal Peirce put it, and improved tense race relations. Although the early black city administrations were important in setting guidelines for minority participation in local government and economy, the more recent generation of southern urban black political leaders understands the importance of brokering the various actors in the political process.

The political sophistication has carried over into state legislative bodies, where the small numbers of black lawmakers necessitate coalition building. Jesse Oliver is a black state representative from Dallas who steered a landmark indigent health-care bill through the Texas legislature during the 1986 session. He accomplished this major victory by carefully building a coalition that included Governor Mark White and House Speaker Gib Lewis. Though powerful opponents, such as the Texas Hospital Association and most Republican lawmakers, including U.S. Senator Phil Gramm, sought to scuttle the bill, Oliver, as one admiring colleague noted, "mastered those details; no one could challenge our facts." Oliver and his allies also subtly warned hostile rural legislators that, if the bill failed, Dallas hospitals would no longer be willing to become the "dumping grounds for charity medical cases referred by rural counties" without some financial restitution. Oliver typified the new, low-key black politician—Neal Peirce referred to him as an "unassuming intellectual." He grew up poor in

A federal registrar places a black citizen on the voting rolls five days after President Johnson signs the Voting Rights Act, Canton, Mississippi, August 11, 1965.

U.S. News and World Report collection, Library of Congress

Waiting to register to vote at the federal courthouse, Birmingham, January, 1966.

From the Archives Collection, Birmingham Public Library, Birmingham, Alabama

Voting in the Alabama Democratic party primary, the first major election in the South after the signing of the Voting Rights Act, May 4, 1966.   Library of Congress

Jackson Ward, a black neighborhood, makes way for the Richmond Coliseum, 1970.

Then-state senator Douglas Wilder (now Virginia lieutenant governor and Democratic party candidate for governor) speaking at a banquet of Richmond's political leaders, 1970. Wilder's success among the state's white electorate results in part from his long years of public service and the moderate image he has cultivated.   Valentine Museum, Richmond, Virginia

Black contractor H. J. Russell talks with a worker at a public housing site, Atlanta, 1974. Federal projects and the guidelines accompanying them have been instrumental in boosting black entrepreneurship in the urban South.

Diverging societies, Atlanta, 1971.
Courtesy of the Atlanta Historical Society

Courtesy of the Atlanta Historical Society

Tom Gilmore, sheriff, Greene County, Alabama, in front of his boyhood home, 1974.

Courtesy of the Atlanta Historical Society

Richmond mayor Henry Marsh III helps host an affair given by the city's Convention and Visitor's Bureau, 1977. Despite occasional conflicts, black politicians have found it necessary to cooperate with white business and political leaders to improve their political longevity.

Valentine Museum, Richmond, Virginia

Lawrence Wade, Memphis banker and entrepreneur, in front of the shopping center he owns. The accommodation in race relations enhanced opportunities for southern blacks already well-positioned to take advantage of them.   Library of Congress

Contemporary southern politics.
Doug Marlette, Charlotte *Observer*, May 10, 1985

Fulfilling the American Dream on Richmond's crabgrass frontier, July, 1983.
Valentine Museum, Richmond, Virginia

Race and metropolitan politics: A white county fends off an unwanted black suitor, July, 1986.

Valentine Museum, Richmond, Virginia

Black political power in Richmond: Mayor Roy West and Vice-Mayor Claudette Black McDaniel enjoy a laugh moments before being reelected to their respective posts, July, 1986.

Valentine Museum, Richmond, Virginia

rural East Texas, a place more like the Old South than the New West. After dropping out of college, he drifted about for nineteen years in a series of odd jobs before becoming an attorney at age thirty-six. He had only a remote connection to the civil rights movement, and his legislative agenda reflected the concern of the 1980s—the poor—much more than the big issue of the 1960s—race.

The background of South Carolina Supreme Court judge Ernest Finney was different from Oliver's, but his political savvy and its positive results were the same. As a young attorney in the 1960s, Finney had defended sit-in demonstrators in Sumter, South Carolina. He eventually became a circuit court judge but coveted a position on the state supreme court. South Carolina is one of the few states where the legislature appoints justices to the high court, and since conservative rural lawmakers had long controlled that body, Finney's selection was highly unlikely. However, during a brief tenure in the legislature, Finney became a desk mate and friend of one of the most influential senators, Ramon Schwartz. When a high-court vacancy occurred in 1984, Finney became a candidate along with three white hopefuls, but he graciously dropped out when it became apparent that he lacked the necessary support in the legislature. The following year when another vacancy occurred, lawmakers remembered his gentlemanly gesture, and he ran unopposed.

Black politicians are beginning to master the often intricate etiquette of state politics and are being rewarded both on their merits and on how well they are playing the game. White lawmakers, for their part, are more comfortable with black colleagues and understand that there is nothing to fear from them in terms of upsetting procedures or in promoting radical legislation. They are also realizing that alliances with black representatives can be helpful to their favorite bills as well. The widespread support for Virginia's Douglas Wilder among the state's Democratic party establishment, for example, stemmed from his long and competent tenure in the state senate. Wilder was not a threat; he was a colleague.

There seems nothing unclear about this picture—the upwardly mobile black politician, the increasingly sophisticated black electorate, and the growing respect for both among establishment whites. Indeed, one could not but help in concurring with Jesse Jackson's statement at the 1984 Democratic National Convention that "the linchpin of progressive politics in our Nation will not come from the North. . . . [It] in fact will come from the South." But although many white southerners were willing to admit blacks to the political game as full-fledged members with all the rights and privileges that this implied, others remained who sought to bend the rules to limit the black political presence.

Voting Procedures: Old Ways and New Quandaries

This opposition was especially notable with respect to electoral procedures. White Mississippi officials in particular continued to utilize a range of techniques to dilute the strength of the state's black electorate. In 1983, Jesse Jackson guided the U.S. assistant attorney general for civil rights, William Bradford Reynolds, through a two-day fact-finding tour of rural Mississippi. Reynolds heard testimony about registrars changing the location of polling places at the last minute, intimidation at the ballot box (including a white man in Greenwood who presented himself as a Justice Department official and dissuaded blacks from voting), and requirements that blacks register in both city and county poll books. In Belzoni, Reynolds learned that whites retained control by refusing to annex a black neighborhood in the center of town; elsewhere, he heard that rural towns were annexing white neighborhoods to dilute black voting strength. Canton officials had built public housing outside the city limits; and whites in Tallahatchee County reportedly paid blacks ten dollars each for returning blank ballots. Mamie Chinn, a black poll watcher from Canton, told Reynolds that she had seen an elderly black man mark his ballot for black candidates when his white employer came over for a brief conversation; the black voter then tore up his ballot and requested another, which he marked for the white candidates. In Jackson, a black service-station attendant was fired from his job for failing to rally black support for a white candidate for sheriff. White Mississippians were not the only violators, merely the worst. After a survey of election procedure abuses across the Deep South in 1981, the U.S. Commission on Civil Rights concluded that "white resistance and hostility by some State and local officials to increased minority participation [was evident] in virtually every aspect of the electoral process."

That these tactics persisted nearly twenty years after the passage of the Voting Rights Act reflected the burden placed on blacks to bring such conditions to the attention of the courts or the federal government. The latter had been nonchalant in its enforcement of the act's provisions in the 1980s, especially of the Section 5 pre-clearance provision. Though the Nixon administration was not a staunch supporter of the act, it did not interfere with the Justice Department's handling of these cases after 1970. The general withdrawal of the Reagan administration from enforcing, much less challenging, procedural changes has placed a significant and expensive burden on local blacks. In 1984, for example, after a strong showing by blacks in a local election, the all-white election commission in Dallas County, Alabama, transferred a polling place from a community center in a black neighborhood of Selma to the county courthouse. In the next election, voting fell from 55 percent of the eligible black voters to 36 percent. When blacks protested to William Bradford Reynolds, he dismissed their claims of discrimination as "fanciful conclusions," adding that the courthouse was merely a "neutral" site and, besides, there was more parking available there. For Selma blacks, the county courthouse had hardly been a "neutral" site in the recent past. Memories were still fresh of Jim Clark and his posse and of intimidation by registrars and assorted white county officials.

The issue of voting procedures, however, was considerably more complex than monitoring the subterfuges of white politicians. Among the assumed verities of voting rights was that single-member districts would enhance the election chances for minority candidates, that district voting was preferable over at-large balloting, and that majority-black districts were better than districts where black voters were in a minority. Elections in the 1980s have called all of these standards into question, throwing courts, black leaders, and white allies into confusion. When court-ordered redistricting occurred in North Carolina in 1984, white Republicans turned out to be the major beneficiaries of the change. The Democrat-controlled General Assembly redrew legislative district lines to create at least one predominantly black district in each of the state's largest cities, with the effect of isolating the traditionally Democratic black vote, while Republicans won in the predominantly white jurisdictions. Republicans picked up fifteen new seats in these redrawn metropolitan districts. Gains by blacks were marginal—they picked up one additional seat in the House and one in the state senate. The day after the election, the Republican state chairman called for single-member districts statewide, and black lawmakers lost important white Democratic allies. The district system also left blacks with less leverage: Republicans competed halfheartedly in the overwhelmingly black districts, and they could ignore black interests in the mostly white jurisdictions. The Democrats, assured of an almost-free ride in black areas, had to compete with Republicans in the white districts, which invariably meant a more conservative stance on issues that blacks support.

The U.S. Supreme Court's quick reversal of itself on the evidentiary support necessary to prove discrimination concerning electoral procedures is symptomatic of the legal confusion attending this area. With the ability of computers to calculate and draw up hundreds of different districting plans, the question of what constitutes minority-vote dilution becomes increasingly complex. Is it sufficient, for example, to create a district with a black electorate of 50 percent to ensure good intent, or is more required? On the other hand, blacks in 1982 petitioned the Texas congressional redistricting committee to maintain two districts in the Dallas area where they comprised a minority of the electorate so they could retain two white liberal congressmen. Though it was unlikely that a black candidate could win an election in these districts, was the status quo discriminatory? In the long run, is it better for the political process not to have isolated, "safe" black districts? The answers are unclear.

The procedural issues would perhaps be less crucial if southern white voters would support black candidates. That has happened on occasion, as the successful campaigns of Virginia's Douglas Wilder and Charlotte's Harvey Gantt attest, but these are unusual cases. Despite Andrew Young's support among Atlanta's white business establishment, the 1981 mayoral race in that city divided clearly along racial lines with 90 percent of the voters of each race casting their ballots for the candidate of their own color. Typically, however, blacks are more willing than whites to cross racial lines in the voting booth—a factor that has cost some black candidates an almost certain election victory. In 1984, the South Carolina legislature established ten majority-black districts throughout the state, and though black candidates ran in all those districts, only three were elected. Few whites voted for blacks. So even in a majority-registration situation, black candidates required virtually unanimous support from the black community—an unusual feat given the numerous class, age, and ideological divisions among blacks—in order to win an election. There was also the factor that some blacks, for a complex set of reasons ranging from tradition to paternalism, did not vote for candidates of their own race. This phenomenon was more prevalent in the rural districts of the Deep South than elsewhere; in 1983, for example, Quitman County (Miss.) blacks had the benefit of sixty-five federal observers for the county supervisors' election and a two-thirds registration advantage over whites, but the white candidates won. A local white official analyzed the result as demonstrating that black voters "know black folks can't give 'em anything. Only white folks can help 'em."

Blacks will win few elections in the South by the strength of numbers. Except for a few cities (Atlanta, Birmingham, New Orleans, and Richmond) and eighty-six rural counties located primarily in the Deep South, white voters easily outnumber blacks throughout the region. Black populations within southern states range from 12 to 35 percent. Overall, whites comprise 83 percent of the southern electorate. Most black voting strength is concentrated in the Deep South (Mississippi, South Carolina, Louisiana, Georgia, Alabama) where blacks constitute nearly one out of four voters, compared with one out of seven in what political scientists Earl and Merle Black call the "Peripheral South" (North Carolina, Virginia, Arkansas, Tennessee, Florida, Texas).

It is not likely that voter registration drives will alter these figures. White voter registration accelerated since 1970 to the point where, by 1985, nearly 80 percent of eligible whites in the South were registered compared with 66 percent of blacks. Some of this surge resulted from the reaction to highly publicized black voter-registration campaigns, especially Jesse Jackson's efforts during the 1984 presidential race. In Georgia, for example, white voter registration had declined by 56,000 between 1980 and 1984, but in the five months prior to the November, 1984, election, 145,000 white Georgians registered to vote. South Carolina also experienced a drop in white voter registration between 1980 and 1984—14,000—but added 19,000 white voters between May and August of the latter year. The increase reflected as well the continued in-migration of whites from other parts of the country, a trend that in the long run is probably more significant than the white backlash, since these new voters are more likely to participate in the political process than working-class whites and poorer blacks.

Republicans and Democrats:
Bodies and Souls

Republicans were counting on the twin appeals to race and economic conservatism to attract a wide spectrum of white support to the party banner. In 1984, political scientist Earl Black spoke to a group of Republicans in South Carolina on the nature and prospects of the party in the South. After his talk, a few businessmen came up to say that they had enjoyed the presentation though they felt that he had overstated the party's racial appeal; they suggested that race was, at best, a minor factor in the party's southern success and that economic reasons were paramount. Before Black could reply, another businessman approached the group and interjected, "Enjoyed the talk. Why don't you leave the niggers behind and come and join us?"

Though Republican leaders would disavow the latter sentiment, race and economics not only became central to party strategy in the South but merged to some degree. A life-long Democratic voter from Mississippi explained his shift to the Republican camp: "It's all this 'gimme' business. . . . What we need now is for the black race to pull themselves up by their own bootstraps." This comment could be neatly catalogued as a reaffirmation of the Republican party's free enterprise philosophy; Democratic party leaders, however, read other meanings into this and similar statements. As Mississippi congressman Wayne Dowdy, a Democrat, observed, "Republicans in Mississippi are . . . [in the GOP] because they like what they think the Republican party now stands for in a racial sense. And that's a strong part of the Republican party in Mississippi. In my district, a lot of the people who are in the Republican party are racists."

Yet there were southern Republican leaders who were anxious to separate out the economic component from the racial appeals and attempt to attract black voters. South Carolina Republican governor Carroll Campbell, elected in 1986, predicted that "the Republican party is going to pick up black voters in the same manner in which it is attracting white voters. And I think that is going to be a philosophy . . . based on concern for human needs and at the same time for the integrity of the free enterprise system. . . . The hope for the Republican party in the South is the growing black middle class, because the Republican party has middle-class values."

Despite Campbell's hope, racial code words still circulate in the rhetoric of some southern Republican candidates. Doug Marlette, award-winning political cartoonist for the New York *Newsday*, penned a drawing in March, 1984, showing North Carolina senator Jesse Helms sitting on a river bank fishing as a Klansman in full regalia stood nearby. Helms says to the Klansman, "Race-Bait? No, Nowadays I Just Use Food Stamps!" Indeed, in Helms's 1984 senatorial campaign against Democratic governor Jim Hunt, the Republican incumbent distributed a newsletter devoted to Governor Hunt's endorsement of the effort to register black voters in the state. Helms's supporters doubtless received the appropriate message, as did a throng of voters in

Philadelphia, Mississippi—the town made notorious for the slaying of three civil rights workers during the Freedom Summer—when Ronald Reagan campaigned there in 1980 and vowed that his administration would defend the principle of "states' rights."

The Republican party in the 1980s has kept race vital as a campaign issue. By making racism respectable through code words and linkages to economic philosophy, Republicans may have inhibited a more thorough-going racial reconciliation in the South. At the least, they have placed Democrats on the defensive concerning race and have given blacks little alternative but to remain almost exclusively in the Democratic party. Blacks gave Democrat Jim Hunt 99.4 percent of their vote in his unsuccessful 1984 Senate campaign against Jesse Helms. Doug Marlette posed the dilemma for Democrats in a political cartoon in May, 1985, that pictured two water fountains, one labeled "White" and the other "Democrat." Such an identification would effectively limit the party to a permanent minority status in the South, a prospect raised by Tom Wicker in a New York *Times* column after the 1984 presidential election. "For the foreseeable future," Wicker perceived the Democrats as "a party of access," and the Republicans as "a party of government."

The pessimism within the Democratic party camp dissipated to some degree with the 1986 elections. The party victory in Virginia the previous year, coupled with the gain of four important Senate seats in Florida, Georgia, Alabama, and North Carolina, indicated that white flight had abated. This came as welcome news to blacks who feared that the party's attempt to compete for white votes would render them politically invisible. But most state Democratic leaders would agree with Mike Daniel, former lieutenant governor of South Carolina, that "we must correct our deficiencies without forgetting our purpose or selling our soul." To accomplish Daniel's objective will require a continuation of the political high-wire act, of balancing blacks' desires for a more interventionist government with white traditions of a low-profile public sector. The victories in Virginia and other parts of the South demonstrate that Democratic candidates who occupy the broad middle with a record of fiscal probity and social progress can maintain their balance.

For those blacks who have made their way into the political arena and have become acculturated to the rules of southern politics, the future is promising in terms of increased power and patronage. As black lawmakers operate within this structured framework, and as long as prosperity persists throughout much of the region, it is also likely that more social legislation such as the indigent health-care bill in Texas will become possible, but the political situation is not likely to provide a quick fix for the majority of southern blacks struggling just above or below subsistence level.

Plenty and Poverty: The Two Worlds of the Southern Black Economy

This is not to say that black economic advance in the South during the late 1970s and 1980s was minuscule. The major economic story of the decade was the rapid expansion of the black middle class—rapid enough for the Republicans at least to consider the development of a different type of southern strategy. Leslie Dunbar wrote in 1980 that the "irreversible achievement of the civil rights movement . . . is that the black middle class has greatly expanded." Earl and Merle Black estimated that by 1980 nearly 30 percent of southern black workers were employed in middle-class occupations (over 40 percent in metropolitan areas) compared with 4 percent in 1940. The best indirect evidence continues to be in-migration: between 1975 and 1985 more than 850,000 blacks moved south, compared with slightly more than 500,000 blacks who left. These in-migrants tended to be younger and better educated as a group than earlier black in-migrants—nearly two out of three held at least a high-school diploma (compared with a 45 percent rate among blacks already living in the South).

Metropolitan areas in the South Atlantic states have been the major beneficiaries of black middle-class migration. Cities such as Atlanta, Charlotte, Richmond, and the Raleigh-Durham-Chapel Hill area with expanding postindustrial economies have been attractive to white-collar, professional blacks—newcomers, returnees, and residents alike. For those returning to the South after many years' absence, the change has been especially noticeable. Diane Freeman, a membership specialist for Discovery Place, a hands-on science museum in Charlotte, left in 1969 to work for Chemical Bank in New York, but returned in 1980 when the employment situation for skilled blacks improved. She found an improved racial climate compared with New York, where "the racial overtones were blatant." William Greene, another black Charlotte native, had a similar experience. Trained as a teacher, he could not find a satisfactory position at a decent salary in his native state, so he accepted a teaching job in Pontiac, Michigan, where the starting salary was nearly double that in North Carolina.

Though the racial situation had improved by the late 1960s, the economic opportunities for educated blacks had not. As Greene noted, "when I left, it was a matter of economics and opportunities." He returned to Charlotte in 1982 to accept an administrative position at a local college, earning more than $30,000 annually.

The South was a frontier of economic opportunity to first-time black migrants as well. These blacks were drawn to the South without ancillary pulls such as kin or place but with the promise of upward mobility. Dick Coleman, a forty-five-year-old manager of pricing services and national accounts for Gold Bond Building Products, moved to Pineville, North Carolina, from Buffalo in 1978. "It's refreshing to be in an area where black entrepreneurship has a chance." He is now attempting to convince his four sisters to move south. Colin Batson is a data-processing researcher for the Royal Insurance Company in Charlotte who moved south when Royal left New York City in 1985. "I was scared about what would come to me down here," he admitted. But now, "I love it down here. I'm sorry I didn't move here ten years ago. . . . I've found that a lot of people treat you nicer here than they do in New York. . . . Quite honestly, I haven't come across anything I don't like about the South."

Some general statistics added substance to these anecdotal testimonials: in 1960, black wages in the South were roughly 20 percent lower than black wages in the North; by 1986, the differential had declined to 6 percent with predictions that by 1990 southern blacks might be at parity or even better paid than blacks elsewhere. Considering the lower living costs in the South, the relative absence of labor unions, and the low pay scales in rural areas and small towns, the effective gap has probably disappeared by now. Even at the lower end of the economic spectrum, there were indications of improvement. Between 1970 and 1982, the percentage of blacks in the South living below the federal poverty standard had declined by 5 percent while increasing by at least 12 percent in other regions of the country; in addition, the unemployment rate for southern blacks was slightly lower than the rate for blacks nationally. Some black leaders argue that part of the brightening economic picture has resulted from the general prosperity of the South over the past decade and, secondarily, from the affirmative action practiced by black political leaders. Atlanta's Andrew Young, for instance, increased minority contracts to 35 percent of the total. These funds, Young claimed, "bubble up to feed the hungry, clothe the naked, and heal the sick"; however, Young's chief black adversary in Atlanta, the Reverend Hosea Williams, questioned the mayor's trickle-down theory and asked "how the mayor plans to cure Atlanta's black inner-city problems, second only to those of Newark on the poverty charts."

Williams' question pointed to another muddle of black life in the South. Black southerners in the 1980s were enjoying their most substantial period of economic prosperity and opportunity in history, but it was a highly uneven advance. It was no longer a question of two black communities emerging side by side, but rather of two separate black worlds, paralleling to some extent the old black-white separation of previous decades. The highly publicized black poverty tours of the late 1960s and early 1970s that first alerted regional and national leaders to the extent of the economic problem in the South were no longer undertaken. They were unnecessary; most white and black leaders were aware of the existence of widespread poverty, but were considerably less optimistic about the possibilities and capabilities of ameliorating it. The federal government had retreated from social services, and state and local governments were increasingly enmeshed in the fierce national competition for economic development.

Black power at the local level counted for even less in the economic realm in the 1980s than it did in the 1970s, because the problems were of such magnitude that only state and federal authorities could begin to address them. The fact that the white business elite still controlled major economic policies meant that black leaders such as Young, Gantt, and Arrington had to limit social engineering or lose the effectiveness of their administrations, and in smaller communities, white elites or no, the economic means remained far below the economic needs of the population. Nearly two decades of black rule in Lowndes County, Alabama, for example, had not changed the fact that it was among the nation's ten poorest counties, or that more than 45 percent of its residents still lived below the poverty line, or that it continued to have one of the nation's highest infant-mortality rates.

Lowndes County was by no means an isolated instance of black poverty amid the Sun Belt South of the 1980s. Thirty-eight black neighborhoods in Houston still lacked indoor plumbing as late as 1985, and in southern cities generally, black median income in 1980 was only 55.8 percent of white median income. Lamond Godwin, former southeastern director of the National Rural Center, noted in 1982 that children of impoverished rural black families were streaming to southern cities that threaten to become a regional "economic dumping ground." By 1980, black slums in Atlanta, New Orleans, Birmingham, Richmond (all four cities had black mayors), and Jackson were among "the most despair-ridden . . . in America," according to journalist Neal Peirce.

But it was the rural South that remained the most shocking exemplar of black poverty. Sammy Lee Jones died in April, 1985, on the 1,200-acre peach farm of Lewis Holmes near Aiken, South Carolina. Jones was an illiterate black farm laborer who, according to relatives, was about sixty years old when he died. He had been suffering from a range of illnesses including tuberculosis, diabetes, alcoholism, and a badly infected leg that never healed after he burned it in a fireplace eighteen months earlier. He lived in a tar-paper four-room shack with his sister and her three sons, none of whom knew how old they were. The shack had no indoor plumbing; water came from an outdoor spigot. Two fireplaces provided heat. There was no telephone. Holmes charged no rent for the dwelling, but deducted $2.50 to $9.00 a week from Jones's pay for utilities, and also subtracted medical expenses. Jones earned $2,566 in 1983, the last full year he worked, yet the family did not know it was eligible for food stamps and other social services. Holmes had urged county health authorities to take the family off his hands and his land: "I don't have to take care of these people when they're not working for me," he explained. An Aiken County government employee noted that the Jones case, though extreme, was not unique in South Carolina. "So many of them out there, they're living like slaves."

Conditions among blacks in rural Mississippi continued to attract national notoriety. In 1983, four out of every ten blacks in the state were living below the poverty level, compared with one in ten whites. In the town of Tunica in the Delta, the typical black dwelling is a two- to four-room wooden shack with a tin roof and cardboard or plastic in place of windowpanes. Only 14 percent of the town's adult blacks have a high-school education, and most are on welfare ($120 a month for a family of four). One especially wretched black district, Sugar Ditch Alley, takes its name from a half-mile trough that runs behind the shacks, where residents dump human waste and other garbage.

Across the South in the 1980s, there was a direct correlation between the proportion of the black population and the relative poverty in a rural county. Rural counties more than one-third black had significantly less employment growth, higher school-dropout rates, and more families below the poverty line than other rural counties. In

1986, sociologist Kenny Johnson tallied the extent of rural black poverty, whose victims are primarily women and children: more than 58 percent of black rural women were poor; 76 percent of rural black children were poor; and black children under six years of age fared worst of all with nearly 80 percent living in poverty.

These counties were not likely candidates for imminent improvement, because they offered little in the way of infrastructure, skilled labor, amenities, school systems, and transportation access that would attract new businesses. Any skilled or educated youngsters would leave these areas. The only realistic economic future for some of these counties is to attract activities shunned everywhere else, such as toxic waste storage.

Sumter County, Alabama, is a case in point. One out of every three residents lives below the poverty line; 93 percent are black. In 1986, the county's unemployment rate was 21.1 percent—welfare is the single most important "occupation." Since 1977, Chemical Waste Management, Inc., has operated a toxic dump in the county, paying roughly half of Sumter's total revenues annually but contaminating the groundwater, creeks, streams, and farmlands. In Alabama, Sumter is derisively known as "the nation's pay toilet." Alabama state district attorney Jimmy Evans, who is conducting an investigation of the hazardous waste industry in several poor, rural Alabama counties, summarized the situation: "The strategy is to find predominantly black, economically distressed areas and make their economies dependent on hazardous waste to the extent that the people who live there become hazardous waste junkies." Policy makers, black and white, have been at a loss at how to deal with either the conditions deriving from poverty or poverty itself. The origins of black poverty, especially in rural areas, are confusing, yet the solutions are truly mystifying.

A similar muddle exists with respect to a policy initially designed to address some of the issues revolving around black poverty—affirmative action. Most southern cities had inaugurated some form of affirmative action program in public employment by 1980. Similarly, southern universities and many businesses in the region had some quota system to comply with federal guidelines, but a combination of growing white resentment and federal opposition threatened adherence to affirmative action principles. Earl Black related that white students in the South today have had some experience with affirmative action programs, "and they do not like them. Every one of them has a friend who didn't get into the University of North Carolina who had higher board scores than blacks who did get in here." Jack Breed, a white businessman from Jackson, Mississippi, called it "overkill. A young white man . . . can't get a job or a promotion because he isn't black." Breed acknowledged that "the doors were locked. They were opened. They *should* have been opened. But they ought not be locked on somebody else now." Breed's scenario was enacted rarely if at all in most firms, but in a region with a strong individualist tradition, where considerable numbers of poor whites are locked out of Sun Belt prosperity (for reasons quite apart from affirmative action), the perception of preferential treatment of a group can create problems. No clear consensus has emerged from the black community on affirmative action, either, but William Julius Wilson contends that its impact is marginal and then only in white-collar occupations where demand for labor of any color generally exceeds supply.

There is another cultural issue involved aside from the South's fierce individualism. The affirmative action principle appeared to contradict the region's religious traditions. Kyle Haselden, the black managing editor of *Christian Century*, argued that quotas leave "with the descendants of the exploiters a guilt they cannot cancel and with the descendants of the exploited a debt they cannot collect." Accordingly, the principle failed "all the crucial tests of a moral struggle for racial justice." In a similar vein, black economist Thomas Sowell declared that "*no* policy can apply to history but can only apply to the present or the future. The past may be many things, but it is clearly irrevocable. . . . Those who suffered in centuries past are as much beyond our help as those who sinned are beyond our retribution."

The Reagan administration attempted to unravel affirmative action agreements in several southern cities, encouraged by a 1984 U.S. Supreme Court decision that upheld the seniority rights of white Memphis firefighters facing layoffs under an affirmative action plan. In 1985, the Justice Department challenged a six-year-old agreement in Birmingham concerning police and fire departments. Yet despite the growing unpopularity of quotas in Washington, as well as among some blacks, a number of white southern leaders have defended the principle. The Birmingham *Post-Herald* scored William Bradford Reynolds for not giving blacks and women, even briefly, "the same edge that white males enjoyed to a much greater degree for many years," and a Charlotte *Observer* editorial allowed that "racial hiring goals are nothing new; for generations, the rigid quota in many places was 100% white. . . . Affirmative action must be understood in the context of

that history. It isn't a perfect tool, but . . . it has been getting results.
. . . Without it some of those people would be shut out again."

The impact on southern blacks of a federal retreat on affirmative
action is unclear, but it is a measure of black political strength in the
urban South that local governments find it inexpedient to follow the
federal example and cancel guidelines and agreements. Indeed, most
urban administrations in the region do not support the federal position
on affirmative action, aware that in the South particularly, the burdens of history are such that hiring goals are the only realistic short-
term solution to increasing black participation in public-sector
employment.

But a greater threat to the economic advancement of blacks may be
the trend of general economic conditions. The expansion of the black
middle class has occurred in the context of an expanding economy; in
fact, some economists argue that black advance in economic status
relates more to these conditions than to civil rights legislation or to
changing attitudes. If that is so, then as new arrivals in the middle
class, blacks in the South could find themselves vulnerable in a recession. Middle-class status among blacks derives in part from husbands
and wives pulling in two incomes, and though in the past immigrant
groups frequently used small businesses to gain initial entry into the
middle class, today southern blacks are inordinately connected to government occupations. If local and state expenditures contract during
hard economic times (and many southern state constitutions prohibit
deficits), then these positions could be threatened.

Economic recession would also, of course, endanger black gains in
the private sector. Some black leaders believe a good deal of these
corporate advances result from tokenism—the elevation of blacks, as
Harvey Gantt put it, "to highly visible but non-profit-centered positions" whose visibility, Gantt argued, aroused "a sense of false comfort." These positions, however, even admitting the charge of tokenism, are vitally important to the overall economic status of southern
blacks. As black writer Albert Murray noted, "the most fundamental
revolutionary changes begin not at the bottom . . . but at the very top.
. . . when you are talking about revolutionary change, tokens and rituals are often more important than huge quantities"—and in the
South, "tokens and rituals" are indelible components of the regional
culture.

Despite the potentially dire impact of a recession on black middle-
class ascension, the persisting and large black underclass remains the

most immediate problem. As Benjamin Hooks, executive director of the NAACP, noted in 1985, "yesterday, we sought the right to check into the hotel. Today, we are fighting to have enough money to check out of the hotel." In assessing the achievements of the civil rights movement up to the 1980s, black novelist Alice Walker observed that "psychologically black people have advanced. . . . But I think that we are also very much out of work, and everything has to have an economic base. You have to be able to feed and clothe yourself and your children before you can really think clearly." Although there seems to be a consensus on what is most wrong about black life in the South, confusion abounds concerning possible solutions. Martin Luther King's warning that "there are no broad highways to lead us easily and inevitably to quick solutions" is even more appropriate today than in 1965.

Middle Class Solutions to Underclass Problems: A Black Monologue

If there is no consensus on policy, there are nevertheless at least two discernible themes in the current debate over the black underclass in the South. First, there is an increasing tendency to discount race as a cause of low economic achievement among blacks, and from this assumption it follows that solutions will not be race-specific. Second, there is a growing inclination to place considerable responsibility on poor blacks themselves—both as causes of their own condition and as resources for their own salvation.

Black journalist William Raspberry quoted Curtis B. Gans, director of the Committee for the Study of the American Electorate, approvingly in a Washington *Post* column in January, 1985: "Blacks . . . must have an economic-class agenda rather than a black agenda." Raspberry went on to claim that "ending racism does not result in significant change for the . . . black underclass." The trick is to devise "programs that speak to the unique problems of the long-term poor" of both races. In the March 28, 1986, issue of the *National Review*, Charles Murray undertook a study of poor whites and discovered that the alleged race-specific problems of poor blacks—teenage pregnancy, crime, school dropout, and matrafocal families—existed among his study group in ratios very similar to those of blacks. His conclusion was that "class, not race, is the more reasonable explanation" for these conditions.

By framing the problem in class rather than in racial terms, black political leaders can scrap narrow and divisive racial agendas and address economic issues in populist terms. This was the tactic of Texas state representative Jesse Oliver when he pushed his indigent health-care bill through the legislature. Southern whites have demonstrated that they respond to populist appeals, so by broadening a racial agenda into a class program, black political leaders could secure passage of some important legislation. Though critics point out that some social-service measures merely serve, in William Raspberry's words, "to make the underclass more comfortable in its poverty," they offer no realistic policy alternatives. Black educator Manning Marable, for example, calls for a "transition in the character of the capitalist economic system" and a "general reallocation of wealth," but as William Julius Wilson noted, fulfilling these objectives "would require far more comprehensive social and economic change than Americans have generally deemed appropriate or desirable."

With such drastic measures unlikely, some observers have begun to focus on the black poor as sources for their own rehabilitation. One major impetus for this new focus has been the growing willingness of black leaders—who realize that black underclass culture is a major obstacle to upward mobility—to discuss aspects of life among the black poor that were generally taboo prior to the mid-1980s. Mary Pringle, a black educator from Virginia, claims that racism is no longer a valid defense for black poverty. Even if it was, the example of recent immigrants from Southeast Asia indicates that culture—in this case, "their traditional background values, their collective achievement orientation, their patience and diligence"—has deflected the impact of racial animosity. Pringle believes that the black poor need "new myths" that depict them as "destined for success rather than doomed to failure."

Some believe that one obstacle to the creation of "new myths" is the dependence of the black underclass on government programs. Shariff Abdullah, chairman of the Mecklenburg County (North Carolina) Minority Affairs Commission, complained that "blacks have become unfamiliar with the problem-solving process. We have asked white society to solve our problems for so long, we no longer have the inner strength to take on our own battles. . . . For too long, we have labored under the false assumption that motivation is something external, someone has to give it to you." Though this rhetoric sounds strikingly similar to the Reagan administration's oft-heard dictum that public assistance robs initiative, it represents a growing sentiment in the black middle-class community.

These critics of black underclass culture perceive self-help as an effective strategy. This is not a new notion for southern blacks, whose initiatives in great part effected changes in racial etiquette and segregation that seemed insurmountable a generation ago. Economic parity, which appears to be another long-distant goal, may require similar involvement. Robert L. Woodson, head of the National Center for Neighborhood Enterprise and chairman of the Council for a Black Economic Agenda, has become one of the leading advocates of the self-help approach. He urges blacks to quit "waiting for a government Moses to save them," for the government will not solve problems like illegitimacy and female-headed households. "If black America is to achieve its rightful place in American society," Woodson argues, "it will not be by virtue of what white America grants to black Americans but because of what black Americans do for themselves."

Woodson's solution is what in the 1960s was called "ghetto enrichment." Specifically, Woodson suggests black enterprise for poor black districts; the use of traditional institutions such as churches to purchase and develop land, upgrade housing, and lease properties; and the formation of tenant groups in public housing to manage these units as is already the case in Louisville and New Orleans. One resident-manager group in New Orleans boasted less than thirty evictions during the past seven years. Woodson holds a low opinion of the quality of some urban school systems and cites the more than three hundred neighborhood-based independent school systems blacks have formed across the nation. Generally, Woodson contends, children's performance in these institutions is better than in the public schools. Taking Woodson's ideas further, Manning Marable advocates black neighborhood government. But if black underclass culture is as deficient as some maintain, from where is this reservoir of self-direction going to come?

Much of this sounds like recycled separatist rhetoric from the late 1960s, which traditionally southern blacks have rejected. The entire thrust of the civil rights movement in the region was integrationist: southern blacks and whites shared a common culture, so they should share each other; blacks had worked too long and hard to end their isolation to turn around and return to an exclusive way of life. But the truth was that southern blacks, even at the height of the civil rights drama, were ambivalent about integration—in their schools, their neighborhood businesses, their churches, and their social clubs. In fact, it can be argued that integration was more a means to the ends of visibility, integrity, identity, and a fuller participation in regional life than an end in itself. Those objectives were largely attained by the 1980s; perhaps it was time to consider other means to obtain other ends more relevant to the present.

But it would be a mistake to equate "bootstrap" ideology with separatism. Most of the advocates of the self-help strategy in the South come from the established black middle class, and drawing on internal resources is to them a temporary phenomenon on the way to a full-fledged economic integration into regional society. It is also consistent with southern culture, harking back to the long frontier period and to the networks on and off the plantations that sustained black life and culture. Self-reliance, by reducing the role of government, moves the individual to greater prominence. Not coincidentally, self-help strategies absolved the black middle class of guilt and responsibility for the condition of the black underclass. If dependence on government or on others was a curse, if the culture of poverty was dysfunctional and impervious to the ministrations of policy, and if self-help was the only viable solution, then there was little that the black middle class could do except to provide moral encouragement and example.

Though rifts between black social classes had always existed, the black upper strata in the South was very small and, in the case of ministers and businessmen, depended too much on a black clientele to become totally aloof. But in the 1970s, the black middle class began to expand and distance itself economically from the black underclass, and by the 1980s, the separation had become physical as successful southern blacks began to move into white neighborhoods and into suburbs. The black entrepreneur in the black district was no longer an important factor in black middle-class life. The new black middle class were bureaucrats and professionals as isolated from the everyday life of the black poor as were their white counterparts.

Intellectual isolation completed the separation. Black Charlotte attorney Mel Watt noted that the attitude of many successful young black urban professionals seems to be "I have made it and I don't owe anybody from the past or future anything." The "me" generation is color-blind. The revival of the Manhattan coalition in politics is another example of black estrangement from black. Eddie Williams, a southern black now head of the Joint Center for Political Studies in Washington, urged blacks to "move from an era of moral persuasion with its non-negotiable demands, to an era of politics, where everything is negotiable," implying that the situation of the black underclass is not a moral issue and is a subject for compromise. The middle-class black attitude that journalist Orde Coombs described in *Black Enterprise* in 1978 perhaps is even more accurate for the present: "What could we really *say* to them, now, except a murmured 'How you doing, bro,' as we hurried along to catch the train that would take us to another appointment, another conference, another step up our frenzied stair of upward mobility. Our eyes would pity them. Our palms would open to them and quickly shut again. And while we hated to talk about it, we knew that we had moved beyond them forever."

How can we make sense of black political and economic life and of the relationship of blacks to whites and to each other? The achievements by the 1980s in politics and in economic status were remarkable compared with the situation just two decades earlier, yet there were glaring elements of regional racial life that remained unchanged. There were even questions about the value, extent, and direction of the achievements themselves. But there is an old and probably overworked saying that confusion precedes understanding. Within the ambivalence and ambiguity that characterized southern race relations in the 1980s there were clues to the future not only that a consensus would emerge to assess race, but that some of the difficult problems uncovered after the cheering stopped could find a solution within the framework of regional culture.

XI / Mountaintops and Green Valleys: Beyond Race in the Modern South

Harry Briggs remembers the long, weary, dangerous battle. It began with a simple request for a school bus and culminated with a historic ruling by the U.S. Supreme Court. Looking back nearly forty years later, Briggs, in his early seventies and still living in Clarendon County, South Carolina, contrasted the hope and striving of his generation with the careless attitude of the current group of black students. "They don't seem to value an education," he said.

But take a walk down to Scott's Branch High School in Summerton, Clarendon County, and see the run-down shacks and dilapidated trailers surrounding the school that is periodically inundated by the runoff from Scott's Branch, and maybe the indifference is more understandable. Take a look at the 590 students—they are all black, and so poor that almost everyone qualifies for free lunches. On a national standardized reading and math exam, the school's tenth-grade class averaged a score of six on a scale of ninety-nine; the national average is fifty.

The county built the school hurriedly after the 1954 *Brown* decision, hoping that a new facility would satisfy blacks and deter them from seeking entrance into all-white Summerton High School. They persisted, however, and under a court order, a few blacks were allowed to attend Summerton High by the mid-1960s. The all-white school board (in a county where blacks outnumbered whites by a ten-to-one margin) refused to go beyond this token gesture, so in 1970 the NAACP filed yet another suit, and a federal district court ordered the county to desegregate its school system totally. The board closed Summerton High, and when the school term began only a half-dozen white children attended the other public schools in the county. A private school, Clarendon Hall, opened to accommodate the white students, leaving the public school system entirely black. The town of Summerton declined along with the public schools, reflecting in part the demise of King Cotton, and in part the reluctance of new industries to come into the county because of the school situation. Harry Briggs's modest and moral proposal forty years ago has ended in bitterness, division, and decay.

The Resegregation of Public Education: A Microcosm of Southern Race Relations

Public education in the modern South exemplifies both the promise and problems of contemporary race relations in the region. As late as 1968, fourteen years after the *Brown* decision, approximately 18 percent of the region's black schoolchildren attended integrated schools. In Atlanta, roughly 90 percent of school-aged blacks remained in segregated schools. Atlanta journalist Ralph McGill complained to a Birmingham audience in 1968, "I am weary of the old hanging on of the dual school systems and the excuses and the evasion. Must we forever keep on? Must a nation which has put a man in space still argue about where and whether a colored child shall go to school?"

Not only McGill but black parents and the federal courts were losing their patience over the dilatory pace of school desegregation. In 1968, the U.S. Supreme Court ruled in a Virginia case, *Green* v. *New Kent County School Board*, that so-called "freedom-of-choice" plans allowing limited numbers of blacks to attend white schools were no longer appropriate means of complying with the *Brown* decision. School boards were now obligated to "come forward with a plan that promises realistically to work . . . until it is clear that state imposed segregation has been completely removed." The *Green* case established a more specific standard than "all deliberate speed" and foreshadowed even stricter guidelines in future decisions.

The following year, the High Court heard a school desegregation suit originating in Mississippi. The Nixon administration, as part of its "southern strategy," had promised a cautious, if not obstructive approach to the issue of school desegregation; accordingly, the Department of Health, Education, and Welfare had granted thirty-three school districts in Mississippi a one-year delay in implementing desegregation plans. The NAACP challenged the delay, and in *Alexander* v. *Holmes County Board of Education*, the Supreme Court ordered these school districts "to terminate dual school systems at once." The Court specifically abandoned the "all deliberate speed" standard as "no longer constitutionally permissible." School boards could not create plans that guaranteed tokenism while delaying complete integration for an indefinite period.

The Court remained silent, however, on the means school boards could employ to comply with the *Alexander* ruling. A suit adjudicated in Charlotte, North Carolina, that same year established a far-reaching precedent on the appropriate method for achieving school desegregation "at once." Darius Swann, a black Presbyterian missionary who returned to Charlotte from an assignment in India during the early 1960s, attempted in 1965 to enroll his six-year-old son in an all-white elementary school. Though Charlotte was operating under a "freedom of choice" plan that allegedly allowed any student to change schools, the transfers mostly involved white students seeking to escape integration. School officials denied Swann's request, and lawyer Julius Chambers filed suit against the Charlotte-Mecklenburg County Board of Education (the city and county school systems had consolidated in the early 1960s) in January, 1965. The suit prompted the school board to initiate a new desegregation plan that would approve freedom-of-choice transfers for all students within specific geographic areas. The U.S. District Court approved the plan rendering the case moot.

But most (66 out of 109) of the schools in the system remained segregated, and Chambers refiled in 1968. Federal judge James B. McMillan heard the arguments and rendered his decision for the plaintiff in the context of the *Green* and *Alexander* cases. From a legal standpoint, his ruling was not difficult: a plan was necessary to desegregate the entire system immediately. Judge McMillan appointed a prominent educator, Dr. John Finger, to draw up a comprehensive desegregation plan for Charlotte-Mecklenburg, and ordered the school system to adopt a busing program. Busing was nothing new to Charlotte-Mecklenburg children—23,600 students rode buses an average of fifteen miles one way—but busing to achieve racial integration was another matter. As Judge McMillan defended his action, "though seemingly radical in nature, if viewed by people who live in totally segregated neighborhoods, it may, like surgery, be the most conservative solution to the whole problem and the one most likely to provide a good education at minimum cost." The school board appealed, and in May, 1971, the U.S. Supreme Court upheld Judge McMillan's decision in *Swann* v. *Charlotte-Mecklenburg Board of Education*. The era of busing to achieve school desegregation was underway.

Many in the white community vilified the judge and his decision, but he was philosophical about the rebuffs and hate mail. As he told a *Time* reporter in 1971, "a judge would ordinarily like to decide cases to suit his neighbors," but he had a legal and moral duty to uphold the law: "Constitutional rights will not be denied here simply because they may be denied elsewhere. There is no Dow Jones average for such rights." It was a lonely time for Judge McMillan. He recalled a hymn that helped him through difficult moments:

> God of justice save the people from the clash of race and creed
> From the strife of class and faction, make our nation free indeed.
> Keep her faith in simple manhood strong as when her life began,
> 'til it find its full fruition in the brotherhood of man.

School desegregation had been a festering controversy in the South for more than fifteen years, but the Supreme Court decisions between 1968 and 1971 left school boards no room for evasion. White parents, confronting what they now knew was inevitable, reacted swiftly and in some cases, as in Charlotte and Greensboro, constructively. Maggie Ray, a white homemaker from an affluent Charlotte neighborhood, helped form the Citizens Advisory Group that participated in preparing a pupil assignment system. The involvement of the city's white community at the initial stage of the desegregation process defused a considerable degree of adverse reaction. In Greensboro, a small group of women led by Joan Bluethenthal decided to study the school situation for their "Great Decisions Club," which worked with Doris Hutchinson of the city school system to initiate a series of weekend retreats for students, parents, teachers, and administrators during the spring of 1971. The retreats became the training ground for hundreds of citizens who began to work for the smooth transition to a totally integrated school system. The climax of the club's efforts was "Public School Sunday," a combination fair and public information program. As historian William Chafe summarized the club's impact, "within days a new world of busing, integrated PTAs and biracial student governments had become routine."

But some places, especially in the Deep South and rural areas, were not so well organized for smooth and uneventful change. Even in these locations, however, few white political leaders advocated resistance, and none advanced veiled warnings of violence. Time had proved the futility of such opposition, and, besides, blacks were becoming a potent political factor. Also, disruption could threaten economic development. Some white leaders even took a forceful stand in support of court-ordered busing. Florida governor Reubin Askew, for example, warned a state PTA conference in 1971 that "we cannot achieve equal opportunity in education by passing laws or constitutional amend-

ments against busing—they could deny us what I believe is the highest
destiny of the American people . . . to achieve a society in which all
races, all creeds, and all religions have learned not only to live with
their differences—but to *thrive* upon them." Extreme protest with
respect to racial matters was no longer fashionable in the South, and
southerners were always careful to conform their public behavior to
the prevailing norm. But there were other ways to register discontent.

For one, whites abandoned public school systems and fled to more
homogeneous schools or systems. Private schools—"seg academies"
as some called them—proliferated. In the first three years after the
Swann decision, the number of private schools in Memphis, for example, more than doubled from forty to eighty-five. White parents generally denied racial motives, citing the issue of "quality education" as
the stimulus for change, but as Mississippi school superintendent
Richard Boyd charged, the private school movement was "100% racial." For those parents who could not afford private school tuition,
flight to the suburbs was another alternative. The white withdrawal
from the Atlanta school system was indicative of a trend throughout
the South: in 1960, Atlanta's segregated school system of 100,000
pupils was evenly divided between black and white, but in 1973, after
busing effected integration, white enrollment dropped to 20,000 and
black students comprised nearly 80 percent of the total school population. As the black population of southern cities continued to grow
during the 1970s, the proportion of black pupils in the public school
system advanced even more.

Sometimes white flight involved considerable hardship to working-
class white parents, who could not afford to send their children to
private academies. In 1970, the Ridgecrest neighborhood in Montgomery, a white working-class area, came under the Carver High School
catchment district as a result of a new court-ordered desegregation
plan. Rather than have their children attend Carver, formerly an all-
black school, many white parents fled the city. The Montgomery *Advertiser* reported "a drastic turnover of housing" in Ridgecrest during
the summer and fall of 1970. Citywide, the plan had pushed 4,000
white children into private schools, but many Ridgecrest homeowners
could not afford the cost of a private education and so sold out to eager
realtors who fueled the panic selling. One white homeowner lamented
to a reporter: "This is our home and we love it, but we just can't stay
here any more. We can never replace what we had here . . . we can't buy
another house as good as this for the price of this one but we are willing

to make the sacrifice." The extent of white flight in Ridgecrest upset the desegregation plan, forcing the school board to redraw district lines less than four years later. The Carver district now included another white working-class area, Bellingrath, and the wave of real estate transfers resumed. By 1980, the school district boundaries had become racial boundaries as well. Never before had Montgomery been so segregated in terms of residence by race.

In many parts of the South in the 1980s, the dual school systems that the Supreme Court had attempted to dismantle a generation earlier were back in place, and there was little the courts could do to reverse the situation. In addition to white flight, the increasing concentration of blacks in central cities encouraged the return of dual systems. In 1984, schools in the city of Durham, North Carolina, were 87-percent black, compared with 55-percent black in 1970; in Durham County, they were 69-percent white. The unwillingness of city and county school systems to merge (as did the Charlotte-Mecklenburg system) has not only re-created segregated school systems but generated financial waste, especially in rural districts that can ill afford such profligacy. Robeson County, a sparsely settled county in eastern North Carolina, has five school systems—one mainly white, one predominantly Indian, two mostly black, and one integrated. Its five superintendents earned a combined salary of $175,000 a year in 1985 and oversaw a total of 25,000 students, whereas the Charlotte-Mecklenburg superintendent led a 70,000–pupil system and earned $66,500 annually.

The costs of dual school systems go beyond budgets. Goldsboro, an important tobacco marketing town in eastern North Carolina's Wayne County, had a school system that was 52-percent black in 1968. In the county, white pupils comprised 70 percent of the school population. By 1984, the city system was 77-percent black, while the county remained at 70-percent white, for despite repeated requests from the city and from a federal court judge, the county balked at merging systems. In February, 1983, the Goldsboro *News-Argus* carried an editorial that reflected on the meaning of the dual school system "in a day in which the law and public enlightenment should find it unacceptable." Noting that within the previous year two major manufacturing plants had closed down in Wayne County, entailing a loss of 600 jobs, the editor stated that the prospects for replacing the departed firms were dim. Though there were many reasons for the uncertain economic future of the county, the editor argued that "there is a millstone around the neck of future progress in this county. It is the problem of maintaining what is tantamount to a segregated public school system. . . . We reap the harvest of economic despair we have planted with the seeds of selfishness and racism."

The re-emergence of segregated education had a significant impact on busing. Increasingly in many cities of the South, busing has become irrelevant since there are no longer sufficient numbers of whites to integrate schools. In 1973, the Supreme Court heard a complaint from Richmond city schools that the only way to avoid a total resegregation of its increasingly black system was to inaugurate a busing plan with the predominantly white Henrico County school system. In a tie vote (Justice William Powell abstained because he had represented the city of Richmond in the lower courts), the Court decided that the *Swann* ruling did not extend to cross-county busing. The implication of this decision and the more sweeping case involving the Detroit school system, *Milliken* v. *Bradley*, was that suburban whites should not be penalized for a city problem. Accordingly, by the late 1970s, urban school districts were scrambling to maintain their white enrollment while at the same time satisfying court desegregation orders. Busing routes were drawn and redrawn, but whites continued to leave the city public school systems.

Ironically, opinion polls demonstrated an increased willingness on the part of southern white parents to send their children to integrated schools. In 1963, approximately 60 percent of white respondents objected to integrated education; by 1970, that figure was down to 16 percent, leading George Gallup to remark that "this finding represents one of the most dramatic shifts in the history of public opinion polling." But white parents' conception of integration may have involved only a token infusion of black students, and even when more than a few black students attended a previously all-white school, segregated classes, lunch hours, and recreation sessions were not uncommon. The southerners' sense of gentility and appropriate behavior may have dictated their responses in the public opinion polls, but their abandonment of urban school systems spoke of other feelings.

For those urban systems that retained some white support, there was considerable effort to devise strategies to maintain the white school population. The concept of neighborhood schools resurfaced as a mechanism to attract and retain white pupils. White parents claimed that they did not object to integration, but rather to the uprooting from neighborhoods and the relatively lengthy journeys required by busing programs. But neighborhood schools reflect their neighborhoods, and in the residentially segregated southern city, a return to neighborhood schools meant a return to segregation. Still, cities such as Little Rock and Norfolk were willing to tolerate a modest resegregation of their systems in order to retain their dwindling white populations.

When cross-town busing began in Norfolk in 1971, the city's school system was 60-percent white. By the time the Norfolk school board unanimously approved a neighborhood school plan in April, 1986, the schools were 60-percent black. The city's black school superintendent, Gene Carter, a strong supporter of the plan, stated that "we are committed to having a stable desegregated system." During the fifteen years of busing, whites had left for private schools and for suburban school districts in nearby Virginia Beach or Chesapeake. Of course, white city residents left Norfolk for many reasons aside from the school situation, but the net effect was to complicate busing routes and increase the likelihood of a resegregated system in the near future. So the city's school officials acted to stem the erosion of white support by abandoning busing for its elementary-school students and creating thirty-five neighborhood elementary schools, ten of which were to be black. Prior to the neighborhood plan there were no all-black elementary schools in the city. School board chairman Thomas Johnson expressed his regret in creating segregated schools, but "I think the facts tell us we're losing the middle class in this city." The local NAACP leader held a different perspective: "They might use fancy, deceptive terms like 'neighborhood schools,' but the bottom line is segregation."

The neighborhood plan, which first emerged in 1982, came under fire from black leaders in Norfolk and wound up in the U.S. District Court. The court agreed with the city that the plan represented "a reasonable, voluntary effort on the part of the school board to insure that the school system retains the greatest degree of integration over the long term," and the U.S. circuit court of appeals in Richmond upheld the lower court ruling as did the U.S. Supreme Court in June, 1986. As superintendent Gene Carter noted in response to the decision, "a youngster of one race need not be seated next to a youngster of the opposite race in order to learn."

Early returns from the Norfolk experiment are not encouraging. The white school population has not increased, nor have the number and length of bus rides diminished. Black parental involvement in the resegregated schools, one of the objectives of the plan, has not materialized. The city has spent $454 more per pupil for materials, teachers, and maintenance in the resegregated schools. Test scores have been disappointing: four of the black schools had lower scores than any school during the year prior to the shift. The scores reflected problems deeper than racial composition. As one teacher said, "the school system bought us nice science books and nice social studies books, but my children couldn't 'Turn to page 138,' because they didn't know what 138 was. We didn't open the science books." Instead, she spent $800 of her own to purchase or make more appropriate materials. Another teacher complained that the children in these schools were not receiving reinforcement at home. Homes lacked crayons or pencils; pupils did not know the meaning of *marshmallow* or *cherry* on standardized tests because they had never seen either. And students often could not go on field trips because they did not have the fifty-cent admission price for a museum. Teachers also noted a deterioration of discipline, perhaps indicating that middle-class children were better role models for deportment and work habits.

Focus on Quality

The Norfolk situation reflects the deepening quandary over public education in the South: obstacles to black educational achievement may be not simply a matter of racial segregation, but rather a function of factors beyond the classroom. Just as the debate over black poverty has shifted from race to class issues, so the discussion over education has broadened to emphasize questions of quality. Durham school superintendent Cleveland Hammond, a black, contended that "quality education—not integration—is the top priority" in his mostly black school system. Tony Brown, a black leader in Charlotte, concurred: "Busing is not a civil-rights issue. Quality education is the issue." These sentiments are not new. A half century earlier, W. E. B. Du Bois said much the same thing: the black child "needs neither segregated schools nor mixed schools. What he needs is Education."

School desegregation was a top priority among southern blacks after World War II because it could enable them to cast off one of the more obvious badges of inferiority. By the 1970s, segregation was vanquished in most parts of the South, enabling blacks to concentrate on improving other aspects of regional race relations. Economic differentials, as we have seen, became the most glaring problem for southern blacks. At the same time, there was a renewed appreciation for black culture and institutions: if southern black churches and southern black schools produced civil rights leaders, then these institutions held strengths within them, segregation or no. So pride and practicality combined to shift emphasis from integration to quality.

There was another reason for the shift—a growing realization that integration has not produced a revolution in the academic performance of black children. A recent study of school desegregation in Nashville and Davidson County, Tennessee, by Richard A. Pride and J. David Woodard concluded that the process had little impact on the academic achievements of blacks or whites. Other school districts noted improved test scores of black students by the 1980s, but this may be more a result of equality of conditions than of integration. In South Carolina, for example, fewer than 25 percent of the state's black schoolchildren scored below average on a standardized reading-skills test in 1986, compared with 36.5 percent in 1983, but it is difficult to attribute the improvement to desegregation since resegregation has been a more prevalent theme in South Carolina public education during the 1980s. Rather, the test scores probably reflect the fact that black children in South Carolina today follow the same curriculum, read the same textbooks, use the same equipment, and learn from the same certified teachers as do white children in the state.

Although this sounds like a restatement of the discredited "separate-but-equal" doctrine, the South of 1986 was considerably different from the South a generation earlier. Segregated schools no longer operated in the context of a totally segregated society framed by a degrading racial etiquette. Just as race-specific policies may be less applicable to the economic problems of the contemporary South, so educational quality may be less a matter of race than of other factors, especially the disparities between urban and rural school systems. A U.S. Navy recruiter visiting Northumberland County in rural eastern North Carolina noted that "ninety percent of the students in this area flunk the Navy entrance test . . . kids up in Guilford County [where Greensboro is located] with just a GED do better than those 'down East' who have a high-school diploma." Urban school systems that are overwhelmingly black are demonstrating that their expenditures and test scores outstrip those in rural school districts. The Durham city school system, for example, which is 87 percent black, leads the state of North Carolina in per-pupil expenditures, and first-graders in the system read at a 2.1 grade level, higher than the reading level of first-graders in predominantly white Durham County. Poor rural jurisdictions can rarely afford more than the basic curriculum. Regardless of the extent of segregation (or its absence), the quality of education in rural areas falls short of urban standards in the region.

The urban-rural dichotomy in education, however, did include a racial as well as a quality component. By the early 1980s, the private school movement in the South that boomed after 1970 was subsiding, especially in urban counties. Though reliable statistics are scarce, journalist Strat Douthat reported in March, 1986, that "the private, secular school movement peaked about 1980 and since has receded." Also, the number of church-affiliated schools has declined since 1980: the Alabama Christian Education Association had seventy-eight member schools in 1982; by 1986, that number had dwindled to fifty-five. Most of the remaining Christian schools admit blacks. As the head of the Calvary Christian Academy in Montgomery noted, "we don't believe you cannot love all people and still serve the Lord." Fifteen percent of the school's student body is comprised of blacks. In the poor, rural, mostly black areas of the South, however, the segregation academies still survive, according to Douthat, adversely affecting the quality of education for both blacks and whites.

The rising concern over quality education among southern blacks includes almost as many nuances as the debate over integration, extending beyond black students to black teachers. Teacher training for blacks had been a haphazard affair, especially in the Deep South, where an eighth-grade education was sufficient to land a teaching position in most black grade schools. Black state teachers' colleges, though obviously an improvement, were considerably below the standards and funding of comparable white institutions, and when black and white faculties were integrated in earnest during the 1970s, the disparities in preparation became evident. The appearance of standardized competency exams by the early 1980s quantified these differences. In 1983, 90 percent of whites who took the Florida teacher competency test passed it; only 35 percent of black candidates attained a passing grade. Some blacks passed off the results as an example of the intrinsic bias of standardized tests as applied to blacks, but for others, William Raspberry related, "the real problem is not the test but the preparation of the prospective teachers." Raspberry argued that "it's unrealistic to expect black children to learn to pass the tests that will get them into quality colleges and decent jobs if their teachers can't pass such tests."

The debate over the quality of black teacher education soon expanded to include discussions about the quality of southern black higher education in general. Dual systems of higher education persist in the South, generating redundancies and diluting quality and expenditures. Although public funding for historically black state colleges and universities has increased dramatically since the 1970s, these institutions started considerably behind their white counterparts, and state spending aside, they are finding it increasingly difficult to maintain pace. Recent black Ph.D.'s are much sought after both within and outside the region, and promising black students are wooed aggressively by historically white universities in the South. White and black educators in the region are beginning to wonder aloud whether the maintenance of a separate and unequal system of higher education is valid any longer.

In June, 1986, the Raleigh *News and Observer* editorialized on the subject of black higher education in North Carolina and reached a startling conclusion. The newspaper had lobbied for a $40-million legislative appropriation to the state's black colleges and universities in 1979. The measure passed, but seven years later, the *News and Observer* was rethinking its position. The editorial catalogued the "proliferation of remedial courses, exceptionally low SAT scores, and higher failure rates on the National Teachers' Examination" at black colleges. Doubting whether vast infusions of money would improve the "inferior education" offered by these institutions, the writer proposed channeling money instead into public elementary and secondary schools to "concentrate on preparing young people for college-level work." While the newspaper acknowledged the traditions and service of black schools, it strongly suggested that their perpetuation reinforced inferiority, quoting black sociologist Kenneth B. Clark on this point: "There is a disturbingly large percentage of blacks who . . . are still arguing for the continued existence of black colleges because they say that black students can't make it anywhere else. That argument represents . . . stagnation. . . . We need to make it clear to black students that they can achieve as well as the average white student."

Clark implied that some of the de-emphasis on integration among southern blacks may evolve from a desire to protect black institutions or from the fear of competition with whites. Integration often meant the closing of black schools and the uprooting of black students, faculty, and administrators since white physical plants were superior to black facilities, and since officials believed that holding white dislocation to a minimum would reduce white opposition to desegregation. Regardless of the motivation of school officials, some black parents and students were concerned that black leadership and black culture would suffer in the new environment. As one black student put it as she entered previously all-white Americus (Georgia) High School in the early 1970s, "it wasn't really our school. Like we had lost our own school, you know, and all we had now was the whites' school." A black parent in Greensboro detected a conspiracy among white leaders as that city prepared its busing plan in 1971. The proposal, he averred, was "a calculated plan to keep our people down" by destroying black pride and black institutions. According to William Chafe, another black parent argued that integration was only a tactic during the early phase of the civil rights movement, and now that blacks had pride and solidarity, whites "want to integrate in order to break this down and control our schools."

These arguments have subsided in recent years as blacks have shifted their focus from integration to the equally elusive concept of quality. However, the protective impulse has surfaced when integration has threatened the integrity or existence of a black school, as in the case of Tennessee State University in Nashville. In September, 1984, a federal court ordered the merger of predominantly black Tennessee State University with the mostly white Nashville branch of the University of Tennessee. The court's objective was the "maximization of educational opportunities for black citizens" of Tennessee. The merged university would retain the TSU name, but would have a 50-50 black-white ratio by 1993.

The ruling resulted from a suit filed by a group of mainly white TSU students and professors who were concerned about the resegregation of the school following a 1979 court order to merge the two campuses. The 1979 merger caused many white students to leave the combined campus and enroll at Middle Tennessee State University, a mostly white institution forty miles south of Nashville, so the TSU group filed suit in 1982 to halt the resegregation trend and commit the state to a fully integrated campus. Most black leaders within and outside the university opposed the 1984 decision claiming that, historically, TSU has been "a haven, run by and for blacks who were unwelcome or uncomfortable in white-dominated schools." TSU's white faculty, while acknowledging the school's historic role, contended that despite generous state financial support, TSU's facilities and standards remained inferior to those of comparable white institutions. John Arthur, a member of the group that filed suit in 1982, argued that "bending the rules" for less-qualified black applicants reflected "a paternalistic racism. . . . You're saying that you've got to have an inferior institution where standards are lower or they [black students] won't compete. The concern for blacks to compete is legitimate, but the solution is to find ways to make them compete, not to lower standards." One of the many ironies of the case appeared during a demonstration by blacks protesting the 1984 court desegregation order. One protester carried a sign that read, "Segregation and Justice for All."

Some whites have commented that black students tested the waters of integrated education and found the going too rough, choosing instead to pull back into the traditional sanctuary of their own institutions. Or perhaps, as Harry Briggs implied, the current generation of black students are unwilling to duplicate the tenacity and courage of their predecessors; to contemporary black youngsters an integrated education is nothing to fight for and maybe even something to fight against. Their experiences with integrated education may have reinforced the view that except for athletic teams there is little interaction with whites socially and, in some cases, academically as well. They may have gone to school in Anson County, North Carolina, and have held separate reunions for their classes; or have seen the beauty pageant at Parker High School in Greenville, South Carolina, where a white contestant withdrew after she discovered that a black ROTC cadet was to escort her during the program; or have read about the cross-burning on Sorority Row at the University of Alabama in protest of the pending move of a black sorority to the vicinity; or have heard of the racial hazing of black cadets at The Citadel in Charleston, South Carolina.

But the struggle over school desegregation, as with voting rights and public accommodations, was always broader than the question of access—it concerned intangibles that have become submerged in the current discussion about quality. Integration of schools, even if superficial, involved some contact: seeing blacks in classrooms lessened the surprise of seeing blacks in boardrooms, and thereby increased the likelihood of black economic mobility. For all its dynamism, a good deal of the southern economy is honeycombed with a good-ole-boy network that extends back to college days and beyond, especially in small and medium-sized urban communities. A segregated education for blacks is not likely to enhance economic opportunities. In addition, the absence of contact tends to feed stereotypes. In 1971, a black girl commented on her first days at newly integrated Americus High School: "After all these years now, we realize the whites are just human beings, not supermen without any faults or weaknesses. . . . Why, a boy in one of my classes, he just sits there all the time eating on pencils—yeah!" Though these revelations are unlikely to occur today—another measure of how far we have come—the danger of re-segregation is that perceptions will grow and fester in a vacuum. Schools remain the greatest contact points for black and white southerners.

The Decline of Race:
A Common Denominator

The status of school desegregation in the South parallels in many respects the status of voting rights and of economic opportunity. These issues no longer seem as clear-cut as they did in the 1960s, nor is there a consensus among black and white southerners on policies related to these issues. The bloom is off integrated education and political power, while black economic status has yet to flower, and there is no agreement on how to nurture it. The decline of race as a factor in each of these issues is a common denominator. In education, black leaders most often stress quality. In voting rights, the prevailing strategy for black elected officials and electorate alike is coalition, compromise politics, and stressing issues that are not necessarily race-specific. And the contemporary wisdom concerning black economic status is that black poverty and its cultural accompaniments result less from racial discrimination than from structural problems within the national economy that have produced an economic, not a racial, underclass.

The recent upsurge in Klan activity and in race-related violence as well as the persistence of traditional patterns of race relations in parts of the rural South seems to contradict the decline of race as a primary element in southern consciousness. Reports of police brutality against blacks surface periodically from Montgomery or Dallas; the lynching of a black youth in Mobile, Alabama, captured national headlines in 1981; and the assault by whites in Forsyth County, Georgia, on peaceful black marchers in 1986 recalls the civil rights clashes of an earlier time. The New York *Times* reported in April, 1985, that in small towns across the rural South "an unwritten code perpetuates what was once enshrined in law and announced by 'Colored Entrance' or 'Whites Only' signs." As a case in point, the *Times* cited Dawson, Georgia, a predominantly black town of 5,700 inhabitants. On the surface, it appeared that some racial progress had occurred in Dawson: in the late 1970s, blacks successfully challenged the at-large system of voting and elected members of their own race to the city council and county commission. In addition, two blacks were named to the school board, and blacks appeared for the first time as bank tellers, in city bureaucracy, and in white-collar positions in local industry and business. But as the *Times* noted, there are "bars where blacks know they cannot buy drinks, restaurants in which they cannot eat, motels in which they cannot get a room." Restrooms are still segregated at the county courthouse, by custom, rather than by law or sign. Most white children attend Terrell Academy, a private school. In tones reminiscent of an earlier era, whites praise the nature of race relations while blacks quietly complain about the situation. As political scientist David Garrow noted, "the distance in time between small rural towns and an Atlanta or a Birmingham is a difference of decades."

But there was a time when Birmingham and the rural provinces of Alabama shared a similar perspective on race in both thought and action. The rural South is the South of yesterday in many more ways than race relations. Declining populations, eroding economic bases, and advancing political impotence have rendered these areas museum pieces that are valuable more in measuring how far the rest of the region has gone than in representing how much more it has to go. Incidents of police brutality, Klan violence, and intimidation are newsworthy for the same reason. They are anachronisms that enable the self-righteous to renew their critique of the South, and the media to fill time on news programs. Twenty years ago, a rag-tag group of whites hurling epithets and a few stones at black marchers would hardly have been news.

More important than such incidents is their swift public condemnation by white leaders and institutions. More important is an all-white jury awarding a black family a multi-million-dollar judgment against the Klan in Mobile for the lynching of Michael Donald. More important is the reaction of a black woman as Glenn Miller and his Klanlike White Patriots Party paraded through Gastonia, North Carolina: "White power," she laughed, "You already got that." More important is the fact that at most Klan rallies, the spectators, law enforcement officers, and media easily outnumber Klansmen. The Klansman is a pitiful figure in the contemporary South, a deluded white often unemployed or underemployed, for whom the Sun Belt remains a *Time* magazine pastiche, and who has been led down the road of great expectations by irresponsible politicians who now wash their hands of him.

This is not to say that we should make light of bigotry and racial violence—indicators of a lingering infection in the region. But southern justice today provides a strong antidote to such antics. Those who perceive a resurgence of racism in the South are wrong on two counts.

First, these incidents represent less a resurgence than examples of something that has existed in the region all along. As journalist Frye Gaillard noted, "the people who cracked open skulls at the Edmund Pettus bridge or turned their dynamite on four little girls in Birmingham aren't the products of an ancient time." Second, the Klan and their ilk operate in a vacuum. Regional institutions have become geared to eradicating the violent aspects of race relations. Subtle changes such as retreats from affirmative action plans are more typically initiated at the federal than at the local level.

Blacks have become too much of a political and an economic force in the South for a retreat from racial progress to advance very far. There is nothing in a recrudescence of racial animosity that the white economic elite would find beneficial, especially since black political leaders have demonstrated a keen interest in and talent for economic development. In addition, the old racial etiquette is gone in the urban South and is changing elsewhere: in the all-important realm of public behavior, blacks and whites are more likely to treat each other with equal cordiality. As John Shelton Reed observed: "More and more, in places like courthouses and stores and schools, Southern whites seem disposed to treat black Southerners as sort of honorary white folks. . . . Southern blacks . . . seem willing to return the favor. The upshot is that on a day-to-day basis . . . , black-white relations in the South seem more cordial, less prickly, than black-white relations in the cities of the North." In the context of southern culture, if individuals treat each other with respect and equality in public, it is less likely that discriminatory behavior will resurface in other public spheres of southern life.

The advances of the civil rights movement have become too ingrained in regional life to be threatened from outside or from within. The leaders, events, victories, and even the violence have become part of southern lore and iconography. A black and silver historical marker, erected in 1980, stands on the corner of Elm Street and Friendly Avenue in Greensboro with the simple inscription: "Sit-ins. Launched the national drive for integrated lunch counters, February 1, 1960. In Woolworth store two blocks South." The Edmund Pettus Bridge in Selma, scene of the bloody voting-rights confrontation in March, 1965, has become an official stop on the city's historic tour. In 1984, the city donated $5,000 toward the restoration of Brown's Chapel, the spiritual headquarters of the voting-rights movement in Alabama. Once refurbished, the chapel will join the bridge on Selma's historical itinerary. Birmingham is in the process of planning for a civil rights museum near the Sixteenth Street Baptist Church, an important shrine for the children's crusade as well as the site of the brutal bombing in September, 1963. The city has already preserved an important artifact from that year—the cell in which Martin Luther King wrote his famous "Letter from Birmingham Jail."

Since 1985, the Mississippi State Historical Museum in Jackson has featured a permanent exhibit, "The Struggle for Equal Rights," the first such permanent display in the nation. It includes a fourteen-minute videotape of police dragging and clubbing demonstrators, and of white mobs taunting sit-in protestors in Jackson. Also included are the complicated voter-registration forms white registrars used for black applicants, posters advertising black protest meetings and Klan rallies, and a glass door panel from a Hattiesburg business on which "White Waiting Room" was neatly lettered, as well as a metal sign from a physician's office in Greenville designating the "Colored Entrance." Just a short time ago, these items were scarcely museum pieces—they represented an active way of life in Mississippi. The exhibit concludes with a quote from James Meredith: "I can love Mississippi because of the beauty of the countryside and the old traditions of family affection, and for such small things as flowers bursting in spring. . . . Why should a Negro be forced to leave such things? Because of fear? No. Not anymore."

Much as tourists make pilgrimages to Civil War battlefields, it is now possible to visit the civil rights battlegrounds, though their commercialization is not yet on a scale with that of their nineteenth-century counterparts. In addition, it is possible to attend commemorative events much like Civil War battle reenactments, with the added attraction that the original cast is often among the participants. On February 1, 1980, for instance, the vice-president of Woolworth served breakfast with a smile to the four initial sit-in demonstrators at the twentieth anniversary of the event in Greensboro. In March, 1985, blacks and whites joined together to reenact the Selma-to-Montgomery march, crossing the Pettus Bridge without incident and meeting Governor George Wallace in Montgomery. And Jackson, Mississippi, holds an annual Medgar Evers Homecoming weekend, which in 1983 featured old adversary Ross Barnett participating in renaming a Jackson street in Evers' honor.

Such commemorations and shrines are no empty symbols; they are the traditional landmarks that southerners have established to designate and cherish their past. In addition, they serve to remind black and white southerners that contemporary race relations have been only recently molded—that a darker heritage lurks in the not-too-distant past. A black nursing student admitted to a reporter covering the Selma-to-Montgomery commemoration that "I just don't know that much about it." Patti Carr Black, director of the Mississippi State Historical Museum, noted that black and white students coming through the civil rights exhibit are surprised to learn that their parents and grandparents attended segregated high schools. "On the one hand," Black observed, "such misperceptions are a positive indication of progress in race relations. . . . On the other hand, they reflect an abysmal lack of knowledge among young people about contemporary history." If the present generation does not know about the costs of the sin of race pride for both black and white southerners and the wrenching process of redemption, then a false security and indifference could settle upon the region. Freedom is more likely lost through neglect than through direct assault.

An encouraging sign, aside from the shrines and commemorations, is that southern whites continue to expiate past sins and expose and eliminate new ones. On the night of May 5, 1960, two white Conway, Arkansas, policemen arrested a black man on suspicion of public drunkenness and placed him in the county jail. By the following morning the man, twenty-year-old Marvin Williams, was dead. According to police reports, Williams and some friends left a high-school prom for the Sunset Café, a popular black night spot in Conway. As Williams and a friend slept in the car, parked outside the café, the police spotted them, illegally parked and drunk. They were transported to the courthouse, and as they walked up the steps, Williams pitched forward striking his head on the concrete steps. A coroner's jury, convened the following day, exonerated the police officers even though they had not seen the autopsy report.

The case resurfaced in 1984 when an Arkansas prison inmate wrote letters to state officials and newspapers claiming that he had witnessed the fatal beating of a Conway jail inmate twenty-four years earlier. The allegations, bizarre as they were after such a long time, prompted the Williams family to obtain a copy of the autopsy report, which indicated no alcohol in Williams' blood and that the cause of death was a large fracture across the back of his skull. In March, 1985, a grand jury of fifteen whites and one black returned first-degree murder indictments against the police officers, long since gone from the force.

On March 1, 1981, a group of Klansmen in Mobile, Alabama, picked out a black at random—nineteen-year-old Michael Donald—savagely beat and strangled him, and hanged his body in a small camphor tree across the street from the home of Klan leader Robert Hays. Their objective was to demonstrate Klan strength in Mobile, but a jury of eleven whites and one black quickly convicted Hays's son of first-degree murder in December, 1983, and recommended a life sentence without parole. Three years later, in rural Iredell County in the North Carolina Piedmont, an all-white federal jury convicted six former Klansmen of conspiring, through a series of twenty-four cross-burnings, to violate the civil rights of blacks and whites in the area who were thought to be "race mixers." Judge Woodrow Jones handed down stiff sentences to the six defendants, including a seven-year prison term for former Klan leader Tony Earp. As he sentenced the Klansmen, Jones, a white, stated, "there's a little cancer here that's got to be blotted out. And you started it."

The point is that community mores, even in rural parts of the South, have shifted with respect to race. Southerners have usually been concerned with doing the right thing, especially for an audience. Race-related shrines and commemorative events are among these proper displays, as are extirpations of improper behavior, violent or rhetorical. Again, these exercises might strike some as empty formalism, but in the South they are integral to a way of life.

A Southern Legacy: To Attempt Things That Might Fail

Indeed, as race relations become routinized in more positive ways, the greatest legacy of the civil rights movement may be its preservation of southern culture. The struggle for racial equality—in segregation, voting rights, economy, and etiquette—never sought to overturn southern culture, but merely to remove the large obstruction of white supremacy from the beneficial operation of that culture for both white and black southerners. How could it have been otherwise? Time, place, and blood had made blacks southerners. Robert Botsch, a political scientist, asked a black North Carolina furniture-store worker why he was supporting Jimmy Carter for president in 1976. He replied that he was "tired of listening to all those slick Yankees who think they know everything and have all the answers." As John Shelton Reed observed, "it is hard to sound more Southern than *that*." It is what blacks returning to the South would say in another way, or what James Meredith meant when he talked affectionately about Mississippi. The heartbreak for blacks was that they could not really leave the land they loved, nor could they stay. The tragedy for whites was that race pride clouded their vision of the land because it cut them off from their companions in nature and history. Blacks offered whites a clearer perception of place, and themselves the ability to love their region unfettered by fear or frustration.

Ultimately, this was a religious movement—not surprising in an evangelical region where biblical rhetoric and imagery suffuse daily speech and writing, and where *redemption* is both a biblical and a political term, and now perhaps even a social term as well. What saved the South may well have been its religion, which had long served as a helpmate for the racial status quo, but which possessed within it the character for change and salvation. This religious element made the movement a moral crusade, lifted it to a higher plane. Southern religion also carried with it the notion of forgiveness. It would have been understandable for blacks to lapse into bitterness and hatred, but they endured the Freedom Rides, the children's crusade in Birmingham, the church bombing, and the voting-rights murders strengthened by their religious convictions. Their fervor filled their songs of freedom, imbued their leaders with resolve, and challenged the beliefs of whites. Martin Luther King wrote in 1965 that "in the quiet recesses of my heart, I am fundamentally a clergyman, a Baptist preacher." That was the essence of his leadership, firmly grounded in evangelical Protestantism, the folk religion of the South.

The moral, religious fervor of the crusade has dissipated, much as the crusade itself has changed. "We must leave the racial battleground," Jesse Jackson implores, "and find the economic common ground." Perhaps economy does not easily lend itself to a moral framework, especially in a prosperous region, but one of the many legacies of the civil rights movement in the South has been to recharge regional theology for moral change. Black churches have historically been dedicated to this end in theory, if not always in practice, and now there is the possibility that white religious institutions can combine with black counterparts to lend a moral framework to the search for "the economic common ground." The successes of the earlier crusade depended to a great extent upon the religious context of rhetoric and action. Perhaps southern religion, white and black, can work similar miracles through a rededication to the moral precepts of evangelical theology. There are indications that this is already occurring in some parts of the South. Doug Oldenburg, former minister at Covenant Presbyterian Church in Charlotte, authored a document, "The Christian Faith and Economic Justice," for a regional conclave in 1984 that stressed biblical support for economic justice and alerted southerners to the "gross inequalities and gross suffering" that occur even in affluent societies. The split early in 1987 in the Southern Baptist Convention resulted in part from a concern among some ministers and congregants that the Convention's emphasis on a political agenda was undermining its historic role of ministering to the poor and performing other outreach services.

In 1980, a church-based organization, Strategies to Elevate People (STEP), formed in Dallas with the intention of drawing on the great reservoir of talent and volunteer spirit in the city's churches and synagogues. STEP mobilized 500 volunteers from its member churches which, by the rules of the organization, include both black and white congregations, and renovated a black housing project in Dallas. In addition, STEP established a college assistance fund for children from low-income families. By 1987, STEP ministries had appeared in Fort Worth, Richmond, Norfolk, Nashville, and Charlotte. Other STEP services include pairing adults with low-income elementary-school children and operating joint programs with local community colleges to provide adult education. STEP churches have succeeded in leveraging business assistance in the form of supplies, funds, and additional voluntary help, demonstrating that religious institutions of the South can bridge the gap between the race relations issues of the past and the economic concerns of the present.

At the 1984 Democratic National Convention, Jesse Jackson, in a typical rhetorical flourish, claimed that blacks have "come from disgrace to Amazing Grace." The same observation could be applied to the South. In 1940, black life in the region was circumscribed by segregation, exclusion, and an elaborate and demeaning racial etiquette. That is mostly gone now, but the South isn't, and southern blacks were largely responsible for both the exorcism and the preservation. Though the agenda of race relations in the South is filled with unfinished business, it is now possible to move beyond race and include such items as part of a larger new crusade for economic justice. If that seems to be a tall order, recall that few southerners, black or white, imagined a new racial order just a short generation ago. The task may be more difficult today less because of the problem than because of our prevailing smugness. It is well to remember Jimmy Carter's admonition in a 1985 interview: "When we . . . are satisfied with what we have accomplished in the eyes of God, we are already far from God. Unless we are attempting things that might fail, we have too little faith—in ourselves or in God."

For the crusade against economic injustice, southern blacks and whites are likely to be partners. Just as the problems are no longer necessarily racial in the South, the means for their solution require an interracial alliance, a connection that already finds a common ground of past, place, religion, and manners, as well as a legacy of ameliorating what Gunnar Myrdal called "The American Dilemma." Perhaps the South can become, after all, that beacon of hope that Faulkner and Dabbs and others predicted decades ago. Perhaps black and white together can descend from "the mountaintops of hope," as Urban League president John Jacob put it in 1985, to "the green valleys of complete equality and justice." That would be the most fitting legacy of the crusade for black equality in the South.

Bibliographical Essay

I. Race Relations and Southern Culture

The struggle for regional redemption was rooted in southern culture. W. J. Cash's *The Mind of the South* (New York, 1941) is the essential starting point for an understanding of southern culture despite its emphasis on the southern Piedmont. Cash effectively connects the attempt to preserve white supremacy with the closed nature of southern society, the "savage ideal," as he called it. Ultimately, all of the South's institutions, including its political and religious institutions, supported the sin of race pride. C. Vann Woodward's *The Burden of Southern History* (rev. ed.; Baton Rouge, 1968) provides an insightful discussion of the ironies, contradictions, and consequent burdens of southern culture. There have been numerous anthologies and surveys of southern culture over the past two decades, among the most useful of which are H. Brandt Ayers and Thomas H. Naylor (eds.), *You Can't Eat Magnolias* (New York, 1972); Louis D. Rubin, Jr. (ed.), *The American South: Portrait of a Culture* (Baton Rouge, 1980); and Stephen A. Smith, *Myth, Media, and the Southern Mind* (Fayetteville, Ark., 1985).

Gunnar Myrdal's *An American Dilemma: The Negro Problem and Modern Democracy* (New York, 1944) remains the classic interpretation of southern race relations in the 1930s. The book is remarkable for discerning the subtleties of race and class etiquette and their impact upon both white and black southerners. Bertram W. Doyle, a black sociologist at Fisk University, wrote *The Etiquette of Race Relations in the South: A Study in Social Control* (Chicago, 1937), a scholarly discourse on the etiquette surrounding segregation. Doyle placed great faith in interracial organizations to ameliorate the demeaning aspects of racial etiquette. Though of an earlier generation, W. E. B. Du Bois, in *The Souls of Black Folk* (Chicago, 1903) and his autobiography, *Dusk of Dawn* (New York, 1940), provides excellent insights on the psychological impact of white supremacy on blacks. Also useful is James Weldon Johnson, *Autobiography of an Ex-Coloured Man* (New York, 1927).

Other, more personal insights into the etiquette of race in the 1930s can be found in Lillian Smith's autobiographical work, *Killers of the Dream* (New York, 1949), which relates the rigid social customs occasioned by white supremacy in the small southern town of her youth. Alabama-born journalist Anne Braden tells how even white liberals became enmeshed in the insidious etiquette of race in Sue Thrasher and Eliot Wigginton, "You Can't Be Neutral: An Interview with Anne Braden," *Southern Exposure*, XII (November-December, 1984), 79–85. Theodore Rosengarten, *All God's Dangers: The Life of Nate Shaw* (New York, 1974), transcribes the reminiscences of a black

Alabama sharecropper (whose real name was Ned Cobb) and his unsuccessful efforts to pursue the American Dream in rural Alabama during the first third of the twentieth century. Another articulate exposition of the limitations imposed on black life by the stifling etiquette of race is Richard Wright's autobiographical *Black Boy: A Record of Childhood and Youth* (New York, 1937). Maya Angelou's childhood in Stamps, Arkansas, provides another autobiographical account of race relations prior to the civil rights movement, *I Know Why the Caged Bird Sings* (New York, 1969). Angelou is particularly good at demonstrating the isolation of the black community and the significant control whites had over the lives of blacks. The Federal Writers' Project undertaken during the 1930s also offers firsthand accounts of racial etiquette from both white and black perspectives. Some of the interviews are available in *These Are Our Lives* (Chapel Hill, 1939) and in Tom E. Terrill and Jerrold Hirsch (eds.), *Such as Us: Southern Voices of the Thirties* (Chapel Hill, 1978). William Alexander Percy's classic memoir, *Lanterns on the Levee: Recollections of a Planter's Son* (New York, 1941), offers a candid white elite perspective on race relations in the Mississippi Delta between the wars. For a different white point of view, both geographically and intellectually, see Percy's contemporary Ben Robertson, *Red Hills and Cotton: An Upcountry Memory* (Columbia, S.C., 1942). Robertson's account is a breezy rendition of life and culture in the South Carolina upcountry prior to World War II. Though he acknowledges the illogic of southern race relations, he is convinced that change can only come within the region.

Scholarly analysis of race relations between 1890 and 1940 would provide a helpful context for examining the ensuing changes, but historians have not studied this important era to the extent that they have written about race in other periods of southern history. There are two helpful case studies that involve this time period: Lester C. Lamon, *Black Tennesseans, 1900–30* (Knoxville, 1977), and George C. Wright, *Life Behind a Veil: Blacks in Louisville, Kentucky, 1865–1930* (Baton Rouge, 1985). In addition, Howard N. Rabinowitz is currently conducting a major study of this era.

Novelists have been especially adept in capturing the nuances of race relations under white supremacy. Ralph Ellison's *Invisible Man* (New York, 1947) is the ultimate statement on black invisibility, though a good deal of the story takes place in the North. Several of William Faulkner's pre–World War II novels make significant statements on the etiquette of race and how it casts a shadow on the lives of white and black southerners. Joe Christmas reflects the tenuous position of mulattoes in the rural South in *Light in August* (New York, 1933), and in *The Sound and the Fury* (New York, 1929), Faulkner distills white perceptions of race relations in the South through the tragic persona of Quentin Compson. Race played an important role in many other novels of the Southern Renaissance. Even when race was not a major theme of Thomas Wolfe, as in *Look Homeward, Angel* (New York, 1929) and *You Can't Go Home Again* (New York, 1940), race relations were part of the New South decadence he depicted. In recent years, Alice Walker has become a leading novelist of black life in the South. On the corroding impact of racial etiquette see especially her novel *The Third Life of Grange Copeland* (New York, 1970).

Walker reminisces about her childhood and the importance of place, despite the hardships of rural southern life, in "The Black Writer and the Southern Experience," *New South*, XXV (Fall, 1970), 23–26. Southern novelists who wrestle with race relations from a white perspective include Ferrol Sams, whose *Run with the Horsemen* (Atlanta, 1982) is a semiautobiographical work on childhood in rural Georgia between the wars, and Olive Ann Burns, whose *Cold Sassy Tree* (New York, 1984) concerns a white teenager growing up in rural Georgia after the turn of the century. For a survey of that group of southern novelists living in the North but writing about race relations and southern culture, see Ruth A. Banes, "Southerners Up North: Autobiographical Indications of Southern Ethnicity," in James C. Cobb and Charles R. Wilson (eds.), *Perspectives on the American South*, Vol. III (New York, 1985).

Several books provide fine surveys of the literary and academic ferment occurring in the South during the twenties and thirties that both uncovered the nature of race relations in the region and built a foundation for future and bolder analyses of the racial problem. Daniel Joseph Singal's *The War Within: From Victorian to Modernist Thought in the South, 1919–1945* (Chapel Hill, 1982) is probably the best of the lot, presenting sharp portraits of the leading academics and literati, including W. T. Couch and Howard W. Odum, though the transition to modernism was less complete than Singal assumes. Other works on the era include Michael O'Brien, *The Idea of the American South, 1920–1941* (Baltimore, 1979), and Richard H. King, *A Southern Renaissance: The Cultural Awakening of the American South, 1930–1955* (New York, 1980).

There were several pioneer academic works on race relations from this period, most published by Couch's University of North Carolina Press. Arthur Raper, a colleague of Odum at Chapel Hill, wrote *The Tragedy of Lynching* (Chapel Hill, 1933), a relatively daring analysis of the psychological and sociological pressures leading to lynching. Odum's *Southern Regions of the United States* (Chapel Hill, 1936) remains the basic sourcebook for scientific insight into southern debilities; though skirting the race issue, the work implies that the biracial society contributed mightily to the South's problems. A more direct summary of Odum's findings is Gerald W. Johnson, *The Wasted Land* (Chapel Hill, 1937). Rupert B. Vance, *Human Geography of the South* (Chapel Hill, 1932), again does not directly address race, but its shadow darkens the southern regions he delineates. Contrast these rather mild expositions on race relations and southern culture with an earlier essay by Odum, "A More Articulate South," *Journal of Social Forces*, II (1924), 730–35, where he explicitly scores the "social fundamentalism" of the region. In this connection, see Wayne D. Brazil, "*Social Forces* and Sectional Self-Scrutiny," in Merle Black and John Shelton Reed (eds.), *Perspectives on the American South*, Vol. II (New York, 1984).

Clarence Cason and Nell Battle Lewis were two of the lesser literary lights of this period, but their works and lives offer reflection on the consuming nature of southern race relations. See John M. Matthews, "Clarence Cason Among the Southern Liberals," *Alabama Review*, XXXVIII (1985), 3–18, and Darden Asbury Pyron, "Nell Battle Lewis (1893–1956) and 'The New Southern

Woman,'" in Cobb and Wilson (eds.), *Perspectives on the American South*, Vol. III.

Evangelical Protestantism was and is a major element of southern culture. Samuel S. Hill, Jr., has been the most prolific writer on the connection between religion and southern culture; in addition, his work emphasizes the role of religion as a support for white supremacy. His most pertinent works include *Religion and the Solid South* (Nashville, 1972); *The South and the North in American Religion* (Athens, Ga., 1980), which offers a strong case for southern exceptionalism; and "The South's Culture-Protestantism," *Christian Century*, September 12, 1962, pp. 1094–96. Two other southern writers who discuss race relations in the context of southern religion are James McBride Dabbs in *Who Speaks for the South?* (New York, 1964) and James Sellers in *The South and Christian Ethics* (New York, 1962), an impassioned brief for the potential positive application of southern religion to race relations. Will Campbell, renegade Baptist preacher, presents a more personal view of the dilemma of race and religion in *Brother to a Dragonfly* (New York, 1977). Charles Reagan Wilson offers a fine background for much of the literature on southern religion in the twentieth century in *Baptized in Blood: The Religion of the Lost Cause, 1865–1920* (Athens, Ga., 1980). The growing bibliography on southern religion in recent years attests to its importance to regional culture, especially to its crucial role with respect to race relations.

II. "A Kind of Sunlight": Depression, War, and Change, 1930–1945

The Great Depression and the New Deal ushered in an era of significant change in the South. Though the changes in southern politics and race relations were not especially evident during the 1930s, the economic upheaval set the stage for the transformations that occurred after World War II. The literature on race relations in the South during the 1930s is increasing, though there is as yet no comprehensive treatment of the subject. George B. Tindall, *The Emergence of the New South, 1913–1945* (Baton Rouge, 1967), Chapter XVI, "New Directions in Negro Life," is a good start. The essays by Pete Daniel on southern agriculture, Wayne Flynt on labor, Alan Brinkley on politics, Harvard Sitkoff on blacks, and Numan V. Bartley on the general impact of the New Deal on the South in James C. Cobb and Michael V. Namorato (eds.), *The New Deal and the South* (Jackson, Miss., 1984), also illuminate the 1930s as an era of transition in southern race relations. For a helpful national perspective on blacks and the New Deal, see Harvard Sitkoff, *A New Deal for Blacks: The Emergence of Civil Rights as a National Issue* (New York, 1978).

Other writers have stressed the theme of continuity—that New Deal programs left race relations and their supporting institutions basically intact. Several studies of states and cities emphasize the entrenched nature of the white political elite and their management of white supremacy. Anthony J. Badger, *North Carolina and the New Deal* (Raleigh, 1981); Ronald L. Heinemann, *Depression and New Deal in Virginia: The Enduring Dominion* (Charlottesville, 1983); and John Robert Moore, "The New Deal in Louisiana," in John Braeman (ed.), *The New Deal: State and Local Levels* (Columbus, Ohio,

1975), are among the better state studies of the New Deal in the South that cover race relations. Roger Biles, *Memphis in the Great Depression* (Knoxville, 1986); Don H. Doyle, *Nashville Since the 1920s* (Knoxville, 1985); and Michael J. McDonald and William Bruce Wheeler, *Knoxville, Tennessee: Continuity and Change in an Appalachian City* (Knoxville, 1983) provide a trilogy for Tennessee during the 1930s, with Biles's book the most aggressive argument for continuity. Charles B. Rousseve's *The Negro in Louisiana: Aspects of His History and Literature* (New Orleans, 1937) includes a section dealing with the economic problems of the New Orleans black community during the early Depression years.

Several articles in recent years have analyzed specific New Deal programs in the South, including their impact on blacks. Generally, the conclusions are that southern white leaders used the federal system and the strength of local customs to rigorously maintain the color line. James A. Burran, "The WPA in Nashville, 1935–1943," *Tennessee Historical Quarterly*, XXXIX (1975), 293–306, and Ronald E. Marcello, "Senator Josiah Bailey, Harry Hopkins, and the WPA: A Prelude to the Conservative Coalition," *Southern Studies*, XXII (1983), 321–39, make that point. The Byrd machine in Virginia, perhaps the most entrenched of southern white power structures, readily weathered New Deal initiatives as demonstrated by A. Cash Koeniger, "The New Deal and the States: Roosevelt Versus the Byrd Organization in Virginia," *Journal of American History*, LXVIII (1982), 876–96.

Though the New Deal altered the nature of labor relations in the United States, labor organizers rarely challenged the color line in the South. Southern textile entrepreneurs in particular had an unwritten bargain with their white workforce to keep blacks out of the mills in exchange for a union-free workplace. However, there was always the danger of labor organization across racial lines, as had occurred in the Reconstruction era in some southern cities and was occurring in parts of the rural South during the 1930s. One of the leaders of the interracial union movement on the farm, H. L. Mitchell, summarized his experiences in *Mean Things Happening in This Land: The Life and Times of H. L. Mitchell, Co-Founder of the Southern Tenant Farmers Union* (Montclair, N.J., 1979). Such interracial alliances were generally short-lived with brutal consequences, especially for blacks. In most instances, there were basic antagonisms between white and black workers that white entrepreneurs did not even need to exploit; see, for example, Charles H. Martin, "White Supremacy and Black Workers: Georgia's 'Black Shirts' Combat the Great Depression," *Labor History*, XVIII (1977), 366–81. Where labor organization made some headway, even under Jim Crow conditions, blacks gained valuable experience in organizing and leadership. See Charles H. Martin, "Southern Labor Relations in Transition: Gadsden, Alabama, 1930–1943," *Journal of Southern History*, XLVII (1981), 545–68, and the most useful essay to date on the subject, Robert J. Norrell, "Caste in Steel: Jim Crow Careers in Birmingham, Alabama," *Journal of American History*, LXXIII (1986), 669–94.

The change in southern agriculture generated by New Deal policies was significant, especially in the cotton South. Though there are no monographic studies focusing on the impact of such legislation on blacks specifically, some general works include this perspective. The best accounts are Pete Daniel, *Breaking the Land: The Transformation of Cotton, Tobacco, and Rice Cultures Since 1880* (Urbana, 1985), and Jack Temple Kirby, *Rural Worlds Lost: The American South, 1920–1960* (Baton Rouge, 1987). Daniel stresses the path not taken by the Roosevelt administration—small farm ownership for tenants and sharecroppers—while Kirby focuses on social disruptions and economic opportunities occasioned by what amounted to a southern enclosure movement. Kirby also makes the good point that race relations varied widely by geographic area and circumstance in the rural South. Pete Daniel's essay "The Transformation of the Rural South, 1930 to the Present," *Agricultural History*, LV (1981), 231–48, is a useful overview. Other works that do not stress the black experience in the changing southern countryside of the 1930s but do provide an important context for understanding that experience are Gilbert C. Fite, *Cotton Fields No More: Southern Agriculture, 1865–1980* (Lexington, Ky., 1984); Paul E. Mertz, *New Deal Policy and Southern Rural Poverty* (Baton Rouge, 1978); and Harry D. Fornari, "The Big Change: Cotton to Soybeans," *Agricultural History*, LIII (1979), 3–21.

World War II, despite the fact that it was one of the most important events in the history of the South, has drawn relatively little scholarship focusing on the region. George B. Tindall's *The Emergence of the New South*, Chapter XX, provides an overview of the era. Pete Daniel is working on a comprehensive study of the war's impact on the South, but there are huge gaps he must fill. Morton Sosna presented a suggestive paper, "More Important Than the Civil War? The Social Impact of World War II on the South" at the Southern Historical Association Convention, November, 1982, that argues for the war's importance in stimulating changes in race relations. John R. Skates argues in a similar vein for Mississippi in "World War II as a Watershed in Mississippi History," *Journal of Mississippi History*, XXXVII (1975), 131–42, and discusses the reaction of the state's white leaders to the Fair Employment Practices Committee (FEPC). H. C. Nixon's *Lower Piedmont Country* (New York, 1946) is a fascinating contemporary account of how the war opened up a relatively isolated region of the South. Flannery O'Connor, who was less optimistic than Nixon about consequences of the war in the rural South, offers a fictional portrayal of his analysis in "The Displaced Person," in Flannery O'Connor (ed.), *The Complete Stories* (New York, 1971).

Though white southerners were generally hopeful about their changing situation during World War II, hints of change in race relations brought about the rabid defense that O'Connor alludes to in her story. "The Deep South Looks Up," *Fortune*, XXVIII (July, 1943), 95–98, 100, 218, 220, 223–24, captures well the mixed feelings of white and black southerners toward the domestic implications of the war. The FEPC provoked the strongest reaction, and Merl E. Reed surveyed both the workings of the committee in the South and the reaction of whites and blacks in two articles, "The FEPC, the Black Worker, and the Southern Shipyards," *South Atlantic Quarterly*, LXXIV (1974), 446–67, and "FEPC and the Federal Agencies in the South," *Journal of Negro History*, LXVI (1980), 43–56. Federal initiatives and black hopes rubbed the passions of some whites raw, resulting in the worst outbreak of violence since the 1890s. The best survey is James A. Burran, "Urban Racial Violence in the South During World War II: A Comparative Overview," in Walter J. Fraser, Jr., and Winfred B. Moore, Jr. (eds.), *From the Old South to the New: Essays on the Transitional South* (Westport, Conn., 1981). Though occurring before American entrance into the war, the Cleo Wright lynching set a precedent for federal involvement. See Dominic J. Capeci, Jr., "The Lynching of Cleo Wright: Federal Protection of Constitutional Rights During World War II," *Journal of American History*, LXXII (1986), 859–87.

When not expressed in violence, white reaction was occasionally highly defensive. The rumor of the "Eleanor Clubs" was one such example chronicled by Howard W. Odum, "The Romance of the Eleanor Clubs," in Odum (ed.), *Race and Rumors of Race: Challenge to American Crisis* (Chapel Hill, 1943). The movement of blacks into southern cities occasioned not only casual violence but increased discrimination. See Chapter 4, "The Sunbelt Cities in World War II," in Carl Abbott, *The New Urban America: Growth and Politics in Sunbelt Cities* (Chapel Hill, 1981). But it would be a mistake to portray southern blacks as victims in this period. A good starting point for an analysis of the southern black during the war is Rayford W. Logan (ed.), *What the Negro Wants* (Chapel Hill, 1944), which makes black aspirations and demands explicit.

Next to the FEPC, the U.S. Supreme Court's decision in *Smith* v. *Allwright* to abolish the white primary agitated southerners the most. The South's political system was as closed as its other institutions—Virginia Durr's difficulties were not unusual. See Hollinger F. Barnard (ed.), *Outside the Magic Circle: The Autobiography of Virginia Foster Durr* (University, Ala., 1985). V. O. Key, Jr., *Southern Politics in State and Nation* (New York, 1949), provides an excellent overview of the restricted nature of southern politics in the 1930s and forties.

The southern white reaction to potential black gains during the war threw liberal southerners into one of their periodic psychological tailspins. Southern liberals, perhaps because historians have sympathized with them, or perhaps because their very existence prompts interest, have received extensive coverage, especially for the 1940s. Morton Sosna's *In Search of the Silent South: Southern Liberals and the Race Issue* (New York, 1977) remains the standard work, demonstrating the ambivalence and divisions of southern liberals on race relations. Gunnar Myrdal's *An American Dilemma: The Negro Problem and Modern Democracy* (New York, 1944) has some excellent passages on liberals' frustrations in the early 1940s, and Fred Hobson's *Tell About the South: The Southern Rage to Explain* (Baton Rouge, 1983) contains insightful sections on liberals Lillian Smith and James McBride Dabbs. Generally, liberals favored local solutions to the race issue and stressed education as the primary means for enlightening southern whites. John T. Kneebone makes this point well in *Southern Liberal Journalists and the Issue of Race, 1920–44* (Chapel Hill, 1985). The loose liberal coalition built up during the 1930s would disintegrate from internal and external pressures by the late 1940s.

III. A Season of Hope, 1945–1954

For a time after World War II it seemed as though the South would cast off its crippling economic, political, and racial institutions. Southern political culture appeared to loosen its ties to white supremacy as reflected both in accelerated black political activity and in the election of whites at local and state levels who abjured appeals to racism. Black political organizing efforts form a major theme of race relations in the immediate postwar era. Black educator Samuel Du Bois Cook's essay "Political Movements and Organizations," in Avery Leiserson (ed.), *The American South in the 1960s* (New York, 1964), provides a good survey of black political organizations, especially in the aftermath of the *Smith* v. *Allwright* decision. Ronald H. Bayor's paper "Race, Ethnicity and Intergroup Relations in the Sunbelt South: Patterns of Change," presented at the Conference on the Sunbelt, Miami, November 3–6, 1985, includes a helpful account of black voter-registration drives in the 1940s and the evolution of the Manhattan coalition in several cities. Henry Allen Bullock, "Urbanism and Race Relations," in Rupert B. Vance and Nicholas J. Demerath (eds.), *The Urban South* (Chapel Hill, 1954), stresses the connection between black urbanization and increased political activity and organization.

The migration of rural blacks to southern cities, part of a general demographic upheaval among southerners just after World War II, was a prerequisite not only for voter-registration drives but for the civil rights movement that followed in the 1950s and sixties. Jack Temple Kirby places the postwar migration in broader perspective in "The Southern Exodus, 1910–1960: A Primer for Historians," *Journal of Southern History*, XLIX (1983), 585–600, and T. Lynn Smith focuses more on the intraregional migration of blacks in "The Redistribution of the Negro Population of the United States, 1910–1960," *Journal of Negro History*, LI (1966), 155–73.

Perhaps Atlanta experienced the political impact of black migration more than any other southern city. Clarence A. Bacote, "The Negro in Atlanta Politics," *Phylon*, XVI (1955), 333–50, is the standard account on black political organizing in Atlanta during the late 1940s. Virginia H. Hein, "The Image of 'A City Too Busy to Hate': Atlanta in the 1960s," *Phylon*, XXXIII (1972), 205–21, includes a section on emerging black political power in the late 1940s and the evolving Manhattan coalition. Harold H. Martin, *William Berry Hartsfield: Mayor of Atlanta* (Athens, Ga., 1978), details Hartsfield's courting of the black vote in Atlanta within the context of segregation. Barry J. Kaplan, "Houston: The Golden Buckle of the Sunbelt," in Richard M. Bernard and Bradley R. Rice (eds.), *Sunbelt Cities: Politics and Growth Since World War II* (Austin, 1985), offers a perspective from another New South city as he discusses the demise of the "8F crowd." Black political influence in the urban South after World War II remains a historiographical frontier, especially for cities other than Atlanta.

At the state level Alabama's political transformation has drawn the most scholarly attention. James E. "Big Jim" Folsom has benefited from two generally favorable biographies: Carl Grafton and Anne Permaloff, *Big Mules & Branchheads: James E. Folsom and Political Power in Alabama* (Athens, Ga., 1985), and George E. Sims, *The Little Man's Big Friend: James E. Folsom in Alabama Politics, 1946–58* (University, Ala., 1985). Grafton and Permaloff's work is the more thorough of the two. Virginia Van der Veer Hamilton looks at other beneficiaries of the short-lived political spring in Alabama in "Lister Hill, Hugo Black, and the Albatross of Race," *Alabama Law Review*, XXXVI (1985), 845–60.

Numan V. Bartley has written extensively and intelligently on the transition that began to occur in southern politics at the state and local levels—the movement away from the dominance of Black Belt elites and their tight-fisted fiscal policies, if not necessarily away from white supremacy. *The Creation of Modern Georgia* (Athens, Ga., 1983) is a model state study that focuses on this transition in Georgia. Two more general essays by Bartley that provide a rich context for the transition are "Another New South?" *Georgia Historical Quarterly*, LXV (1981), 119–37, and a review essay, "Beyond *Southern Politics*: Some Suggestions for Research," in Merle Black and John Shelton Reed (eds.), *Perspectives on the American South*, Vol. II (New York, 1984). For a general summary of the southern political spring along with some interesting vignettes on the leading politicians of the era, see Jack Bass and Walter De Vries, *The Transformation of Southern Politics: Social Change and Political Consequence Since 1945* (New York, 1976). Atlanta journalist Ralph McGill offers a few contemporary profiles in a collection of essays edited by Calvin M. Logue, *Southern Encounters: Southerners of Note in Ralph McGill's South* (Macon, Ga., 1983).

The increasing amount of formal interracial cooperation in the postwar years paralleled the political thaw. Morton Sosna, *In Search of the Silent South: Southern Liberals and the Race Issue* (New York, 1977), has an excellent discussion on the era's interracial organizations. Howard W. Odum offers the perspective of the Southern Regional Council (SRC) and its new integrationist approach in "An Approach to Diagnosis and Direction of the Problem of Negro Segregation in the Public Schools of the South," *Journal of Public Law*, III (1954), 8–37. Arnold Shankman's fine essay "Dorothy Tilly and the Fellowship of the Concerned," in Walter J. Fraser and Winfred B. Moore, Jr. (eds.), *From the Old South to the New: Essays on the Transitional South* (Westport, Conn., 1981), demonstrates the connection among women, churches, and racial reform in the South. Anthony P. Dunbar, *Against the Grain: Southern Radicals and Prophets, 1929–1959* (Charlottesville, 1981), deals with some of the bolder interracial organizations of the postwar era.

Many of the "radicals and prophets" had formal seminary training, continuing a lengthy tradition of religious-oriented reform in the South; however, the institutional church did not play a major role in leading the South toward a new era of race relations after World War II. Donald W. Shriver, Jr., "Southern Churches in Transition," *New South*, XXV (Winter, 1970), 40–47, includes material on the Southern Baptist Convention (SBC) and race. A more specific analysis of Southern Baptists and race relations is Leon McBeth's essay "Southern Baptists and Race Since 1947," *Baptist History and Heritage*, VII (1972), 155–69.

The federal offensive on behalf of civil rights reinforced regional trends. The report of the Committee on Civil Rights, *To Secure These Rights* (Washington, D.C., 1947), called for a direct federal assault on segregation. Historians are still assessing President Harry Truman's role in promoting civil rights legislation. Harvard Sitkoff, "Harry Truman and the Election of 1948: The Coming of Age of Civil Rights in American Politics," *Journal of Southern History*, XXXVII (1971), 597–616, stresses the political motivations behind Truman's efforts, especially the growing black presence in the northern wing of the

Democratic party. Monroe Billington, "Civil Rights, President Truman and the South," *Journal of Negro History*, LVIII (1973), 127–39, focuses on Truman's deteriorating relations with southern political leaders and their constituents.

The federal judiciary became an important part of the federal offensive in the late 1940s and early fifties. Much of the pertinent litigation revolved around the wretched inequalities of southern schools, a clear violation of the Supreme Court's 1896 ruling in *Plessy* v. *Ferguson*. Gunnar Myrdal in *An American Dilemma: The Negro Problem and Modern Democracy* (New York, 1944) provides some telling statistical and qualitative evidence for the inequalities in southern education. The regional costs of such inequalities were a favorite topic of Howard W. Odum, expounded especially in *The Way of the South: Toward the Regional Balance of America* (New York, 1947), which in many respects, though not as boldly, echoes Lewis Harvie Blair's *A Southern Prophecy: The Prosperity of the South Dependent upon the Elevation of the Negro*, ed. C. Vann Woodward (Boston, 1964). David W. Southern, "Beyond Jim Crow Liberalism: Judge Waring's Fight Against Segregation in South Carolina, 1942–52," *Journal of Negro History*, XLVI (1981), 209–27, includes a discussion of the landmark Briggs case, and Frye Gaillard, *Race, Rock & Religion: Profiles from a Southern Journalist* (Charlotte, 1982), contains an interesting profile of Harry Briggs. For the relatively lengthy precedents leading up to the 1954 *Brown* decision, see Richard Kluger, *Simple Justice: The History of Brown v. Board of Education and Black America's Struggle for Equality* (New York, 1976).

As promising as the immediate postwar era was, ambivalence reigned among white moderates and liberals, who recognized the need to expiate the sin of white supremacy but were plagued by uncertainty, fear, and even unwillingness. Their feelings are captured with skill in William Faulkner's first postwar novel, *Intruder in the Dust* (New York, 1948).

IV. Flight from Reality: The Rise of White Resistance, 1945–1956

Historians, political scientists, and journalists have documented well the attempt of old-line leaders to retake the political ramparts and repair Fortress South. Many of the essays and books that examine the southern political spring also relate the flight and splintering of liberals and the resurgence of traditional forces. Virginia Hamilton's article "Lister Hill, Hugo Black, and the Albatross of Race," *Alabama Law Review*, XXXVI (1985), 845–60, discusses the Boswell Amendment and the narrowing options for Hill and Sparkman. Jack Bass and Walter De Vries, in *The Transformation of Southern Politics: Social Change and Political Consequence Since 1945* (New York, 1976), trace the rise of the Dixiecrats and the Smith-Graham U.S. Senate race in North Carolina in 1950 that doomed the political spring over most of the South.

Traditional white southern leaders used the Truman administration's civil rights initiatives to stir up racial and patriotic sentiments. See Harvard Sitkoff's "Harry Truman and the Election of 1948: The Coming of Age of Civil Rights in American Politics," *Journal of Southern History*, XXXVII (1971),

597–616, and Monroe Billington's "Civil Rights, President Truman and the South," *Journal of Negro History*, LVIII (1973), 127–39. These tactics made less an impression on the administration than on southern liberals, some of whom disavowed integrationist organizations and spokesmen, while others were harassed into silence or exile. Morton Sosna, *In Search of the Silent South: Southern Liberals and the Race Issue* (New York, 1977), deals with the splintering of white liberals in the late 1940s. Arnold Shankman's essay "Dorothy Tilly and the Fellowship of the Concerned," in Walter J. Fraser, Jr., and Winfred B. Moore, Jr. (eds.), *From the Old South to the New: Essays on the Transitional South* (Westport, Conn., 1981) and David W. Southern, "Beyond Jim Crow Liberalism: Judge Waring's Fight Against Segregation in South Carolina, 1942–52," *Journal of Negro History*, XLVI (1981), 209–27, detail the ostracism suffered by these individuals. Irwin Klibaner, "The Travail of Southern Radicals: The Southern Conference Educational Fund, 1946–1976," *Journal of Southern History*, XLIX (1983), 179–202, emphasizes red-baiting as a strategy to discredit southern integrationists, as does Virginia Durr in her memoir, edited by Hollinger F. Barnard, *Outside the Magic Circle: The Autobiography of Virginia Foster Durr* (University, Ala., 1985). Wilma Dykeman and James Stokeley, in *Seeds of Southern Change: The Life of Will Alexander* (Chicago, 1962), study the impact of such methods on a pioneer of interracial cooperation in the South. The religious motivation of southern reformers is particularly evident in John A. Salmond, *A Southern Rebel: The Life and Times of Aubrey Willis Williams, 1890–1965* (Chapel Hill, 1983). William H. Nicholls, *Southern Tradition and Regional Progress* (Chapel Hill, 1960), written just as massive resistance was peaking, provides a useful discussion on the relationship between white supremacy and the traditional political structure. Robert Sherrill, *Gothic Politics in the Deep South* (New York, 1968), offers vivid portraits of the era's more virulent race-baiters. Given the widespread reaction in the South, Hodding Carter, who counted himself among the enlightened liberals, warned outsiders not to attempt to solve southern racial problems. These issues could and must be handled from within, he argued—an old but surprisingly resilient line. See his book *Southern Legacy* (Baton Rouge, 1950).

This drawing inward, both by southern liberals and by the region, was in stark contrast to the open, optimistic, almost complacent attitude among most whites immediately after World War II. This perspective heightened the shock of subsequent events and necessitated a major re-education campaign on the part of the old-line leaders. On the southern psyche after World War II, see C. Vann Woodward, "From the First Reconstruction to the Second," *Harper's*, CCXXX (April 1965), 127–33.

Blacks, of course, received increasingly rougher treatment as white resistance mounted. Manning Marable, *Race, Reform and Rebellion: The Second Reconstruction in Black America, 1945–1982* (Jackson, Miss., 1984), has a discussion of the suppression of black voting rights in the late 1940s and early fifties. Ronald H. Bayor's paper "Race and Urban Development: The Shaping of Twentieth-Century Atlanta," presented at the Organization of American Historians Convention, Minneapolis, April, 1985, focuses on the hypocrisy of the

Hartsfield administration in wooing black voters while at the same time trying to limit their influence.

Southern white resistance accelerated after the *Brown* decision. Numan V. Bartley, "Massive Resistance in Retrospect," *New South*, XXIV (Winter, 1969), 6–16, is a helpful overview. For a more detailed account, see his monograph *The Rise of Massive Resistance: Race and Politics in the South During the 1950's* (Baton Rouge, 1969). Neil R. McMillen provides the definitive study of organized resistance in the Deep South in *The Citizens' Council: Organized Resistance to the Second Reconstruction, 1954–64* (Urbana, 1971). Judge Tom Brady's *Black Monday* (Jackson, Miss., 1955) was among the earliest and most striking defenses of southern racial traditions in the wake of *Brown*. William D. Workman, Jr., *The Case for the South* (New York, 1960), attempts a more reasoned approach marshaling the voices of leading clerics and politicians to defend segregation. James J. Kilpatrick's *The Southern Case for School Segregation* (New York, 1962) is a more legalistic though not less staunch defense. Kilpatrick's emphasis on litigation made some of the resistance appear respectable, even genteel to outsiders. William Chafe, *Civilities and Civil Rights: Greensboro, North Carolina, and the Black Struggle for Freedom* (New York, 1980), is the most exhaustive analysis of dilatory strategies in a single community, one with a reputation for benign race relations. Steven E. Barkan, "Legal Control of the Southern Civil Rights Movement," *American Sociological Review*, XLIX (1984), 552–65, demonstrates the corollary of Chafe's argument—the difficulty of advancing school integration through the courts.

Not all white southern leaders wrote books attacking the federal government and misguided southerners while defending regional traditions. Ralph McGill groped warily throughout the mid- and late-1950s to locate some common ground. His attempts are collected in *No Place to Hide: The South and Human Rights*, ed. Calvin M. Logue (2 vols.; Macon, Ga., 1984), I. James McBride Dabbs was more forthright than McGill in setting down his disappointment at white resistance. *The Southern Heritage* (New York, 1958) is a strong indictment of the hypocrisy of southern white leaders, especially in their professions against violence. Mississippi congressman Frank E. Smith recounts the storm he created as a result of advising his constituents to obey the law in *Look Away from Dixie* (Baton Rouge, 1965).

Dabbs laments the silence of the institutional church, as does Marshall Frady in "God and Man in the South," *Atlantic Monthly*, CCXIX (January, 1967), 37–42. For a summary of Jerry Falwell's racial views, see Myra MacPherson, "The Many Voices of Jerry Falwell," *Washington Post*, October 7, 1984. Most churchmen, unlike Falwell and Mississippi's liberal bishop Duncan Gray, chose to remain silent.

The silence of the federal government was especially regrettable, leaving whatever white progressive forces that remained in the South thoroughly isolated. Robert Frederick Burk, *The Eisenhower Administration and Black Civil Rights* (Knoxville, 1984), is a balanced account that reveals the president's genuine constitutional inhibitions about activity in the civil rights area, yet his willingness to end segregation in those places directly under his jurisdiction. Michael S. Mayer, "With Much Deliberation and Some Speed: Eisenhower and the *Brown* Decision," *Journal of Southern History*, LII (1986), 43–76, is more specific on, and more critical of, the president's lack of public effort in 1954 and 1955. The growing isolation of the Supreme Court is a major theme in Harrell R. Rodgers, Jr., "The Supreme Court and School Desegregation: Twenty Years Later," *Political Science Quarterly*, LXXXIX (1974), 751–76.

V. The Limits of Endurance: Buses, Books, and Balance Sheets, 1954–1960

The literature on the early phases of the civil rights movement is extensive, and the sources discussed in this portion of the essay are not meant to be exhaustive. The following titles, rather, are particularly helpful in connecting the civil rights movement to southern culture.

Several works include interviews with participants of the major events in southern race relations during the late 1950s. New York *Times* reporter Howell Raines's *My Soul Is Rested: Movement Days in the Deep South Remembered* (New York, 1977) is one such compilation. Raines features interviews with Montgomery bus boycott figure E. D. Nixon, as well as accounts of the lynching of Edward Aaron. A less comprehensive collection is William R. Beardslee, *The Way Out Must Lead In: Life Histories in the Civil Rights Movement* (Atlanta, 1977), which includes an interview with John Lewis who would play a prominent role during the 1960s as an SNCC official. The Public Broadcasting System documentary series "Eyes on the Prize," which aired in January and February, 1987, utilized extensive footage and interviews from the late 1950s. Part 1, "Awakenings, 1954–1956," dealt with the Emmett Till lynching and the Montgomery bus boycott; Part 2, "Fighting Back, 1957–1962," included material on the Little Rock school desegregation crisis. Clayborne Carson *et al.* (eds.), *Eyes on the Prize: America's Civil Rights Years* (New York, 1987), is an excellent source book for movement writings and commentary.

The civil rights movement in the South as a religious movement has received increased support from scholars in recent years. Historically, black ministers have provided leadership and formed the bulwark of a small, primarily urban black middle class in the South. Gunnar Myrdal, in *An American Dilemma: The Negro Problem and Modern Democracy* (New York, 1944), offers a thorough discussion of black leadership and occupational structure in the 1930s that provides a context for the events that followed. Also important from a contextual point of view is black educator Benjamin E. Mays's work *The Negro's God* (Boston, 1938), which takes a dim view of the southern black church as a progressive institution in the 1930s. In a similar vein, Lester M. Salamon, "Leadership and Modernization: The Emerging Black Political Elite in the American South," *Journal of Politics*, XXXV (1973), 615–46, notes the ties of middle-class blacks in the 1950s to a segregated society, hence their ambivalence toward protest and reform. But with a new generation of leadership and with increased migration to the city, the black church began to take a more activist role in the 1950s. W. Sherman Jackson, "The Civil Rights Movement and the Black Church: A Conservative or Militant Force?" *Negro History Bulletin*, XXXVI (1984), 41–42, presents a strong argument for the militancy case.

Most observers regard the Montgomery bus boycott as the opening event of the civil rights movement. J. Mills Thornton III, "Challenge and Response in the Montgomery Bus Boycott of 1955–1956," *Alabama Review*, XXXIII (1980), 163–235, is the most thorough account of the boycott. Thornton's great contribution is to tie the effort to the local political situation, a connection that would become a common theme for other key events throughout the civil rights era. Martin Luther King, Jr., *Stride Toward Freedom: The Montgomery Story* (New York, 1958), is a valuable personal insight into the boycott, as well as a confession of faith. See also "Montgomery Bus Boycott," *Southern Exposure*, IX (Spring, 1981), 13–21.

The boycott, of course, was intimately connected with Martin Luther King, Jr., and with the formation of the Southern Christian Leadership Conference. Aldon D. Morris, *The Origins of the Civil Rights Movement: Black Communities Organizing for Change* (New York, 1984), includes a discussion of King and the SCLC, emphasizing that the organization was more than merely a personal vehicle for King. Morris also argues that the role of the SCLC reflected the fact that the events of the civil rights movement were more orchestrated and centralized than some historians believe. The most extensive analysis of the SCLC and King is Adam Fairclough, *"To Redeem the Soul of America": The SCLC and Martin Luther King, Jr.* (Athens, Ga., 1987), in which Fairclough depicts King as a reluctant leader and agrees with Morris that the organization did not solely revolve around King. For a briefer overview of the SCLC, see Fairclough's article "The SCLC and the Second Reconstruction, 1957–1973," *South Atlantic Quarterly*, LXXX (1981), 177–94.

Despite the emphasis on the SCLC, most writers have noted the key role played by King not only in the bus boycott but for the movement in general. Among the numerous biographical studies of King, the most thorough covering the civil rights era is David Garrow, *Bearing the Cross: Martin Luther King, Jr., and the Southern Christian Leadership Conference* (New York, 1986). Garrow stresses the religious aspect of King's crusade and details his Christian-driven mission, especially after the kitchen revelation during the Montgomery bus boycott. The man that emerges from these pages is heroic, yet filled with doubt, guilt, and loneliness. Stephen B. Oates, *Let the Trumpet Sound: The Life of Martin Luther King, Jr.* (New York, 1982), is a hortatory work that provides good coverage of King's pre-Montgomery years. See also Oates's article on the Christian derivation of King's philosophy, "The Intellectual Odyssey of Martin Luther King," *Massachusetts Review*, XXII (1981), 301–20. For a more detailed perspective on King's intellectual background, see Frederick L. Downing, *To See the Promised Land: The Faith Pilgrimage of Martin Luther King, Jr.* (Macon, Ga., 1986). Downing, like Oates, does not see Gandhi as a major influence on King's intellectual development. Charles Wellborn, "The Bible and Southern Politics," *Religion in Life*, XXXIII (Winter, 1975), 418–27, demonstrates how King exploited the common religious backgrounds of white and black southerners in his demonstrations.

The controversy over school desegregation peaked around 1961, only to revive by the late 1960s when it became apparent that many school districts had not advanced beyond tokenism. The Little Rock controversy brought the desegregation issue to national attention as much as the *Brown* decision had three years earlier. Elizabeth Huckaby, English teacher and assistant principal at Central High School in Little Rock, presents a personal account of the event in *Crisis at Central High: Little Rock, 1957–58* (Baton Rouge, 1980). Elizabeth Eckford, one of the nine blacks admitted to Central High, offers her perspective in an essay in the *Eyes on the Prize* volume. Tony Freyer, in *The Little Rock Crisis: A Constitutional Interpretation* (Westport, Conn., 1984), provides a more scholarly orientation as he emphasizes the legal aspects of the Little Rock situation. Elizabeth Jacoway's essay on Little Rock in Jacoway and David R. Colburn (eds.), *Southern Businessmen and Desegregation* (Baton Rouge, 1982), presents a more comprehensive version of the controversy as Jacoway notes the leadership vacuum and the belated stirring of the business community after Governor Faubus closed the schools. There are essays of lesser merit on school desegregation in New Orleans and Atlanta in this volume, as well as a fine essay by Carl Abbott detailing the school-closing controversy in Norfolk. For an interesting if uncomplimentary profile of Governor Faubus, see Harry S. Ashmore, *An Epitaph for Dixie* (New York, 1957).

Aside from the numerous studies of the Little Rock affair, there is a growing literature on school desegregation in other cities. Morton Inger, *Politics and Reality in an American City: The New Orleans School Crisis of 1960* (New York, 1969), is an adequate summary of the crisis in that city. On the business fallout from the New Orleans situation, see "New Orleans Rift Takes Trade Toll," New York *Times*, December 6, 1960. And Margaret Conner's story is told by Alan Wieder, "One Who Stayed: Margaret Conner and the New Orleans School Crisis," *Louisiana History*, XXVI (1985), 194–201. Virginia Hein's article, "The Image of 'A City Too Busy to Hate': Atlanta in the 1960s," *Phylon*, XXXIII (1972), 205–21, covers the peaceful school desegregation in Atlanta. For a laudatory account of the effort, see "A Proud City," *Newsweek*, September 11, 1961. On the school closings in Virginia, see "The Lost Class of '59," *Life*, November 3, 1958. Robert Coles, *Children of Crisis: A Study in Courage and Fear* (Boston, 1964), is a Yale psychiatrist's perspective on the heroic yet unassuming roles played by black children pioneering the desegregation movement. Coles spent several years in the South gathering material for this book and its sequel, *Farewell to the South* (Boston, 1972), which includes a profile of one of the three black children who integrated New Orleans' schools in 1960.

There have been relatively fewer pieces written on the desegregation of the University of Mississippi and the University of Alabama. Ed Williams, associate editor of the Charlotte *Observer* and a student at Ole Miss in the 1960s, wrote down some useful observations in "Oct. 1, 1962: The Last Battle of the Civil War," Charlotte *Observer*, October 1, 1982. See also Kevin Pierce Thornton, "Symbolism at Ole Miss and the Crisis of Southern Identity," *South Atlantic Quarterly*, LXXXVI (1987), 254–68, which demonstrates how white students attempted to develop instant "traditions" as a mechanism to ward off change, and how black enrollment at the university challenged those symbols. For a summary of Governor Wallace's stand in the schoolhouse door at the University of Alabama in 1963, see Hoyt Harwell, "The Schoolhouse Door," Charlotte *Observer*, June 10, 1983. There is need for a comprehensive study on the desegregation of higher education in the South in the 1950s and sixties.

Many of the school-desegregation confrontations resulted from actions related to court orders. Black litigants were fortunate in having sympathetic justices in some key federal districts in the South, especially the fifth district covering the Deep South. Jack Bass, *Unlikely Heroes: The Southern Judges Who Made the Civil Rights Revolution* (New York, 1981), is the definitive study of the fifth circuit court of appeals. Tinsley E. Yarborough, *Judge Frank Johnson and Human Rights in Alabama* (University, Ala., 1984), profiles a frequent adversary of Governor Wallace. Though the legal process generated considerable frustration, delays, and expense for blacks, the victories stemming from that process further legitimized the cause of southern blacks both in Washington and in national public opinion.

VI. The Crusade Against Segregation, 1960–1964

The sit-ins were the first major regionwide protests. Though there is no comprehensive study of the sit-in movement, there are helpful analyses of sit-ins in specific cities. William Chafe's *Civilities and Civil Rights: Greensboro, North Carolina, and the Black Struggle for Freedom* (New York, 1980), provides an excellent interpretation of the dignified protest in Greensboro. Howell Raines interviewed one of the Greensboro principals, Franklin McCain, in *My Soul Is Rested: Movement Days in the Deep South Remembered* (New York, 1977). The Charlotte *Observer* had a twenty-five-year reminiscence with the participants that appeared in the paper on February 1, 1985. For the follow-up to the initial demonstrations in February, 1960, see "I'm Gonna Sit at the Welcome Table One of These Days," *Southern Exposure*, IX (Spring, 1981), 22–33. Jack L. Walker, *Sit-Ins in Atlanta: A Study in the Negro Revolt* (New York, 1964), is an adequate study of the movement in Atlanta, though without the interpretative sophistication of Chafe's study of Greensboro. Part 3, "Ain't Scared of Your Jails," of the PBS documentary "Eyes on the Prize," focuses in part on the student-led sit-in demonstrations in Nashville and offers a fine example of the moral confrontation involved in those demonstrations. For a more general account of the sit-ins and the crucial role of students, see J. Allen Williams, Jr., and Ruth Searles, "Negro College Students' Participation in Sit-Ins," *Journal of Social Forces*, XL (1962), 215–20. Chapter 3 in Harvard Sitkoff's *The Struggle for Black Equality, 1954–1980* (New York, 1981) provides a fine summary of the demonstrations throughout the South. The definitive study of the Student Nonviolent Coordinating Committee that emerged from the sit-ins is Clayborne Carson, *In Struggle: SNCC and the Black Awakening of the 1960s* (Cambridge, Mass., 1981).

The sit-in demonstrations had dramatic impact on both black and white southerners. For the black perspective, see "The Image Makers," *Ebony*, XVI (April, 1961), 88. White liberals such as Ralph McGill, Leslie Dunbar, and James McBride Dabbs applauded the demonstrators and their southern protest.

See especially Dunbar's essay "The Changing Mind of the South: The Exposed Nerve," in Avery Leiserson (ed.), *The American South in the 1960s* (New York, 1964). James A. Rogers, editor of a small-town newspaper in South Carolina, did not share the liberals' enthusiasm, but the demonstrations awakened him to the injustice of segregation. See his recollection of the revelation, "Striking the Balance in the Sixties," *Furman Magazine*, XXII (Spring, 1985), 2–7.

Although the sit-ins provoked sporadic violence, the first serious attacks to draw national attention occurred during the Freedom Rides. On the first Freedom Ride in 1947, the Journey of Reconciliation, see August Meier and Elliott Rudwick, "The First Freedom Ride," *Phylon*, XXX (1969), 213–22. Howell Raines in *My Soul Is Rested* interviews James Farmer of CORE, who was involved in both Freedom Rides. Harvard Sitkoff's *The Struggle for Black Equality*, Chapter 4, summarizes the rides. The violence associated with them brought the federal government closer to direct action, though the Kennedy administration remained reluctant to protect the riders. On this latter point as well as the ambiguous role of the FBI during the Birmingham-Montgomery phase of the rides, see Kenneth O'Reilly, "The FBI and the Civil Rights Movement During the Kennedy Years—From the Freedom Rides to Albany," *Journal of Southern History*, LIV (1988), 201–32. For a dramatic visual presentation of the violence associated with the rides, see Part 3 of the documentary "Eyes on the Prize." See also Virginia Durr's account of the violence she witnessed in Montgomery, in Hollinger F. Barnard (ed.), *Outside the Magic Circle: The Autobiography of Virginia Foster Durr* (University, Ala., 1985).

The Albany demonstrations beginning in 1961 underscored the limitations of nonviolent protest. John A. Ricks III, " 'De Lawd' Descends and Is Crucified: Martin Luther King, Jr., in Albany, Georgia," *Journal of Southwest Georgia History*, II (1984), 3–14, presents the local context for the Albany demonstrations, the conflicts within the city and between local groups and the SCLC, and the role of police chief Pritchett. Steven E. Barkan, "Legal Control of the Southern Civil Rights Movement," *American Sociological Review*, XLIX (1984), 552–65, focuses on the tactics of Pritchett that eventually squelched the demonstrations. Adam Fairclough, "Martin Luther King, Jr., and the Quest for Nonviolent Social Change," *Phylon*, XLVII (1986), 1–15, stresses Albany as a valuable learning experience for King, as a prelude to Birmingham. The failure of Albany, Fairclough argues, was not in the nonviolent method but in the scattergun approach to issues taken by the demonstration leaders.

The role of the business community in facilitating the integration of public accommodations in the urban South was mixed. As the essayists note in Elizabeth Jacoway and David R. Colburn (eds.), *Southern Businessmen and Desegregation* (Baton Rouge, 1982), southern businessmen rarely took the lead in pushing for integration. Typically, a combination of black pressure and image-consciousness (as well as the negative examples of cities where violence erupted) moved these men to action. Once they supported integration, however, it usually became a *fait accompli*. James C. Cobb, in *The Selling of the South: The Southern Crusade for Industrial Development, 1936–1980* (Baton Rouge, 1982), makes these points in less equivocal terms than the essayists, and also disputes the conventional wisdom that racial strife adversely affected economic development. Cobb claims that the results were mixed. Atlanta's image-conscious business elite were among the earliest converts to downtown integration. See Art Harris, "Atlanta, Georgia: Too Busy to Hate," *Esquire*, CIII (June, 1985), 129–32, which, though focusing on the aggressive development policies of Mayor Andrew Young, traces the success of those policies to the racial accommodations worked out in the early 1960s. Harris notes especially the roles of Coca Cola's Robert Woodruff and Mayor Ivan Allen, Jr., in implementing integration. Charlotte offered a similar scenario, though lagging behind Atlanta in its timing. Cobb discusses the Charlotte case as does then-mayor Stanford Brookshire in a memoir published in the Charlotte *Observer*, "Keep Doing What We've Done Well," December 14, 1985. That many southern business leaders acted less out of conviction that segregation was wrong than out of expediency is emphasized by David Alan Horowitz, "White Southerners' Alienation and Civil Rights: The Response to Corporate Liberalism, 1956–1965," *Journal of Southern History*, LIV (1988), 173–200. Even national business leaders sometimes found it difficult to discuss integration with their colleagues in the South, who suffered from fear of reprisal as well as from the understandable delusion that segregation was the natural order of things.

Birmingham was of major importance in the civil rights movement both for the violence the campaign there provoked and for underscoring the connection between violent white intransigence and the attainment of demonstration objectives. Despite the campaign's importance, there is as yet no book-length scholarly analysis of the Birmingham demonstrations. David Garrow offers one of the more insightful accounts in *Protest at Selma: Martin Luther King, Jr., and the Voting Rights Act of 1965* (New Haven, 1978), where he contrasts Birmingham with Selma and contends that the sporadic violence of blacks (primarily black youths), though provoked, limited the impact of the Birmingham campaign. Events in the city were not, therefore, directly responsible for the 1964 Civil Rights Act. Adam Fairclough in *"To Redeem the Soul of America": The SCLC and Martin Luther King, Jr.* (Athens, Ga., 1987) disagrees, stressing that Birmingham convinced President Kennedy of the moral imperative of federal legislation to guarantee integration in public accommodations. As with most major civil rights events, local political and economic issues directly affected the outcome. See Robert Corley's essay in Jacoway and Colburn (eds.), *Southern Businessmen and Desegregation*, and Sitkoff, *The Struggle for Black Equality*, Chapter 5. The tragic Birmingham church bombing is covered in *Life*, September 27, 1963. See also "No Easy Walk, 1961–1963," Part 4 of the documentary "Eyes on the Prize." The "Letter from Birmingham Jail" is one of many eloquent documents that Martin Luther King gave to the movement and to the South. For a collection of these works, see James M. Washington (ed.), *Testament of Hope: The Essential Writings of Martin Luther King, Jr.* (San Francisco, 1986), and Coretta Scott King (ed.), *Words of Martin Luther King, Jr.* (New York, 1983), as well as King's own account of events in Birmingham in *Why We Can't Wait* (New York, 1964).

Writers have not dealt extensively with the South's ready acceptance of the 1964 Civil Rights Act. Those who have sought to explain it have usually focused on the widespread cultural tradition of fighting the good fight, on the general feeling of relief, or on the realization that integration was inevitable. John Hope Franklin, in a videotape, "Public Education: The Reality and the Vision," North Carolina Center for the Advancement of Teaching, March, 1988, contends that since white southerners had no time to develop the subtle methods of discrimination within the law that white northerners had perfected over the years, they adopted the openness of public accommodations with the same conscientiousness that they had followed segregation. A good deal of credit must go to black southerners who conducted the struggle for regional redemption within a context understood by all southerners. On the relation between culture and acceptance of change, see Leslie Dunbar, "The Annealing of the South," *Virginia Quarterly Review*, XXXVII (1961), 495–507. See also Ralph McGill, *No Place to Hide: The South and Human Rights*, ed. Calvin M. Logue (2 vols; Macon, Ga., 1984), II. None of this surprised C. Vann Woodward, whose *The Strange Career of Jim Crow* (New York, 1955) argued that segregation was not a hoary tradition in the South and therefore did not preclude other forms of race relations from emerging. For an astute assessment of Woodward's contentions, see Howard N. Rabinowitz, "The Woodward Thesis and More: Three Contributions of *The Strange Career of Jim Crow*," presented at the American Historical Association Convention, December 29, 1986, Chicago.

Historian David Donald has argued that the codification of segregation on a wide scale during the 1890s, as well as the growing militancy of southern blacks in combating discrimination, may have been a generational phenomenon, the coming of age of a new post–Civil War generation of whites and blacks with different expectations and concerns. In a similar fashion, the demise of segregation may have owed to a new generation of blacks—the demonstrators—and a new generation of whites who grew up in a more optimistic, more urbanized, and less isolated region than their parents. Southern music, rock 'n' roll, in particular, was one manifestation of generational preferences. For a discussion of the black and white blending of southern music in the country genre, see Kent Blaser, "'Pictures from Life's Other Side': Hank Williams, Country Music, and Popular Culture in America," *South Atlantic Quarterly*, LXXXIV (1985), 12–26. Courtney Haden, "Dixie Rock: The Fusion's Still Burning," *Southern Exposure*, V (Summer-Fall, 1977), 37–43, includes an analysis of racial tensions generated in the South by early rock 'n' roll. Columnist Kays Gary delves into the black influences on Elvis Presley in an interview conducted with Presley that appeared in the Charlotte *Observer*, June 27, 1956. See also "Rock 'n Roll: The Revolution Turns 30 and Ever-New Beat Goes On," Charlotte *Observer*, July 9, 1985, and musicologist John Grooms on the defiance of early black rock 'n' rollers, "It Took Courage to be an Early Rocker," Charlotte *Observer*, June 18, 1986.

VII. The Last Crusade: Voting Rights, 1962–1965

Of all the racial barriers disfranchisement was among the most humiliating and frustrating. It barred southern blacks from effective citizenship and rendered them invisible to policymakers, which in turn helped to reinforce their inferior place in southern life. Steven F. Lawson, *Black Ballots: Voting Rights in the South, 1944–1969* (New York, 1976), is the essential introduction to the legal and federal context of voting rights in the South and a clear statement on the crucial role of southern blacks in pressing for their constitutional rights through a variety of channels. Chapter 6 of Harvard Sitkoff, *The Struggle for Black Equality, 1954–1980* (New York, 1981), offers a shorter summary that concentrates on the 1960s. Chapter 6 of Clayborne Carson *et al.* (eds.), *Eyes on the Prize: America's Civil Rights Years* (New York, 1987), has useful documentary sources for the period 1962–64.

The most important provisions of the 1957 and 1960 Civil Rights Acts related to voting rights. Allan Lichtman, "The Federal Assault Against Voting Discrimination in the Deep South, 1957–67," *Journal of Negro History*, LIV (1969), 346–67, is a helpful analysis of the passage, strengths, and weaknesses of these measures. David Garrow, *Protest at Selma: Martin Luther King, Jr., and the Voting Rights Act of 1965* (New Haven, 1978), includes material on the difficulties of enforcing federal voting-rights legislation during the early 1960s, especially the obstreperous behavior of some of President Kennedy's federal court nominees in the Deep South.

The first extensive organized effort at voter registration in the South occurred under the auspices of the Voter Education Project. Though the full story of this effort during the early 1960s remains to be told, Lawson, Sitkoff, and Garrow provide useful discussions. Howell Raines, *My Soul Is Rested: Movement Days in the Deep South Remembered* (New York, 1977), contains some material on the VEP and its ambivalent relationship with the Kennedy administration, as well as the unsuccessful Delta campaign undertaken by SNCC as part of the VEP effort. Raines includes an interview with SNCC Delta worker Lawrence Guyot. Perhaps the most revealing account of the hardships of voter-registration drives prior to the Freedom Summer of 1964 is Anne Moody's autobiographical *Coming of Age in Mississippi* (New York, 1968). Moody, a black college student from Canton, Mississippi, tells of the constant fear and harassment that stalked VEP workers, as well as the reluctance of rural blacks to press for their rights in the repressive atmosphere of the Delta. Mississippi, in fact, became a national symbol of voting-rights intransigence. White leaders there were so fearful of change that they imposed a constricting conformity of rhetoric and action; James Silver, an academic casualty of this regime, summarized the atmosphere in *Mississippi: The Closed Society* (New York, 1964). The madness and sadness of Mississippi is the theme of novelist Walker Percy's essay "Mississippi: The Fallen Paradise," *Harper's*, CCXXX (April, 1965), 166–72. John R. Salter, a participant in the state's voter-registration drives prior to 1964, chronicles the struggle and offers a profile of slain NAACP leader Medgar Evers in *Jackson, Mississippi: An American Chronicle of Struggle and Schism* (Hicksville, N.Y., 1979). Neil R. McMillen, "Black Enfranchisement in Mississippi: Federal Enforcement and Black Protest in the 1960s," *Journal of Southern History*, XLIII (1977), 351–72, provides some background for the repressions of the early 1960s and includes a profile of Fannie Lou Hamer.

Voter-registration drives in Mississippi culminated with the COFO effort during the Freedom Summer of 1964. The "Eyes on the Prize" documentary,

Part 5, "Mississippi: Is This America?" covers this episode in chilling detail. Char Miller (ed.), "The Mississippi Summer Project Remembered—The Stephen Mitchell Bingham Letter," *Journal of Mississippi History*, XLVII (1985), 284–307, an account by one of the northern white college students who came to the state that summer, conveys the pervasive fear that overtook the workers, especially after the murders of Chaney, Schwerner, and Goodman. Sally Belfrage, *The Freedom Summer* (New York, 1965), is an adequate summary of events, though there has been no book-length study placing the summer in the context of black and white Mississippi society and previous voting-rights movements.

The drive for voting rights reached its culmination at Selma, and David Garrow's *Protest at Selma* is the definitive account of that drama. Garrow is adept at placing Selma in the broader context of civil rights protest and ably assesses the roles of King, white officials, and black demonstrators. Howell Raines's *My Soul Is Rested* contains a section on Selma in Chapter 4, including an interview with John Lewis, one of the march leaders. Steven Lawson provides a well-written summary of the march and events immediately preceding it in *Black Ballots*. For memorable footage of the March 7 protest, see Part 6, "Bridge to Freedom, 1965," of the documentary "Eyes on the Prize." Anne Nall Stallworth, *Go, Go, Said the Bird* (New York, 1984), includes a compelling fictional account of the Selma affray as seen through the eyes of her mulatto protagonist.

In recent years, historians have begun to emphasize the local dimensions of the civil rights movement. Even such national events as Selma were rooted in local organizations and leaders. Clayborne Carson has been a leading advocate of this school of thought most recently expressed in "Martin Luther King, Jr.: Charismatic Leadership in a Mass Struggle," *Journal of American History*, LXXIV (1987), 448–54. Robert J. Norrell, *Reaping the Whirlwind: The Civil Rights Movement in Tuskegee* (New York, 1985), is another strong statement for the importance of localism. These and other works were necessary correctives to a civil rights historiography that tended to concentrate on the national leaders and their organizations. Still, the importance of Martin Luther King, Jr., and the SCLC should not be underestimated. King provided an extremely valuable service for the movement (among many others) in articulating black concerns for the white community, a liaison that was essential for the implementation of legislative remedies. David Garrow makes this point especially well in *Bearing the Cross: Martin Luther King, Jr., and the Southern Christian Leadership Conference* (New York, 1986).

Writers are still assessing the impact of the 1960s on the white South, and *liberation* is one word they use frequently to describe the experience. As Ralph McGill wrote in the *Saturday Review*, March 9, 1968, civil rights legislation "freed the Southern white man more than the black man." Contrast McGill's comment with the episodes related by C. V. Roman in *American Civilization and the Negro* (Philadelphia, 1916) and Pat Watters, *The South and the Nation* (New York, 1969), that raised conformity above humanity. The civil rights movement, at the least, enabled the southern white to bring behavior in line with principles. Joel Williamson, *The Crucible of Race: Black-White Rela-*

tions in the American South Since Emancipation (New York, 1984), is a brilliantly written, pessimistic, and often personal analysis of southern race relations. Williamson contends that white southerners felt considerably more depressed than liberated in 1965. Walker Percy, in *The Last Gentleman* (New York, 1966), discerned a happy, relaxed region and people: the burden of race had been lifted and southerners could go about their business, literally. If Percy is correct, then part of the reason for the good mood must be the civil rights movement itself.

Although race relations changed dramatically, the South did not. Southerners, as George B. Tindall noted in *The Ethnic Southerners* (Baton Rouge, 1976), did not lose their identity by changing; they found it.

VIII. The First Hurrah: Black Ballots

For the first time in the twentieth century, southern blacks looked forward to full political participation with the passage of the 1965 Voting Rights Act. Steven F. Lawson, *In Pursuit of Power: Southern Blacks and Electoral Politics, 1965–1982* (New York, 1985), is the basic work on the implementation of the act. Though the ballot has not helped southern blacks overcome all obstacles to racial equity, Lawson contends that voting rights significantly altered the southern political landscape and removed race as the major qualification for registration, voting, and officeholding. William C. Havard, "Intransigence to Transition: Thirty Years of Southern Politics," *Virginia Quarterly Review,* LI (1975), 497–521, places these changes within the broader context of southern politics since World War II.

The most immediate impact of the black ballot was in voter-registration figures and in the numbers of black elected officials. David Campbell and Joe R. Feagin, in "Black Politics in the South: A Descriptive Analysis," *Journal of Politics,* XXXVII (1975), 129–62, provide a helpful overview of these quantitative gains. On the upsurge in black elected officials, see Monroe Billington, "The Solid South: A Moribund Political Institution?" in James C. Cobb and Charles R. Wilson (eds.), *Perspectives on the American South,* Vol. III (New York, 1985).

Did this increase in political power translate into policy? The consensus seems to be, "Yes, but not much." Milton D. Morris, "Black Electoral Participation and the Distribution of Public Benefits," in Chandler Davidson (ed.), *Minority Vote Dilution* (Washington, D.C., 1984), discusses several empirical studies that tend to support this viewpoint. See also the comments of Ivan Allen, Jr., on the difficulties of reversing generations of service neglect, in Southern Regional Conference on Urbanization, *Proceedings* (Athens, Ga., 1967). Still, Atlanta's first black mayor, Maynard Jackson, and his successor, Andrew Young, have been able to effect some redistribution of city funds in the black community. On this point, see Bradley R. Rice's essay "Atlanta: If Dixie Were Atlanta," in Richard M. Bernard and Bradley R. Rice (eds.), *Sunbelt Cities: Politics and Growth Since World War II* (Austin, 1985). See also F. Glenn Abney and John D. Hutcheson, Jr., "Race, Representation, and Trust: Changes in Attitudes After the Election of a Black Mayor," *Public Opinion Quarterly,* XLV (1981), 91–101, on Maynard Jackson's administration. Campbell and Feagin pointed out that black elected officials in smaller communities were able to tap federal and foundation funds much better and more frequently than their white predecessors, but Peter Schrag, in "A Hesitant New South: Fragile Promise on the Last Frontier," *Saturday Review*, February 12, 1972, pp. 51–57, observed that these transfusions cannot alleviate the grinding poverty in the rural South. Christopher Silver, *Twentieth-Century Richmond: Planning, Politics, and Race* (Knoxville, 1984), noted that though black elected officials campaigned on a platform of change, their policies did not differ greatly from those of their white predecessors. For a balanced assessment of the impact of the black ballot on services and policies in general during the first decade of the Voting Rights Act, see Steven F. Lawson, "Preserving the Second Reconstruction: Enforcement of the Voting Rights Act, 1965–1975," *Southern Studies*, XXII (1983), 55–75.

Blacks had more success in electing white politicians sympathetic to their needs than in electing candidates of their own color or in implementing policies directly beneficial to the black community. On the new southern political spring after 1970, see Jack Bass and Walter De Vries, *The Transformation of Southern Politics: Social Change and Political Consequence Since 1945* (New York, 1976). One aspect of this spring was a sharp decline in race-baiting, as noted by Earl Black, "Southern Governors and Political Change: Campaign Stances, on Racial Segregation and Economic Development, 1950–69," *Journal of Politics*, XXXIII (1971), 703–34. Perhaps the most dramatic change in campaign tactics and rhetoric occurred in Mississippi, as chronicled by Tip H. Allen, Jr., and Dale A. Krane, "Class Replaces Race: The Reemergence of Neopopulism in Mississippi Gubernatorial Politics," *Southern Studies*, XIX (1980), 182–92. Roy Reed, New York *Times*, September 27, 1974, offers a more critical perception of the new generation of southern governors. According to Charles S. Bullock III, "Congressional Voting and the Mobilization of a Black Electorate in the South," *Journal of Politics*, XLIII (1981), 662–82, blacks have had more success influencing their U.S. congressmen and senators—witness the 1975 extension vote on the Voting Rights Act—than their state officials.

Though the policy implications of the new southern politics were hardly revolutionary, some white leaders persisted in efforts to limit black political participation. Steven F. Lawson's *In Pursuit of Power* offers a fine summary of these efforts. The essays in Chandler Davidson (ed.), *Minority Vote Dilution*, provide an excellent summary of the tactics employed by white officials to circumvent the letter and intent of the Voting Rights Act. Howard Ball, Dale A. Krane, and Thomas P. Lauth, in *Compromised Compliance: Implementation of the 1965 Voting Rights Act* (Westport, Conn., 1982), focus on federal enforcement efforts and their limits. Marshall Frady recounts whites' fears in Greene County, Alabama, in *Southerners: A Journalist's Odyssey* (New York, 1980). Charles S. Bullock III, "The Election of Blacks in the South: Preconditions and Consequences," *American Journal of Political Science*, XIX (1975), 727–39, suggests that racial gerrymandering combined with traditional low black voter turnout can perpetuate white power structures even where there are significant numbers of blacks. Also, most whites do not vote for blacks, while blacks often cast ballots for white candidates. In this connection, black voter-registration drives have also mobilized white voters, sometimes cancel-ing the impact of increased black registration. See John Hammond, "Race and Electoral Mobilization: White Southerners, 1952–68," *Public Opinion Quar-terly*, XLI (1977), 13–27. Carl Abbott, *The New Urban America: Growth and Politics in Sunbelt Cities* (Chapel Hill, 1981), offers some helpful insights into the use of annexation for racial purposes. For a case study (Richmond, Virginia) of this strategy, see John V. Moeser and Rutledge M. Dennis, *The Politics of Annexation: Oligarchic Power in a Southern City* (Cambridge, Mass., 1982).

The institutional framework surrounding American politics provided an-other limiting factor for black political power. John Dittmer, "The Politics of the Mississippi Movement, 1954–64," in Charles W. Eagles (ed.), *The Civil Rights Movement in America* (Jackson, Miss., 1986), presents an early exam-ple of how this framework helped to squelch the Mississippi Freedom Demo-cratic party (MFDP). In addition, the political system tended to favor those blacks who did not veer abruptly from the policies of their white predecessors; hence, the new black political leadership did not openly and consistently embrace a so-called black political agenda. See Lester M. Salamon, "Leader-ship and Modernization: The Emerging Black Political Elite in the American South," *Journal of Politics*, XXXV (1973), 615–46. Not surprisingly, southern black voters began to lose confidence in both the system and their leaders, as Virginia Durr found at Tuskegee in the early 1970s.

The rise of the Republican party in the South after 1965 was, of course, closely connected to the ambiguous status of black political fortunes. Alex-ander P. Lamis, *The Two-Party South* (New York, 1984), presents the clearest case of Republican resurgence in the South, especially its connections to the race issue. Just as Willie Morris in *The Last of the Southern Girls* (New York, 1973), found some Republican "good ol' boys" in Virginia, Lamis asserts that the party had achieved parity in many states by the mid-1970s, particularly in federal elections. Brothers Earl and Merle Black, in *Politics and Society in the South* (Cambridge, Mass., 1987), make a similar point, framing their analysis with more extensive historical data. In addition, the Blacks note that migra-tion of middle-class northern whites into the region reinforced the trend of whites to vote Republican. These factors have kept the Democratic party in the South close to the political center, which means that the large-scale social activism favored by most blacks became out of the question. The Blacks also make a helpful distinction between the Peripheral South where the Republi-can party is on more or less equal footing with the Democrats, and the Deep South where the Democratic party, because of the higher concentration of black voters, remains the dominant party on a consistent basis.

IX. The Rough Side of the Mountain: The Black Economy, 1965–1976

Though there have been several comprehensive analyses of black political fortunes after 1965, works on southern black economic conditions in this period are relatively scarce. General works on southern agriculture such as Pete Daniel's *Breaking the Land: The Transformation of Cotton, Tobacco, and Rice Cultures Since 1880* (Urbana, 1985) and Gilbert C. Fite's *Cotton Fields No*

More: Southern Agriculture, 1865–1980 (Lexington, Ky., 1984) include post-1965 developments but do not focus on black rural life. Indeed, most southern agricultural historians view the basic rural adjustments as over by 1960. It is nevertheless possible to piece together a portrait of southern black rural life in the decade after 1965, primarily from articles.

The letter to the Sumter County, Alabama, sharecropper Charlie quoted in the text appeared as "Charlie: This Letter Is to Advise You . . . ," *New South*, XXIII (Winter, 1968), 14–19. Charlie, of course, was part of a much larger picture, of which Janet K. Wadley and Everett S. Lee, "The Disappearance of the Black Farmer," *Phylon*, XXXV (1974), 276–83, provide a statistical overview (up to 1970). For more-personal accounts of the impact of mechanization and the attractions of so-called public work (non-farm employment), see Theodore Rosengarten, *All God's Dangers: The Life of Nate Shaw* (New York, 1974), where Ned Cobb offers a poignant epitaph to his family's farming tradition, as all of his children but one have left the rural South. Ernest J. Gaines, *A Gathering of Old Men* (New York, 1983), is a bittersweet fictional farewell to black sharecropping in Louisiana. Of course, as in Charlie's case, the leaving was often more bitter than sweet, especially as the civil rights movement provided white landlords with another excuse to mechanize. On this point, see Chapter 2 of John Egerton, *The Americanization of Dixie: The Southernization of America* (New York, 1974). On other occasions, black farmers had been unable to keep up with new scientific farming or technologies, nor were state extension agents particularly helpful in educating and assisting them. Paul Good covers this point in *The American Serfs* (New York, 1968). F. Ray Marshall and Virgil L. Christian, Jr., "Human Resource Development in the South," in H. Brandt Ayers and Thomas H. Naylor (eds.), *You Can't Eat Magnolias* (New York, 1972), make a similar argument concerning the education and information gap confronting black agriculturists. Roger Beardwood, "The Southern Roots of Urban Crisis," *Fortune*, LXXVIII (August, 1968), 80–87, 151–56, focuses on racial discrimination within state extension services.

For those blacks left behind in small country towns and on farms in the 1960s, poverty, inadequate housing, poor education, and ill health characterized their existence. Robert Elgie, "Industrialization and Racial Inequality Within the American South, 1950–70," *Social Science Quarterly*, LXI (1980), 458–72, notes that low education, skill levels, and income made rural blacks the least likely candidates to find alternative employment in their localities, assuming such alternatives existed. Though not focusing specifically on blacks, F. Ray Marshall makes a similar point in "Some Rural Economic Development Problems in the South," *American Economic Review*, LXII (1972), 204–11. The 1980 Commission on the Future of the South, *The Future of the South* (Research Triangle Park, N.C., 1981), offers some statistical support for these arguments. The housing crisis was especially acute among rural blacks in the 1960s and seventies, but again, no book-length account of this problem is available. Black writer Don Anderson offers a vivid description of the poor quality of black rural dwellings in Piedmont Virginia in "At Daniel's Mountain," in Fifteen Southerners (eds.), *Why the South Will Survive* (Athens, Ga., 1981). Eventually the most publicized condition of rural blacks in the late

1960s was their hunger. Senator Ernest F. Hollings, *The Case Against Hunger* (New York, 1970), is a shocking recounting of his poverty tours. See also Jack Bass, "Hunger? Let Them Eat Magnolias," in *You Can't Eat Magnolias*. Not all rural blacks, of course, lived in these conditions; in the 1970s in the North Carolina Piedmont, for example, there remained black tenant farmers who had good relations with their white neighbors. Cooperation and sharing between the races had enabled both to survive the major agricultural changes. See Steven Petrow, "The Last of the Tenant Farmers in the Old New South: A Case Study of Tenancy in Franklin County, North Carolina," in Robert L. Hall and Carol B. Stack (eds.), *Holding On to the Land and the Lord: Kinship Ritual, Land Tenure, and Social Policy in the Rural South* (Athens, Ga., 1982).

Life in southern towns and cities offered an improvement for southern blacks seeking economic advancement, as had been the case since the eighteenth century, and blacks migrated to southern cities in substantial numbers during the 1960s and early seventies. See John D. Reid, "Black Urbanization of the South," *Phylon*, XXXV (1974), 259–67. But for many, especially new arrivals, the improvements were slight. Those who arrived in the cities in the late 1960s were generally unprepared for urban occupations. See Anne S. Lee and Gladys K. Bowles, "Policy Implications of the Movement of Blacks Out of the Rural South," *Phylon*, XXXV (1974), 332–39. In addition, they more than likely faced some form of discrimination as reported in Wayne King, "Southern Blacks, Women Found in Low City Jobs," New York *Times*, May 25, 1978. In some industries, however, such as textiles and steel, blacks found new opportunities. See Cliff Sloan and Bob Hall, "Home in Greenville," *Southern Exposure*, VII (Spring, 1979), 83–100, and Robert J. Norrell, "Caste in Steel: Jim Crow Careers in Birmingham, Alabama," *Journal of American History*, LXXIII (1986), 669–94. These were not industries with bright futures, however.

Housing conditions in the cities generally were better than those in rural areas, but buildings were likely to be crowded, poorly serviced, and vermin infested. Joel Garreau offers a vivid portrait of black housing in Houston in Chapter 5 of *The Nine Nations of North America* (Boston, 1981). Christopher Silver, in *Twentieth-Century Richmond: Planning, Politics, and Race* (Knoxville, 1984), provides extensive evidence of the reinforcement and creation of black slums through city planning policies, especially urban renewal policies. Ronald H. Bayor's paper "Race and Urban Development: The Shaping of Twentieth-Century Atlanta," presented at the Organization of American Historians Convention, Minneapolis, April, 1985, covers Atlanta's urban renewal policies through the 1960s. One result of urban renewal in Atlanta (and elsewhere) was increased residential segregation. See Dana F. White and Timothy J. Crimmins, "Urban Structure, Atlanta," *Journal of Urban History*, II (1976), 231–52, on this point. For a survey of black residential patterns in the urban South, see Robin Flowerdew, "Spatial Patterns of Residential Segregation in a Southern City," *Journal of American Studies*, XIII (1979), 93–107. On the decline of Atlanta's "Sweet Auburn," see "Auburn Street a Victim of History's Spotlight," Charlotte *Observer*, January 11, 1984. James McPherson provides a touching portrait of the scattering of his kin in his old Savannah neighborhood, "A Belief in Electricity," *Southern Magazine*, I (January, 1987), 51–55, 85–89.

The impact of black economic impotence on race relations remains largely unexplored. Steven F. Lawson, *In Pursuit of Power: Southern Blacks and Electoral Politics, 1965–1982* (New York, 1985), found continuing discrimination in rural areas of the South, as the Sammy Younge incident demonstrated. William Least Heat Moon found Selma blacks dispirited and suspicious in his journey through the Deep South, *Blue Highways* (Boston, 1982). Peter Schrag, "A Hesitant New South: Fragile Promise on the Last Frontier," *Saturday Review*, February 12, 1972, pp. 51–57, encountered lingering patterns of segregation and discrimination in the small-town South where blacks form a dense economic underclass. Perhaps more frustrating was the fact that the economic plight of southern blacks was difficult to dramatize, a point made effectively by David Halberstam, "The Second Coming of Martin Luther King," *Harper's*, CCXXXV (August, 1967), 39–51. *Time* magazine in its September 27, 1976, issue, "The South Today," proclaimed a general prosperity over the region, making it difficult to fasten on the persistence of poverty.

Martin Luther King, Jr., recognized the importance of economic justice. In fact, it became his major objective after 1965, though he had stressed it earlier. See especially *Where Do We Go from Here: Chaos or Community* (New York, 1967). William H. Chafe, "The End of One Struggle, the Beginning of Another," in Charles W. Eagles (ed.), *The Civil Rights Movement in America* (Jackson, Miss., 1986), is a useful summary of King's economic philosophy. David Garrow, *Bearing the Cross: Martin Luther King, Jr., and the Southern Christian Leadership Conference* (New York, 1986), has helpful material on King's post-1965 programs and ideas, as he began to espouse a version of Christian socialism and sought to address other issues that he felt were interrelated with the basic cause of freedom and justice. His outspoken opposition to the Vietnam War beginning in 1967 further splintered what was already a fractured black leadership and rank-and-file. Black columnist Carl T. Rowan took King to task in "Martin Luther King's Tragic Decision," *Reader's Digest*, XLVI (September, 1967), 37–42. For a scholarly perspective on the controversies that surrounded King during his last years, see Henry E. Darby and Margaret N. Rowley, "King on Vietnam and Beyond," *Phylon*, XLVII (1986), 43–50. The criticism he received added to King's burden at the same time it stiffened his resolve to broaden the issues. See David Garrow, "Martin Luther King, Jr., and the Cross of Leadership," *Peace and Change*, XII (1987), 1–12. King's final campaign in Memphis is covered by Joan Turner Beifuss, *At the River I Stand: Memphis, the 1968 Strike, and Martin Luther King* (Memphis, 1985). David M. Tucker places the Memphis campaign in its local context in *Memphis Since Crump: Bossism, Blacks, and Civic Reformers, 1948–68* (Knoxville, 1980).

King's assassination underscored the drift of civil rights objectives that had been going on since 1965. Paul Delaney, "A New South for Blacks?" in John B. Boles (ed.), *Dixie Dateline: A Journalistic Portrait of the Contemporary South* (Houston, 1983), includes a discussion of the disarray of the civil rights organizations in the 1970s, as well as a brief account of journalist Chet Fuller's travels through the South. Marshall Frady chronicles attorney Warren Fortson's lonely journey through Mississippi in 1967 in *Southerners: A Journalist's Odyssey* (New York, 1980), as both the spirit and the flesh of the movement had vanished. Adam Fairclough, *"To Redeem the Soul of America": The SCLC and Martin Luther King, Jr.* (Athens, Ga., 1987), discusses the reduced circumstances of the SCLC.

It was apparent by the mid-1970s that, despite organizational problems and economic difficulties, a solid black middle class was emerging in the South. The story of this group and how it differed from its more limited predecessor in black communities across the region remains to be told. There are some suggestive comments from black middle-class individuals in Howell Raines, *My Soul Is Rested: Movement Days in the Deep South Remembered* (New York, 1977), and in William R. Beardslee, *The Way Out Must Lead In: Life Histories in the Civil Rights Movement* (Atlanta, 1977) (especially the interview with John Lewis). Some statistical evidence of this group's satisfaction with the South and with their lives is cited in John Shelton Reed, "Up from Segregation," *Virginia Quarterly Review*, LX (1984), 377–93. Journalist Fred Powledge also encountered optimism among middle-class blacks, even in Mississippi, as described in *Journeys Through the South: A Rediscovery* (New York, 1979). Southern states attempted to take advantage of these new images through aggressive advertising campaigns aimed not only at corporate investors but at tourists and conventions. See, for example, the series of ads put together by Mississippi in the March, April, and May issues of *Southern Living* magazine in 1976.

Perhaps the best quantitative information confirming enhanced opportunities and living conditions for blacks in the South (and not only for middle-class blacks) during the 1970s was the net in-migration. See Kevin E. McHigh, "Black Migration Reversal in the United States," *Geographical Review*, LXXVII (1987), 171–82. See also a comparison of 1970 and 1980 census figures and their implications in an Associated Press story, "North Carolina Natives Return, but Not for Money," in the Charlotte *Observer*, February 20, 1984, that emphasizes ties of place and kin. For a general discussion of the black middle class in a national perspective, see William Julius Wilson, *The Declining Significance of Race: Blacks and Changing American Institutions* (Chicago, 1978).

X. No Broad Highways: Class and Race in the South Since 1976

The difficulty of writing about the contemporary is the difficulty of perspective. I drew most of the material for Chapters X and XI from newspaper and magazine articles; there were, however, a few helpful books, especially in the area of southern politics. Earl Black and Merle Black, *Politics and Society in the South* (Cambridge, Mass., 1987), and Alexander P. Lamis, *The Two-Party South* (New York, 1984), are excellent in describing the ambiguities of black political power. The Blacks particularly demonstrate the simple demographic obstacles confronting black voters and candidates quite aside from prejudice, vote dilution, and poverty.

Among the more positive aspects of black voter participation in the 1980s has been the growing independence and sophistication of black voters, as Martin Kilson points out in "Blacks and Politics: A New Maturity," *Wilson*

Quarterly, VIII (1984), 66–67. Black support for George Wallace represents a combination of independence and religious belief in redemption, with a good dose of common sense as far as state appointments are concerned. See "Sizeable Black Support Aids Wallace Comeback," Charlotte *Observer*, September 9, 1982, and Wendell Rawls, Jr., "Segregation Then, Unity Now: Wallace Sings New Tune," New York *Times*, January 18, 1983. Blacks are not averse to voting for Republican candidates under the right circumstances, as they demonstrated in the Talmadge-Mattingly U.S. Senate race in 1980. See James C. Cobb, "Cracklin's and Caviar: The Enigma of Sunbelt Georgia," *Georgia Historical Quarterly*, LXVIII (1984), 19–39. Increasing sophistication is also apparent among black elected officials such as Birmingham's Richard Arrington, who followed a rocky first term with a solid second and is now in his third, building alliances with different political and economic groups. But Arrington still receives only a small percentage of the white vote. See Dale Russakoff, "Turnabout in Birmingham," Washington *Post*, October 14, 1983, and "Arrington Reelected to 3rd Term as Mayor of Birmingham," New York *Times*, October 12, 1987. A more successful example of coalition building among black elected officials is the case of Jesse Oliver, as related by Neal Peirce, "New-Style Black Legislators: Hope of the Poor?" Washington *Post*, March 1, 1986. Peirce implies that by not espousing a race-specific agenda, black political leaders could accomplish considerably more for their constituents.

Though some black politicians have been adept at coalition building, voter coalitions across racial lines have sometimes been difficult to achieve. This factor has made redistricting a double-edged sword for blacks, on the one hand guaranteeing at least some black elected officials and on the other isolating black voters and eliminating friendly white candidates. See Robert Harmel, Keith Hamm, and Robert Thompson, "Black Voting Cohesion and Distinctiveness in Three Southern Legislatures," *Social Science Quarterly*, LXIV (1983), 183–92; "A Changing of the Old Guard? South Carolina Remapping Puts Incumbent Senators in Tough Races," Charlotte *Observer*, September 30, 1984; and "Democrats' N.C. Losses Linked to Redrawn Districts," Charlotte *Observer*, November 10, 1984. There are occasions, of course, when voting in the South does not break along racial lines, indicating that factors other than race may be operating. The 1985 statewide election in Virginia was a case in point: successful black Democratic candidate Douglas Wilder received significant white support in the South's most Republican state. See "Black Takes No. 2 Post in Virginia," New York *Times*, January 12, 1986. The failed Bork nomination is another example of how black voters, despite their apparent isolation, can affect white lawmakers; apparently, black voting power was particularly influential in the negative vote of Alabama's Democratic senator Howell Heflin. See Tom Wicker, "Bork and the Black Voters," New York *Times*, October 7, 1987. On the considerable behind-the-scenes power of Alabama's black political leaders see Wayne Greenhaw, "The Man," *Southern Magazine*, I (February, 1987), 24–25.

Unfortunately, some black politicians have not been any more virtuous than their white counterparts, a fact that breeds cynicism among blacks and confirms prejudices among some whites. See Michael Hirsley, "FBI Charges

Criticized in Augusta," Chicago *Tribune*, January 15, 1984, and "Augusta Mayor Convicted in Federal Extortion Case," Charlotte *Observer*, April 28, 1984. For the rise and fall of a corrupt black political boss in rural Georgia, see John Rozier, *Black Boss: Political Revolution in a Georgia County* (Athens, Ga., 1982).

Though blacks occasionally vote for Republicans, their overwhelming support for Democratic candidates limits their political power. Southern Republicans have made few overtures to black voters, and a subtle appeal to racial prejudice is one aspect of Republican strategy in the South. See Haynes Johnson, "The South's Racial Climate Turns Ugly and Raw," Washington *Post*, October 7, 1984, on the use of racial code words by Republican candidates in the South during the 1984 campaign. Of course, not all Republicans who oppose black policy are motivated by race; some genuinely oppose the significant government intervention that many blacks favor. See Ronald Smothers, "Racial, Philosophical Differences Mark Campaign in Mississippi," New York *Times*, October 23, 1984. Still, there is room for black-Republican coalition building, especially on family and law and order issues. See Milton Coleman, "Does Political Loyalty Pay Off for Blacks?" Washington *Post*, July 14, 1985. If Republicans were to attempt to woo at least middle-class blacks, this would add to the growing headaches of the Democratic party in the South. See Tom Wicker, "A Dilemma for Democrats," New York *Times*, November 23, 1984.

Opportunities for Republicans may also come along economic lines. Black elected officials, especially in the larger cities of the South, have pursued vigorous economic development policies in recent years while casting off race-specific agendas. See Art Harris, "Atlanta, Georgia: Too Busy to Hate," *Esquire*, CIII (1985), 129–32, on "Andynomics." On a new version of the Manhattan coalition in Durham, North Carolina, see "Durham Takes On Progressive Image with New Leaders," Charlotte *Observer*, November 17, 1985. But subsequent events demonstrated the fragility of the black part of the coalition, which is threatening to split along class lines as noted in Bill Finger, "Poised for Power," *Southern Magazine*, I (March, 1987), 22–26. On the criticism of Harvey Gantt's black constituents toward his emphasis on downtown development, see Lynn Haessly, "'We're Becoming the Mayor,'" *Southern Exposure*, XIV (March-April, 1986), 44–51.

The perceived indifference of the Reagan administration toward black voting rights in the South has encouraged circumvention of the Voting Rights Act in some areas. Moving or closing polling places, the persistence of run-off primaries, and various forms of intimidation still occur, especially in a few Deep South precincts. See Art Harris, "The 'Justice Buggy' Journeys into Mississippi," Washington *Post*, June 16, 1983, on the Jesse Jackson–escorted tour of communities where voting-rights abuses allegedly occurred, and "Failed Voter Revolution for Blacks," Washington *Post*, August 6, 1983. On the legal ramifications of these subterfuges, see Chandler Davidson (ed.), *Minority Vote Dilution* (Washington, D.C., 1984). Tom Wicker discusses the problems black candidates faced with runoff primaries in "The Delicate Issue of Runoffs," New York *Times*, May 1, 1984.

The black economy, like black political power, gives mixed signals on the status of southern blacks. For the growing black middle class, times are good as reflected in migration patterns and job growth. On recent trends, see "Blacks Moving Back to South," Charlotte *Observer*, June 8, 1986. For the personal observations of some North Carolina migrants, see "Returning Blacks View South as Land of New Opportunities," Charlotte *Observer*, January 30, 1983. The trend of more first-time migrants among the total migration pool became evident in the late 1970s. See Bernard L. Weinstein and Robert E. Firestine, *Regional Growth and Decline in the United States: The Rise of the Sunbelt and the Decline of the Northeast* (New York, 1978). On the improvement of black income in the South during the 1970s, see Albert K. Karnig and Paula D. McClain, "The New South and Black Economic and Political Development: Changes from 1970 to 1980," *Western Political Science Quarterly*, XXXVII (1985), 539–50. Albert Murray, *South to a Very Old Place* (New York, 1971), emphasizes the importance of tokenism as a black entrée to higher white-collar occupations in the South.

The other black society in the South is the poor. Studies on particular aspects of black poverty in the 1980s abound, both from government agencies and from scholars. Some of the more helpful discussions are Robert K. Whelan, "The Impacts of Reagan Administration Budget Cutbacks on States and Cities in the Sunbelt," presented at the Conference on the Sunbelt, Miami, November, 1985, and Kenny Johnson, "The Southern Stake in Rural Development," in the 1986 Commission on the Future of the South, "Rural Flight/Urban Might: Economic Development Challenges for the 1990s," Research Triangle Park, N.C., 1986. Johnson provides especially telling figures on the poverty of rural black women and children. See also in this connection the 1986 Commission on the Future of the South, "Equity: The Critical Link in Southern Economic Development," Research Triangle Park, N.C., 1986. On persisting black-white wage differentials, see Stuart Rosenfeld, "A Divided South," *Southern Exposure*, XIV (November-December, 1986), 10–17. On how black poverty translates into adverse policy, see Johnny Greene, "The Poisoning," *Southern Magazine*, II (February, 1988), 26–29, 59–65, on toxic waste in Sumter County, Alabama. See also the story on Sammy Lee Jones, "Life, Death in Poverty," in the Charlotte *Observer*, July 6, 1985.

Whether affirmative action is one method of alleviating poverty is a matter of debate. William Julius Wilson, *The Declining Significance of Race: Blacks and Changing American Institutions* (Chicago, 1978), maintains that it is irrelevant for poor blacks, whereas southern whites like Jack Breed think it is bad policy. See Fred Powledge's conversation with Breed in *Journeys Through the South: A Rediscovery* (New York, 1979). Some blacks are equally unenthusiastic about the policy. See the excellent discussion in Hugh Davis Graham, *The Era of Civil Rights: Race, Gender, and Equality, 1960–1972* (New York, 1989). On the other hand, significant advances in state and local government employment of blacks have been attributed to affirmative action policies (though most of these positions require educational and technical skills beyond those of the black underclass). See the editorial "Ignoring History: The

War on Hiring Goals," Charlotte *Observer*, May 1, 1985, referring both to the advantages of affirmative action and the Reagan administration's largely unsuccessful efforts to undermine such programs.

Though the black economic picture in the South remains a muddle, there is a clear awareness that poverty is a major obstacle to the advance of southern blacks. See the comments by Benjamin Hooks, "The Road Ahead," in Clayborne Carson *et al.* (eds.), *Eyes on the Prize: America's Civil Rights Years* (New York, 1987), and Alice Walker in Krista Brewer, "Writing to Survive: An Interview with Alice Walker," *Southern Exposure*, IX (Summer, 1981), 12–15. An increasing number of middle-class blacks are disavowing racial agendas for broader economic policies as well as advocating self-help strategies. See William Raspberry, "The Dilemma of Black Politics," *Washington Post*, January 9, 1985. Charles Murray, "White Welfare, White Families, White Trash," *National Review*, March 28, 1986, pp. 30–34, revives Oscar Lewis' "culture of poverty" argument, suggesting that culture (shared by both white and black poor) rather than race accounts for the persistence of poverty. Raspberry discusses and approves of Mary Pringle's contentions on the need for new myths among blacks in his "Why Blacks Need a New Myth," *Washington Post*, July 19, 1985. For two strong statements of the self-help ethic, see Shariff Abdullah, "Blacks Must Acquire Self-Help Skills," Charlotte *Observer*, July 15, 1986, and Robert L. Woodson, "Self-Help Is the Answer for Poor Blacks," *Washington Post*, May 12, 1985. On the warning that self-help ideology may become a black middle-class cop-out, see Mel Watt's comments in a Charlotte *Observer* editorial, August 7, 1985. Orde Coombs is quoted on the same point in an article on the black middle class by Gary Puckrein, "Moving Up," *Wilson Quarterly*, VII (1984), 74–87.

XI. Mountaintops and Green Valleys: Beyond Race in the Modern South

Just as there are no easy solutions to, or even definitions of, southern black politics and economy, school desegregation presents a labyrinth of dilemmas. There are a few useful book-length studies of busing particularly: Raymond Wolters, *The Burden of Brown: 30 Years of School Desegregation* (Knoxville, 1984), a negative view of busing's impact on education; the solid case study by Richard A. Pride and J. David Woodard, *The Burden of Busing: The Politics of Desegregation in Nashville, Tennessee* (Knoxville, 1985), another critical work; and the more positive books on the Charlotte-Mecklenburg busing-for-desegregation case, Bernard Schwartz's *Swann's Way: The School Busing Case and the Supreme Court* (New York, 1986), and Frye Gaillard's compelling volume *The Dream Long Deferred* (Chapel Hill, 1988). But There is no comprehensive analysis of the effect of school desegregation on the South and especially on blacks and whites.

There have been numerous essays on resegregation, especially in the press. On the Clarendon County, South Carolina, situation, see "A School Struggles On," Charlotte *Observer*, December 17, 1983; on the landmark Norfolk case, see Marjorie Mayfield, "At All-Black Schools, Teachers Hurdle Tasks Unique to New System," *Virginian-Pilot and Ledger Star*, August 16, 1987. The flight of whites to private academies and suburbs has been partially responsible for resegregation. See Strat Douthat's Associated Press story, "Private Academies Declining: Many Nonpublic Schools Remain Segregated," Charlotte *Observer*, March 18, 1986. A. P. Rogers, "Patterns of Racial Residential Segregation in Montgomery, Alabama," Montgomery, 1982, on file at Auburn University, provides vivid documentation of the white flight pattern in Alabama's capital city. On the economic consequences of segregated school systems, see the editorial in the Goldsboro *News-Argus*, February 16, 1983. For a useful summary of the U.S. Supreme Court's liberation of suburbia from responsibility for inner-city-school racial composition, see Chapter 27 of Richard Kluger, *Simple Justice: The History of Brown v. Board of Education and Black America's Struggle for Equality* (New York, 1976).

Though resegregation is obviously a concern among black leaders, there has been increased emphasis on quality in recent years. See D. L. Cuddy, "A Better Remedy: Beginning of End for Busing?" Charlotte *Observer*, October 22, 1984, and William Raspberry, " 'Whither Black America' Debate," Washington *Post*, January 16, 1985. Linda Flowers will soon publish a book with the University of Tennessee Press that ties together rural and urban educational differences, resegregation, and issues of quality: *'Throwed Away': Lessons in Eastern North Carolina*. The concern over quality extends to higher education, dual systems of which prevail throughout the South. The quality of historically black institutions of higher learning is often marginal. See the Raleigh *News and Observer* editorial for February 14, 1986. On the controversy over Tennessee State University, see Peter J. Boyer, "Fighting for Black Identity," Charlotte *Observer*, December 13, 1984.

There are still remnants of resistance (perhaps *isolation* is a better word) in the South. See E. R. Shipp, "Across the Rural South, Segregation as Usual," New York *Times*, April 27, 1985, and, on the Forsyth County confrontation, Christopher Phillips, "Aftermath of a March," *Southern Magazine*, II (January 1988), 44–49. Still, there is considerable hope and evidence that the revitalized southern culture can not only maintain the advances made in race relations but improve upon them in the South. See John Shelton Reed on the role of manners in attaining this goal, "Up from Segregation," *Virginia Quarterly Review*, LX (1984), 377–93.

The sense of the past, as it becomes enshrined and symbolized, becomes shared. See William E. Schmidt, "Civil Rights Movement Chronicled," New York *Times*, December 7, 1984, on the exhibit in the Mississippi State Historical Museum, and Schmidt, "20 Years After the March," New York *Times*, March 1, 1985. See also Steve Blow, "Trial Out of the Past," Charlotte *Observer*, August 12, 1985, on the Arkansas murder case, and "Klansman Convicted in Murder," Charlotte *Observer*, December 11, 1983, on the Michael Donald case. There is also evidence that the sense of place is appearing in a renewed southern pride among blacks. See John Shelton Reed, *Southerners: The Social Psychology of Sectionalism* (Chapel Hill, 1983).

Perhaps most important for the future of race relations in the South is the common religious bond between black and white that is reflected not only in theology but in good works as well. Unfortunately, this remains the least explored aspect of contemporary race relations in the South. Helpful essays include Frye Gaillard's interview with Jimmy Carter, "Carter's Hopes Unclouded by Defeats of the Past," Charlotte *Observer*, July 11, 1985; "A Giant STEP," Charlotte *Observer*, May 10, 1987; and Louis L. Knowles, "Faith, Trust & Movement," *Southern Exposure*, V–VI (November-December, 1986), 93–94. John Jacob's religious metaphor appeared in the Charlotte *Observer*, January 29, 1985.

Index

Aaron, Edward, 88
Abdullah, Shariff, 252
Abernathy, Ralph David, 10, 217
Affirmative action: President Johnson's
statement on, 212–13; in local govern-
ment employment, 248, 249; white ob-
jections to, 248–49; black objections to,
249; federal court decisions on, 249; op-
posed by Reagan administration, 249;
support in cities for, 249
Agricultural Adjustment Act (AAA), 26
Agricultural Stabilization and Conserva-
tion Service (ASCS), 200
Alabama: censorship in, 87; decline in
private school enrollment, 266
Alabama Christian Movement for Human
Rights (ACMHR), 126
Alabama, University of, 115–16
Albany, Ga., 130–32
Alexander, Kelly, Sr., 227
Alexander v. *Holmes County Board of
Education* (1969), 257
Alexander, Will, 21
Allen, Ivan, Jr., 192–93
Almond, J. Lindsay, 67
Anderson, Don, 202
Angelou, Maya, 6, 10
Anniston, Ala., 125
Arkansas, 106–107
Arnall, Ellis, 49, 71
Arrington, Richard, 228, 229, 236
Askew, Reubin, 179, 259–60
Atlanta, Ga.: black political power in, in
1930s, 46; school expenditures, 55;
school desegregation, 113, 114; role of
business leaders, 113, 133; preparations
for desegregation, 113–14; transforma-
tion of politics, 177–78; urban renewal,
182; suburban opposition to, 186;
lynching in, 211; decline of black business district, 205; as good place for
blacks, 220; segregated schools in, in
1960s, 257; white flight from public
schools, 260–61; resegregation of public
schools, 260
Augusta, Ga., 204
Austin, Tex., 46

Aycock, Dr. E. Kenneth, 203
Ayers, H. Brandt, 209

Baker, Ella, 123
Baker, Wilson, 162, 167
Barnett, Ross: ties to White Citizens'
Council, 82; attempts to block de-
segregation of University of Mississip-
pi, 114; attends Medgar Evers
Homecoming, 273
Barry, Marion, 123
Batson, Colin, 245
Beaumont, Tex., 36
Berry, Chuck, 147
Bevel, James, 140
Bilbo, Theodore G. (D-Miss.), 34, 73
Bingham, Stephen Mitchell, 158
Birmingham, Ala.: SCHW meeting in
1937, p. 29; school expenditures, 55;
reputation for violence, 126; Freedom
Rides, 126; change in government
structure, 135; demonstrations in, 135,
139, 140; Ku Klux Klan in, 140; black
retaliation in, 140–41; desegregation
accord, 140–41; decline of black business district, 205; importance of local
civil rights organizations, 217; and
commemoration of civil rights demonstrations, 272–73
Birmingham, Dave, 47, 93, 94
Black church: role of, 10, 89–90; dependence on white community, 90; new
generation of leadership in 1950s, 105
Black elected officials: access to federal
funds, 176; geography of, 176; increase
in number of, 176, 228; and improved
services in black neighborhoods, 176,
181, 230; in Black Belt, 182–183, 230–
31; black disillusionment with, 191,
192, 193–94; limits of, 191–92, 193,
206, 255; and growth of black government bureaucracy, 219–20; backgrounds of, 228; and affirmative action,
229, 250; and coalition politics, 229–
30; changes in priorities of, 236. *See
also* Black political power
Black middle class: during segregation

313

era, 58; political differences from other blacks, 189; importance of government bureaucrats in, 219–20; advance of, in 1970s, 220; estrangement of, from underclass, 221–22, 254–55; targeted by Republicans, 235, 242; advance of, in 1980s, 244; precarious nature of, 250; suggestions for underclass, 254
Black Panthers, 224
Black, Patti Carr, 274
Black political power: helps white liberals, 178–80; in state legislatures, 179; in congressional delegations, 180; and neighborhood groups, 182; in Black Belt, 182–83, 230–31; white resistance to, 184–87, 193; urban-rural differences, 188, 192; divisions in, 189, 190–91; revival of "Manhattan coalition," 228–29; in statewide contests, 230, 231; cultural influences on, 232–33, 275; sophistication of, 233, 235, 236, 237; and Voting Rights Act extension, 1982, pp. 233–34; and Judge Bork's nomination, 234; black majority does not ensure black victory, 240–41
"Black Power," 223–24
Black schools: positive aspects of, 10–11; disparities in public spending for, 55–56; preparation of students and teachers, 56; curriculum of, 56–57; negative aspects of, 57–58; higher education, 58–59; neighborhood-based independent school systems, 253. *See also* Education; School desegregation
Blair, Lewis Harvie, 57
Bluethenthal, Joan, 259
Bond, Julian: elected to Georgia legislature, 179; on voter registration tour, 183; and other black elected officials, 192; on white liberals, 194; on "Black Power," 224
Boswell Amendment, 64
Boutwell, Albert, 135
Boynton, Amelia and Samuel, 218
Braden, Anne, 13–14, 21
Brady, Tom, 75–76
Breaux, John (D-La.), 234
Briggs, Harry: challenges inequalities in public education, 60; persecution of, 72; on attitudes of black youths, 256
Briggs v. *Elliott* (1954), 60–61
Brookshire, Stanford, 133
Brown, Tony, 264
Brown v. *Board of Education of Topeka, Kansas:* U.S. Supreme Court decision, 61–62; initial reaction to, 75–77; leadership vacuum in response to, 78; legislative resistance, 79–80; school board

resistance, 80; *Brown II*, 81; "massive resistance" to, 84–86; raises black consciousness, 91–92
Buchanan, John (R-Ala.), 175
Bumpers, Dale, 179
Busbee, George, 179

Cameron, Ben, 129
Campbell, Carroll, 242
Campbell, Rev. Will, 14, 170
Carmichael, Stokely: on relation between economic and political power, 206; on need for major economic changes, 213; and Meredith March Against Fear, 224
Carter, Hodding, 70, 71
Carter, Jimmy: refuses to join White Citizens' Council, 82; governor of Georgia, 178; black votes and 1976 presidential victory, 179; warns against smugness, 277–78
Cashin, John, 187
Cason, Clarence, 19
Chandler, A. B. ("Happy"), 77
Chaney, James, 159
Charlotte, N.C.: business leaders of, and desegregation, 133; urban renewal, 182; freedom-of-choice plan, 258; busing, 258, 259
Cherry, Francis, 77
Cities: black political power in, 45–48, 182, 186; importance of economic development, 46–47; new leadership in, after 1945, p. 48; annexation, 73–74, 185–86; political changes in, after Voting Rights Act, 182; black urbanization, 203; black employment in, 204; black housing in, 204–205, 246; black migration to, 208; black poverty in, 246–47
City of Mobile v. *Bolden* (1980), 234
Civil Rights Act of 1957, pp. 110, 150–51
Civil Rights Act of 1960, pp. 150, 151
Civil Rights Act of 1964: provisions, 145; impact on South, 145, 146; reasons for swift compliance with, 146–48
Civil Rights Commission, 150, 151
Civil rights movement: local dimensions of, 168–69, 217–19; impact on whites, 169, 170, 171, 172; impact on blacks, 172; meaning for South, 173
Civil rights organizations, 130, 216–17, 223, 224
Clark, Jim, 162, 163, 164–65, 167
Clement, Frank, 49, 77
Clifford, Clark, 54
Cloud, Maj. John, 164, 165
Cobb, Ned (Nate Shaw), 6, 30, 31
Cochran, Thad (R-Miss.), 235
Coleman, Dick, 245

Coleman, James P., 76
Collins, Leroy, 121
Committee on Interracial Cooperation
(CIC), 41–42
Congress of Racial Equality (CORE), 124,
127
Conner, Margaret and Jim, 111
Connor, Eugene ("Bull"), 126, 134, 135,
139, 140
Conway, Ark., 274
Cooper v. *Aaron* (1958), 110
Couch, W. T., 17, 18, 19, 42
Council of Federated Organizations
(COFO), 156, 157–60
Cox, W. Harold, 129, 154, 159
Culture: shared by blacks and whites, 1;
components, 15–18; importance of con-
formity, 17–18; dissent from, 18–20;
consequences of dissent from, 19–20,
116, 134; positive attributes of, 21–22;
consequences of conformity to, 87–88;
and civil rights movement, 170–72,
275–78; infuses black political perspective, 232–33; promotes civility in race
relations, 272. *See also* Religion (southern); Southern history

Dabbs, James McBride: on racial reconciliation, 22; despair during WWII, 41;
attacks White Citizens' Councils, 84;
notes decline of paternalism, 89; on
shared culture, 171–72
Dabney, Virginius, 41, 89
Dallas County Voters' League (DCVL),
218
Daniel, Mike, 243
Dawson, Ga., 270–71
DeLaine, J. A., 73
Delta (Voting Rights) Campaign: economic pressures, 153; origins, 153; violence,
153–54, 155; failure, 154; accomplishments, 156
Democratic party: tension between
southern and national wings in WWII,
37; power of southerners in Congress,
54; growing influence in, of northern
urban blacks, 54; Dixiecrat revolt, 66–
67; change in southern wing after 1965,
p. 180; interracial composition, 196; response to Republican challenges, 197–
98; black leadership in, 231; hurt by redistricting, 239–40; perceived as party
of blacks, 243
Dennis, David, 157, 160, 189, 190
Dixiecrats (States' Rights Democratic party), 66–67
Doar, John, 127, 128
Dombrowski, James, 21, 50

Domino, Fats, 147
Dowdy, Wayne (D-Miss.), 242
Du Bois, W. E. B.: on impact of racial etiquette on whites, 4; on reaction of
blacks to white supremacy, 116–17;
quality education more important than
desegregation, 264
Dunbar, Leslie, 122, 146, 244
Durham, N.C.: coalition politics, 229–30;
resegregation of public schools, 261;
black students' test scores, 265
Durr, Virginia: on impact of racial etiquette on whites, 12; on voter registration procedures, 39–40; on white
supremacy, 64; and Rosa Parks, 96; and
Freedom Ride violence, 127–28; on
black politics, 191; on attitudes of
black youths, 222

Eastland, James O. (D-Miss.): supports
poll tax, 40; in U.S. Senate, 54, 70; attacks southern liberal organizations,
70; supports White Citizens' Councils,
83; and Freedom Ride, 129; on voting
rights in Mississippi, 154; reconciles
with black political leaders, 190
Eckford, Elizabeth, 109
Education: blacks emphasize quality, 264;
urban-rural differences in, 265; black
teacher training, 266; black higher education, 266–67, 268–69. *See also* Black
schools; School desegregation
Edwards, Edwin, 175
Egger, Rev. Henry E., 76
Eisenhower, Dwight D.: response of to
Brown, 78, 80–81; and Little Rock crisis, 109, 110; judicial appointees of, 116
Ellison, Ralph, 5
Employment, black: narrowing of, in
1930s, 26; and mechanization before
1940, p. 27; and labor unions, 28; during WWII, 34—36; in declining industries, 204; advances in white-collar,
209; diminishing North-South differences, 245
Engelhardt, Sam, 100
Ervin, Sam (D-N.C.), 84–85
Ethridge, Mark, 33, 34, 41, 70
Etiquette of race: functions of, 1, 2, 6;
components, 2–3; impact of, on whites,
3–5, 12–13, 14, 15, 171–72; impact of
on blacks, 5–9, 116–17; modification
noted in 1930s, 29; variability of, 41;
changes in, 169, 272; persistence of old
patterns, 207
Evers, Charles: secures grant for Fayette,
177; on political changes in Mississippi,
183; congressional campaign, 185; on

political strategy, 187–88; gubernatorial races, 189, 235–36

Fair Employment Practices Committee (FEPC): origins, 33; limitations, 34–36; white opposition to, 34, 36; Truman's support of, 53

Falwell, Rev. Jerry, 76

Farmers, black: during 1960s, 199–200, 201; hampered by institutional discrimination, 200; loss of community, 201; new labor patterns of, 201

Faubus, Orval: early years, 107; as progressive governor, 107; and Little Rock, 108, 109, 110–11; loses gubernatorial bid (1970), 179; in 1970s, 225

Faulkner, William: racial perspectives in novels, 3, 5, 45, 52; on black aspirations during WWII, 32; hesitancy on integration, 87

Federal Bureau of Investigation (FBI), 127, 159

Fellowship of the Concerned, 51

Finney, Ernest, 237

Flowers, Walter, 180

Folmer, Emory, 232

Folsom, James E., 48, 64, 119

Fortson, Warren, 216

Freedom Rides: Journey of Reconciliation, 124; origins, 124; violence, 125, 126, 128; federal involvement, 126–27, 128, 129; SNCC involvement, 127; conclusion, 128–29; results, 129, 130

Freedom Summer: plans for, 157–58; and northern white college students, 158; local blacks' fears, 158–59; murders, 159; other violence, 159–60

Freeman, Diane, 244

Fulbright, J. William (D-Ark.), 67

Gaines, Ernest J., 6, 201

Gantt, Harvey: impact of *Brown* on, 91–92; white support of, in mayoral campaigns, 228, 229; on white-collar tokenism, 250

Gayle et al. v. *Browder* (1956), 102

Gayle, W. A. ("Tacky"), 94, 100

Georgia, 152

Goldsboro, N.C., 261

Goldwater, Barry (D-Ariz.), 195–96

Gomillion v. *Lightfoot* (1969), 185

Goodman, Andrew, 159

Gore, Albert (D-Tenn.), 49

Graham, Rev. Billy, 85–86

Graham, Frank Porter (D-N.C.): and SCEF, 50; President's Committee on Civil Rights, 53, 54; senatorial campaign, 67–69; mentioned, 49

Gray, Duncan, 76, 84

Gray, Fred D., 97, 101

Grayson, George, 231

Green, Ernest, 225

Green v. *New Kent County School Board* (1968), 257

Greene, William, 244–45

Greensboro, N.C.: efforts to evade *Brown*, 80; sit-ins, 119; "Death-to-the-Klan" rally, 211; black institutions in, 219; preparations for school desegregation, 259; commemorates sit-ins, 272, 273

Greenville, S.C., 46

Guyot, Lawrence, 153–54, 183

Hamer, Fannie Lou: on black ambitions, 6; on Mississippi, 155, 158; on Delta Campaign, 156; on Voting Rights Act, 177; memorialized by Mississippi legislature, 225

Hammond, Cleveland, 264

Hartsfield, William B.: and black voters, 46; protection of Dorothy Tilly, 72; seeks to dilute black votes, 73–74; and school desegregation, 113; limits of coalition with blacks, 177

Heflin, Howell (D-Ala.), 234

Helms, Jesse (R-N.C.), 68–69, 242

Henry, Aaron, 190

Highlander Folk School, 96

Hill, Bobby, 198

Hill, Lister, 67

Hill, Oliver, 48

Hollings, Ernest F. (D-S.C.), 170, 203

Holly, Buddy, 147

Holton, Linwood, 196

Hood, Jimmy, 115

Hooks, Benjamin, 251

Horton, Miles, 96

Housing for blacks: federal, in the 1930s, 29; in rural areas, 202, 247; in cities, 204–205, 247; tenant management, 253

Houston, Tex.: black political power in, 47; political changes in 1950s, 47; housing, 246

Humphrey, Hubert H., 189, 190

Hunt, Jim, 242, 243

Jackson, Jesse: and SCLC, 217; on underclass, 226; meets with George Wallace, 231–32; on progressive South, 237; voting rights tour, 238; on importance of economic issues, 276; on black advances, 277

Jackson, Jimmie Lee, 163

Jackson, Maynard: on importance of ballot, 174; mayoral administration, 177–78; exploits class issue, 180; and neighborhood power, 182; and garbage strike, 192; on Atlanta, 220

Jackson, Miss.: blacks in white-collar employment, 209; killings at Jackson State, 210; Medgar Evers Homecoming, 273
Jacksonville, Fla., 29
Jacob, John, 278
Johnson, Charles S., 30
Johnson, Frank M., 116
Johnson, Gerald W., 20, 71
Johnson, Guy, 49
Johnson, James Weldon, 58
Johnson, Leroy, 191
Johnson, Lyndon B.: and civil rights legislation, 144–45, 150; and Voting Rights Act, 165–66, 167; and Mississippi Freedom Democratic Party, 189–90; supports affirmative action, 212–13
Johnston, Olin D. (D-S.C.), 38
Jones, Sammy Lee, 247
Jordan, Barbara, 176

Katzenbach, Nicholas, 115
Kefauver, Estes (D-Tenn.), 49
Kennedy, John F.: and desegregation of the University of Alabama, 115–16; and Freedom Rides, 126, 127; judicial appointees, 129; and Birmingham demonstrations, 141
Kennedy, Robert F., 127
Kilpatrick, James J., 79, 80, 120–21
King, Coretta Scott, 232
King, Ed, 189, 190
King, Rev. Martin Luther, Jr.: background, 97–98; and Montgomery bus boycott, 98–99, 101, 103–104; founding of SCLC, 104; founding of SNCC, 123; Albany campaign, 130, 131–32; in Birmingham, 134, 139–41; "Letter from Birmingham Jail," 135–38; on unmerited suffering, 139, 144; March on Washington, 141–43; on Birmingham church bombing, 144; Selma demonstrations, 160–63; "Tuesday Turnaround," 165; Selma-to-Montgomery march, 166–67; on importance of ballot, 175, 193; on economic equality, 212, 213; Poor People's Campaign, 213, 214; broadens nonviolent agenda, 214; in Memphis, 216; ability to mobilize blacks, 218; middle-class values of, 221–22; concern over "Black Power," 223, 224; no easy solutions, 251; on religious calling, 276
Ku Klux Klan, 211, 271, 274–75

Lafayette, Bernard, 218
Lawson, Rev. James, 214
Leadership, black: during segregation era, 90–91; divisions in, 212; new leaders in

1970s, 219–20; backgrounds of leaders, 228; priorities of, 229. *See also* Black elected officials
Lewis, John (D-Ga.), 124–25, 142
Lewis, Nell Battle, 19–20
Liberals (before mid-1950s): challenge cultural conformity, 18–20; avoid race issues, 20; hostility toward outside intervention, 20; despair during WWII, 41–42; organizing efforts in postwar era, 49–51; splintering of, 70–72
Lightner, Clarence, 182
Little Rock, Ark.: Blossom Plan, 106, 108; integration and class issues, 108; desegregation of Central High, 109, 110–11; economic impact of desegregation crisis, 132
Liuzzo, Viola, 167
Loeb, Henry, 215
Logan, Rayford W., 42
Long, Earl, 48
Lowery, Rev. Joseph, 227
Lucy, Auterine, 115, 225

McCain, Franklin, 119, 122
McGill, Ralph: on postwar politics, 49; denounces SCHW, 70; on inviolability of segregation, 71, 85; on leadership vacuum, 116; on how legislation can change attitudes, 145–46; on guilt over segregation, 147; on how civil rights movement liberated whites, 171; on subtle racism of Republicans, 196; on persistence of segregated schools in Atlanta, 257
McKnight, C. A. ("Pete"), 61, 133
McMillan, George, 232
McMillan, James B., 258–59
McLaurin v. *Oklahoma Board of Regents* (1950), 58–59
McMath, Sid, 48
McNeill, Joseph, 118–19
McNeill, Rev. Robert Blakely, 116
McPherson, James, 205
Malone, Vivian, 115
March on Washington, 141–43
Marsh, Henry L., III, 182, 186, 236
Marshall, Burke, 126, 152
Massell, Sam, 177
Mattingly, Mack (R-Ga.), 233, 235
Mays, Benjamin, 49, 50, 89–90
Memphis, Tenn.: black neighborhoods, 27; and WPA, 29; PWA housing program, 29; sanitation workers' strike and local politics, 215; white flight from public schools, 260
Meredith, James: integrates University of Mississippi, 114; March Against Fear, 222–24; on Mississippi, 273

Meredith March Against Fear, 222–24
Miami, Fla.: black political power in
　1939, p. 46; racial violence in, 229
Migration of blacks: to the North, 9; from
　farm to farm, 25; induced by AAA, 26;
　to southern cities, 26; to the South,
　208, 220–21, 244–45
Milliken v. *Bradley* (1974), 262
Mississippi: black electorate in 1950s, 47,
　73; stiffens voter registration in 1950s,
　152; "closed society," 154; political
　changes in, 183; voting rights abuses in
　1970s, 184–85; campaign to change im-
　age, 225; voting rights abuses in 1980s,
　238; state museum depicts civil rights
　era, 273
Mississippi, University of, 114
Mississippi Freedom Democratic Party
　(FDP), 189–90
Missouri ex rel. Gaines v. *Canada* (1938),
　58
Mobile, Ala., 35–36, 274–75
Montgomery, Ala.: black political power
　in, in 1940s and 1950s, 47, 93–95;
　White Citizens' Council of, 81–82, 83,
　100; bus segregation in, 93–94; demo-
　graphic changes after WWII, 94–95; po-
　litical divisions in, 95; Freedom Ride,
　127, 128; white flight from public
　schools, 260–261
Montgomery bus boycott: origins, 95–97;
　leadership, 98; implementation, 99–
　100; entanglement with local politics,
　100; lawsuit challenges segregation,
　101, 102; implications of, 102–104
Montgomery Improvement Association
　(MIA), 100
Moody, Anne, 7, 8, 155
Morgan, Chuck, 143–44
Morgan v. *Virginia* (1946), 124
Morris, Willie, 6, 197, 209
Morrison, de Lesseps, 111
Moses, Bob: and SNCC Delta Campaign,
　153; on building political base from lo-
　cal Delta blacks, 155–56; on voting
　rights as foundation for other rights,
　157; and Freedom Summer, 157–58; and
　FDP, 189, 190
Murray, Albert, 250
Music: black and white influences on,
　146–47; segregationist opposition to
　rock 'n' roll, 147
Myrdal, Gunnar: on racial etiquette, 3, 7,
　13, 29, 119; on uses of southern history,
　15; on black schools, 55–56; on invis-
　ibility of black middle class, 58

Nash, Diane, 121

Nashville, Tenn.: black political power
　in, in 1940s, 48; sit-in demonstrations,
　121; academic results of school de-
　segregation, 265
National Association for the Advance-
　ment of Colored People (NAACP): ha-
　rassed by state legislatures after *Brown*,
　79, 80; and *Brown II*, 91; time and ex-
　pense of legal challenges, 92; challenges
　delays in school desegregation, 257
National Recovery Act (NRA), 28
Negro Voters Leagues, 46, 47
New Deal: growing southern political op-
　position to, 30; and lessening of black
　dependence on whites, 31. *See also* in-
　dividual legislation
New Orleans, La.: employment for blacks
　in 1930s, 26; school desegregation and
　class issues in, 111, 112; economic im-
　pact of school desegregation crisis, 112;
　white flight from desegregated schools,
　112; black political divisions in, 190–
　91; tenant management experiments,
　253
Nixon, E. D., 94, 96, 97
Nixon, H. C., 43–44
Norfolk, Va.: "Lost Class of '59," 113;
　consolidation of suburbs, 186–87;
　school resegregation, 263–64
North Carolina, 239
Nunn, Sam (D-Ga.), 198

O'Connor, Flannery, 44, 138–39
Odum, Howard W.: on pressure for con-
　formity, 17, 18; supports southern solu-
　tions to racial problems, 20; despairs
　during WWII, 41; and SRC, 49–50
Oliver, Jesse, 236–37
Oldenburg, Rev. Doug, 276–77
Orangeburg, S.C., 210

Parks, Rosa, 95–96
Patterson, John, 127
Patterson, Robert, 82
Penniman, Richard ("Little Richard"),
　147
Pepper, Claude, 38, 49, 65
Percy, Walker: on southern religion, 137;
　on surfeit of violence, 147; on "insane"
　Mississippi, 155; on Goldwater in Mis-
　sissippi, 196
Percy, William Alexander, 4
Perez, Leander, 111
Petersburg, Va., 193
Pickett, Delores, 233, 234
Place, sense of, 22
Political system: role of Black Belt, 38,
　182–83; restrictive franchise, 38–39,

73–74, 149–50; new leadership after WWII, 48–49; old-line challenges, 64–70; race-baiting, 65, 149; red-baiting, 65; transformed by Voting Rights Act, 175, 177, 178, 179, 180, 182–83; limits of new leadership, 194; rise of Republican party, 195–97; votes follow racial lines, 240. *See also* Voting Rights; Voting Rights Act (1965)
Poor People's Campaign, 213, 214, 217
Poverty, black: in rural areas, 202–203, 247, 248; denied by some white leaders, 203; decline, 1970–1982, p. 245; in Lowndes County, Ala., 246; policy constraints in addressing, 246, 255; in cities, 246–47; triggers other problems, 247–48; as racial problem, 250–51; not a racial problem, 251–52
President's Committee on Civil Rights, 53–54
Presley, Elvis, 147
Price, Cecil, 159
Prichard, Ala., 193
Pritchett, Laurie, 131–32, 133
Public Works Administration (PWA), 28, 29

Race relations (since 1965): as perceived by whites, 209; and violence, 210, 211, 270; compounded by social class, 211; as perceived by black leaders, 220; as perceived by middle-class blacks, 225–26; confusing nature of, after 1976, p. 227; as perceived by black in-migrants, 244–45; urban-rural differences, 270–71; official reaction to violence, 271, 274, 275; civility in, 272
Rainey, Lawrence, 159
Rankin, John E., 3–4, 34
Raper, Arthur, 132
Ray, Maggie, 259
Reagan, Ronald, 249
Reeb, Rev. James J., 166
Reese, Rev. Frederick, 220
Religion, southern: role among whites, 16–18, 137; positive aspects of, 21, 276–77; response of white churches to *Brown*, 76–77, 85–86; use of, by Martin Luther King, Jr., 103; influence of, on black political power, 232–33; activist role of white churches, 276–77
Republican party: "southern strategy," 195–96; Goldwater candidacy, 195–96; use of racial code words, 197; black support for, 235; attempts to solicit black votes, 235, 242; aided by redistricting, 239–40; racists attracted to, 241–42, 243

Reynolds, William Bradford, 238, 239
Richmond, Va.: black political power in 1940s, 48; annexation, 186; city-county relations, 262
Richmond v. *U.S.* (1975), 186
Ricks, Willie, 223
Rivers, L. Mendel (D-S.C.), 34
Robertson, Ben, 20
Robinson, Jo Ann, 93–94, 96–97
Rock Hill, S.C., 125
Rockefeller, Winthrop, 108, 198
Roman, C. V., 171
Roosevelt, Eleanor, 29
Rousseve, Charles B., 26
Russell, Richard (D-Ga.), 54
Rustin, Bayard, 104, 206

St. Augustine, Fla., 133, 145
Sanford, Terry (D-N.C.), 209
School desegregation: white opposition to, prior to *Brown*, 57, 77–78, 81; court cases, 58–62; alleged sexual repercussions of, 76, 77; early efforts, 77; and white class divisions, 108, 111, 112; role of white leaders in, 111, 113–14, 116; in higher education, 113, 114–16; by 1960, p. 114, 116; resegregation, 256, 260, 261, 263–64; and freedom-of-choice plans, 257; and busing, 258–60, 262–63; white flight from public schools, 260–62; white support for, 262; ambiguous academic benefits of, 265; decline in private school movement, 266; black questioning of, 267–68; segregation within desegregated schools, 269; intangible benefits of, 269–70
Schwerner, Michael, 159
Scott, William L. (R-Va.), 197
Segregation: residential, 10, 27, 205, 208; institutional, 10–11; origins, 11; impact of, on blacks, 11–12, 89; in New Deal agencies, 28, 29; white support for, 87; black business districts, 90, 205; on buses, 93–94; public accommodations, 119, 124; white perceptions of changed, by sit-ins, 122; whites see downfall of as inevitable, 146; white guilt over, 147; and southern culture, 170; persistence in small towns, 206–207, 208, 270–71; strengths of segregated institutions, 219, 254
Seigenthaler, John, 127, 128
Sellers, Clyde, 94, 100
Sellers, James, 170
Selma, Ala.: White Citizens' Council in, 83–84; description, 161; new political leaders in, 162; voting rights demon-

strations in, 162–63; persistent racial problems of, 207–208; importance of local voting rights organizations in, before 1965, p. 218; as good place for blacks, 220; altering registration procedures in, 239; march landmarks incorporated into historic tour of, 272

Selma-to-Montgomery march: first attempt on March 7, p. 163–65; "Tuesday Turnaround," 165; violence attracts media attention, 165; as stimulus for Voting Rights Act, 165–66; final attempt, March 21, pp. 166–67; reenactment of, in 1975, p. 174; reenactment of, in 1985, p. 273

Shelby, Richard (D-Ala.), 234

Sherrod, Charles, 131

Shuttlesworth, Rev. Fred L.: aids Freedom Riders, 125; activities with ACMHR, 126; and Birmingham campaign, 134; organizing activities of, in 1950s, 217

Sit-ins: in Greensboro, 118–20; religious nature of, 119, 121; spread throughout the South, 120; white opposition to, 120; white support for, 120, 121; civility of demonstrators, 120–21; moral implications of, 121, 122; and changed white perceptions about segregation, 122; impact on blacks, 122–23

Smathers, George (D-Fla.), 65

Smith, Frank E. (D-Miss.), 78

Smith, Lillian: on southern traditions, 2; *Strange Fruit,* 43; attacks White citizens' Councils, 84; mentioned, 70

Smith, Willis, 68–69

Smith v. *Allwright* (1944): origins, 33–34; opposition of whites to, during WWII, 37–38. *See also* Voting rights

Smitherman, Joe, 162, 181, 230

South Carolina, 240, 265

Southern Baptist Convention, 51–52, 277

Southern Christian Leadership Conference (SCLC): origins, 104–105; close ties to black churches, 105; decision to target Birmingham, 134; divisions in, 214; and Meredith March Against Fear, 223–24. *See also* King, Rev. Martin Luther, Jr.

Southern Conference Education Fund (SCEF), 50–51, 70

Southern Conference on Human Welfare (SCHW): and Eleanor Roosevelt, 29; connection with SCEF, 50; victim of red- and race-baiting, 70

Southern history: myths of, 15–16; positive attributes of, 21–22; clarified by civil rights movement, 170–71; civil rights artifacts and locales incorporated into, 272–73; importance of historic

symbols, 273–74; ignorance of young blacks and whites about recent, 274. *See also* Culture

"Southern Manifesto," 84, 85

Southern Regional Council (SRC), 49–50, 70, 211

Sparkman, John (D-Ala.): and black votes, 47; and repeal of Boswell Amendment, 64; adherence to racial orthodoxy, 67; on impact of Voting Rights Act, 175; mentioned, 48

Stennis, John (D-Miss.), 233

Strategies to Elevate People (STEP), 277

Student Nonviolent Coordinating Committee (SNCC): origins and philosophy, 123–24; and Freedom Rides, 127, 129–30; activities in Albany, 130, 131, 132; Voter Education Project and Delta Campaign, 152–56; role in COFO, 156; and Freedom Election, 156–57; angered at "Tuesday Turnaround," 165; divisions in, 216, 217; activities in Dallas County, Ala., before 1965, p. 218; and Meredith March Against Fear, 223–24

Summerton, S.C., 256–57

Swann v. *Charlotte-Mecklenburg Board of Education* (1971), 258

Sweatt v. *Painter* (1950), 59

Talmadge, Eugene: complains about WPA wages, 31; ties to urban elites, 65; race-baiting, 71

Talmadge, Herman (D-Ga.): elected governor, 65; attacks *Brown* decision, 77; black votes help to defeat, 233

Tate, Allen, 18

Tennessee State University, 268–69

Tennessee Valley Authority (TVA), 29

Thurmond, Strom (D-S.C.; R-S.C.), 67, 234

Till, Emmett, 88–89

Tilly, Dorothy, 51, 54, 72

Truman, Harry S.: establishes President's Committee on Civil Rights, 53; supports FEPC, 53; introduces civil rights package to Congress, 54; seeks votes of northern urban blacks, 54; abolishes segregation in the armed forces, 55; southern opposition to, 65–67

Tunica, Miss., 247

Tuttle, Elbert, 116

U.S. v. *Lynd* (1962), 151

Urban renewal, 181–82, 205

Vance, Rupert, 1

Vandiver, Ernest, 113

Vardaman, James K., 57

Voter Education Project (VEP): origins, 152–53; accomplishments, 154; fail-

ures, 154; in post-1965 Mississippi, 183
Voting rights: abolition of white primary,
33–34; restrictions to black franchise,
38, 73, 74, 82, 149, 151–52, 184, 188,
238, 239; increased voter registration in
cities during 1940s and 1950s, 45–48;
Boswell Amendment, 64; violence
against blacks seeking to exercise, 73,
184; and Civil Rights Act of 1957, p.
110; importance of, for whites, 149; and
Civil Rights Act of 1960, 150; voter
registration figures, 151, 161, 175–76,
227–28; as a priority of Kennedy
administration, 151; and VEP, 152–53;
Delta Campaign, 153–56; Freedom
Election, 156–57; Freedom Summer,
157–60; Dallas County demonstrations,
161–63, 218; Selma-to-Montgomery
march, 163–67; Voting Rights Act,
165–66, 167; importance of, for blacks,
174, 175; vote dilution, 184–86
Voting Rights Act (1965): drafted and submitted, 165–66; impact on Dallas
County, 167; provisions, 167; as conclusion of civil rights movement, 168,
169; impact on race-baiting, 175, 179;
impact on voter registration in deep
South, 175–76; and black elected officials, 176; impact on Atlanta politics,
177–78; aids white liberals, 178–79,
180; impact on state legislatures, 179;
enhances power of urban neighborhoods, 182; impact on Black Belt, 182–
83; operation of preclearance provision,
187, 238–39; procedural requirements
aid Republicans, 239; 1982 extension,
233–34; evidentiary burdens on plaintiffs eased, 234

Walker, Alice: on powerlessness of
blacks, 8; and black-on-black violence,
9; on sense of place, 22; on impact of
Brown, 92; on psychological advances
of blacks and economic shortcomings,
251
Walker, Wyatt Tee, 98, 131, 134
Wallace, George C.: attempts to block desegregation of University of Alabama,
115; condemns 1964 Civil Rights Act,
146; prohibits Selma-to-Montgomery
march, 164; refuses to meet with
marchers, 166; repentance of, 225;
blacks in administrations of, 231, 232;
meets with Jesse Jackson, 231–32;
courts blacks votes, 232; policies aid
blacks, 232, 234; and 1985 march commemoration, 273
Waller, William, 179
Waring, J. Waties, 60–61, 71–72

Warren, Earl, 61–62
Warren, Robert Penn, 20
Washington, Booker T., 12
Watt, Mel, 254
West, Ben, 121
West, Roy, 236
Wheeler, Dr. Raymond, 203
White, Charlie, 199
White Citizens' Councils: origins, 81, 82;
opposition to, 81–82, 84; tactics, 82–
83; prominence in Deep South, 84, 100;
attack rock 'n' roll in Alabama, 147
Wilder, Douglas, 230, 237
Williams, Aubrey, 21, 50, 70
Williams, Eddie, 254
Williams, Hank, 146–47
Williams, Hosea, 163, 164, 246
Williams, John Bell, 183
Winter, William, 179, 235
Woodruff, Robert W., 133
Works Progress Administration (WPA),
29, 31
Wolfe, Thomas, 44
World War I, 18
World War II: blacks perceive oppor-
tunities provided by, 31, 32; federal ex-
penditures in the South during, 32;
federal civil rights initiatives, 33; job
discrimination during, 34–36; racial vi-
olence during, 35–36, 37; white con-
cern about black aspirations, 37–38;
alters southern isolation, 43–44
Wright, Cleo, 33
Wright, Fielding, 67
Wright, J. Skelly, 116
Wright, Richard: on white racial stereotypes, 3, 5; impact of racial etiquette on
blacks, 5, 6, 7–8; on migration, 25

Young, Andrew: on King as reluctant
leader, 98; and Birmingham campaign,
134; on white response to 1964 Civil
Rights Act, 145, 146; recruits whites for
Selma-to-Montgomery march, 165;
elected to Congress, 176; on importance of southern black vote in 1976
presidential race, 179; on disillusionment of black voters, 191; and King's
death, 216; on politicians as new black
leaders, 219; on great changes in race
relations by 1970s, 220, 226; elected
mayor of Atlanta, 228; and affirmative
action, 229; economic development priorities, 229; black complaints about
policies of, 236; on trickle-down prosperity, 245
Younge, Sammy, 206–207

Zellner, Robert, 134